1599 ELE

EERL Withdrawn
Surplus/Duplicate

D1016959

MARIANO DE
LARRA
AND SPANISH
POLITICAL
RHETORIC

MARIANO DE
LARRA

AND SPANISH
POLITICAL RHETORIC

Pierre L. Ullman

The University of Wisconsin Press
MADISON, MILWAUKEE, AND LONDON

PQ
6533
Z5
U35

PROPERTY OF
UNIV. OF ALASKA LIBRARY

Published 1971
The University of Wisconsin Press
Box 1379, Madison, Wisconsin 53701

The University of Wisconsin Press, Ltd.
27-29 Whitfield Street, London, W.1

Copyright © 1971
The Regents of the University of Wisconsin
All rights reserved

First printing

Printed in the United States of America
Kingsport Press, Inc., Kingsport, Tennessee

ISBN 0-299-05750-x; LC 72-133239

Frontispiece:
Mariano José de Larra

From a drawing by Federico de Madrazo, housed in the Museo Nacional de Arte Moderno, Madrid.
Photograph by José Domínguez Ramos.

To NORMAN EYSTER
former Spanish master
at
The Wooster School

CONTENTS

	ACKNOWLEDGMENTS	ix
	NOTE ON BIBLIOGRAPHY AND ORTHOGRAPHY	xi
1	LIFE AND TIMES OF LARRA	3
2	THE POLITICAL SCENE FROM FERDINAND'S DEATH TO THE OPENING OF THE CORTES	46
3	LARRA'S PREPARLIAMENTARY ARTICLES	65
4	THE QUEEN OPENS THE CORTES	101
5	A REPLY TO THE CROWN	111
6	ABSENTEEISM AND INACTION	139
7	A BILL OF RIGHTS	149
8	THE GUEBHARD LOAN	182
9	CIVIL SERVANTS	213
10	THE EXPULSION OF BURGOS	244
11	MACHINATIONS IN THE CABINET	257
12	THE POST-OFFICE MUTINY	281
13	FUNDS FOR THE SECRET POLICE	320
14	CLIMAX BEFORE DEPARTURE	354
	NOTES	369
	BIBLIOGRAPHY	403
	INDEX	415

Acknowledgments

I wish to express my gratitude to Professors Vicente Lloréns and Edmund King for their precise and painstaking examination of the first draft of this book, and to José Barrio Garay, for his kindness in making available a photograph of the portrait of Larra used on the jacket and in the frontispiece. I am also grateful to Ampliaciones y Reproducciones Mas, Barcelona, for permission to reproduce this portrait. Many thanks are due Mrs. Vonnie Whitbeck for her care in the preparation of the manuscript. A summer grant from the University of Wisconsin—Milwaukee Graduate School was partly applied to the research time which the book required. To my wife, who was always there to aid in many ways, I express my appreciation for her help and patience.

Pierre L. Ullman

Milwaukee, Wisconsin
July 1970

Note on Bibliography and Orthography

References to Larra's works are indicated by volume (1–4) and page number in *Obras de Mariano José de Larra*, ed. Carlos Seco Serrano, in *Biblioteca de Autores Españoles*, vols. 127–130 (Madrid: Atlas, 1960), henceforth indicated as *BAE*. For a detailed recommendation of this edition for scholarly purposes, see my review in *Revista Hispánica Moderna* 29 (1963): 298–299.

The source for parliamentary speeches has been the *Diario de las sesiones de Cortes, legislatura de 1834 a 1835*. The page number in these references is preceded by the abbreviation *Ilus.* for the *Estamento de Ilustres Próceres* (Madrid: Imprenta Nacional, 1865), and by *Pr.* for the *Estamento de Procuradores* (Madrid: J. A. García, 1867).

The orthography of quotations has been modernized in accordance with the "Nuevas normas de prosodia y ortografía," which may be found in Real Academia Española, *Grámatica de la lengua española* (Madrid: Espasa-Calpe, 1959), pp. 537–540. Words found in the *Diario* in the form *gerarquía, geroglífico, Gerónimo*, and *prorogar* have been respelled. "Zea Bermúdez" is used in the body of the text, but "Cea" has been retained in quotations which originally carried this version. The orthography of nineteenth-century historians and of the preamble to the Estatuto Real has likewise been changed: for example, *esponer, esperiencia, lijero, Rei, frayle, doile*.

To differentiate between ellipsis dots indicating omissions from the text and the suspension dots employed by Larra, ellipsis dots have been set with more space between them than the suspension dots throughout the body of this book.

MARIANO DE
LARRA
AND SPANISH
POLITICAL
RHETORIC

1

LIFE AND TIMES
OF LARRA

ON February 13, 1901, a group of young intellectuals who
would come to be known as the Generation of '98 held
their first public function, a visit to a Madrid cemetery
which had long before been closed down. There, in front of his
tomb, they paid homage to Mariano José de Larra, whom they
considered their master. Yet they knew Larra only through his
writings, for he had committed suicide just sixty-four years previously at the age of twenty-seven. Thus it was, and still is, that people tend to remember the anniversary of Larra's death rather than
his birth. This should not surprise us; his life was, after all, a model
of Romantic tragedy. Even the year of his birth, 1809, seems un-
important compared to the preceding one, which overshadows it
historically. At least it can be said that he was conceived in 1808,
the fateful year which marks the beginning of modern Spain.

"Modern," to be sure, necessarily implies intellectual freedom,
normally the result of a nation's internal struggle. Nevertheless,
unlike their French neighbors, Spaniards heard the first sound of

3

liberty proclaimed not by native revolutionaries but by foreign invaders. If we should find this historical circumstance ironic, it must be added that the Spanish literary scene presents a condition no less puzzling. Larra, Spain's greatest Romantic author, was renowned not as a poet, playwright, or novelist, but as a satirical essayist. No other genre would appear, on the surface, less Romantic. Yet, when we look back upon his era, this incongruity aptly reflects the anachronistic nature of Spanish Romanticism; for if Spain was literarily two decades behind the times, socially and politically she was out of step with France by fifty years. Therefore her Romantic movement was an anachronism internally as well as externally.

It is much too facile to attribute the phenomenon merely to political retardation. In 1789 the French people had revolted against a government that had managed to concentrate almost all political power in the person of the king. The Spanish Bourbons, on the other hand, never could obtain from their subjects the obedience enjoyed by their French cousins. Suffice it to say that all of Charles III's ministers were summoned before the Inquisition, which even managed to punish one of them severely. The Bourbons encountered considerable opposition from the moment they acceded to the throne in 1700. They encouraged reform where the Hapsburgs had allowed stagnation, and at every step their good intentions met with resistance by established interests. Even when the king succeeded in foiling the designs of the Inquisition, it still retained overwhelming support among the clergy and peasantry. Charles III made himself highly unpopular when he expelled the Jesuits in 1767 and curtailed the autonomy of the Holy Office by demanding to be fully informed of its secret proceedings. Spain was thus a "moderate monarchy," as later historians designated the form of government she traditionally possessed; the term is intentionally vague. But the limitations on the sovereignty of the Crown cannot be deemed constitutional, as the expression is understood nowadays. It was the Church and its branches that held a balance of power, not the old aristocracy, which had ceased to exercise political influence. This arrangement can hardly be called constructive, and many eighteenth-century Spaniards who yearned for progress placed their hope in a truly absolute monarchy patterned on the French system. Consequently, when their neighbors were proclaiming the Rights of Man, many progressive-minded Spaniards were still advocating enlightened despotism.

The Inquisition, understandably, looked askance at enlightened despotism. Its role in Spanish history should never be underestimated, since it gives the social and political scene a dimension that exists nowhere else in Europe. The Inquisition perpetuated a caste system based on "cleanliness of blood," disadvantageous to the descendants of anyone punished for heresy, which coexisted with the standard nobiliary system. It also helped to maintain unchallenged the traditional religious concepts pertaining to the person of the king, who was looked upon with awe as a sort of vice-God. Divergent views constituted a fatal offense, and intellectual competition to the religion that proclaimed these percepts was consistently stifled. Nevertheless, the Holy Office did not consider that its ideological service to the king was gratuitous, and it defied his power through the authority it held over his ministers.

Another important factor set Spain apart from the rest of Europe. Generally speaking, the nation had no bourgeoisie. It is true that in the eighteenth century a middle class of persons not in government employ began to form in some cities, especially ports like Cádiz. They eventually acquired social and economic importance along with the intellectuals who looked to the French Encyclopedists. Nevertheless, Spain had no geographically distributed middle class which might aspire to take power from aristocratic and rural elements and unite the country economically. In the 1830s, while French Romantics took up their pens to attack the bourgeoisie, Larra was complaining that

> apenas tenemos una clase media, numerosa y resignada con su verdadera posición; si hay en España clase media, industrial, fabril y comercial, no se busque en Madrid, sino en Barcelona, Cádiz, etc.; aquí no hay más que clase alta y clase baja . . . (1: 411)

> (we can hardly be said to have a middle class, numerous and resigned to its real position. If there is in Spain a middle class, industrial, manufacturing, commercial, it should not be sought in Madrid but in Barcelona, Cádiz, and so forth. Here there is only an upper class and a lower class . . .)

Consequently, the only genuine rebels on the Peninsula were the legendary gentlemen highwaymen, whom the government tried in vain to tame or exterminate. Some, like Jesse James and his brothers in the United States, attained lasting fame; one such group was the notorious clan nicknamed Los Niños de Écija. Larra once wrote with his characteristic wit that Spain was a country where for years the Niños had given orders.

In 1808 there sat on the throne of what was still the world's largest empire a sixty-year old monarch, the decrepit Charles IV, immortalized in the masterpieces of Goya beside his consort María Luisa, who undoubtedly held sway over him. The greatest influence on the queen, in turn, was her paramour Manuel Godoy, whom she had gradually promoted from bodyguard to prime minister. Charles and María Luisa were terrified of the French revolution, and Godoy had managed to preserve Spain from its fury by damping the reforming current set in motion by his predecessors and by exercising diplomatic moderation in dealing with France. Later he allied Spain with Napoleon against England, a move which cost Spain its fleet at Trafalgar in 1805.

This shattering defeat did not disillusion Godoy about such alliances. In 1808 new arrangements with Bonaparte allowed French troops to enter the Peninsula in great numbers under pretext of preventing a possible British invasion of Portugal. Alarmed by Godoy's policies, a group of nobles staged a coup at Aranjuez which forced Charles to abdicate in favor of his eldest son, Ferdinand VII. Napoleon seized the opportunity. He refused to recognize Ferdinand's sovereignty, played the two sides against each other, and finally tricked both parties into handing the crown over to his brother, Joseph Bonaparte.

Joseph "the Intruder" was a decent man. He had the makings of a good ruler, but his kingdom, like Maximilian's, established sixty years later in Mexico by another Napoleon, rested on the might of French armies. Ferdinand's confessor told Bonaparte that the king's person was sacred to the Spanish people, who would never forgive his ruse. This prediction proved correct. On May 2, 1808, the citizens of Madrid displayed their courage to the whole world, rising against the French garrison, which retaliated with bloody reprisals.

For the first time in recent history, civilians had defied a foreign army, and Europe could hardly believe the news that a people in such circumstances would dare or even care to challenge the unvanquished Imperial troops. Spain, previously regarded as a nation of religious fanatics, an object of banter and scorn in eighteenth-century writings, now became the Romantic land par excellence.

All Spaniards, however, did not fit this nostalgic image. Some chose to collaborate with the French and rallied to the cause of Joseph I. One of these Afrancesados, or Josefinos, was Dr. Mariano de Larra y Langelot, father of our author. It should not surprise us that many persons joined the invaders. After all, the Bourbons had abdicated, and besides, Napoleon gave the country its first modern charter, the Constitution of Bayonne, which, among other things, abolished the Inquisition. Fanatic traditionalists would unhesitatingly fight against the Imperial armies, but the reformers were divided. One group, led by Manuel José Quintana and Gaspar Melchor de Jovellanos, felt that the future held hope for Spain only if progressive elements joined the struggle against the invader and invigorated the resistance movement with modern ideas. Many of these men, prominent during the reign of Charles III, had fallen from favor under Charles IV and been persecuted by Godoy, who curtailed reforms as a reaction to the French Terror. The other group, led by the playwright Leandro Fernández de Moratín, aligned themselves with what they considered the winning side.

The division of the educated classes into two camps had repercussions on the family level, to be sure. Dr. Larra, a physician in his thirties, joined the medical corps of the Imperial Army, a decision which, some biographers aver, caused a break in relations with his father, Antonio Crispín de Larra. But this account is not backed by sufficient evidence. Mariano José's grandfather, director of the Royal Mint, did not abandon his post when the effigy of Joseph I appeared on the coinage; he was therefore in no position to condemn his son. Antonio Crispín de Larra had been born in Lisbon, and his wife, Eulalia Joaquina da Concepçaõ Langelot, was Portuguese by birth. Doña Eulalia's interest in Castilian literature developed as a result of her zeal to learn the language and in turn probably influenced her famous grandson, who learned how to read at the age of three. The physician's first wife and her seven children had all died before he married Dolores Sánchez de Castro y Delgado, an Aragonese. It appears that she was frivolous and lacked affection for her only child, born in Madrid on March 24, 1809.

This bright and precocious boy was to endure more hardship than his mother's indifference. During the War of Independence the people of Madrid went through a famine, and his family must have been affected. In 1813 the four-year-old and his parents joined the long caravan of refugees who hastily left Spain under the protection of the retreating French, harassed by guerrillas and pressed by Wellington's victorious armies. The family lived for some time in Bordeaux while Dr. Larra worked at the military hospital of that city. He was later transferred to Strassburg, whither he took his wife. Young Mariano, however, was left in a Bordeaux boarding school and soon forgot his native language. After the war Dr. Larra practiced in Leipzig, Berlin, Vienna, and Holland, where he could study and move in prominent medical circles. He translated into Castilian Mateo Orfila's famous toxicological treatise and part of Augustin de Candolle's botanical research; he also concocted some pills and elixirs held in high repute at the time. In 1817 Ferdinand granted at last an amnesty to the Josefinos, and Dr. Larra returned home with his family and the Order of the Lily, with which Louis XVIII had decorated him.

Much had happened to Spain in the meantime. During the War of Independence a congress assembled at Cádiz (in spite of military and political obstacles) in order to pass, among other things, the famous Constitution of 1812, nicknamed "la Pepa" because it took effect on St. Joseph's day. This charter later became a model for constitutional monarchies throughout Europe. It gave the legislative power to the Cortes and the executive to the monarch (or, at the time of its inception, the Council of Regency), who could not be held accountable, because decrees would be valid only if signed by the ministers. It also specified that Roman Catholicism was the sole acceptable faith on Spanish territory, even though the Cortes had abolished the Inquisition. The Constitution of 1812 was mostly the work of a group of young men known as Liberals. The opposite political faction got to be called the Serviles because they seemed unswerving in their vassalage. But in spite of conflicting ideologies, the two parties united for one goal, to restore Ferdinand to the throne.

Patriots referred to him as "el Deseado," a cognomen he hardly deserved, for he turned out to be Spain's most dastardly ruler. As early as 1806 he had conspired against his parents, perhaps even consenting to their assassination. He loathed his oversexed mother, to whom he referred in his letters as "la bête puante," and hated Godoy. Yet Ferdinand VII did not belie his heredity; as king he would walk almost every night from the palace, accompanied by his procurer the Duke of Alagón, toward the poorer quarter of Madrid. His sister (and later mother-in-law) Isabella Maria, queen of Sicily, enjoyed being whipped by her lovers. His brother Carlos, on the other hand, became a religious fanatic. During his comfortable captivity in France, Ferdinand would never miss an occasion to send Napoleon congratulations on every victory obtained over the Spanish people. When the war was over he promised, before reentering the country, that he would uphold the constitution; but once in Spain he surreptitiously accepted the support of a coalition of Inquisitorials and absolutists, sent the Liberals to penal colonies, and enthroned himself as absolute monarch.

Conditions had changed since 1808, however. Ferdinand came back to a nation ruined by the incessant ravages of French, British, and even Spanish troops. Moreover, the only men capable of putting things aright either had been forced to flee for having collaborated with the French, or had been driven out, imprisoned, or executed for their liberal views. Six years of mistakes ensued. The Spanish ambassador met with rebuffs at the Congress of Vienna, and Spain received no reparations from France. In order to restore the economy, the king was persuaded that the rebelling American colonies had to be reconquered. All available funds were invested in a fleet to transport troops to the New World. When the ships, bought from Russia, arrived at Cádiz, they proved to be rotten and unseaworthy. It was the Russian ambassador, Tatitscheff, who arranged the transaction. Tatitscheff had become a member of the camarilla, almost gaining control of foreign affairs, and had encouraged such admiration for Russian despotism that even the uniform of the czar's soldiers was copied by some units, fur caps being worn under the blazing Andalusian sun.

Between 1814 and 1820 five attempts to overthrow the government were uncovered, including the Triangle Conspiracy of 1816, supposedly aimed at the king's life. Ferdinand's ministers not only feared plotters but the monarch himself; during this six-year period thirty secretaries went in and out of the five secretaryships. The king, remembering the example of his parents with Godoy, decided never to have a favorite. Any person who showed talent would soon arouse his distrust, and courtiers recognized affectionate behavior on Ferdinand's part as a sign of danger. The affairs of state were at such an ebb that a revolt was imminent.

This was the condition of the native land to which Mariano José de Larra returned at the age of nine. His father had obtained the enviable position of physician to Don Francisco de Paula, Ferdinand's youngest brother, and could afford to enroll him at the Piarist school of San Antonio Abad in Madrid, where he finished his primary education in 1819 and his secondary in 1822. Besides religious studies, the program consisted of Castilian and Latin grammar, poetics, mythology, arithmetic, algebra, geometry, and rhetoric, the latter course having considerable significance for the formation of Larra's style. Many years later Mariano was still remembered by some teachers as the best pupil in his class, a serious child who preferred reading and chess to playing with his classmates. Like the other boarders, he had permission to go home on Thursdays and Sundays, where he spent his free time in such diversions as translating the Iliad, making a compendium of Castilian grammar, and versifying a geography of Spain. This early fascination with language would persevere till the end of his life.

While the child thus busied himself, the body politic underwent a major tremor. It started at Cádiz among the troops waiting to embark for America, many of whom had already served their time and were being unjustly conscripted. Their discontent, stirred by some liberals, erupted into a rebellion led by Rafael de Riego, who proceeded to march on Madrid. To save his crown, Ferdinand hypocritically welcomed the revolution with the unforgettable pronouncement, "Marchemos francamente, y yo el primero, por la senda constitucional" ("Let us frankly advance, and I first of all, on the constitutional path"). Whether these words impressed the eleven-year-old Larra at the time we cannot know. In any case, he did not fail to perceive a decade and a half later that they could be used as a symbol of betrayal and disillusionment, for he parodied them to describe the turmoil of 1836: "Marchemos todos francamente, y yo el primero, por la senda de presidio" (2: 194—

"Let us frankly march, and I first of all, on the way to prison");
or "Marchemos francamente, y yo el último, por la senda del extranjero" (2: 321—"Let us frankly march, and I last of all, on the
path of exile"). But now Larra was merely younger than the
young men who came to power in 1820. They were a generation
"schooled by harsh oppression to a fanaticism in the cause of liberty as exaggerated as that of their opponents in the cause of absolutism. Their mental food was the political Utopias of revolutionary doctrinaires . . . They had of course no experience of
public life."[1] This new generation of liberals brought the nation
three turbulent years of freedom known as the Triennium.

It is the tragedy of Spanish governments to be consistently
anachronistic, and this time fate had it that liberals should rise to
authority when the rest of the continent was gripped by despotism. Following their example, Naples and Piedmont rebelled, but
their liberty was promptly crushed by the Austrian Empire. Spain
consequently stood alone. Notwithstanding, her young and enthusiastic legislators, disregarding their country's isolation, chose
to push blindly forward. It was impossible that under such circumstances the régime could function normally, because its primary
requirement for survival, the monarch's good faith, was utterly
lacking. Indeed, the king's frequent visits to his country estate
served as a pretext to plot against his government. He may also
have conspired in ignoble ways to discredit the system, encour-
aging popular disorders in order to put the Liberals to shame.

Yet the Liberals were also plotters, unlike their predecessors of
1810–1814. Antonio Alcalá Galiano, who a dozen years later
would be Larra's editor, was then the leader of Los Amigos del
Orden, one of a few Masonic societies that dominated political
parties behind the scenes. Headquarters for these societies were
large Madrid cafés, where orators stood on the tables to harangue
their audiences. Nevertheless, the Liberals could be grouped into
two factions, Exaltados and Moderados. The principal clique
among the latter was led by Francisco Martínez de la Rosa; José
María Queipo de Llano, Conde de Toreno; Bernardino Fernández
de Velasco, Duque de Frías; and José María Calatrava. Three of
these would be prime ministers during Larra's adulthood, and the
Duque de Frías one of his early patrons. The Moderates aimed to
let matters stand now that constitutional rule had been restored,

whereas the Exaltados looked upon this as but a starting point.

When, after several months, the Exaltados gained a majority, their vehemence imperiled the whole Liberal movement. Having imposed order by means of the National Militia, the left-dominated legislature authorized the imprisonment of reactionaries, expelled the Jesuits, revived a project to secularize Church property, and forced people to take a loyalty oath to the constitution. The Cortes also abolished the religious orders, a bill which the king at first vetoed on instructions from the pope, but was eventually tricked into signing after an organized riot. This sort of change, however, was not the only form of secularization in evidence, for even religious modes of expression were dissociated from their customary content; during the riot of 1821, people gesticulated before the king, pressing to their hearts copies of the constitution as one would a crucifix or holy image.

Later, *La Trágala* and *El Lairón*, two vulgar revolutionary hymns, were sung at Ferdinand. Crowds would jeer the royal person. The press showed a total lack of responsibility. Libelous sheets like *La Cotorrita* ("Little Gossip"), *La Tercerola* ("Little Carbine"), and the infamous *Zurriago* ("Whip") provoked the populace, redress being well-nigh impossible because juries chosen for slander cases were invariably rigged.

Dr. Larra must have sensed that Madrid would shortly be unsafe and, on Mariano's graduation from the Piarist school, obtained the position of town physician at Corellas in Navarre. There the boy zealously studied on his own, without formal instruction, buried in his books. The doctor's decision proved all too well-founded. Discontent at legislative boldness and administrative arbitrariness was growing. At the Congress of Verona the absolutist powers, including Orthodox Russia, pacted with the pope to preserve the ascendancy of the Roman Catholic Church in Spain. The pope's warning, however, was met with spiteful pride in the Cortes, where one Exaltado went so far as to request "Pido que se lea esa bula, edicto o como se llame ese papelote"[2] ("that this bull, edict, or whatever it is this broadside is called, be read forthwith"). In the meantime Ferdinand's agents duped the French into believing that he would favor a very limited constitution similar to their *charte octroyée*. Then the reactionaries rebelled. An Army of the Faith, under the command of a Trappist monk, seized Seo de Urgel on June 21, 1822. Many supporters of this revolt were upstarts with purchased titles of nobility. They purported to reinstate medieval felicity and inaugurated a temporary regency with sham pageantry. At this signal the absolutist nations at the Congress of Verona, which had agreed to let the French intervene, gave their blessing to an invasion of eighty thousand troops sent by Louis XVIII under the Duc d'Angoulême. The Hundred Thousand Sons of Saint Louis, as they were called, took Spain with little effort. Most Spanish generals sent to fight them were cajoled into acquiescence with promises of the aforementioned charter. Ironically enough, Angoulême's first care on entering Madrid was to post guards outside the houses of liberals to prevent atrocities, for the populace had grown accustomed to having its discontent whetted by all sides. The crowd now chanted, "¡Vivan las caenas!" ("Long live fetters!"). The French pressed on; the constitutional government moved first to Seville, then Cádiz. When the king refused to go along, the Exaltado majority voted him insane and forced him to make the journey. After a last stand at the Trocadero the Liberals capitulated.

Perhaps Ferdinand had called upon the French in order not to be totally indebted to the extreme rightists, the so-called Apostolic party. Much to their chagrin, he kept one promise to his foreign allies; he failed to revive the Inquisition. But then Spain had changed intellectually during the Triennium. Modern ideas had circulated freely, French fashions appeared, translations flooded the book market. The absolute monarchists had been sufficiently enlightened to break their alliance with the Apostolics. The latter got the upper hand at first. A short reign of terror ensued, during which people who committed atrocities could walk into churches and be summarily pardoned by confessors. Even the absolutist powers protested these crimes and intervened, though in vain, to avert the shameful torture and execution of El Empecinado, peasant hero of the War of Independence. As for the press, partly in the hands of monks, it became even more abusive and vitriolic than any paper the extreme left had put out. At last Ferdinand gained partial control of the nation, betrayed the Apostolics, and deposed their ministers, including his wicked ex-confessor Víctor Sáez. Nevertheless, the king was still powerless to discipline the provincial ecclesiastical authorities which autonomously instituted

Juntas de Fe to replace the Inquisition. In 1826 one of these illicit tribunals publicly executed the Valencian schoolmaster Ripoll on outlandish grounds and flimsy evidence, an action which shocked all Europe.

Ferdinand, to be sure, did not keep his promise to give the nation a charter; on the contrary, he went so far as to declare all legislative and administrative acts of the Triennium null and void. This summary abrogation caused vast confusion, as could be expected. It entailed nonrecognition of foreign loans transacted between 1820 and 1823, a dearth of national integrity that likewise caused an outcry throughout Europe.

Inasmuch as the monarch could now rely on neither the Inquisitorial party nor the persecuted Liberals, he called upon the former Josefinos, who had been mistreated by both sides. They now formed the bulwark of the nonecclesiastical absolutist party and it was fortunate for Ferdinand that many of them were good administrators. Dr. Larra presently felt that he could return to Madrid safely, enrolling his son at the Colegio Imperial of the Society of Jesus, where he completed a course in mathematics in 1824. At the same time, Mariano took courses in stenography and economics at the Real Sociedad Económica de Amigos del País.

After the reign of terror the universities reopened. The quality of education they offered, however, can be inferred from a publication of the University of Cabrera, which began thus: "Lejos de nosotros la peligrosa novedad de discurrir . . ."[3] ("Far from us the dangerous novelty of reasoning . . ."). But the young man did not go to Cabrera. For one year he attended Valladolid, where he finished courses in Greek, botany, mathematics, logic, and metaphysics. It was there, at the age of sixteen, that Larra went through an experience which changed his character profoundly. The boy found himself attracted to a flirtatious young woman in her early twenties. She encouraged his affection and soon the ingenuous student fell in love. Now, while Larra attended Valladolid, his father was practicing in Aranda del Duero, as attested in a certificate of good conduct issued by the parish priest on May 16, 1825, such a document being indispensable in Spain. Aranda was sixty miles away and the doctor traveled frequently to Valladolid to visit his son; or so it seemed, for Larra discovered one day

that the young woman was his father's mistress. For the first time in his life Mariano was seen weeping profusely. Twelve years later, another love affair would be the decisive factor in his suicide.

Larra decided to leave immediately, going to Madrid to seek the aid of his paternal uncle Eugenio, assayer of the Royal Mint. The relationship proved lasting, for it was this uncle who adopted Larra's children after his suicide. Once in the capital the young man went back to school, at the Reales Estudios de San Isidro, located in the aforementioned Colegio Imperial. There he completed in 1826 courses in Greek and experimental physics. Some sources suppose that he then attended the University of Valencia for a few months. In any case, 1827 found him employed as a civil servant in Madrid, a job obtained through the influence of friends and relatives, which he soon quit from boredom. He thereupon began to frequent literary circles, becoming a friend of the playwrights Manuel Bretón de los Herreros and Ventura de la Vega and enjoying the protection of the Archdeacon of Madrid, a patron of the arts.

On October 1, 1827, Larra's first published work appeared, a mediocre ode, "A la exposición primera de artes españolas," for which his fellow writers bantered him. What Larra praised was nevertheless an important event, and we should return to our historical digression to understand its significance.

The years 1823 to 1833 are known as the Ominous Decade, a tyrannical era followed, inevitably, by a seven-year civil war. Ferdinand's ministers were at great pains to keep the Apostolics at bay on the one hand and to repress liberal elements on the other. This is borne out by numerous plots to dethrone him, crushed by his fawning and merciless premier Francisco Tadeo Calomarde through a ramified political police. In 1824 the Federation of Pure Royalists, a clerical faction, issued a manifesto which some historians consider the first Carlist document. Resentful over a frustrated scheme of Calomarde's to ensnare Apostolic leaders through a feigned conspiracy, these extreme rightists now pinned their hopes on the king's brother Carlos. Also about this time an abortive plot was fomented from abroad by exiled Moderates. In 1827 came the short-lived Guerra de los Agraviados, whose instigators, feeling the king had betrayed them, announced a crusade to

sostener y defender con la vida los dulces y sagrados nombres de Religión, Rey e Inquisición, y arrollar y exterminar a cuantos masones, carbonarios, comuneros, y demás nombres inventados por los maquiavelistas que no han obtenido el indulto que Su Majestad se dignó dispensarles si dentro de un mes no se retractaban de sus errores.[4]

(sustain and defend with our lives the sweet and sacred names of Religion, King, and Inquisition, and crush and exterminate all Masons, Carbonari, Comuneros, and other names invented by the Machiavellians, who have not obtained the amnesty that His Majesty deigned to grant them if within a month they do not recant their errors.)

Though professing loyalty to Ferdinand, the leaders secretly entertained the idea of placing Carlos on the throne. The revolt occurred in Catalonia and the king had to go there himself to put it down. On seeing the monarch in person subduing the revolt, most of the ignorant people who had been beguiled into thinking they were actually fighting for him put down their arms.

Of primary concern at the time was the treasury, bankrupted by Ferdinand's policy toward the rebellious American colonies. A new secretary recommended the long-overdue recognition of the American republics in order to revive the national economy, because Andalusian wine and oil, and the coarse products of Catalan industry, found no market in Europe. But the king showed not the slightest interest in industry. One of his ministers had organized with great zeal the exhibition about which Larra composed his first published poem. On opening day the minister escorted Ferdinand to an exhibit of Catalan textiles which, it was hoped, might compete with smuggled English goods. The king took one look, exclaimed "¡Cosas de mujeres!" ("Women's frippery!"), and left hurriedly for his walk in the Prado. The monarch's words, to be sure, made a greater impression than Larra's poem. But industry was not the only activity which the sovereign ostentatiously scorned. When news of a French revolution reached Spain in 1830, he shut down the universities for fear of student revolt and allowed Calomarde to open bullfighting schools in their stead.

The plan for American trade was rejected; but the economy

survived by means of a loan from the Paris-based banker Aguado, negotiated for the Regency of Urgel by Francisco Javier de Burgos, a former Josefino. In 1835 this loan would become the subject of a lengthy parliamentary debate and of two Larra essays. No loan, however, could remedy the many ills of the body politic. Bandits roamed the countryside, while exiles, in touch with dissatisfied elements, attempted several incursions.

Emigré groups were active. The Freemasons, headed by the guerrilla hero Francisco Javier Espoz y Mina, formed the right wing of the Liberal expatriates, while the former Comuneros, led by José María Torrijos and Flórez Calderón, made up the left. Louis-Philippe, installed by the revolution of 1830, tolerated military expeditions from French territory but only until Ferdinand belatedly recognized him, whereupon such activities were curbed. The exiles, however, failed to profit from this short-lived opportunity. Mina's incursion in the Basque provinces ended in the rout of his decimated band, which, incidentally, included the poet José de Espronceda. Joaquín de Pablo, the famous guerrillero who went by the nickname Chapalangarra, died in an attempt to cross the Pyrenees. Torrijos's invasion plans were betrayed and he and his partisans shot. Mariana Pineda was executed after a denunciation by a seamstress from whom she had ordered a flag embroidered with the word "libertad." Miyar, a bookdealer, was hanged for being party to a plot. For shouting "¡Viva la libertad!", Carlos Latorre, an inebriated cobbler's apprentice, suffered torture for three days, then death. These are only the best-known examples of what befell persons with liberal ideas. Some of these people were later memorialized in Larra's essays.[5]

It was in this environment, and when Larra was not quite nineteen, that he began to publish *El Duende Satírico del Día*. This one-man paper, of which only five numbers appeared, each one except the last two done by a different Madrid printer, lasted from February to December 1828. The *Duende* ("Goblin") contained in its first issue an *artículo de costumbres*, a kind of descriptive essay dealing with the social scene and local color. This piece, "El café," can be called the best of its genre written in Spain up to that time, because of what from the very beginning differentiated Larra's *costumbrista* essays from all others: his mordant manner of criticizing what he described. We can imagine perhaps the state of Spanish culture under Ferdinand VII by considering that these youthful attempts far outshone anything else produced at the time. Notwithstanding, the young author exhibited certain defects which he would later have to eliminate, especially those profuse epigraphs and quotations that, according to F. Courtney Tarr, "reveal a serious-minded and somewhat pedantic youth, with a classical and eighteenth-century background, a preoccupation with correct diction, and a decided leaning toward the critical and the satiric."[6] After lambasting a bad Ducange comedy being staged in one of Madrid's two theaters and painting bullfights in unflattering colors, Larra decided, for his fourth number, to focus on another aspect of the local scene, *El Correo Literario y Mercantil*, Madrid's only paper, a triweekly. Judging from the *Duende*'s profuse and comically annotated quotations from the *Correo*, it must have been a hodgepodge of ill-written trivia. The *Duende*, of course, ceased publication; the *Correo* had too many friends at court. For three and a half years Larra desisted from journalistic ventures, but he did not stop writing. Several unpublished poems came from his pen in 1829, and another was published, a dirge for the victims of some serious earthquakes. The piece was praised by the *Correo*, indicating that Larra had been forgiven by its editor, perhaps through the mediation of the benevolent Archdeacon of Madrid.

On May 18, 1829, Ferdinand's third wife, Amalia of Saxony, passed away—to the great relief of all liberals. A religiously zealous woman who ran the palace according to the canonical hours, she had pressed the king into saying the rosary every evening before retiring (Ferdinand, to be sure, only feigned retiring, then went out on his nocturnal assignations). Amalia had also shown the temerity to publish her execrable poetry, which became the object of great merriment for some and chagrin for others. Worst of all, she was barren, and many Spaniards dreaded the day when Carlos would ascend the throne. The reactionary Carlos, however, was balanced by Ferdinand's other brother, Francisco, who had sided with Moderate elements, becoming himself a Mason. His wife Luisa Carlota was ready to do almost anything to prevent Carlos's consort, María Francisca of Braganza, from becoming queen. She bore her a deep personal grudge because, when the royal family was evacuated during the siege of Cádiz in 1823,

María Francisca had had white dresses embroidered with fleurs-de-lys specially fashioned for the queen and herself so that they might make a resplendent impression on the Duc d'Angoulême when he received them on the French flagship. But Luisa Carlota had not been in on this plan, and climbed aboard in her everyday clothes! Now Ferdinand, it appeared, wanted to remarry. María Francisca proposed another devout German princess like Amalia, and the king answered laconically, "¡No más rosarios!" At last it was Carlota's turn. She swayed the king toward her younger sister, María Cristina, whose portrait he found quite fetching. The royal wedding took place on December 11, 1829. The lovely new queen exuded grace and kindness, and her benign spell on Ferdinand caused many small reforms that partially dispelled the stifling atmosphere. The music conservatory she founded, for example, soon vied with Calomarde's bullfighting schools. It was even reported that on her way from Naples, Cristina had turned a kind ear to the implorations of Spanish exiles in Provence.

Soon after the wedding the king learned that he would have an heir. He then decided on March 27, 1830, to publish the Pragmática Sanción of 1789 which abolished the so-called Salic Law, or French tradition disallowing queens regnant. This custom, unknown in Spain until the Bourbons, was foisted on the nation by Philip V through his Auto Acordado of 1713, in order to avoid the possibility that France and Spain might some day be ruled by one head. In 1789, however, Charles IV revoked the Auto Acordado with his Pragmática Sanción, approved by the Cortes but kept secret at the insistence of María Luisa and Godoy, for no one could tell at the time whether Ferdinand was healthy enough to live. Carlos never accepted his brother's decision to publish their father's edict, and he managed to be absent at the ceremony of June 20, 1833, proclaiming Ferdinand's daughter Isabel Princess of Asturias and accordingly heiress to the throne. Born on October 10, 1830, she had to be constantly guarded, as well as her mother Cristina, against Carlist foul play.

In September 1832 the king fell seriously ill, and several groups, expecting his impending demise, began to plot vigorously. One leftist faction hoped to topple the Bourbon dynasty and make Peter of Braganza emperor of the whole Peninsula, but the scheme was halted through the mediation of Martínez de la Rosa. The

Apostolics, to be sure, used all means at their disposal to facilitate Carlos's ascension to the throne. They managed to convince the queen that her daughter's cause was lost, and won her reluctant cooperation in swaying the king to contravene the Pragmática Sanción through a codicil to his will. Carlist designs were frustrated, however, by Ferdinand's recovery and Carlota's return from Seville, where she had been sojourning with Don Francisco, whom Calomarde had failed to inform of the king's illness. In fact, Cristina herself had not even written to Carlota. She found out through the newspapers and, thoroughly irked, returned on September 24 to the royal residence at La Granja post haste, burst into the palace, calling her sister the queen a "pazza" and "regina di galleria." When Calomarde presented her with the codicil, she tore it to bits, spit on the floor, slapped him, and exclaimed: "Siempre te tuve por un bruto, pero por un pícaro traidor no hasta ahora" ("I always took you for a brute; but a dastardly traitor, not until now"). Calomarde replied to the slap with the famous phrase: "Manos blancas no ofenden'" ("Lily-white hands cannot offend"). Meanwhile, the capital seethed in rumor and anti-Carlist citizens set out to march on La Granja. At this juncture a palace coup against the Carlists forced Calomarde to flee to England.

On October 6 the convalescent Ferdinand appointed María Cristina to head the Council of State. The next day she ordered the universities reopened and pardoned a number of prisoners. Two weeks later, realizing that her daughter's cause needed immediate support, the queen decreed a partial amnesty to the exiles. The Carlists secretly welcomed this amnesty in the belief that it would frighten absolute monarchists into joining forces with the Apostolic party. But this did not occur to any significant degree; all those who opposed Carlism united, though not too solidly, under the designation of Cristinos. Finally, on December 31, Ferdinand announced that he had signed the codicil when not in control of his senses. The nation at last began to enjoy some cultural progress, though with a tenuous political balance.

During those years Larra was not idle. The *Correo* published his sonnets hailing the birth of Isabel and Cristina's second pregnancy. On April 29, 1831, Madrid saw his first play represented, an adaptation from Augustin Scribe. Thus began our author's career as translator of third-rate French comedies, just what needy writers did to eke out a living, since the pay was the same as for originals, this being a major cause of Spain's literary decline. Larra, however, boldly decided to undertake once more the creation of a satirical paper like his defunct *Duende*. On August 17, 1832, the first number of *El Pobrecito Hablador* went on sale. By March 14, 1833, the date of its fourteenth and last issue, this young man had established himself as the wittiest writer and most refined prose stylist of the day. Not only did Larra demonstrate unusual proficiency at eliciting double entendre in his ambiguous praise of the government, but he painted the Spanish character in such deep color throughout his essays that they have gained lasting fame by being deemed all too true ever since. One engaging facet of Larra's work is his ability to laugh at himself along with his fellows. At the close of the essay, "¡Vuelva usted mañana!" (January 14, 1833), a satire of bureaucratic procrastination, he offers excuses for giving it to the public long after the date promised, pretending that it is three months late. There is indeed something quite subjective about all his writings. In one issue of *El Pobrecito Hablador* he condemns bad "occasional," or ad hoc, poetry; we cannot help but wonder whether he alludes in part to his own verse. Another piece, "El casarse pronto y mal" (November 30, 1832), seems inspired by the author's own conjugal situation.

On August 13, 1829, Larra had taken to wife Josefa Anacleta Wetoret y Martínez. Neither family was especially pleased; two famous friends of the bridegroom, the Duque de Frías, soon to become ambassador to France, and the playwright Bretón de los Herreros, signed the church register as witnesses. Their distinguished company at the wedding, however, did not exorcise what made this marriage unsuccessful. From the union were born Luis Mariano de Larra, author of musical comedies and potboilers, for which he had to bear the epithet of "Larra el Malo," besides the curse of his father's suicide; and Adela, who married her first cousin, Eugenio's son. Baldomera, the third child, reputedly not Larra's—which may explain the couple's eventual separation—became the mistress of Amadeo I during his brief reign, and later perpetrated a notorious financial swindle. In any case, the adultery in Larra's marriage was double. His liaison with Dolores

Armijo de Cambronero began in 1832 or perhaps earlier. Dolores's husband, who held a government position, was the son of Manuel María de Cambronero, an eminent jurist. Whatever the tension this affair may have produced within the social circle frequented by Larra, there is no doubt that he retained the friendship of persons with growing political influence.

Francisco Zea Bermúdez, the man who eventually replaced Calomarde, was anti-Apostolic and a firm believer in absolute monarchy and enlightened despotism. Accordingly, intellectuals could breathe more freely, even though Ferdinand recuperated and took charge of the affairs of state on January 4, 1833. With the advent of a cultural renewal, Larra's good fortune began to rise. On November 17, 1832, an anonymous theatrical review, obviously from his pen, appeared in *La Revista Española*, successor to *El Correo*. Thus began his long association with the nation's finest newspaper, as drama critic. When Ramón de Mesonero Romanos, who had charge of the *artículos de costumbres*, left for Paris in March 1833, Larra was made associate editor and also became the newspaper's *costumbrista*. If Larra contributed anything to Spanish culture besides his immortal essays, it is the reform of the theater, through his unrelenting, scathing attacks on the tasteless spectacles and execrable acting which dominated the Madrid stage. And in coming years, with a relaxation of censorship, his social, political, and theatrical criticism would become indistinguishable as he linked world and stage in burlesque metaphors. For his now new role with *La Revista Española* the young satirist adopted his definite pen name, Figaro, inspired by a quotation from Beaumarchais that he used as an epigraph, ending with the words, "Je me presse de rire de tout, de peur d'être obligé d'en pleurer" (1: 173—"I hasten to laugh at everything, in fear of being driven to weep over it").

A jester like Figaro was precisely what the Spanish people needed to keep up their spirits during such trying times. Everyone foresaw a civil war. The Madrid police had uncovered a junta attempting to make Carlos regent during Ferdinand's lifetime. Then a new Carlist secret society, La Legitimidad, on learning of the king's decision to exile his brother to Portugal, started to plan a regency consisting of Joaquín Abarca, bishop of León, General José O'Donnell, and the superior general of the Jesuits. Faced with growing defiance, Zea surreptitiously armed the Masons and placed the Voluntarios Realistas (a sort of national guard), whose administration heretofore had been independent, under the secretary of war. Their leaders were then promptly purged, a most important step, for their power had grown to such proportions that the ministers—even the king on occasion—were subject to their will. The measure met with some resistance, as evidenced by a rebellion, which was finally put down, of the Voluntarios Realistas in León on January 14, 1833, under the aegis of its bishop.

What proved most problematic were relations with Portugal. In view of several Larra essays on this question, we must turn briefly to Spain's policy concerning her neighbor. After Brazil declared its independence in 1821, it became impossible for the same person to wear both crowns. Accordingly, when Peter I, Emperor of Brazil, inherited Portugal on his mother's death in 1826, he abdicated that throne in favor of his seven-year-old daughter Maria da Gloria, allowing his brother Miguel to be regent. But the latter, backed by clericals and absolutists, abolished the constitution and seized the crown. England, under Lord Charles Grey, declaring itself against the usurper, aided the Liberals and Peter to regain the kingdom for his daughter. The British government hoped that Spain would follow suit, but Stratford Canning, a notoriously clumsy ambassador, could not sway Ferdinand from the influence of Carlos and the Russian and Austrian diplomats. When Ferdinand, owing to the troubles occasioned by his brother's presence, finally sent Carlos off to Lisbon, Portugal was in the throes of a civil war. Even after the Liberal forces had obtained several victories, Spain persevered in recognizing Dom Miguel, hoping in vain that he might reciprocate by extraditing Carlos. Now that the maneuvers of Carlos's partisans had been checked, the Spanish government wanted him back in Madrid where he could be watched; but he refused to obey the king's orders to return for an indispensable ceremony, the nation's pledge of allegiance to Isabel on April 20, 1833.

This matter was still unresolved when Ferdinand died unexpectedly on September 29, 1833.[8] He had once compared Spain to a beer bottle, with himself as the stopper, which would spill over when uncorked. His uncouth metaphor proved appropriate, for the nation immediately seethed in a civil war that was to last seven years. Zea Bermúdez could not long remain in power, and María Cristina, now regent for her daughter, appointed Martínez de la Rosa prime minister on January 4, 1834.

Because Martínez became the principal target of Larra's satire, it behooves us to examine his character in detail. The new minister had begun his political career in the Cortes of Cádiz. Persecuted as a liberal on Ferdinand's return to Spain, he spent part of the 1814–1820 period in a penal colony, where he meditated upon the effects of overenthusiasm. Accordingly, the Triennium found him in the Moderate camp, eventually as prime minister. In 1823, though not the object of reprisals, he chose to emigrate to France, joining those who were forced to flee. There he became even more moderate.

Descriptions of the new premier can be found in several accounts. In his memoirs Mesonero Romanos tells us that in 1813, as a child of ten, he first saw Martínez de la Rosa, whose handsomeness and elegance made a lasting impression. Thirty years later the statesman Edgar Quinet, writing for a French audience conditioned by the Romantic vision of Spain, embroidered his portrait:

> Il a la vieillesse élégante et jeune des poètes. Loin que son talent poétique ait été pour lui une cause de défaveur dans les assemblées, c'est à cette élévation de l'âme qu'il doit sa juste prépondérance. Ses grands traits sont en même temps pleins de finesse; ses cheveux blonds tempèrent le feu de ses yeux d'Andalou. Ajoutez la taille haute et fière d'un hidalgo de Grenade, un naturel charmant, une voix de sirène, à laquelle manque, sans doute, le cri africain, mais qui le rachète par un atticisme continu. Personne n'a mieux concilié avec l'humeur indigène l'imitation des formes étrangères. Il est cosmopolite, si un Espagnol de l'Alhambra peut l'être. Sa véhémence correcte est tout l'opposé de la furie de [Joaquín María] López; sa phrase se balance *paladinamente*, avec la souplesse d'un cheval andalou dans un tournoi; il semble combattre à mort, non pour les passions d'un parti, mais pour l'honneur et la devise de sa dame.[9]

(He possesses the youthful elegance of poets in their old age. Far from being hampered in political assemblies by his poetic talent, he owes to this elevation of his soul the preponderance due him. His features are broad, yet fine. His fair hair tempers the fire of his Andalusian eyes. Add to this the straight and proud bearing of an hidalgo from Granada, natural charm, a siren's voice, perhaps lacking in the African blare, but compensated by a sustained atticism. No one has better attuned to the native temperament the imitation of foreign forms. He is cosmopolitan, if indeed a Spaniard from the Alhambra can be this. His correct vehemence is the very opposite of López's fury; his periods are balanced *paladinamente*, with the suppleness of an Andalusian horse at a joust; he seems to fight to the death, not for the passions of a party, but for the honor and emblem of his lady.)

Even those who wrote unflatteringly of Martínez will not deny him those qualities. George Villiers, the British ambassador, sent home a letter that bespeaks closer acquaintance:

He is the most difficult man I have yet had to deal with; he has many estimable qualities; he is a just, benevolent and honorable man, but certainly possesses vanity and littleness in his composition enough to spoil ten good men. He is determined to be what Providence has denied to anyone—excellent in all things; accordingly, as a poet, a statesman, a dramatist, a Lovelace, a financier, an orator, an historian, he assumes for himself the first places and can endure no competition. Accordingly with that unerring sign of a little mind, he seeks to surround himself with men miserably inferior to himself, who feed his vanity . . . Most things are consequently left undone, and those that are not are, for the most part, ill done . . . Therefore I never appear even to advise . . . I merely throw out my ideas . . . and you would laugh, as I have done over and over again, if I told you how often he has given me, three or four weeks later, my ideas as his own, adding *que c'était une idée qui lui a passé par la tête*. . . .
 . . . The gentle insinuation that he had broken his word of honor he could not stand . . .[10]

Also of interest are the remarks of a man who became his personal secretary at a later stage in Martínez's career:

Martínez de la Rosa ganaba mucho en ser conocido. Su aire un tanto desdeñoso y la costumbre que tenía de dedicarse casi exclusivamente a la sociedad de las señoras, no le hacía simpático a la generalidad del sexo fuerte. Pero tratado en la intimidad descubría un fondo de bondad y rectitud que le atraía los corazones. No había sido volteriano ni masón; era un liberal a la inglesa, que respetaba y amaba la religión y el trono. Unía, sin embargo, lo sagrado con lo profano, y aunque no faltaba nunca a la misa que se decía los domingos en la capilla de la Embajada, eso no le impedía tener después citas con mujeres. No le faltaba orgullo, pero desconocía la vanidad . . . Habiéndome tomado mucho afecto, me llevaba a menudo a su palco y me daba una agradable lección de literatura dramática, explicándome las bellezas y defectos de la pieza representada. También me prefería para amanuense, porque yo escribía entonces con mucha velocidad, y me dictaba sus despachos, parándose de cuando en cuando para que le leyese lo escrito, y preguntándome luego: ¿Suena? ¿suena?; porque su grande empeño era que los períodos fuesen armoniosos.[11]

(The more one knew Martínez de la Rosa, the more one got to like him. His slightly disdainful air and his habit of devoting himself almost exclusively to the company of ladies did not generally win him sympathy among the stronger sex. Yet those who knew him intimately discovered in him a profound goodness which captured their hearts. He had been neither Voltairian nor Mason; he was a liberal in the English manner, who respected and loved the Faith and the Crown. Nevertheless, he combined the sacred with the profane; and though he never missed Sunday mass at the Embassy chapel, this did not keep him from assignations with women afterwards. He had no lack of pride, but vanity was alien to him . . . Having taken a liking to me, he would often invite me to his box and give me a pleasurable lesson in dramatic literature, explaining the virtues and defects of the play being staged. He also preferred me as his amanuensis because I wrote rapidly, and he dictated his dispatches, stopping from time to time so I could read back what was written, and then asking me, "How does it sound?", because his great desire was for harmonious phrasing.)

Later historians are less benign. Wenceslao Ramírez de Villa-Urrutia states that, although Martínez de la Rosa dressed like Lamartine, he was politically inspired by Chateaubriand. Had he not been disposed to poetic tenderness in a puerile manner, his horror of demonstrations, riots, and anarchy would have been commendable. But he lacked energy, exhibited a faint will, and resorted too often to compromise. Accordingly, he was easily duped, as Ferdinand VII found out quite early. Perhaps Villa-

Urrutia exaggerates, for Martínez possessed considerable diplomatic skill.

Since the present volume deals mainly with Larra's work during the Martínez ministry, it will only be touched upon cursorily at this point. During this ministry censorship was relaxed, though by no means did Spain enjoy freedom of the press. Martínez produced a charter known as the Estatuto Real, but it could hardly be called a modern constitution. After a decade of absolutism the country again possessed a parliament, whose inaugural ceremony on July 24, 1834, was conducted with great pomp. The revived Cortes eventually weakened the power of the Throne, not only institutionally, but incidentally. When the queen rose to deliver the Crown speech, one detail was noticed by the whole assemblage. She was pregnant. The king, let us remember, had died on September 29, 1833. People did not easily forget that the private lives of María Cristina's mother and grandmother had provoked scandal.

Nevertheless, Cristina faced a terrible dilemma at the time because Ferdinand's will stated that she could remain regent only if she did not remarry. The queen was a faithful Catholic and abhorred the thought of taking a lover; yet she fell in love anew, which, for a young widow, should hardly surprise us. The woman in her finally prevailed over the queen, and on December 28, 1833, the palace chaplain married her privily to Fernando Muñoz, one of her bodyguards, the handsome son of a peasant woman who held the tobacco concession at Tarancón. The union was legally and canonically invalid, but Cristina and "Fernando VIII," as people dubbed him, chose to disregard those drawbacks. The affair could not long remain a secret, and neither could the mystery of the queen's frequently large waist, and a series of several small children sent off to France, the first one born on November 7. Yet, officially, the union did not exist, nor was the act of marriage common knowledge. She could therefore be intimidated with threats of its disclosure, and indeed was blackmailed into sanctioning the suppression of monasteries in 1836, a measure she abominated. In 1840 Manuel de la Cortina forced the queen regent to abdicate by pointing out that the Constitution of 1837 forbade the sovereign to marry without the Cortes' permission. Such confrontations, to be sure, did not occur until long after Martínez de la Rosa's ministry. What proved even more detrimental was the effect of the queen's behavior on public opinion. In order to keep up appearances the government adopted a strict policy. The slightest hint in any newspaper about the affair resulted in the editor's immediate banishment.

Martínez de la Rosa's failure to end the war, to grant more freedom, and to bring about needed reforms led to his replacement by the Conde de Toreno on June 7, 1835. But by that time his wittiest critic, Figaro, had been away for two months. We know that Larra gave up his Madrid apartment on March 25 and left the capital on or about April 5, the date Dr. Larra arrived from Navalcarnero to sign a power of attorney allowing his son to collect an old debt in Belgium. There is, of course, much speculation among biographers about the author's trip. Was it a quarrel arising from professional rivalry, or was Larra avoiding a duel with Dolores's husband? Young Cambronero, it seems, had just been granted a government position in Manila. Could he have sent his wife off to a convent in Badajoz? In any case, the journalist's first stop on his trip was Badajoz, where he stayed as a guest of his close friend José Negrete, Conde de Campo-Alange, as well as at Mérida and the count's estates in Extremadura. From there he traveled to Lisbon, where he embarked for London. After three days in England he crossed the channel to Belgium, recovering only a small part of the debt. We then find him in Paris, received with open arms by his old friend and protector the Duque de Frías, now ambassador, who forthwith facilitated Figaro's entry into French literary circles. Yet these experiences were hardly all pleasure. Larra worked hard, sending essays and the customary translations of Scribe and Ducange to Madrid. Strangely enough, the comedies Larra chose often bore significant titles that could be taken to allude to his amorous vicissitudes: *Un desafío, Las desdichas de un amante dichoso, Los inseparables, Partir a tiempo, ¡Tu amor o la muerte!* If such possible allusions were taken seriously, the plots of these plays might conceivably offer indications that Larra was virtuous in spite of widespread rumors. Did he purposely do this to throw people off the track, or was it part of an ineluctable obsession to exhibit allegorically his inner struggles? The nature of Figaro's life and work makes the latter plausible, as some critics suggest.

Larra probably entertained the idea of making his literary fortune in France, but his hopes were soon dashed. He fell ill and ran out of funds. On December 23, 1835, Figaro was back in Madrid. The nation had a new prime minister, Juan Álvarez Mendizábal, successor to the short-lived Toreno ministry. Mendizábal belonged to the New Christian caste and certain reactionary cartoonists would place a tail on him in their caricatures. He had served with distinction in the War of Independence, then emigrated to England where his financial talent earned him a small fortune; he spent the greater part of it on the Liberal cause, notably the Portuguese revolt.

The new prime minister moved boldly. Having pledged an end to the Carlist War within six months and initiation of sweeping administrative and fiscal reforms, he found himself compelled to take the unavoidable step of selling Church lands; and although corruption among his followers prevented the treasury from reaping the benefits it expected, this measure created an established middle class committed to anticlericalism. After a few months, the failures of Mendizábal's program brought about a realignment in Liberal politics which profoundly affected Larra's future. The journalist had aligned himself with the somewhat moderate and protectionist clique led by Francisco Javier Istúriz and backed partly by Catalan enterprise, while Mendizábal relied for his support on libertarians and Cádiz sea merchants. Though Figaro during this régime took up his pen mostly for literary criticism, he eventually joined in the attack on the prime minister, who was ousted in May when people got wind of plans for a trade treaty with Britain that would have ruined Catalan industry.

Mendizábal was replaced by Istúriz on May 15, 1836, and Larra now found himself in a dilemma. How could he use his literary talents against the government when his friends were in power and moreover would not accept such opposition in their own newspaper, *El Español*? Furthermore, Figaro, satirical champion of the Spanish people, could obviously see that Mendizábal, whose fall was really caused by palace intrigue, had much broader popular support than Istúriz. After much protestation, however, the dilemma was resolved. The author decided that Figaro would limit himself to literary criticism while Mariano José de Larra's political writings in *El Español* could go unsigned. And besides, we suddenly encounter him as a government candidate for *procurador* (member of parliament) for Ávila, the very city where Dolores now lived, in the care of her uncle. Interestingly enough, the individual working hardest for his candidacy was a municipal employee in Ávila, the same person who had been acting as Cupid's messenger for Figaro. As evidenced by extant patronage correspondence, Larra found himself, after his election, enabled to repay both favors, or so it seems. The new position, however, could gain only prestige for its occupant, for it provided no salary. Not only had the young author stanched his satirical vein—by which he would have maintained a more lasting prestige—but the political compromise did nothing to relieve him of debt. And Larra never seemed to be out of debt. His sincerity drove him to be a paragon of elegance while he criticized his countrymen for their slovenliness; and at the same time he had a family to support. Perhaps the new position was sought in order to impress Dolores; we do not know whether her dying love revived.

Unfortunately for Larra all his plans came to nought, for he never took his seat in Cortes. Since suffrage was not universal, these new national elections went against liberal opinion generally, which strongly favored Mendizábal and his supporters. Spain now found itself in the throes of a revolution within a revolution. A Madrid mob killed the captain general of Castile, and Istúriz and his ministers had to flee. Even the garrison at La Granja rebelled under the leadership of its sergeants while the officers were at the opera, and on August 12, 1836, the queen was forced to proclaim the Constitution of 1812. The previous elections were annulled and José María Calatrava named prime minister. Calatrava belonged to the group known as Doceañistas, advocates of the 1812 constitution.

Figaro's writing, let us not forget, is highly subjective and imparts to the reader a sense of deep personal pain at Spain's ills. It is hard to know whether at this point Larra interpreted the political situation in terms of his own misfortunes. The new régime, though leftist, maintained censorship and incarcerated conservative journalists just as previous governments had persecuted Progressive-oriented writers. Not satisfied with selling Church lands, it confiscated monasteries and convents, turning out the religious. Corruption became widespread, while victorious troops went unpaid and the wounded forgotten. Figaro sensed that this leftist rebellion against a Liberal régime had set a terrible precedent. The pessimistic tone of his last essays is precisely what ranks him not only as a great Romantic but as a prophet of modern Spanish politics, which has turned out to be a succession of rebellions, anarchy, military coups, and strong-arm rule.

Politically disillusioned, heavily in debt, condemned by his former fans who now saw Figaro's articles in ultra-Moderate newspapers, he held on to one hope, a lasting reconciliation with Dolores. The morning of Tuesday, February 13, 1837, Larra received a note from her asking if she could come for a short visit. This elated him immediately and he spent a good part of the day on preparations. Dolores arrived, accompanied by her husband's sister, who sat in the parlor while the two former lovers spoke at length in the adjoining room. After an hour Dolores came out with the packet of love letters that the young man had so fondly saved. As the two women left the building they heard a shot. Dolores vacillated a moment, then hurried on. Meanwhile Adela, the author's six-year-old daughter, went into his room to kiss her father good-night; she found his body in a pool of blood.

Larra's funeral was a major event, not so much because of his popularity as a writer but because he had committed suicide. The Church at the time was so uninfluential with the régime that the ecclesiastical authorities had to accede to the author's burial in a regular cemetery. Consequently, the ceremony turned into a *cause célèbre*, a covert expression of anticlerical humanism. Among those who delivered eulogies at Figaro's grave, an unknown youth of nineteen started to fascinate the audience with one of the most beautiful odes they had heard, but a friend had to finish the reading for him. The young man had fainted, not only from emotion, but from hunger, having gone two days without a meal. Were it not for this chance which brought him instant fame, the man who became Spain's most beloved Romantic bard would have starved to death and perished in oblivion. Thus, like the phoenix, did José Zorrilla rise from the ashes of Mariano José de Larra. A few days later Dolores boarded a ship to join her husband in the Philippines. The ship sank in a storm, with no survivors.

While it is evident that Larra killed himself for love's sake, one cannot deny that other failures in his personal life brought him to the point where he was disposed to take this final step. But we must also allow for a genuine political disillusionment, deeply rooted in the vicissitudes of liberal ideas on the Peninsula. The French Revolution and Napoleonic invasion, let us remember, interrupted and irretrievably damaged the nation's normal growth, when enlightened despotism was just beginning to bear good fruit. The conflict among the several liberal ideologies of the nineteenth century was thus aggravated by external circumstances, just as enlightened policies, from which they derived, had been arrested in the eighteenth century when Charles IV feared the spread of revolutionary ideas from France. The division of Liberals into Moderates and Progressives during the Martínez ministry may perhaps parallel in part the schism between the Moderados and Exaltados of the Triennium. Yet the Triennium situation seems more plausible as a pattern for the political scene after August 1836. Likewise, when we seek precedents for the two broad camps of the Martínez period, we obtain better theoretical explanations by tracing them back to the eighteenth century, when, after Jovellanos's imprisonment, Spanish intellectuals split into two groups. One, headed by Moratín, was so appalled by the French Terror that its zeal for reform was damped; it continued to seek the favors of Godoy and the court. The other group, gathering about Quintana, decided that the old régime could never provide a suitable climate for intellectual reform and development. Moratín's followers believed that progress could be achieved within the existing institutions; but for Quintana, the institutions had to be changed. During the War of Independence, the former became Josefinos, while the latter fought the French and drafted the Constitution of 1812 in Cádiz. Jovellanos himself, however, though choosing Cádiz, displayed a more conservative bent than his admirers. Perhaps the first indicator of the deepening rift among men of modern ideas is the disillusionment of Joseph Blanco White with Jovellanos during the early days of the Junta Central, as Vicente Lloréns has demonstrated.[12] Jovellanos, acceding to the indignant demands of ancient-régime officeholders, suspended Blanco's controversial *Semanario Patriótico*, the first newspaper which dared to express views divergent from the government's. Larra's ideas can be compared with Blanco's, while Jovellanos's became the creed of the Moderates.

Jovellanos's conservatism, it must be noted, increased with age, and this type of ideological change occurred likewise among those who were Progressives in Larra's day, though for them it was harsher and involved guilt-ridden palinodes. Larra's editor-in-chief, Alcalá Galiano, writing in 1846 about his political role in 1834–1835, described his former self as an imprudent distorter of fact, arrogant, contributing to malevolence, hurling invectives, and putting on airs of fatuous solemnity.[13] Such *mea culpa* can only be comprehended by reflecting on the growing disillusionment of many Progressives after the Martínez era, which may likewise partly explain Larra's suicide. Again, we can turn to Edgar Quinet for a perceptive analysis of the problem:

On demande toujours pour quelles idées, pourquoi sont morts les hommes qui ont résisté à l'ancienne monarchie espagnole. Ils étaient eux-mêmes passionnés de royauté; ils ne haïssaient ni l'Eglise ni la noblesse, qui n'avait jamais eu l'arrogance de la nôtre. Que voulaient-ils donc? Que l'Espagne cessât d'être muette. Ils voulaient eux-mêmes lui délier la langue, et entendre le son de la parole humaine, dont ils étaient sevrés depuis le moyen âge. Ils croyaient que tout serait gagné, et que le miracle s'accomplirait dès que la vérité ensevelie pourrait sortir, sans mélange, des lèvres de l'homme de bien. Cette foi dans la puissance de la parole sincère est le fondement de la vie nouvelle des Espagnols.[14]

(People always seem to be asking, for what ideas, for what purpose, the men who resisted the old Spanish monarchy gave their lives. They were themselves impassioned royalists, hating neither Church nor nobility, which had never shown the arrogance of ours. What then did they seek? They wanted Spain to cease being mute. They themselves wanted to loose its tongue, to hear the sound of human speech, of which they had been deprived since the Middle Ages. They believed all would be won, that the great miracle would be accomplished, once the truth, lying buried, should come forth unadulterated from the lips of men of good will. This faith in the power of sincere speech is the basis of Spain's new life.)

On the strife for social change, Quinet also observed that "parquée dans le catolicisme, cette révolution se heurte çà et là contre elle-même"[15] ("this revolution, confined in Catholicism, constantly collides with itself"). How could a man become a progressive liberal without abjuring many traditions deemed sacred? But progressives necessarily broke with tradition, braving the stigma of heresy, turning into exaltados and, finally, iconoclasts as fanatical as their opposites. On the other hand, the moderates who attempted to compromise with tradition soon found themselves to be advocates of stagnation, giving lip service to the new ideas while averring that they were not yet practicable. At the age of twenty-eight Larra perceived the ineluctability of the politicians' dilemma and, after creating his famous tetralogy of pessimistic essays,[16] committed suicide. By February 13, 1837, the only thing left for Larra to believe in—so he felt—was Dolores's love, as evidenced by his essay on the exequies of the Count of Campo-Alange, who had lost his life in the war as a colonel in the infantry. Less than a month before his own demise, the journalist included the following lines in the eulogy of his friend:

> Pero era justo; Campo-Alange debía morir. ¿Qué le esperaba en esta sociedad? Militar, no era insubordinado; a haberlo sido, las balas le hubieran respetado. Hombre de talento, no era intrigante. Liberal, no era vocinglero; literato, no era pedante; escritor, la razón y la imparcialidad presidían a sus escritos. ¿Qué papel podía haber hecho en tal caos y degradación?
>
> Ha muerto el joven noble y generoso, y ha muerto creyendo; la suerte ha sido injusta con nosotros, los que le hemos perdido, con nosotros cruel; ¡con él misericordiosa!
>
> En la vida le esperaba el desengaño; ¡la fortuna le ha ofrecido antes la muerte! Eso es morir viviendo todavía; pero ¡ay de los que le lloran, que entre ellos hay muchos a quienes no es dado elegir, y que entre la muerte y el desengaño tienen antes que pasar por éste que por aquélla, que ésos viven muertos y le envidian! (2: 294)

(Campo-Alange had to die. What awaited him in this society? As a soldier, he was not insubordinate; had he been so, the bullets would have spared him. A man of talent, he was no intriguer. A liberal, he was not vociferous; a man of letters, he was not pedantic; as a writer, reason and impartiality guided his pen. What role could he have played in such chaos and degradation?

The young and generous youth is dead, and he died believing. To us who lost him, fate has been unjust. Cruel to us, merciful to him!

In life, disillusionment awaited him; Fortune offered him death first. This is to die when one is still alive. But woe unto those who mourn him, for among them are many who cannot choose, who will have to pass through disillusionment before going to their deaths; these are the living dead who envy him!)

Figaro proved a good prophet. His other friends lived on, turned moderate and opiated their intellect, a process keenly observed by Quinet during the parliamentary debates of 1843:

Quel dommage que le découragement perce sous ces splendeurs de langage! Et que cet esprit de réaction suppose de mécomptes, de bouleversements, d'exils, de douleurs publiques et privées! J'ai entendu M. Galiano combattre l'une après l'autre toutes les définitions qui ont été données de la liberté; comme il ne les remplaçait par aucune autre, il s'ensuivait tacitement que l'Espagne, à travers tant de rivières de sang, a poursuivi un fantôme qui se trouve être un mot. C'était l'éloquence d'un homme sincère, qui brise ce qu'il a élevé, et, dans un désespoir tout viril, s'indigne de la stérilité de ses anciennes idoles. Que devait-il être dans le temps où il croyait à l'avenir! Hier il renversait l'idée d'égalité, aujourd'hui celle de la souveraineté du peuple. La révolution tombait pièce à pièce, et l'assentiment public accompagnait chacune de ces immolations. On applaudissait la lassitude, l'épuisement, le désespoir même, comme autrefois l'espérance. Est-ce que l'Espagne songe à se dépouiller de la révolution, comme de la robe de Déjanire? . . . Quand on les presse sur ce sujet, la plupart avouent, sans tergiversation métaphysique, qu'ils sont désabusés, *desengañados*. C'est le mot qui revient le plus souvent.[17]

(What a pity that discouragement shows through these verbal splendors! And how many misfortunes, tumults, exiles, public and private sorrows, must underlie this spirit of reaction! I heard Mr. Galiano challenge one after the other all known definitions of liberty, and since he failed to replace them by any other, it followed implicitly that Spain, after so many rivers of blood, had pursued a phantom which turned out to be but a word. This was the eloquence of a sincere man, who shatters what he has exalted and, in virile despair, becomes indignant at the barrenness of his

ancient idols. What he must have been like in those days when he
believed in the future! Just yesterday he rebutted the concept of
equality; today, the sovereignty of the people. The revolution
was falling piece by piece, and public assent accompanied each im-
molation. People were applauding lassitude, exhaustion, despair itself, as they had once cheered hope! Does Spain dream of casting
off the revolution like the robe of Deianira? . . . When you press
them on the subject, most will avow, without metaphysical eva-
sion, that they are disillusioned, *desengañados*. This is the word
which comes back most often.)

Perhaps such disenchantment was bound to result from the impo-
sition of foreign ideas by force, if only because too many Spaniards would not forget that liberty, equality, and fraternity had
been first proclaimed at the points of Napoleonic bayonets. One
group, though, did not let itself be overcome by disillusionment:
those who had helped to write, despite the French threat, a constitution to rival that of Bayonne—the faithful Doceañistas like
Agustín Argüelles and Quintana, who always worked unfailingly
toward the goal of plain political regeneration, which they viewed
as their country's primary need. Larra's circle, on the other hand,
eventually had to reckon with the inapplicability of the modern
beliefs they had so faithfully held. It is sad to discern, with historical hindsight, that long before this reappraisal occurred to progressives like Galiano, the moderates who followed Martínez de
la Rosa already understood the irrelevancy of those ideas. Yet the
moderates did not perceive the harm caused by the utterance of
this type of skepticism. Its damaging effect is another aspect of
Spanish political life so well described by Quinet:

> Quand la parole se flétrit chez un peuple qui a placé toute sa
> dignité dans la parole, le désordre est au comble; car, si le men-
> songe à voix basse finit par stériliser la bouche qui le profère, que
> l'on se figure ce qui doit arriver quand la tribune publique, qui est
> la bouche d'un peuple, ne proclame plus que des fictions, des am-
> bages, des propos tortueux. . . . Je n'imagine rien de plus cor-
> rupteur qu'une tribune d'où se répand, avec convenance, un
> brillant verbe de mort . . .[18]

(When, among a people which has put all its dignity in the
word, the word withers, then disorder is at its height; because, if

the whispered lie ends by sterilizing the mouth which utters it, imagine what must happen when the public rostrum, which is the mouth of a people, proclaims nothing further than fictions, equivocations, tortuous propositions. . . . I can imagine nothing more corrupting than a platform from which is spread with propriety a brilliant language of death . . .)

Shortly before leaving Madrid in 1835, Larra wrote an essay entitled "Por ahora," where he humorously showed how, by dint of political abuse, *palabras buenas* ("good words") turned into *buenas palabras* ("bons mots"). Figaro assigned himself the task of ridiculing the bons mots of the Moderates. Though his efforts did not halt the spread of brilliant verbiage, he did expose its incongruities and put his countrymen on their guard against it.

The present volume demonstrates in part how Larra set about demolishing Moderate oratory. In order to do this, the scholar needs a clearer concept of the journalist's opus than can be derived from most collections, which usually divide his work into *artículos de costumbres*, political articles, and literary and theatrical essays, often without indicating the date of composition. Such is the persistence of ill-founded routine that this arrangement has prompted the public to categorize the author himself in this manner. Thus, anyone doing research on Figaro will often be asked whether he is dealing with the *costumbrista*, the theatrical critic, or the political essayist.

All these erroneous notions can be refuted immediately. Larra himself makes it quite clear in the preface to the first edition of his collected articles that the only appropriate arrangement is chronological:

Con la publicación del Pobrecito Hablador empecé a cultivar este género arriesgado bajo el ministerio Calomarde; la *Revista española* me abrió sus columnas en tiempo de Cea, y he escrito en el *Observador* durante Martínez de la Rosa. Esta colección será, pues, cuando menos, un documento histórico, una elocuente crónica de nuestra llamada libertad de imprenta. He aquí la razón por qué no he seguido en ella otro orden que el de las fechas.[19] (1: 5)

(With the publication of *El Pobrecito Hablador*, I started to cultivate this hazardous genre under the Calomarde ministry; *La Revista Española* opened its columns to me at the time of Zea, and I wrote in *El Observador* during Martínez de la Rosa. Our selection, therefore, will be at least a historical document, an eloquent chronicle of our so-called freedom of the press. This is the reason why I have adopted no order other than that of the dates.)

Not only does the author's statement evince his own preference for a chronological arrangement, but it indicates the proper basis for scholarly research into his production; namely, that the various periods of his literary activity coincide precisely with the régimes under which he wrote. Figaro's very words thus justify the nature of the present study, which covers a period delineated by the essayist himself, that of Martínez de la Rosa.[20]

The pitfalls of any other approach were clearly perceived by the critic Emilio Pastor Mateos, who commented twenty years ago on the difficulty of classifying many of Larra's *artículos de costumbres:* "se resisten a ser clasificados como tales, ya que la crítica política o literaria asoma frecuentemente en ellos, y en muchas ocasiones llega a invadirlos, e incluso a suplantar su condición originaria . . ."[21]

F. Courtney Tarr posed the problem even more radically:

> The outmoded style and subject-matter of the *artículo de costumbres* as practiced by his contemporaries are the perfect antithesis of the eternal timeliness—and timelessness—of thought, feeling, and expression to be found in the best work of *Fígaro*. To him manners and customs, events and phenomena, are of no interest *per se* (hence the minimum of description in his work), but intensely so as manifestations of underlying human verities, historical, social, and psychological. For Larra, the *artículo de costumbres* is a means, not an end . . . a form at once light in tone and serious in implication, partaking of all the advantages of the critical essay and the formal satire, but with none of their disabilities of limited public and personal and intellectual responsibility. In times of strict censorship and high partisan passion, the very pretense of unpretentiousness was for Larra the *artículo's* most effective (and protective) arm. As the people's jester—for such, in effect, was *Fígaro*—he could permit himself liberties of critical expression impossible in any other form.[22]

Noteworthy in the above quotation is Tarr's mention of the *artículo de costumbres* and the censor in the same paragraph. Tarr understood fully why the essayist called his work "an eloquent chronicle of our so-called freedom of the press." Indeed, a thorough examination of Larra's work must postulate the censor as a factor in its genesis, like the Church fathers for Dante, or Freud for Joyce. The influence of the "umbrageous eye of the all-powerful censorship" was recognized in 1855 by the French critic Charles de Mazade: "Il semble que, sous l'oeil ombrageux de la censure encore toute puissante, l'esprit de l'auteur redouble de souplesse et de vivacité déliée pour se frayer une issue et regagner, par une stratégie savante de réticences et de concessions, la liberté de la satire."[23]

The essayist himself must have felt this factor intensely. The censor's very presence became for him a fount of inspiration, and it is not unlikely that he dreaded the disappearance of the antagonist in the struggle against whom he had refined and specialized his artistic talents. Seven months before his suicide, Figaro wrote:

> Géneros enteros de la literatura han debido a la tiranía y a la dificultad de expresar los escritores sus sentimientos francamente una importancia que sin eso rara vez hubieran conseguido. La alegoría, por ejemplo, sobre cuya base se han fundado tantas obras eminentes, y acaso en las más han brillado los esfuerzos del ingenio, la alegoría expira ya en el día a manos de la libertad de imprenta. La lucha que se establece entre el poder opresor y el oprimido ofrece a éste ocasiones sin fin de rehuir la ley, y eludirla ingeniosamente; y sobre vencerse tal dificultad, no contribuye poco a dar sumo realce a esas obras el peligro en que de ser perseguido se pone el autor una vez adivinado.[24] (2: 242)

> (Whole genres in literature owe to tyranny and to obstacles faced by writers in expressing themselves frankly, an importance which they would not have otherwise acquired. Allegory, for example, on whose foundations so many eminent works have been created, perhaps those works where the striving of wit has shone brightest —allegory is expiring in our day at the hands of freedom of the press. The struggle arising between the oppressing power and the oppressed offers the latter infinite occasions to evade the law, to circumvent it ingeniously; and besides the conquest of such a hurdle, the danger of persecution in which an author puts himself, once it has been guessed, contributes in no small way to the splendor of those works.)

The attainment of the cause for which Figaro struggled would accordingly remove his *raison d'être*. Perhaps his comprehension of the problem made him feel more keenly his own tragedy, for among the winds of political change that swayed the journalist's opinion, there exists one unchanging principle: a desire for liberty of the press. Larra's poetry is minor, his novel is of little merit, and his best play overshadowed by other Romantic productions; but, as Tarr observes, the art of satire was "a form peculiarly suited to Larra's equivocal and paradoxical personality and genius, to his hyperlogical mind and supersensitive soul."[25]

But what of the essays treated in the present volume? Here opinions have differed considerably. José R. Lomba y Pedraja feels they are the least meritorious of Larra's production, because of their peculiar political nature, which obliged the essayist to stray from his principles. Their only saving grace lies in their literary qualities, says the timorously conservative Lomba, who finds Figaro's "steel-tipped darts" flying off from his pen in all directions: "Los dardos acerados saltan de su pluma en todas direcciones; vuelan, fulguran, hieren"; and "De ser una de las partes inconsistentes y caducas de su obra total la salvan solamente sus cualidades literarias."[26] But this is a misconception. The darts were flung in only one direction, at Martínez de la Rosa and his adherents. Another critic, Ismael Sánchez Estevan, praises these essays highly for journalistic instinct, though he assumes like Lomba that Larra was not a party man: "no se sabe qué elogiar más en ellos, si el fino instinto perodístico que revelan o la intención política o la habilidad o el gracejo insuperable de la forma. Con todo lo que se ha escrito sobre política en la prensa española, nada hay comparable a los artículos de Fígaro . . ."[27]

It is Tarr who again seems to come closest to the source of their perennial appeal, when he states that Figaro's "creative gift lies in adaptation and expression—rather than in innovation."[28] Adaptation and expression are indeed our main concern here, for to spoof oratory is primarily to adapt for satirical expression the ideas uttered in a parliament. This is the basis of several essays written between July 1834 and March 1835. Accordingly, the procedure followed in this book has been what, for lack of a better word, might be called "interdisciplinary." Parliamentary history and stylistic analysis will be found side by side.

As for the first, the significance of parliamentary events cannot be overlooked. In Chapter 4 we shall see how the opening of Cortes after a decade of tyranny brought about a grand revival of oratory. Congressional speeches became the talk of the town and filled three-quarters of the average newspaper. This phenomenon must be taken into account if we are to understand Larra's political writings, which originally appeared beside the speeches they ridiculed. Examine the party organs containing his essays and it becomes evident that Figaro's pen was as much a part of the political scene as the oratory. The author himself could hardly underestimate his impact on public opinion. Had his influence and that of his colleagues not been feared, there would have been no censorship, and he would not have developed the ironic and ambiguous style that got his articles past the censor. Form in Larra's work is consequently more than ever inseparable from content; they determine each other, and so our method of analysis must be both historical and stylistic.

Yet even the stylistic aspect of this study has a historical basis. One of the subjects taken by Larra at the Piarist school he attended as a boy was rhetoric, which he learned "with application and proficiency."[29] The significance of rhetoric in any scholarly investigation of Figaro's style cannot be overlooked, for it informs his writing in a twofold manner. In the first place, Spanish orators of the nineteenth century knew their rhetoric well. If by any chance they had missed out on the detailed manuals used by schoolboys, they could always turn to Antonio de Capmany's more modern and grown-up *Filosofía de la elocuencia*, whose many editions attest to its popularity. Now, as we shall see, several of Larra's essays contain parodies of speeches delivered in Cortes, so that what he burlesqued was itself composed according to the principles of rhetoric. Since Figaro likewise knew his rhetoric quite well, he could not only recognize its presence in oratory, but construct his parodies with its help. To state this in a more abstract manner, one might suggest that above the rhetorical oratory stood Larra's rhetorical parody of rhetorical oratory. Now, the mark of a great orator is that his speeches do not appear construed. The technique is there, but the consummate artist has rendered it unobtrusive. This is true of the orators; and so it must necessarily be true of their satirist. In order to oppose them efficiently, Figaro had to be as adept as they at their own tricks. Tarr must have perceived this process clearly when he wrote that satire "allowed the fullest play to [Larra's] extraordinary rhetorical talent."[30]

Although a rhetorical analysis of Larra's work is beyond the scope of the present volume, rhetorical terms are occasionally used in describing his style. By doing this we deal with Larra on his own "terms," and the more so because the textbook he studied as a boy is identifiable. The Piarists seem to have assigned throughout their schools a particular manual written by one of their own members, Fr. Calixto Hornero.[31] Its short prologue is immediately followed by one hundred thirty quotations from Classical Latin authors to be learned by rote, lest pupils slip into Church Latin, one of the author's tactfully stated concerns. The same care is evidenced in the next eighteen pages, designed to teach elegant syntax, but dealing solely with Latin grammar. Then comes something more significant for our purposes, the forty pages devoted to progymnasmata, since most of them are applicable to Castilian as well as Latin prose.[32]

Exercises in creating climax are especially noteworthy, because we could easily find a close stylistic kinship between the examples given and some passages of *El Pobrecito Hablador*. All the examples in Hornero's book are from Cicero and Fray Luis de Granada. A great deal has been said by critics concerning the influence of various authors on Larra, but up to now no one has mentioned Fray Luis in this conection.

Fr. Hornero, moreover, mentions three kinds of fable, the rational (or parable), moral, and mixed. There are several instances of the first in Larra; moreover, in *El Duende Satírico del Día*, we find examples of the last two quoted from Iriarte, a famous eighteenth-century fabulist.

Almost all of Figaro's stylistic devices are of the kinds listed by rhetoricians. Nevertheless, there is one, frequently used by him, which they have not touched upon, simply because rhetoric was intended for oratory, not satire. The device in question is a sort of ironic simile to which I have given the name "pregnant vehicle." This term is patterned on "pregnant construction" (q.v. in H. W. Fowler, *Modern English Usage*), and on I. A. Richards's denomination of the two elements of a metaphor as "tenor" and

"vehicle."[33] Since Richards devised his terminology mainly to analyze English poetry, its application to other literatures is not quite
adequate; still, these two words are the most appropriate we have.
Thus, when we say, "God is like a father," *God* is the tenor and
father the vehicle. Now, Larra's similes are often found in an
ironically structured context. For example, his article on a bad
performance of Gaetano Donizetti's *Ana Bolena* provides him
with an opportunity to comment on the dismal political situation:

> Por otra parte, es indudable que fue ópera: muchas señales hubo
> de ello por lo menos; estaba el teatro concurrido, en primer lugar;
> el público, en segundo, estaba tan frío y descontadizo como si le
> estuvieran gobernando y haciendo feliz, y tan callado y tan de mal
> humor, como en tiempo de Calomarde; la orquesta estuvo tan dis-
> corde y llena de contradicciones, como nuestra legislación; las
> comparsas estaban en ala, a manera de adornos paralelos que nunca
> han de encontrarse, y tan separados los sexos como liberales y
> carlistas . . . (1: 398)

> (Indubitably it was an opera; at least there were many signs of
> it. In the first place, the theater was full; secondly, the public was
> cold and dissatisfied, as if it were being governed and conducted
> to pursue happiness; and quiet and ill-humored as in the days of
> Calomarde. The orchestra was as discordant and polyphonous as
> our laws; the extras, forming two wings like parallel decorations
> never bound to meet, with the sexes separated like Liberals and
> Carlists . . .)

If the vehicle of this passage is not the dominant element, it is
thematically at least at an equal level with the tenor, because Figaro never tires of relating most defects and misfortunes to the
political situation, the foremost topic in his mind.

As Tarr has pointed out, "in Larra's best and most characteristic articles the point of departure often lies in a single happy
phrase or concept—frequently the title—the implications of
which are developed with amazing agility of wit and originality
of application."[34] Accordingly, Larra will use a word or phrase to
join several ideas in such a manner that this word or phrase deter-
mines the form of his essay, whereas the content is dispersed
among the several ideas he brings together. We could say, from a
stylistic point of view, that the phrase in question is explicated by

an accumulation of similes; nevertheless, we must add that the whole process is ironic, because what results is not a clarification of the theme but a witty combination of ideas. The vehicle of each simile therefore becomes more significant than the tenor, which is the theme phrase.

Two illustrations of the pregnant vehicle will serve as a conclusion to this introductory chapter. The first occurs in an early work, the second at the end of Larra's career. On March 1, 1833, Figaro published an essay entitled "Yo quiero ser cómico," through which he exposed the plight of the Madrid stage and the incompetence of its players, who, he implies, do their job so badly that they are truly ne'er-do-wells. Almost at the beginning of his essay we read:

> Columpiábame en mi mullido sillón, de estos que dan vueltas sobre su eje, los cuales son especialmente de mi gusto por asemejarse en cierto modo a muchas gentes que conozco, y me hallaba en la mayor perplejidad sin saber cuál de mis numerosas apuntaciones elegiría para un artículo que me correspondía injerir aquel día en la *Revista*. (1: 187)

> (I was rocking in my well-padded armchair, the kind that turns on its axis, which is especially to my liking because it somehow resembles many people I know; and I found myself in the greatest perplexity, not knowing which of my numerous notes to choose for an article that it was my turn to interject into *La Revista* that day.)

What is the swivel chair? The journalist himself, who, frustrated by severe censorship, cannot decide what topic will bear marketable fruit? The ignorant young ne'er-do-well who comes to see him for a recommendation, hoping to succeed as an actor because he is a failure at everything else? Perhaps even the despotic, warily alert government? Why not the whole stagnant nation itself? But notice that they are not like the swivel chair; the swivel chair is like them.

As Larra grew older he became more adept at this type of simile. Less than four months before killing himself he produced a pessimistic essay entitled "El día de difuntos de 1836. Fígaro en el cementerio," written on the occasion when Roman Catholics remember their dead. Figaro tells his audience that they waste their time going to the cemetery; all they need do is look in the mirror, since Madrid itself is a huge graveyard. Yet even here the author injects political satire. The "ultraliberal" government has taken, among other measures, two which he highly disapproves of, confiscation of convents and monasteries and abolition of the gallows, reinstating the garotte in their stead. We may observe how a sarcastic Larra combines linguistically these two apparently unrelated pieces of legislation, turning the tenor into its own vehicle, as he ponders the approaching silence of the bells in the deserted convents:

Y el bronce herido que anunciaba con lamentable clamor la ausencia eterna de los que han sido, parecía vibrar más lúgubre que ningún año, como si presagiase su propia muerte. Ellas también, las campanas, han alcanzado su última hora, y sus tristes acentos son el estertor del moribundo; ellas también van a morir a manos de la libertad, que todo lo vivifica, y ellas serán las únicas en España ¡santo Dios! que morirán colgadas. (2: 280)

(And the stricken bronze which announced with mournful clamor the eternal absence of the departed, seemed to vibrate more gloomily than ever, as if to presage its own death. They too, these bells, have reached their last hour; their grievous accents are the stertor of the moribund; they too shall die at the hands of liberty, which instills new life into everything, and they will be the only ones in Spain, oh God!, to die hanging.)

2

THE POLITICAL SCENE
FROM FERDINAND'S
DEATH TO THE
OPENING OF CORTES

W HEN Ferdinand died on September 29, 1833, the liberals hoped that María Cristina, now queen regent for her young daughter Isabel II, would form a new ministry. They were immediately disappointed, however, because she kept Zea Bermúdez, who reiterated his belief in enlightened despotism. The prime minister was backed mainly by the aristocracy and several persons who had profited from the government's clumsy handling of its foreign debt through Aguado, a Spanish banker in Paris. Perhaps the queen retained Zea also out of spite for Carlota, who hated him; the two sisters were not on good terms at the time. Yet María Cristina always trusted Zea more than anyone else, and his decision to abide strictly by Ferdinand's will appealed to her. After all, she was regent by virtue of Ferdinand's desire as expressed in this will, and the more closely the document was observed, the more it would be held in esteem. This soon proved impracticable, however, because it specified who should serve on the Council of State, and several of these individuals were hostile to the queen. Yet Zea Bermúdez's uncompromising position prevented his obtaining additional support to offset this hostility. He is reported to have said in October 1833 that the possibility of recovering Spain's American colonies was greater than ever.[1] Then, in order to assuage the misgivings of Russia and Austria, he issued the famous manifesto of October 14 which stated that the political system would not allow dangerous innovations ("admitir innovaciones peligrosas").[2] This did not pacify the Carlists. It may have kept the absolutist nobles from showing alarm; it may have met with approval from the London *Times* and *Globe* and some French newspapers; it may have satisfied the British and French ambassadors; but it outraged the liberals. This decree, which Léonce-Victor, duc de Broglie, called an irremediable mistake ("une faute irrémédiable"), did not even afford Isabel the recognition of Russia or the Holy See, and least of all that of Cristina's brother, the king of the Two Sicilies, who recognized Carlos. As for France, she had already declared for the queen. Moreover, the manifesto was not really needed to obtain the support of many absolutists whose allegiance sprang from sentimental rather than political considerations. Spaniards, after all, saw France as a frequent enemy and honored the memory of Isabel the Catholic. Carlists would therefore encounter difficulty in persuading people that women could not rule in Spain owing to a French law. Serafín Estébanez Calderón, one of Larra's fellow *costumbristas*, would thus use traditional arguments against those of the supposedly traditional Carlists. A second Isabel appealed to his historical and poetic inclinations.[3] Luis Fernández de Córdoba, who would later command the queen's troops, acted from sheer loyalty.[4]

Although he compounded with more blunders the mistakes made under Ferdinand, Zea Bermúdez did take some effective measures. He obtained the recognition of three constitutional monarchies, replaced unreliable government officials, reopened the universities, issued another amnesty, restored their property to former exiles, rescinded the *cédula* of 1824 which had annulled purchases of entailed estates effected during the Triennium, and attempted to revise the civil code. Nevertheless, most liberals were far from satisfied, even after a new decree issued on January 4, 1834, concerning the press. All scientific, technical, artistic, and literary works could now be printed without prior censorship as long as they did not contain political, historical, or philosophical remarks. But works dealing with geology, history, and travel, as well as poems, novels, and plays were still censored.[5] In practice, censorship turned out to be almost as onerous as before the decree; it was even impossible to teach the natural sciences, with scholasticism still in vogue.[6] Meanwhile, French politicians repeatedly admonished the Duque de Frías, ambassador to Paris, to proceed slowly at reforms ("N'allez pas trop vite!"). The principle of immutability, however, could not long apply in a country that had been repressed for so many years.

Under these circumstances some liberal groups became extremely restless. Very shortly after Ferdinand's death a coup was proposed by Eugenio de Aviraneta, founder of the Isabelina, a secret society with which Larra may possibly have been associated. The plan was rejected by Aviraneta's fellow progressives, who deemed it unwise to inflict additional sorrow on María Cristina; the regent would not have forgiven such an act. They decided instead to issue an apocryphal *Gaceta de Madrid*, announcing Carlist rebellions in several parts of Spain, in the hope of arousing people to demand arms. This did not work, but the fake *Gaceta*'s news turned out to be fortuitously authentic.[7] These leftist liberals also indicated their attitude in other ways. For example, when Isabel II was proclaimed queen of Spain, Larra, in an article describing the ceremonies, insinuated his liberal—they could even be called progressive—views for the first time. Zea Bermúdez, still prime minister at the time of these ceremonies (October 25, 1833), was relying for support on Masonic groups who were merely anticlerical conservatives, not sufficiently numerous to take on the Carlists. The liberals, on the other hand, wanted the regent to hasten reform and create a constitutional government. One way to force her hand was to withhold their cooperation, thus foisting on her a political allegiance with them. In their outlook we might find an analogy with that of certain liberals during the Napoleonic War. For the Jacobins who helped create the Constitution of 1812, the War of Independence was inseparable from what they called the Spanish Revolution, that is, a change to representative government and a higher degree of liberty. Such an equation was out of the question for the more conservative

Junta Central, merely interested in seeing Ferdinand returned to the throne as an enlightened despot.[8]

In the meantime Carlism was gaining. Just when the cause seemed lost, Tomás de Zumalacárregui reorganized the rebels in the Basque provinces and put to rout several loyal army units. What drew so many Basques to Carlos was the not wholly unfounded fear that the Cristinos would revoke their *fueros*, the pseudoconstitutional privileges of the old kingdom of Navarre. Yet rebellion was by no means limited to the northeast. Bands of the factious roamed other provinces and a Carlist plot was unmasked in Madrid. The monks, most of whom sympathized with the pretender's cause, were hiding weapons behind church altars and even engaging in open attack. Calomarde formed a junta in Toulouse while a loan from the house of Enero was being negotiated by Carlos in Portugal. During both the Zea and Martínez ministries, progressive liberals insisted on more governmental action against the rebels, but the latter's terrible reprisals eventually induced the opposite course of issuing exaggerated pardons.[9]

Alarmed at the Carlist danger, the French proceeded to deploy armies along the Pyrenees to impede the flow of supplies and reinforcements to the rebels. As for the British, their ambassador, George Villiers, who had at first supported Zea, began to hope for his removal. Henry John Temple, Third Viscount Palmerston, formulated the Quadruple Alliance, and Spain found herself again torn between several foreign policies as well as by internal strife. At last even the Masons became impatient with Zea. Two letters were addressed to the regent, one ghost-written by Salustiano Olózaga and signed by General Vicente Jenaro de Quesada, and another by General Manuel Llauder, who would later become secretary of war. Though never acknowledged by the government, copies of them were circulated in Madrid. They called for Cortes and a liberal régime. Even conservatives like General Luis Fernández de Córdoba and the Marquis of Miraflores, Manuel Pando Fernández de Pineda, sent such notes to the queen, so that finally, after some blunt persuasion, Zea understood his situation and resigned.[10]

The ministry which succeeded Zea Bermúdez took office on January 15, 1834. It lasted about sixteen months. A year after its demise, Larra curtly summed up the latter part of the régime in

"Buenas noches": "pasamos largos meses haciendo una comedia de capa y espada, que no ha sido otra cosa el año 35" (2: 143—"we spent seemingly endless months composing a cloak-and-dagger comedy, which is just what the year 1835 has been"). The government at the time had six secretaryships—its members were not even officially designated as ministers—and the posts were occupied as follows:

Secretario del Despacho de

Estado: January 15, 1834—Francisco Martínez de la Rosa.

Gracia y Justicia: January 15, 1834—Nicolás María Garelly; February 19, 1835—Juan de la Dehesa.

Marina: January 15, 1834—José Vázquez Figueroa.

Guerra: November 16, 1833—Remón Zarco del Valle; November 2, 1834—Manuel Llauder (Martínez de la Rosa acting for one month); January 24, 1835—Martínez de la Rosa, acting; February 17, 1835—Jerónimo Valdés.

Hacienda: January 15, 1834—José Aranalde; February 7, 1834— José de Imaz; June 18, 1834—Conde de Toreno.

Fomento (renamed lo Interior on May 13, 1834): October 21, 1833—Francisco Javier de Burgos; April 17, 1834—Nicolás María Garelly, acting; May 2, 1834—José María Moscoso de Altamira; February 17, 1835—Diego Medrano.

The change from "Fomento" to "lo Interior" should be noted. The latter denomination had a certain symbolic significance because it first appeared during the regency installed by the Duc d'Angoulême in 1823. When his troops departed, the Despacho de lo Interior was abolished owing to pressure from the extreme right. Then, in 1833 the queen, upon assuming responsibility while Ferdinand was ill, reactivated this branch of government, placing at its head Javier de Burgos, but, in order to avoid alarming Francophobic elements, with the title of *Ministro de Fomento*.[11] When the importance of the office had grown considerably, it was felt that loyal citizens would not be outraged by a reversion to the original title, and the *subdelegados de Fomento* became *gobernadores civiles*. Besides, the title of minister had by that time been changed to secretary, so that there was no cause for alarm.[12] As we shall see, these changes in denomination became the butt of Larra's railleries.[13]

The first thing Martínez did upon assuming power was to inspect the treasury. When he saw that it was empty, he turned to the French Rothschilds, the only alternative to a tax raise, which would have lost the queen considerable support, or a national loan, which would have been unfruitful. Baron James Rothschild thus became *Banquero de España*, and after some delay funds were sent to the Ejército del Norte.[14] It is therefore obvious that Martínez did not have the resources to extinguish the Carlist rebellion immediately, as some historians retrospectively suggest he ought to have done. He defended himself honorably when accused by General Fernando Butrón of laxity in this matter. On September 9, 1834, Martínez explained in Cortes:

No basta decir *levántese un ejército:* es menester ver cómo se levanta, cómo se arma, cómo se mantiene: es menester ver hasta dónde alcanzan los recursos del Estado, cuál es el déficit que hay en el Ministerio de Hacienda, cuál es el desnivel de entradas y salidas, en las necesidades y presupuestos. (*Pr.,* p. 214)

(To say *let's raise an army* does not suffice. It is necessary to determine how it can be raised, armed, maintained; how far the resources of the state can be extended, what is the deficit in the treasury, what is the discrepancy between income and expenses, needs and budgets.)

As for the nonfiscal measures taken by Martínez, they include the formation of a new civil code, the confiscation of the Bishop of León's property (an effective warning to the other Carlist clergy, for this bishop, who was now one of the pretender's ministers, had been fomenting dissension even before Ferdinand's death), a decree to send captured noncommissioned rebels on overseas duty, a reform of the judiciary, and a project to reform the clergy. The latter, however, was doomed from the start because Gregory XVI did not recognize Isabel II. The most important religious measure was the definitive abolition on July 15, 1834, of the Inquisition, which, as we have seen, Ferdinand had failed to revive in 1823. Larra humorously alludes to the decree in "El ministerial" (September 16, 1834) (1: 438).[15]

Although prior censorship was not abandoned, new regulations made it less arbitrary. Still, they were far from lenient, and when

Larra satirized them in October, his article remained unpublished, most probably because of the regulations themselves.[16] Nevertheless, they could be interpreted broadly and some benevolent censors could be found. Others, like Juan Nicasio Gallego, were strict; but none resembled the officeholder of 1832, "el infame fraile censor, que es un bribón e idiota carlista"[17] ("the infamous monk-censor, who is a scoundrel and a Carlist idiot").

In order to suppress Carlist uprisings in Madrid, the Milicia Urbana was instituted by decree on February 15, 1834. It corresponded to the defunct absolutist Voluntarios Realistas abolished by Zea. Certain provisions were made in its charter, however, to avoid alarming conservative elements. The new corps was not given the name of Milicia Nacional, too suggestive of its role in the Triennium. Moreover, each town or city could have only one *urbano* for every hundred inhabitants, a requirement that elicited the banter of the *Boletín del Comercio*, which demonstrated that the one percent law ("ley del uno por ciento") would leave many towns and large areas defenseless.[18] The law soon had to be revised, of course, and Larra did not fail to incorporate the blunder into his satirical repertory.[19]

Another step taken by the new régime was the amnesty of February 24 to liberals still in exile. Unfortunately, the government's attitude thoroughly irked the progressive faction because, by issuing an acquittal, it assumed a charitable and patronizing pose. The proper course, many felt, would have been to declare null and void the expatriation decrees which had originally forced these persons into exile when the constitutional régime was overthrown in 1823.[20] A further source of annoyance was the existence of many government posts still occupied by Calomarde's and Zea's former staff. The Progressives wanted the appointments of the Triennium revalidated, and the controversy developed into a long parliamentary debate that soon found echoes in Larra's writings.[21]

The ministry's best-known accomplishment was the Estatuto Real, sanctioned by the queen on April 10, 1834.[22] Owing to the prime minister's hesitancy, liberals had to wait four months for the promulgation of this document, which could not even be called a constitution. Although the Estatuto Real resembles the French charter of 1814, in spirit it is not really a *charte octroyée* (a charter granted by the monarch as a privilege rather than a right). The French Crown, affirming its right to absolute power, conceded to the nation the privilege of representation. The Spanish government, on the other hand, claimed that it renewed a medieval institution, an opinion asseverated by Martínez de la Rosa: "No es gracia de la Corona, sino un derecho de la nación que se restablece"[23] ("It is not a favor from the Crown, but a right of the nation which is being reestablished"). Nevertheless, many liberals did not share this view. For them, since a national assembly did not draft it, the Estatuto was still a *carta otorgada*.[24] All considered, the Estatuto Real was a hybrid of the French charter and the statutes of Spain's medieval Cortes, allowing for two chambers given the traditional name of Estamentos. Perhaps Martínez de la Rosa's ideas on medieval political revival have much in common with those of the so-called Ocistas, a group of Spaniards exiled in England during the Ominous Decade who aired their views in the journal *Ocios de Españoles Emigrados*. The Ocistas' tenets can be traced back to Jovellanos. Though Martínez revered Jovellanos, he was likewise greatly influenced by Victor Cousin. Perhaps Martínez de la Rosa decided on the bicameral system after observing the English and reading Jeremy Bentham, who enjoyed a great vogue in Spain at one time.[25] Nicolás María Garelly also favored this system, but apparently not Toreno, the most liberal of the triumvirate which drafted the Estatuto.[26] The members of the lower house, the Estamento de Procuradores, were to be elected in the following manner: In each town that was a *cabeza de partido*, an electoral junta was to be established, composed of

> todos los individuos del ayuntamiento, incluso los síndicos y diputados, y agregándoles un número igual de los mayores contribuyentes. Cada una de estas juntas nombrará dos electores para que concurran a la capital de la respectiva provincia, pudiendo nombrarlos, no sólo entre los mismos individuos del ayuntamiento, y entre los mayores contribuyentes que hayan concurrido a la elección, sino entre todos los que tengan las condiciones que requiera la ley.[27]

(all the individuals in the municipal government, including the syndics and deputies, and adding to them an equal number of the largest taxpayers. Each one of these committees shall name two electors who are to meet in the capital of the respective province; these may be appointed not only from among the municipal government members themselves, and from among the largest taxpayers who have assisted in the election, but also from among all those who satisfy the requirements of the law.)

The electors meeting in the capital of their province would then name the *procuradores* for that province. To qualify for the office, one had to be over thirty, a native of Spain or son of Spaniards, have an income of twelve thousand reales, and be, moreover, a native of the province represented, or have resided there two years, or receive six thousand reales in income from property within it. The electoral system was not fixed in the Estatuto itself, however, but in the preamble, which added:

> Por fortuna, el sistema de elecciones es de suyo variable y sujeto a enmiendas y mejoras; y así nos ha parecido preferible comprenderle en una ley aparte: ya para no darle cierto carácter de perpetuidad, entrelazándolo con disposiciones fundamentales, ya para anunciar desde luego que irá perfeccionándose insensiblemente con el arreglo de la administración pública y con los consejos de la experiencia.[28]

> (Fortunately the electoral system is by its very nature variable and subject to amendments and improvements. Accordingly it has seemed preferable to us to include it in a separate law, in order not to impart to it a certain character of perpetuity, as well as to announce at the outset that it will perfect itself imperceptibly as the public administration is put in order and with the counsels of experience.)

The upper house, called the Estamento de Próceres, consisted of (1) all grandees in good standing, over twenty-five years old, possessing an income over two hundred thousand reales; and (2) holders of nonhereditary *procerazgos*, chosen by the Crown among men of distinction, including the ecclesiastical hierarchy. One category of *prócer* had to have an annual income of sixty thousand reales, a requirement which did not escape Larra's banter.[29] It should be obvious that the Próceres was a "rubber stamp" chamber. The only dissenters in the upper house turned out to be Ángel Saavedra, Duque de Rivas; Ramón Gil de la Cuadra; and

Antonio Cano Manuel. The lower house, on the other hand, became the scene of considerable opposition, in spite of Martínez's electoral precautions, cleverly described by his biographer:

> Postérieurement les gouverneurs civils reçurent l'ordre de faire proclamer en grande pompe le Statut Royal et le décret d'élections. Le Ministère leur adressa aussi quelques conseils sur l'honnêteté et la liberté nécessaires dans les opérations électorales, afin que les élus "soient des personnes aimant sincèrement leur pays, résolument décidées en faveur des droits de la reine, et animées de ces principes conservateurs qui, dans un gouvernement monarchique, identifient la splendeur et la fermeté du Trône à la liberté et à la gloire de la Nation." Autrement dit, le Ministère voulait qu'on lui préparât une majorité. On sait avec quelle fidélité cette méthode a été suivie en Espagne jusqu'à nos jours.[30]

> (Subsequently the civil governors were ordered to proclaim with great pomp the Royal Statute and the election decree. The minister also directed to them some advice on the honesty and liberty necessary in electoral procedures, so that those elected "would be persons who sincerely loved their country, were resolutely decided in favor of the queen's rights, and motivated by those conservative principles which, in a monarchical government, identify the splendor and firmness of the Throne with the glory of the Nation." In other words, the minister wanted a majority prepared for him. How faithfully this method has been followed in Spain to our day is well known.)

Martínez de la Rosa was most successful in foreign policy. It should not be forgotten that his domestic policy was designed to some extent to please foreign governments, or at least, as in the case of the Northern Powers, to avoid offending them. The latter nevertheless recalled their ambassadors from Madrid. According to Martínez de la Rosa, had it not been for the Treaty of Quadruple Alliance, a commendable achievement, the Northern Powers would have recognized Carlos to boot. The results, then, were felicitous, but the negotiations leading up to the treaty were fraught with errors. For one thing, England still considered herself France's rival. She therefore took advantage of French hesitation about Spain and purposely strained Anglo-French relations in order to keep France out of Portuguese affairs. Moreover, wishing to retain commercial influence for themselves, the British looked askance at the possibility of French intervention in the Peninsula (this was to become obvious two years later when the English ambassador, George Villiers, signed a secret treaty with Mendizábal which so angered the French and Catalans that it led to Mendizábal's downfall). At first the English looked with some satisfaction upon Louis-Philippe's vacillating attitude; because of it the Marqués de Miraflores was persuaded to sign a separate treaty with England which excluded France from Portuguese affairs and merely invited it to aid Spain voluntarily. This in turn angered the French and tended to make them indifferent to the civil war,[31] although they soon perceived the disadvantage of such a course. On April 22, 1834, the separate treaty was dropped and the Quadruple Alliance formed. Its signature had diverse effects. Miraflores is reported to have remarked later that "entre naciones cuya fuerza es desigual, las estipulaciones escritas no tienen otra aplicación ni inteligencia que la que quiere prestarles la nación más fuerte entre las contratantes" ("among nations whose power is unequal, written stipulations have no other application or meaning than that which the strongest nation among the contracting parties wants to give it"). Marliani attributes to Talleyrand the observation that the treaty "es nada, para nosotros; algo, para las Potencias del Norte; mucho, para los tontos"[32] ("for us, nothing; for the Northern Powers, something; for fools, a great deal"). The opinion prevailing in Vienna was reported in a letter from the Comte de Saint-Hilaire dated March 17, 1834:

On est ici très soucieux, mais on n'en parle qu'académiquement. Je ne crois à aucune démonstration des puissances, mais seulement à un redoublement d'intimité qui se manifestera dans quelque autre affaire. Pour tout ce qui arrivera en Espagne, on ne se fâchera que si le contre-coup se faisait sentir en Italie. C'est à cela qu'il importe de prendre garde.[33]

(People are very worried, but speak of it only academically. I don't believe any power play will take place, but only an increase in cordiality which will show up in some other affair. People will get angry at everything that may happen in Spain only if the backlash should show up in Italy. That's what one has to be careful about.)

Nevertheless, according to Elie, Duc Decazes, the French king was still hesitant, even in the face of Carlist growth encouraged by the Pretender's secret entry into Spain in August:

> Le duc d'Orléans est très fortement prononcé pour l'intervention; le roi contre. Le roi s'en explique même trop avec les ambassadeurs étrangers. Le duc d'Orléans dit que si don Carlos entre à Vittoria [sic] et marche sur Burgos, nous ne devons pas hésiter, parce qu'à aucun prix nous ne devons laisser une restauration s'établir à Madrid. Thiers est de cet avis. Guizot en était au moment même de l'entrée en Espagne de don Carlos. Rigny n'en est pas éloigné. En résumé, je crois que le cas prévu par le duc d'Orléans arrivant, l'intervention aura lieu. Le roi est plus favorable dans son for intérieur à don Carlos qu'à la reine. La loi salique l'emporte de beaucoup dans son coeur sur la question constitutionelle ou d'usurpation.[34]

> (The Duke d'Orléans has come out very strongly in favor of intervention; the king, against it. The king even argues his point too much with foreign ambassadors. The Duke d'Orléans says that if Don Carlos enters Vitoria and marches on Burgos, we must not hesitate, because at no price must we allow a restoration to be established in Madrid. Thiers is of this opinion; Guizot was at the very moment that Don Carlos entered Spain; Rigny is not far from it. In sum, I believe that if the situation foreseen by the Duke d'Orléans should occur, intervention will take place. The king, deep down inside, favors Don Carlos more than the queen. In his heart the Salic law prevails over the question of constitution or usurpation.)

Miraflores, on his part, persevered in seeking more guarantees, until the Additional Articles were signed on August 18, 1834. These were deemed even more important than the treaty itself, for in them England pledged arms, munitions, and naval support; France swore to stop supplies for the Carlists at her frontier; and Portugal promised all possible aid.[35] Nevertheless, the Spanish liberals' hopes began to fade because the expected results were not forthcoming. Larra expressed his disillusionment as early as October.[36] The following year he sent from abroad to his newspaper an article portraying "una *cuasi* intervención, resultado de un *cuasi* tratado, *cuasi* olvidado, con naciones *cuasi* aliadas" (2: 122—

"a quasi-intervention, resulting from a quasi-treaty, in quasi-oblivion, with quasi-allied nations").

While diplomacy lingered the Carlist menace grew. There were frequent plots as well as rebel bands throughout the country. In the Basque provinces, Zumalacárregui's army won its first battle at Alsasua. Since the Cristinos had decided to treat Carlists as traitors who deserved execution, Zumalacárregui retaliated by shooting prisoners too. Even a grandee suffered this fate.

Mention must be made of the affairs of Portugal. On Ferdinand's death, many adherents flocked to the neighboring nation, rallying to the cause of Don Carlos, who began issuing decrees as if he were king. When the Spanish government finally recognized Maria da Gloria, General José Ramón Rodil and his Ejército de Observación were invited to drive out Dom Miguel, who capitulated on May 26, 1834, and agreed to embark for Italy. The Spanish pretender, on the other hand, managed to obtain safe-conduct to England on a British frigate whose captain had been persuaded to lend his aid by Auguet de Saint-Sylvain, Carlos' French admirer and adviser.[37] The prince's escape from England on June 1, 1834, was likewise planned by Saint-Sylvain. Carlos passed through France secretly and arrived on the 12th at Elizondo, where he met Zumalacárregui and named him lieutenant-general and commander of his army, reserving for the Virgin Mary the title of Generalissima of all the Loyal Defenders of the Faith.[38] There were medieval precedents for this decree, of course, but we must admit that it was an anachronism, especially under the circumstances, even though Carlos firmly believed that divine intervention would make him king. As always, he surrounded himself with clergy, since "la voix d'un homme en soutane, fût-il sacristain, lui paraît toujours la voix de Dieu"[39] ("the voice of a man in a cassock, even a sacristan, always seemed to him to be the voice of God"). The Carlist goals were the restoration of the Inquisition, the preservation of clerical interests, and the maintenance of the special privileges or *fueros* of Navarre. Carlos Seco Serrano, in his preface to Larra's work, reproduces an editorial from the official Carlist newspaper which praises "la sencilla y virtuosa ignorancia de las gentes, ignorancia saludable que las hiciera vivir contentas sin ambicionar destinos de superior jerarquía" ("the simple and virtuous ignorance of the common people, a wholesome ignorance which would allow them to live contented without aspiring to positions of higher category"), and which "la revolución" was destroying. "¡Cuánto más conveniente hubiera sido continuar bajo el pretendido *oscurantismo,* y dejarse el pueblo conducir por la voluntad de los Reyes!" (1: xlvii—"How much more convenient it would have been to continue under so-called *obscurantism,* and for the people to let itself be led by the will of Kings!").

The Carlists were not the Madrid government's sole plague, however. The other side of the political spectrum also vexed it considerably with conspiracies in Seville and Jerez on March 2 and May 6, 1834, respectively. The capital itself was the scene of riot on May 11 and later of the great plot of July 23 in the midst of a population demoralized by cholera. An epidemic had swept the country, reaching Madrid during the first half of July, and at first causing only isolated cases of illness. A sudden wave of death came on the morning of the fifteenth, reaching its apogee on the seventeenth. A mass exodus ensued, not only from Madrid but from Spain, to which many families did not return for several years. To account for the casualties a rumor spread that monks had poisoned the water. Mobs broke into the monasteries to slaughter the friars, even before their altars. Among them were Jesuit educators such as the noted Arabic scholar Artigas. Some of Larra's Piarist teachers also perished. In general, the monks were in sympathy with the pretender's cause, which they secretly aided, but this cannot justify the suspicious delay of action by the civil authorities in putting down the disorders. Augusto Conte relates in his memoirs Martínez de la Rosa's recollection of these events:

> tenía Martínez fija en la memoria la matanza de los frailes. Veíase que aquel suceso *manebat alta mente repostum.* Y motejaba con amargura al *Ministro de la Guerra* Zarco del Valle, el cual llegó al Consejo de ministros a hora tarda y colocándose en un sofá, como si estuviera muy cansado, exclamó: "Ya he visitado todos los puestos y estoy seguro de que no habrá motín." Pero no había casi acabado de hablar cuando se oyeron los primeros tiros. "Una sola cosa me faltó entonces y me ha faltado toda mi vida, seguía diciendo Martínez de la Rosa, y es ceñir una espada."[40]

(Martínez kept the massacre of the monks fixed in his memory. It could be sensed that the event was buried in the depths of his mind. And he would bitterly rail at the War Minister Zarco del

Valle, who arrived at the cabinet quite late and, getting down on a sofa as if he were very tired, exclaimed, "I have already inspected all the posts and I am certain there shall be no insurrection." But he had hardly finished speaking when the first shots were heard. "I needed one thing then which I have lacked all my life," Martínez de la Rosa would keep on saying, "and that's to gird on a sword.")

Some historians have pointed to the Sociedad Isabelina as the propagator of the rumor, but the truth will probably never be known. It should be noted that this sort of defamation had precedents, especially in the Middle Ages when the Great Plague was blamed on the Jews for the same reasons. In 1831 some monks in Paris were also slaughtered for supposedly poisoning the water.[41]

The society blamed for inciting the slaughter was a revival of the Comuneros of 1821. Its founder, Eugenio de Aviraneta, who had already been dissuaded from a previous plot against Zea, was now planning to overthrow the Martínez ministry, with which the Progressives were thoroughly dissatisfied. Burgos and other former Josefinos would be exiled, and the queen forced to disavow the Estatuto Real and to sign a more liberal constitution, drawn up by Olavarría.[42] It would have abolished all monastic orders and land privileges. Property belonging to the state would be freely distributed, one-third as recompense for military service, two-thirds to the needy. It also proposed a ceiling on government salaries and the independence of the Spanish Church from the Roman Curia. It must not be forgotten that the Cortes were about to open. As part of the plot, several *procuradores*-elect had agreed to propose to the Estamento that it constitute itself into a National Assembly, which indicates that Martínez's apprehensions were well-founded. The plot was denounced, but at the moment of his arrest Aviraneta managed to eat the list of those involved. José de Palafox y Melzi, whom the queen had just named Duke of Saragossa, was also arrested. Reams of pamphlets and articles had been distributed, and though everyone believed the existence of a conspiracy, the leftist press, especially *El Eco del Comercio*, attempted to prove that there had been none.

Don Eugenio de Aviraneta oscureció de tal manera el proceso, durante la sustanciación [which occurred months later], que nada pudieron averiguar los tribunales; y el fiscal don Laureano de Jado se vio precisado a declarar inocente a todos, y reconocer como únicamente culpable a Aviraneta. Éste, que no deseaba otra cosa que quedar solo, en un artículo comunicado inserto en el *Eco del Comercio,* contestó a la acusación fiscal, diciendo entre otras cosas . . . "que conspiración reducida a un solo individuo, no es conspiración, porque es implicatorio conspirar más de un solo hombre."[43]

(Eugenio de Aviraneta confounded the case in such manner, during the substantiation, that the courts could ascertain nothing. The prosecutor Laureano de Jado found himself compelled to declare everyone innocent, and to recognize Aviraneta as the only guilty person. Aviraneta, who desired nothing more than to remain alone, replied to the accusation of the prosecution in a communication printed by the *Eco del Comercio,* saying among other things . . . "that a conspiracy which reduces to one individual is not a conspiracy because by definition it is contradictory for one man to conspire alone.")

Larra's attitude toward this incident will be examined in the next chapter.

An account of Martínez de la Rosa's character has been given in the previous section. It now behooves us to examine several judgments concerning his ministry during the years that Larra criticized him. Jean Sarrailh, who wrote the statesman's biography and edited his dramatic works, makes the following general appraisal:

Pendant les premiers mois de son ministère, Martínez se recueille, réfléchit aux solutions les plus favorables. Il ne prend que des décisions partielles . . . Pour ce qui est des relations de l'Espagne avec les autres puissances, Martínez semble avoir fait preuve d'une grande activité: il aimait mieux les déclarations historiques, les grandes considérations politiques que les actes et les décisions promptes . . . les premières démarches révèlent un sens exact de la situation diplomatique de l'Espagne et un vif souci de fortifier le trône de la jeune souveraine. Comme elles ne furent pas connues du public, elles ne purent pas calmer la déception causée par les mesures administratives adoptées par le cabinet.[44]

(During the first months of his ministry, Martínez collected his thoughts, reflecting on the most favorable solutions. He made partial decisions only . . . Concerning Spain's relations with the other powers, Martínez appears to have displayed much activity. He preferred historic declarations and broad political considerations to prompt acts and decisions . . . his first moves reveal an exact appraisal of Spain's diplomatic situation and intense concern with strengthening the throne of the young sovereign. Since the public was not aware of them, they could not allay the disappointment caused by the cabinet's administrative measures.)

Being a skillful diplomat, Martínez de la Rosa assured foreign governments that no perilous innovations would be undertaken. His prudence was vindicated the next year by the hapless example of Mendizábal, whose radical policies frightened Louis-Philippe to such an extent that the French allowed convoys and supplies for the Carlists to pass the frontier. Yet Martínez's inclination to go at reforms slowly does not appear sufficiently justified, and H. Butler Clarke's statement that "he proved a good transition minister"[45] is somewhat exaggerated. On the other hand, the attacks of his contemporaries, including Larra, must be judged with care. Antonio Cánovas del Castillo shows a profound understanding of the situation when he writes:

> Los gabinetes que se sucedieron en los primeros años del nuevo reinado eran débiles de necesidad, y sin culpa de los que los componían, porque, más o menos explícitamente, entraba en el programa de todos la condenación y aun execración de los actos de resistencia que llevó a cabo el régimen anterior . . . De destierros o deportaciones no se hable, que gobiernos nacidos de una amnistía y consolidados a poder de otras, no sonaba todavía bien a los principios del nuevo reinado, que decretasen tales castigos, ni parecía bien que el aplicárselos a los liberales honrase a los mismos que acababan de volver al suelo patrio, después de largas y maldecidas emigraciones. No encontraba, pues, el gobernante más enérgico, tratándose de resistir a los desmanes anárquicos, aquel apoyo moral en la opinión pública, sin el cual se hace tarde o temprano inútil toda resistencia desde el poder. Da lástima ahora de pensar por cuan cortos motivos perdían las autoridades entonces la fama de liberales, aunque estuviese ganada en cien motines, pasando a ser déspotas y tiranos aborrecibles. Ni quiere esto decir que alguna que otra vez no se llevasen a ejecución, al fin, sangrientas represiones, y se diese áspero tratamiento también a los liberales impacientes.

La debilidad, es bien sabido que llega ser, de cuando en cuando, mucho más violenta y cruel que la energía de la voluntad verdaderamente firme y segura de sí misma.[46]

(The cabinets which succeeded one another during the first years of the new reign were necessarily weak, and not through the fault of those who made them up, because the condemnation and even execration of the previous régime's acts to resist change entered into their very programs . . . Certainly banishments and deportations could not be seriously considered, for governments born of one amnesty and consolidated through others would hardly have found it acceptable at the beginning of the new reign to decree such punishments, nor would it have seemed likely and fitting that applying them to liberals should have redounded to the honor of those who had themselves just returned to their native land after long and accursed emigrations. Thus the most energetic of rulers, in attempting to resist anarchical excesses, would not have found in public opinion the moral support without which any resistance on the government's part eventually turns out to be useless. One's pity is aroused nowadays by the thought of the scant reasons for which the authorities at that time lost their liberal reputation, though it might have been earned through a hundred insurrections, and became despots and hateful tyrants. To be sure, this does not mean that on occasion bloody repressions were not, after all, carried out, and that impatient liberals were not harshly treated. It is well known that weakness gets to be, now and then, much more violent and cruel than the energy of truly firm and self-assured will.)

Whatever the government might undertake to appease one, it would invariably offend another, of the mutually antagonistic factions of monarchists, rich landowners, ecclesiastics, and conservative Catholics on the one hand, and persecuted liberals on the other. "Corría la suerte de España por entre dos abismos, y quienquiera que se despeñara hacia cualquiera de ellos merece disculpa a la verdad . . ."[47] ("The fate of Spain wended its way between two chasms, and whoever plummeted down to either one truly deserves exculpation"). Consequently, the remarks of the Duc Decazes, in a letter to Baron Guillaume-Prosper de Barante, dated March 24, 1834, concerning the prime minister's capacity, must be based on a somewhat faulty appraisal of the situation:

Martínez de la Rosa manque de virilité et d'habileté; il y a absence complète d'action et même de pensée dans le conseil, s'il y a réellement conseil. La reine le sonne, au retour de la chasse, comme un valet de pied; on lui transmet des ordres par un secrétaire. Il n'ose convoquer les Cortes, même par Estamentos, dans la crainte qu'ils ne se constituent en Convention.[48]

(Martínez de la Rosa lacks virility and ability; there is a complete absence of action and even thought in the council of ministers, if indeed it does constitute itself. On her return from the hunt, the queen rings for him as for a footman. Orders are transmitted to him through a secretary. He does not even dare to summon the Cortes, even by *estamentos*, in fear that they might set themselves up as a constitutional convention.)

In defense of Martínez de la Rosa, it must be said that by going at reforms slowly he avoided alarming the nobles and the wealthy and brought them to the side of Isabel, giving them a place of honor in a bicameral parliament.

3

LARRA'S PREPARLIAMENTARY
ARTICLES

THE preceding chapter dealt with the political situation
from Ferdinand's death to the opening of Cortes. Now we
shall turn to Larra's production during this period. An
immediate question in that respect is whether, as some scholars
have felt, Figaro's writings betray a gradual disillusionment with
Martínez. It seems to me that a thorough examination of the essays,
with adequate knowledge of historical sources, would obviate such
a conclusion. An increase in the essays' evident animosity should
be attributed not so much to growing disillusionment as to a probable relaxation of censorship in the latter half of 1834. Yet this is
only a hypothesis, because no one has studied the fluctuation of
censorial severity during that year. Nevertheless, there is evidence
of such a relaxation. A new censorship regulation did go into effect
on July 1, 1834, and we can assume that it was a step toward freedom. It could be argued, of course, that the interpretation and application of the law in such cases is more significant than the law
itself; and no study of the practical application of censorship exists.
Moreover, the information necessary for this sort of work would be

well-nigh impossible to gather, not to speak of a reasonable doubt that the pertinent data are even extant.

Yet, after an examination of all the relevant materials, Larra's stance does give the appearance of constant and systematic opposition to Martínez de la Rosa, espousal of the Progressive cause, and perhaps even sympathy with the Sociedad Isabelina. Julio Nombela y Campos reached a similar conclusion:

> Fue aquélla una campaña en toda regla, que hace época en los anales de nuestro periodismo, porque Fígaro echó mano de todos los recursos de su fértil ingenio para combatir sin tregua ni cuartel al autor del Estatuto real.[1]

> (It was indeed a campaign in due form, the kind that opens a new era in the annals of our journalism, because Larra availed himself of all the resources of his inventive wit to combat without truce or quarter against the author of the Estatuto Real.)

We may have reservations about some further statements of Nombela's however:

> Se adhirió a la opinión liberal, que juzgaba nefasta la continuación en el poder de Martínez de la Rosa; pero sin llegar a ser un verdadero hombre de partido, sin avenirse a sacrificar su carácter independiente, sin aceptar una disciplina, que repugnaba a su esquiva naturaleza.[2]

> (He became an adherent of liberal opinion, which deemed Martínez de la Rosa's continuance in power to be ominous; but without becoming a real party man, without allowing himself to sacrifice his independent character, without accepting a discipline, which would have gone against his elusive nature.)

In the first place, had he written "progresista" instead of "liberal," Nombela would have been more accurate and just; the Moderates, after all, were also Liberals. Then the assertion concerning Larra's political independence smacks of sentimentality. Who can prove that the journalist was not a party man? All this shows, in short, that extreme care must be taken not to reach a hasty conclusion.

Larra's first essay after Ferdinand's death is "Varios caracteres" (October 13, 1833), where the customary pose of disinterested observer adopted by typical *costumbristas* is exaggerated into bitter indifference. It is quite possible that this literary stance reflects the uncooperative position of the Liberals mentioned in the last chapter. What will later underlie the very structure of "El hombre menguado" (October 27) is now only an insinuation:

> Cualquiera me conocerá en estos días en que el fastidio se apodera de mi alma, y en que no hay cosa que tenga a mis ojos color, y menos color agradable. En estos días llevo cara de filósofo, es decir, de mal humor; una sonrisa amarga de indiferencia y despego a cuanto veo se dibuja en mis labios . . . (1: 290)

> (Anyone can recognize me nowadays when ennui dominates my soul, when nothing appears to my eyes as having color, and least of all an agreeable color. I go around looking like a philosopher; in other words, in a bad humor. A bitter smile of indifference and detachment from everything I gaze upon is drawn on my lips. . . .)

On October 18, however, Figaro turns to banter in his anti-Carlist "Nadie pase sin hablar al portero." After "Los amigos" (October 20), a simple adaptation of Etienne-Antoine Jouy, he publishes "El hombre menguado," which masterfully combines anti-Carlism with indifference to the Zea régime. It reveals a studied nonchalance about the proclamation ceremonies and a skeptical attitude toward the "entusiasmo popular." The narrator has not dressed in keeping with the glorious occasion. On the contrary, "por hablar a estas gentes [Carlists] aquel día, y explorar su parecer sin miedo de parecerles sospechoso, púseme una capa vieja y un viejísimo sombrero" (1: 302—"in order to speak to those people that day, and search out their opinions without fear of appearing suspicious, I put on an old cape and a very old hat"). Figaro is more interested in cajoling the Carlist than in cheering Isabel II. Not that he is against the latter, but the circumstances are such that the attitude of a disinterested observer (viz., a *costumbrista*) in this case suits him politically. He poses as the mere spectator of a popular celebration, since the people he depicts cheering the new queen are not men of social stature but "las gentes":

> En esto venía ya andando hacia nosotros la proclamación, y gritaban las gentes por delante: "¡viva Isabel II!"
> —¡Qué dice usted a esto, amigo?—le pregunté.

—No oigo nada, caballero. Y si acaso oigo, que no estoy seguro, ¡gente pagada!
—Por supuesto—dije yo para mí—los de Merino[3] no es gente pagada, porque donde hay dinero se cobran ellos... (1: 303)

(At this point the proclamation began to come close, and the folk in front were shouting, "Long live Isabel II!"
—What do you have to say about this, my friend?—I asked him.
—Sir, I don't hear a thing. And if by chance I do, and I'm not even sure about that, I'll tell you what: they're paid to do it!
—Of course,—I said to myself—Merino's raiders aren't paid, because where they find money they collect it on their own...)

As we can see, the accusation "¡gente pagada!" is not refuted; it is merely offset by an ironic *tu quoque*. Moreover, a few lines further the "turba entusiasmada" is shown grasping for coins thrown to them, a note which implies a corroboration of the Carlist's assertion. There is also a hint of inducement in the use of "entusiasmada" rather than "entusiasta." As for Figaro, far from being ecstatic, he stands aloof like many other liberals. And when the proclamation passes by, it is not Isabel II who absorbs his thoughts but the ridiculous appearance of the Carlist, at whom he laughs hilariously. "El hombre menguado" is a tour-de-force. The anti-Carlism, from a structural point of view, may be considered the main theme of the essay. Nevertheless, it is also a device to obviate the censorship of another political message, since it allows the author to imply his detachment from the event, thereby insinuating that the new queen has the support only of the unreliable and impressionable masses, not of the dedicated liberal intelligentsia.

Another anti-Carlist satire appeared on November 10, "La planta nueva o el faccioso," whose technique of botanical similes would be used again by Larra in "El hombre pone y Dios dispone" (April 4, 1834) and in "El ministerial" (September 16, 1834), along with zoological similes. In "La junta de Castel-o-Branco," published on November 19, Figaro portrays the pretender almost alone and bereft of followers. This may have made efficient propaganda at the time, but it was false. The same can be said of "El fin de la fiesta" (December 1). The other articles printed during the last days of the Zea régime are theatrical reviews, except for two. "Las circunstancias" (December 15, 1833) is the first sign of our author's concern with the government-employees problem, which will be taken up in chapter 9 of this book. "La educación de entonces" (January 5, 1834) pokes fun at old-fashioned moralists.

Among the essays published during Martínez de la Rosa's ministry there are several significant passages that will be examined in detail. We should also note some others, which seem to deal with social issues but have no direct bearing on politics, though they may in places appear to do so. Of this type are Larra's complaints of the crowds flocking to the masked balls organized in January:

> porque saber de dónde venían las más [máscaras] que en el teatro, en la citada noche se vieron, ni es tan fácil como parece ni nos ofrecería acaso un origen tan limpio y de tan preclara nobleza, puesto que la nobleza no es más que la antigüedad. . . . Para pintar las tres cuartas partes de la concurrencia, bástanos decir que necesitaríamos el pincel de Murillo con toda la verdad que ostenta en el cuadro de Santa Isabel. Bastará decir que las pocas señoras que asistieron, que las pocas elegantes que en aquel día se hallaron, engañadas sin duda, ni pudieron bailar ni osaron descubrirse; que vimos infinitas mujeres sin guantes . . . Ese fue el baile y ésa la concurrencia; nosotros, que en materia de sociedad somos enteramente aristocráticos, y que dejamos la igualdad de los hombres para la otra vida, porque en ésta no la vemos tan clara como la quieren suponer . . . (1: 334–336)

> (because knowing where most masks seen in the theater that night came from is not as easy as it appears. It might not necessarily show us a limpid origin, or of eminent nobility, since nobility is nothing more than antiquity. . . . In order to paint three quarters of those present, suffice it to say that we should need Murillo's brush with all the realism it displays in the picture of Saint Elizabeth. Suffice it to say that the few ladies who were present, the few elegant women who came, undoubtedly deceived, could not dance and did not dare to reveal themselves; that we saw innumerable women without gloves . . . So that was the ball and the crowd. We who are, with respect to society, entirely aristocratic, and who leave equality of mankind for the other life, because in this one we cannot see it quite as clearly as some would suppose . . .)

Such passages should not be used to demonstrate political conservatism on Larra's part. On the contrary, a pseudoaristocratic attitude and superciliousness in manners and refinement was quite consistent with liberalism. Those who objected to the rustic customs of the average Spaniard, those who yearned after urbanity, were often accused of *afrancesamiento*. During the Triennium, for example, the Duke of Rivas, a well-known liberal, formed a political circle noted for its aristocratic and refined deportment.[4] On the other hand, the tyrannical Ferdinand VII is notorious for his vulgarity and his humiliation of the aristocracy.[5] The polish of the liberals contrasted with the crass plebeianism of the tyrannophiles.[6] The meaning of the word "society" in an article on masked balls is thus quite different from that in "Los barateros" (April 19, 1836), for example. Larra probably shared the attitude expressed by José Cadalso in the seventh of the *Cartas marruecas*, as well as a belief in the aristocracy of talent.[7] Consequently, it can be said of these accounts that their primary value consists in the vocabulary and metaphorical setting that masked balls provide for political satire, as in "Los tres no son más que dos y el que no es nada vale por tres—mascarada política" (February 18, 1834).

On January 24, 1834, Larra wrote a review of a Scribe play, *Julia*, which he had himself translated anonymously. The review's only political note is an allusion using the "pregnant vehicle" trope. While pointing out that Scribe's work is based almost entirely on stock characters and situations, Larra explains ironically that

> no hay nada más parecido a un hombre que otro hombre, nada más semejante a un pueblo que otro pueblo, nada más parecido a un parte oficial que otro parte oficial, nada, en fin, más semejante a una comedia que otra comedia. El tipo general es uno, y la verdad primitiva de las cosas una; lo que llamamos novedades son pequeñísimas modificaciones de ellas, y si se especula con esas modificaciones es porque felizmente no suele el vulgo profundizar y buscar debajo de las superficies exteriores el principio general de todas. Póngase usted sobre una sola cara cien caretas diferentes, mil si usted quiere, hasta el infinito, y especule usted con la pública seguridad bien seguro que nadie ha de arrancarle una sola de ellas para verle la cara verdadera. (1: 338)

> (nothing resembles one man more than another man, one people more than another people, one official communiqué more than another official communiqué, and, lastly, one comedy more than

another comedy. The general type is one, and the primary truth of things is one. What we call innovations are their tiny modifications, and if these modifications are speculated about, it is because fortunately the common herd is not given to fathoming and searching below the exterior surfaces the general principle of them all. Put on one face a hundred different masks, if you wish a thousand, or ad infinitum, and you can speculate with public security quite sure and secure that no one is going to rip off a single one of them to look at your real face.)

The mention of "parte oficial" brings to mind the government issuing it and therefore hints at the application of the next sentence to slowness at reforms and to the possibility that with Martínez liberalism is but a mask. The latter figure is fully developed a few days later in the "mascarada política" (1: 347).

Two days after the review of *Julia*, Figaro wrote another theatrical article, "Primera representación de la comedia refundida y puesta en cuatro actos titulada *Juez y reo de su causa o Don Jaime el Justiciero*" (January 26, 1834). Here we witness once more the playful conjunction of the politics of the theater and the theatricality of politics:

> Mucho tiempo hace que dimos en la *Revista* a nuestros lectores una idea exacta de lo que ha solido entenderse en nuestro teatro por refundición de comedias. De entonces acá hemos adelantado mucho en el país en materia de refundiciones, a Dios Gracias; pero según las muestras, el teatro es el único que se queda hasta ahora rezagado. ¿Será más difícil refundir un teatro que una nación? Tentados estamos de creer que sí. (1: 340)

> (A long time ago we gave our readers in *La Revista* a precise idea of what in our national theater has been understood by the term rifacimento. Since then the country has progressed considerably with respect to rifacimenti, by the Grace of God. But, as we can see from the samples, only the theater now finds itself at the rear. Could it be more difficult to recast a theater than a nation? We are tempted to believe so.)

The discourse on theatrical adaptation mentioned above is found in his review of a rifacimento of Agustín Moreto's *A cada paso un acaso* (May 10, 1833):

Preguntaríamos a estos *arrimones* literarios que refunden trabajos ajenos, si quieren hacer las comedias de Moreto, Tirso, etcétera, o si quieren hacer las suyas. . . . Si refundir es hacer bajar y subir los telones en otros pasajes de la acción diversos de aquellos en que Moreto creyó subdividir su intriga; si consiste en añadir algunas trivialidades a las que desgraciadamente puede encerrar el original, haciendo desaparecer de paso algunas de sus bellezas; si consiste en decir *cinco actos* en vez de *tres jornadas;* si estriba en estropear la versificación haciendo consonar *trato* con *cinco y cuarto,* entonces esta refundición es de las más completas que en estos teatros hemos visto . . . (1: 224)

(We ought to ask these sponges of literature who recast the works of others, whether they want to write the comedies of Moreto, Tirso, and so forth, or their own. . . . If recasting means making the curtains go up and down at passages of the action different from those where Moreto thought of subdividing his plot; if it consists in adding some trivialities to those which the original might unfortunately include, removing in the process some of its beauty; if it consists in saying *five acts* instead of *three "jornadas";* if it depends on damaging the prosody by having *trato* rhyme with *cinco y cuarto* in consonance, then this rifacimento is one of the most complete ever seen on these boards . . .)

We can deduce then that Larra did not think much of rifacimenti; his allusion on January 26 to political change in such terms must be burlesque, and "hemos adelantado mucho" cannot refer to the type of progress he felt to be desirable.

In "Representación de *La mojigata*" (February 2) the journalist calls attention to the relation between political freedom and the development of the arts. Since *La mojigata* had been forbidden for several years, there was apparently reason to be thankful, in all fairness, to the new government for allowing its production. Yet the more we examine the passage, the more its subtle ambiguity becomes evident:

Al verla representar de nuevo en el día, no sabemos si sea más de alabar la ilustrada providencia de un Gobierno reparador que la ofrece de nuevo a la pública expectación, que de admirar la crasa ignorancia que la envolvió por tantos años en la ruina de una causa momentáneamente caída. (1: 341)

(Seeing it performed again nowdays, we are at a loss to know whether we should praise the enlightened providence of a restoring Government which offers it anew to public expectancy, more than we should wonder at the crass ignorance that implicated it for so many years in the ruin of a suddenly fallen cause.)

The government, by permitting the performance, is being provident; its enlightenment is outstanding, but it is only relatively so, in contrast to the previous obscurantism. After all, the public has been awaiting this permission eagerly, almost expecting it as a matter of course. Larra hints, moreover, that the cause of freedom had only lost ground temporarily, thus implying that in order to keep pace with the now irrevocable course of public sentiment, Martínez would have to make more concessions. And in the previous paragraph Larra does caution the government about the risk of losing public support:

Sólo un Gobierno fuerte y apoyado en la pública opinión puede arrostrar la verdad, y aun buscarla: inseparable compañero de ella, no teme la expresión de las ideas, porque indaga las mejores y las más sanas para cimentar sobre ellas su poder indestructible. (1: 341)

(Only a strong government, supported by public opinion, can face the truth, and even seek it. Since truth is its inseparable companion, it does not fear the expression of ideas because it investigates the best and soundest in order to base on them its indestructible power.)

Next comes the first patently anti-Martínez essay, "Los tres no son más que dos, y el que no es nada vale por tres—mascarada política," published in *La Revista Española* on February 18. As Nombela y Campos clearly demonstrates, all the political articles from this time until the author's departure in March 1835 were aimed specifically at the prime minister.[8] Even the title of this first one implies that the political field has become polarized and that the government must choose sides. There are now two active parties, says Fígaro, "blancos" and "negros," neither of which he paints in glowing colors, though the latter is deemed preferable. There is also a third group, the majority, which is uncommitted and therefore worthless as a political force, or so reasons Larra.

They appear to have a leader, but since they are not people of action, any attempt to direct them is futile:

> Era el resto de la concurrencia la mayoría; pero se conservaba a cierta distancia del que parecía su jefe . . . Éstos no decían nada, ni aplaudían, ni censuraban; traían caretas de yeso, miraban a una comparsa, miraban a otra, y ora temblaban, y ora reían. En realidad no hacían cuenta con su jefe; éste era el que contaba con ellos; es decir, con su inercia. (1: 348)

> (The rest of the crowd was the majority, though it kept itself at a certain distance from the man it considered its leader . . . These people said nothing, neither did they applaud or censure. They wore plaster masks, looked at one masquerade retinue, then at the other. Now they trembled, now they laughed. In truth they did not reckon with their leader. He was the one who counted on them; that is, with their inertia.)

The leader, as Nombela clearly saw, is obviously Martínez, neither "blanco" nor "negro," but "atornasolado claro" ("clear litmus") (the latter adjective pointing to liberal tendencies).[9] His followers seem to walk but are merely marking time, with "lead feet" ("pies . . . de plomo"). The leader himself is described: "de medio cuerpo arriba venía vestido a la antigua española, de medio cuerpo abajo a la moderna francesa, y en él no era disfraz, sino su traje propio y natural" (1: 348—"from the waist up he was dressed in the old Spanish manner, from the waist down in the modern French fashion, and on him it was not a disguise but his proper and natural clothing"). This personage refuses to judge; he only wants to reconcile. He shies away from strong language: the Carlists are not hypocrites, revolutionaries, and fanatics, as the leftist press calls them, but rather "seductores, . . . fautores de asonadas, . . . ilusos, incautos . . . —Señores, todos tienen ustedas razón; la unión, la cultura, un justo medio... ni uno ni otro... las dos cosas..." (1: 350—"deceivers, . . . abettors of riots . . . deluded gulls . . . —Gentlemen, you are right, all of you; union, culture, a just middle road... neither one nor the other... the two things..."). As for Figaro, he chaffs the Progressives as well as the other groups, but in the end states clearly that he is on the Progressive side: "—No hay para qué hablar más, que ya me habéis conocido—dije yo apresurándome a interrumpir a los míos, que me iban tratando peor que los contrarios" (1: 349—"—No point saying one thing more, since you have recognized me—I said, hastening to interrupt my own crowd, who were now treating me worse than my opponents").

A few lines further down Larra portrays the figure we assume to be Martínez de la Rosa, holding aloft a copy of *La Revista* (1: 350). It is quite possible that the author adds this descriptive note to advise us indirectly that he stands to the left of the newspaper he writes for. Fortunately for Figaro, *La Revista*'s attitude was one of loyal opposition rather than hostility. Those papers which did express hostility, *El Siglo, El Universal, El Eco de la Opinión,* and *El Tiempo,* were ultimately abolished.[10]

Larra's next essay is *"El Siglo* en blanco" (March 9, 1834), where the government is chided after having closed down a newspaper and jailed its editors, Antonio Ros de Olano, Ventura de la Vega, Isaac Núñez Arenas, and Espronceda.[11] It should be kept in mind that by printing (on March 7, 1834) a newspaper with blank columns bearing only titles, these young men were not violating any existing regulation, except that technically they did break a law by not submitting the titles themselves to the censor. It was not until June 1 that a censorship regulation applying specifically to newspapers was issued, and it contained one article designed to avoid the recurrence of such an incident:

> Art. 16. Los prospectos se sujetarán a censura, y los periódicos no podrán publicarse con ninguna parte de sus columnas en blanco. Los editores de los periódicos en que por este medio, el de líneas de puntos o cualquiera otro semejante se indique la supresión de artículos presentados a la censura, pagarán por primera vez una multa de 2.000 rs., de 4.000 reales por la segunda, y a la tercera vez serán suprimidos los periódicos.[12]

> (Art. 16. Prospectuses will be subject to censorship, and newspapers shall not be published with any parts of their columns blank. The editors of newspapers in which the suppression of articles submitted to censorship is indicated by this means, or that of lines of dots, or any other, will pay for the first time a fine of 2000 reales, the second time 4000 reales; the third time the newspapers will be suppressed.)

The only guide at the time of the *Siglo* affair was the general "Reglamento de Imprentas" drafted by Javier de Burgos and decreed on January 4 during the Zea régime, whose Article 7 states that

> se declaran . . . sujetas a previa censura . . . todas las obras, folletos y papeles que versan sobre moral, política y gobierno, abrazando esta palabra cuanto tenga relación directa o inmediata con nuestra legislación.[13]

> (all works, pamphlets, and papers which treat of morals, politics, and governments—the latter word including anything having direct or immediate relation to our laws—are declared subject to censorship.)

What probably occurred was that Espronceda, after several issues had undergone heavy censorship, proposed a number bearing titles only, and without asking the authorities for permission.[14] Larra's comments about the affair are extremely clever. His essay begins with a pseudophilosophical prolegomenon, a type used again in "El ministerial." He then states that a blank article can mean all things to all men, and thereupon relates the blankness to Martínez's empty pronouncements:

> Un artículo en blanco es además picante, porque excita la curiosidad hasta un punto difícil de pintar . . . Este sistema de hacer gozar haciendo esperar, del cual pudiéramos citar en el día algún sectario famoso . . . (1: 353)

> (A blank article is rather sharp, since it excites the taste for curiosity to a point difficult to describe . . . This system of giving delight through expectation, of which we might mention in our day a famous partisan . . .)

Larra thus hints ironically that Espronceda and his friends were following the government's example, heeding, by means of the blank columns, a precept likewise embodied in the vacuity of official verbiage. Figaro therefore amuses us by implying that *El Siglo* emulates the government. Yet this piece of irony ultimately reflects Larra's deepest conviction: freedom of speech and of the press are fundamental principles from which all else in politics emanates, a virtual concept by the light of which all verbal manifestations of the political scene find themselves reflected in each other. Viewed thus, in a seemingly unwitting Neoplatonic context, the irony may reveal an ultimate truth in Figaro's statement that *El Siglo* is a "periódico enteramente platónico," in the sense that during the Ominous Decade

> nos sucedía precisamente lo mismo que en la cátedra de Platón, a saber, que sólo hablaba el maestro, y eso para enseñar a callar a los demás, y perdónenos el filósofo griego la comparación. (1: 352–353)
>
> (the same thing happened to us as in Plato's class, to wit, that only the master spoke, and moreover for the purpose of teaching the others to keep quiet—may the Greek philosopher pardon the comparison!)

After "Ventajas de las cosas a medio hacer" (March 16), an ironic essay without reference to any special event, we proceed to the review of *Hernán Pérez del Pulgar* (March 30), a book published by the prime minister in March of 1834. On examining the circumstances under which Larra wrote the article, I have come to believe that his mordacity in this instance was probably exacerbated by Antonio María Segovia. Segovia also reviewed Martínez's book but, unlike Larra, he extolled it. Moreover, in searching for a foil, he seems to have made derogatory insinuations about Larra's *El Doncel de don Enrique el Doliente* (3: 5–205). Evidence still points to the probability that Larra's review was published after Segovia's, who, according to Tarr, "never lost an opportunity to take an underhand fling at Figaro."[15] The first volume of Larra's only novel came off the presses on January 23, 1834, the second on February 13, the third on March 16, and the fourth on March 29. The prime minister's book also appeared about this time, so that there was bound to be a comparison of the two. Segovia's eulogy of *Hernán Pérez* in the columns of *La Abeja*, the unofficially ministerialist paper, not only compares quixotically Spain's glorious past to its miserable present, but also reveals a no less quixotic preference for archaic language over the "degenerate" modern idiom:

> El lenguaje es puro y castizo: esto no había que decirlo, pero sí hay que añadir la observación de que el autor convencido sin duda de

que aquellas esclarecidas hazañas no merecen ser tratadas en el habla de los castellanos degenerados, se retira todo lo posible, y tomando en edad menos remota y discordante de su objeto la lengua hermosísima de nuestros padres, la maneja de un modo incomparable, y descubre su gala y lozanía toda, consintiendo más bien tal o cual arcaísmo que el uso de las palabras nuevas que pudieran manchar su escrito lastimosamente.[16]

(Its language is pure and correct; this goes without saying. But one needs to add the observation that the author, no doubt convinced that those resplendent deeds do not deserve to be painted in the tongue of the degenerate Castilians, recedes as much as possible; and taking from an age less remote and discordant from its object the beautiful language of our fathers, handles it in an incomparable manner and displays all its grace and freshness, allowing himself the use of an archaism here and there rather than new words that might sadly taint his writings.)

Segovia, in praising the prime minister's book, shows, moreover, his disapproval of historical novels, and for moral reasons. It is likely that he had in mind *El Doncel,* where the figure of Macías, enamored of a married woman, is more tragic than exemplary, as opposed to Pulgar, an epic hero:

Pero este retrato histórico de Hernando del Pulgar, en nada se parece a esas *novelas históricas,* género monstruo resucitado, si no creado, por algunos ingenios que en él malgastan sus bellísimas y acreditadas disposiciones. Con sus libros fatales dañan a la historia, porque adulterando los hechos y delineando retratos caprichosos de personas, y cuadros ideales de costumbres, forman en las cabezas ignorantes un caos, una confusión de ideas que difícilmente podrán ya desembrollar. Dañan a la literatura, porque ni sus composiciones son verdaderas novelas, ni poemas, ni aun tienen la pureza de lenguaje y elegancia de estilo que resplandecen en el Amadís de Gaula. Dañan también a las costumbres, porque no son los que presentan a la juventud modelos dignos de imitarse, ni jamás por el carácter falso de uno de sus héroes, podrán formarse otros que alcancen eterna fama para sí, para su edad y para su patria.[17]

(But this historical portrait of Hernando del Pulgar does not resemble in the least those *historical novels,* a monstrous genre revived, if not created, by a few wits who waste on it the aptitude for which they have acquired such a fine reputation. With their baleful books they harm history, because, by adulterating the facts and drawing whimsical portraits of personages, and by painting idealized customs, they form in ignorant minds a chaos, a confusion of ideas which the latter will indeed find difficult to unravel. They harm literature, because their compositions are not true novels, nor poems, nor even have the purity of language and elegance of style that shine forth in *Amadís of Gaul*. They also do harm to customs, because they are not of the kind that offers to youth models worthy of imitation. Whoever would attain eternal fame for his age and his country could never fashion himself after the false character of one of their heroes.)

Now, on reading Larra's review after Segovia's, we shall find that everything Segovia praises Figaro condemns:

No faltará quien llame la obra entera un arcaísmo; no faltará quien crea, acaso con razón, que se descubre el artificio que en tal escrupuloso remedo ha debido emplear su autor; nosotros nos limitaremos [typical Larra paralipsis] a indicar que, a nuestro débil entender, las lenguas siguen la marcha de los progresos y de las ideas. (1: 359)

(Undoubtedly somebody will call the whole work an archaism; there will always be someone who believes, perhaps rightly, that the artifice which the author must have used in such a scrupulous imitation is too patent. As for us, we shall limit ourselves to indicating that, in our faint understanding, languages follow the march of progress and ideas.)

It should be rather evident that Figaro agrees with "quien crea, acaso con razón"; and he is probably justified in doing so. Was it necessary for Martínez in the year 1834 to use an archaism like "della"?[18] And what of the jejune tautological simile, "las oleadas de gente semejaban a las del mar"[19] ("the waves of people resembled those of the sea")? But let us return to Segovia, who now praises the book's documentation:

Comenzó a hallar el señor Martínez de la Rosa monumentos preciosos y auténticos, que con los rebuscados en otros archivos, secretarías, bibliotecas y academias, forman por apéndice de la obra pruebas irrecusables de su narración. Así, con el convencimiento de la verdad de los hechos, encuentra el corazón tal deleite . . .[20]

(Mr. Martínez de la Rosa began to find precious and authentic documents which, along with those sought out in other archives, offices, libraries, and academies, constitute as an appendix to his work irrefutable proofs of his narration. Thus, convinced of the truth of these facts, the heart finds such delight . . .)

Larra, on the contrary, expresses his contempt for all of this in a delicately mordacious antithetical conclusion:

Por lo demás, échase bien de ver cuánta sea la erudición del señor Martínez al advertir que llenan dos terceras partes del tomo las notas y apéndices con que ha creído deber autorizar las increíbles hazañas de Pulgar. (1: 359)

(Furthermore, the erudition of Mr. Martínez de la Rosa becomes evident indeed when we notice that two thirds of the volume is filled by the notes and appendices with which he has believed it necessary to authenticate the unbelievable deeds of Pulgar.)

And where Segovia says, "¡Ah! ¿Por qué no han logrado todos los castellanos ilustres un Plutarco como el señor Martínez de la Rosa?"[21] ("Ah! Why is it that all illustrious Castilians have not enjoyed a Plutarch such as Mr. Martínez de la Rosa?"), Figaro observes mischievously:

No luce en él la enérgica concisión de Tácito, ni la profunda filosofía de Plutarco; pero puede rivalizar su estilo con lo mejor de nuestro siglo de oro. Tan cierta es esta proposición, que al leer *Hernán Pérez del Pulgar* hemos creído más de una vez tener entre manos un libro desenterrado de aquella época. (1: 359)

(The vigorous conciseness of Tacitus does not shine in him, nor the profound philosophy of Plutarch, but his style can rival with the best of our Golden Age. This assertion is indeed so true, that on reading *Hernán Pérez del Pulgar* we felt more than once that we were holding in our hands a book disinterred from that epoch.)

The above passage is a typical slice of Larra's review, embodying as it does the passage's main satirical device. The essay is, first of all, an expertly conceived anticlimax containing subsidiary anticlimaxes. The main anticlimax occurs with respect to literary matters only, and begins with the words "quisiéramos tributar nuestra alabanza y respeto" (1: 359—"we should like to render our praise and respect"), where "quisiéramos" seems to imply the inhibition of a complaisant gesture. Simultaneously, however, there is a climax, but with respect to political matters, as an attack on Martínez's régime gradually develops. The attack is quite subtle. For instance, when he writes "aquella misma Granada, de él tan querida y privilegiada"[22] ("that very Granada, by him so beloved and privileged"), Figaro may be alluding to political favoritism. Likewise, he points out "aquellas reflexiones políticas o morales que suelen nacer tan naturalmente a veces de la misma relación de los hechos bajo la pluma del historiador" (1: 359— "those political or moral reflexions that at times are wont to arise so naturally from the very relation of facts under the historian's pen"). From the ironic "naturalmente" we can infer the book's tendentiousness. It cannot be denied that Martínez de la Rosa betrays a quixotic tendency to draw parallels between his own times and the past. Here are some typical passages from his book:

> Había nacido Hernando del Pulgar en tan buena sazón y coyuntura, que le duraba, al llegar a la edad viril, el horror que despertaran en su ánimo las revueltas y discordias civiles, cuando exhaustos los pueblos, desmandados los nobles, el trono mal seguro, se desgarraba el reino con sus propias manos; y al mismo tiempo en que se miró huérfano, dueño de mediana fortuna y cabecera de su ilustre casa, vio Pulgar que se iba despejando el cielo de Castilla, y que las prendas y virtudes de la Reina Doña Isabel presagiaban largos días de prosperidad y de gloria. Anublóse no obstante la común alegría, cuando apenas estaba en el solio aquella esclarecida princesa; se amontonaron en derredor tantas y tan recias tormentas, hasta el punto de renacer en la propia tierra antiguas parcialidades y bandos, de traspasar huestes extrañas los opuestos confines del reino, y de disputarse la corona a punta de lanza en el mismo corazón de Castilla.
> Entonces fue cuando por primera vez salió Hernando del Pulgar a probar en el campo sus armas; y con tan buen éxito hubo de hacerlo, que sin más recomendaciones que su espada, y cuando apenas entre tanta muchedumbre de guerreros se distinguían los capitanes más esforzados, logró un simple escudero llamar la atención de los Reyes, que fáciles y prontos a galardonar el merecimiento, le nombraron *continuo de su casa*. . . .
> ¡Días de ventura y gloria, eternos en los fastos de España:

cuando en el mismo campo de batalla, a la vista de tantos héroes, un poderoso Príncipe recompensaba una victoria con el solo título de caballero! Hoy se mendiga, si no es que se compra. . . .

En los miserables tiempos que alcanzamos, apocados los ánimos y enmohecidos con el vil interés, casi miramos con sonrisa de lástima la extraña demanda de Pulgar, cual si ya frisara en locura; pero en aquella era de gloria y de heroísmo, se creían los españoles, como los antiguos romanos, destinados al imperio del mundo.[23]

(Hernando del Pulgar was born at such an opportune juncture in history that, on reaching manhood, he could not put in oblivion the horror that civil discords and revolts had awakened in his mind when the kingdom, torn apart by its own forces, revealed a people exhausted, a nobility disobeying its monarch, and a throne insecure. And just when he found himself orphaned, lord of no mean estate and head of his illustrious house, he saw that the skies of Castille were beginning to clear, and that the qualities and virtues of Queen Isabel foretold long days of prosperity and glory. Nevertheless, hardly had this eminent princess mounted the throne than the common felicity was again beclouded. Many a severe storm accumulated over Spain, to the point that the old factions and bands were reborn in the land, hostile armies crossed the kingdom from one end to the other, and the crown was disputed at the point of the lance in the very heart of Castille.

It was then that for the first time Hernando del Pulgar came forth to test his arms in the field; and he must have carried it out so successfully that, though only a simple squire, with only his sword as a recommendation, and among such a multitude of warriors that the bravest captains could hardly be made out, he managed to catch the attention of the Monarchs, who, eager and prompt to reward merit, named him *yeoman of the household*. . . .

Days of fortune and glory, eternal in the annals of Spain, when on the field of battle itself, in the sight of so many heroes, a powerful Prince recompensed a victory with the mere title of knight! Nowadays it is begged, if not bought. . . .

In the miserable times that we have come upon, when the will is attenuated and corroded by vile interest, we almost look with a smile of pity upon the strange request of Pulgar, as if it came just too close to insanity. But in that era of glory and heroism, Spaniards, like the ancient Romans, believed themselves destined to rule the world.)

Is it any wonder that the final remark in Figaro's review should be:

> *Aut agere scribenda, aut legenda scribere,* decía un célebre romano: *o hacer cosas dignas de ser escritas, o escribir cosas dignas de ser leídas.* Ya que no podemos ser Hernando del Pulgar, quisiéramos ser su historiador. (1: 359)

> (a famous Roman said *either do things worthy of being written down, or write things worthy of being read.* Since we can't be Hernando del Pulgar, we should like to be his historian.)

It is noteworthy that Larra's *El Doncel de don Enrique el Doliente* also contains comparisons between the past and the present. In Figaro's work, however, an ambiguous resemblance of the two eras is ironically insinuated:

> Tiempos felices, o infelices, en que ni la hermosura de las poblaciones, ni la fácil comunicación entre los hombres de apartados países, ni la seguridad individual que en el día casi nos garantizan nuestras ilustradas legislaciones . . . (3: 7)

> (Happy or unhappy times, when neither the beauty of cities, nor easy communication between men of faraway lands, nor the individual security which nowadays our enlightened legislations almost guarantee . . .)

Of course, Larra was describing an earlier period than Martínez. Yet, where both authors explored the past, they found different ambiences therein.

All of this brings us back to the question of the Medieval Revival, the interest in the Middle Ages that comprised an important facet of the Romantic ethos. In Martínez's case, such interest may have originated in part from the need to find precedents for parliamentary institutions. Nevertheless, for most Romantics it has a profound significance, consisting in a vague notion that there existed an affinity between the two epochs. But beyond this Larra and Martínez diverge radically. The latter extols the hero who brings the Middle Ages to an end by defeating with medieval ardor a supposedly foreign enemy for the benefit of a nationalistic ideal. Figaro, on the other hand, discusses ironically the dissimilarity of the two periods, thus implying the tragic resemblance of their internal dissensions. He asks the reader of *El Doncel* to imagine himself transported

> a siglos remotos, para vivir, digámoslo así, en otro orden de sociedad en nada semejante a este que en el siglo XIX marca la adelantada civilización de la culta Europa (3: 7),

> (to remote centuries, to live, so to speak, in another order of society not resembling in the least this one which is marked in the nineteenth century by the advanced civilization of educated Europe),

in which "la seguridad individual que en el día casi nos garantizan nuestras ilustradas legislaciones" was inexistent. *Casi* is almost always ironic with Figaro. In another passage, also from chapter 1, there is obvious irony in the use of the words "milagro" and "extremadas":

> Nuestra nación, como las demás de Europa, no presentaba a la perspicacia del observador sino un caos confuso, un choque no interrumpido de elementos heterogéneos que tendían a equilibrarse, pero que por la ausencia prolongada de un poder superior que los amalgamase y ordenase, completando el gran milagro de la civilización, se encontraban con extraña violencia en un vasto campo de disensiones civiles, de guerras exteriores, de rencillas, de desafíos, y a veces de crímenes, que con nuestras extremadas instituciones mal en la actualidad se conformarían. (3: 7)

> (Our nation, like the rest of Europe, presented to the perspicacity of the observer only a confusing chaos, an uninterrupted clash of heterogeneous elements that tended to balance each other, but which, owing to the prolonged absence of a superior power that might amalgamate and put them in order, thus completing the great miracle of civilization, found themselves violently thrust in a vast field of civil dissensions, foreign wars, feuds, duels, and sometimes crimes, which at the present would hardly conform to our consummately good institutions.)

The Romantic Larra presents an analogy of tragic disorder, curable only by disbelieved miracle, whereas Martínez the romantic, the spinner of romances, attempts to demonstrate the plausibility of the miracle. Of the two, it is Larra who best reflects the intellectual atmosphere, as evidenced by memoirs of the period. Augusto Conte, reminiscing in 1901 about his childhood, observed that

la generación actual apenas puede figurarse el desorden moral y material, ni la división de los ánimos, ni el encono de los partidos que reinaba en nuestro país. . . . Diríase que habíamos vuelto a la Edad Media, a la época de los güelfos y gibelinos, de montescos y capuletos.[24]

(the present generation can hardly imagine the moral and material disorder, the division of opinion, or the party strife which reigned our nation. . . . One could have said that we had gone back to the Middle Ages, to the era of Guelphs and Ghibellines, Montagues and Capulets.)

In July 1833 Quintana wrote that "las turbulencias políticas y morales son lo mismo que los grandes desórdenes físicos"[25] ("political and moral turbulences are the same thing as great physical disorders"), a statement that should be interpreted with an understanding of medical backwardness at the time. Andrés de Arango, in a letter dated December 31, 1835, compared the state of the nation to an uncontrollable disease:

La [enfermedad] de esta Península ya observará V. por la lectura de nuestros periódicos que se ha mejorado algún tanto después del crecimiento que tan de punto subió durante los meses de Agosto y Septiembre último, pero la enfermedad siempre es muy grave y de cura muy tardía y delicada, pero como en estas graves dolencias suele haber sus crisis favorables que no dependen de cálculos humanos, en ella está fija mi esperanza ya que no puedo tenerla en otra cosa.[26]

(You probably observe by reading our newspapers that the illness of this peninsula has improved somewhat after peaking so much during the past months of August and September, but the illness is still quite serious and in need of a slow and delicate cure; but, as these serious maladies are wont to have their favorable crises, independent of human calculations, in this do I place my hope, for I cannot do so in anything else.)

Nevertheless, Arango, whose only hope for Spain lay in Providence, according to the above, had expressed on September 26 of the same year another basis of confidence:

> Sin embargo de todo no crea V. que yo me abandone al desconsuelo de un fatal y definitivo resultado porque cuento con la nulidad de nuestros enemigos que también son españoles, porque si no lo fuesen, ya hace tiempo que estaría aquí Don Carlos.[27]

> (In spite of everything, don't think that I abandon myself to the disconsolateness of a fatal and definitive result, because I count on the incompetence of our enemies, who are also Spaniards, because if they were not, Don Carlos would have been here a long time ago.)

Optimism springing from profound pessimism concerning the very nature of the national character is a stage that Larra does not appear to have reached.

Let us now return to Larra's essays. On April 4, 1834, the *Revista Española* printed "El hombre propone y Dios dispone, o lo que ha de ser el periodista." Two theatrical reviews without political overtones had preceded it. "El hombre propone," a subtle attack on censorship, uses the same sort of pseudoscientific (that is, pseudonaturalist) enumeration as "La planta nueva" and "El ministerial." About two days later Figaro found another opportunity to address a gentle rebuke to the government for its action against *El Siglo* and other newspapers. Criticizing the *Diario de Avisos* for not bothering to list actors' names in its theatrical announcements, he adds:

> No sabemos cuál sea la causa de la reserva de nuestro hermano; acaso cobrando miedo a la muerte que acecha a los periódicos en el día, temerá comprometerse y... ¿quién sabe? (1: 366).

> (We know nothing concerning the cause of our colleague's reserve; perhaps through fear of the death that threateningly lurks near newspapers in our day, it is afraid to commit itself and... who knows?)

In truth, the omission was probably due to indifference.

After a smattering of other theatrical reporting and a review of the third volume of Quintana's *Vidas*, we come to an article of considerable political interest, "Representación de *La niña en casa y la madre en la máscara* de Don Francisco Martínez de la Rosa" (April 14). Here Larra praises the playwright's linguistic refinement and good taste and the sensitivity with which his characters are drawn. On the other hand, the plot fares badly at the journalist's hands, owing mainly to some excessively protracted scenes and to the inclusion of a personage whose main purpose is to moralize.

> Nosotros entendemos que la moral de una comedia no la ha de poner el autor en boca de [este o de aquel] personaje; ha de resultar entera de la misma acción. . . . *qui ne sait se borner ne sut jamais écrire,* ha dicho un famoso crítico. Sin que queramos hacer una aplicación exacta de este axioma al señor Martínez, confesamos que es sensible que se haya dejado llevar de la antigua tradición . . . (1: 372–373)

> (It is our understanding that the moral of a play should not be put by the author in the mouth of this or that character; it should come wholly from the action itself. . . . *he who cannot limit himself never found out how to write,* a famous critic once said. Without wishing to apply this axiom exactly to Mr. Martínez, we must admit that it is regrettable for him to have let himself be guided by the old tradition . . .)

Larra, though extremely careful, had no qualms about criticizing the prime minister's plays when he could introduce mitigating praise about a secondary aspect.

The next essay, "¿Qué hace en Portugal Su Majestad?" (April 18), a pungent burlesque of the pretender's court and his decrees, is followed by a highly favorable review of Juan María Maury's *Espagne poétique.* Then comes the well-known article about *La conjuración de Venecia* (April 25). In spite of abundant evidence of Larra's political hostility to Martínez, many critics have misunderstood Larra's views. Basing their arguments mainly on his praise for one play (which is undeniably good) and on a supposedly favorable mention of the Estatuto Real, these critics pay little heed to the circumstances. For example, in his biography of Figaro, Ismael Sánchez Estevan concludes that Larra's kind word for the Estatuto in the review of *La conjuración* indicates that the journalist may still have been a supporter of Martínez at the time, and only later became disillusioned with him.[28] But when we consider that before his review of *La conjuración de Venecia* Larra wrote five articles directly or indirectly against Martínez,[29] and then shortly after this play wrote two more such articles,[30] Sánchez Estevan's inference becomes untenable.[31] It is indeed obvious that Larra's praise of the play is superlative; but it is also clear that Figaro's statements are justified in view of the moment. "No hemos visto nada mejor en Madrid" (1: 387—"we have seen nothing better in Madrid") may imply adverse criticism of the Spanish stage and thus indicate only relative excellence. The assertion, moreover, should be understood as referring to theatrical productions in their totality and not just to the quality of the plays in written form.

Keeping this review in mind, let us turn momentarily to later events before its political significance is explained. On May 3, in his article on Giudita Grisi's performance of *I Capuletti ed i Montechi*, Larra again mentions the Estatuto Real, but his tribute to it is seemingly ironic. He insinuates that it does not satisfy his political yearning and complains openly about the time it took the government to draft it. It is true that at a later date he apparently wrote an article in praise of the Estatuto and an *octava* "En loor de la Reina Gobernadora," both published in the *Revista Española* (June 14, 1834). Yet they are unsigned, a highly significant detail. The poem, meant as a contribution to the celebration of the Estatuto's solemn proclamation, was reproduced the next day by *La Abeja*, but with the author's name. Let us remember that the celebration was part of a well-organized campaign, with paeans for the benevolent queen who had granted the charter.[32] It was also desirable to play safe, especially when the government had recently set an example by suppressing the extreme newspapers that might have contained unfavorable criticism. The true nature of all the encomium is hinted at by a contemporary historian:

No conviene a nuestros fines examinar detenidamente las imperfecciones o aciertos del nuevo código; sólo diremos que en nuestro sentir se hallaba muy distante de satisfacer los deseos que mucho antes de su publicación se habían ya generalmente manifestado. Por prudencia, por ignorancia o por lisonja, se tributaron a su autor

grandes encomios en un principio; éstos se convirtieron después en quejas y severas críticas con daño del mismo hombre que había creído asegurarse en aquella obra la eterna estimación y reconocimiento de los españoles.[33]

(It does not suit our purpose to examine at length the imperfections or merits of the new code. We shall only say that in our opinion it came far from satisfying the desires which, long before its publication, had been generally manifested. Through prudence, ignorance, or flattery, great praise was heaped upon its author in the beginning. These later turned into complaints and severe criticism to the detriment of the very man who had thought to assure himself, by means of this work, the eternal esteem and gratefulness of Spaniards.)

Is Larra's praise due to prudence, ignorance, or flattery? Some scholars have ascribed to him a sort of enthusiastic delusion. Again, I feel they have not properly examined the circumstances. Prudent flattery seems more likely here. In order to understand what Larra was up against and why he lauded somewhat the Estatuto, let us turn to Fermín Caballero. Caballero should be a reliable historian. He was not only a witness to these events but also a *procurador* and the editor of the *Eco del Comercio*:

Los que consideran a la imprenta como un poder en los gobiernos representativos, hablan de la prensa libre: nosotros durante el *Estatuto* la hemos tenido bajo la dura férula de la censura previa, y mal podía creerse un poder del estado. Ha hecho bienes inmensos, porque el continuo empeño del escritor lograba disfrazar algún día sus sentimientos hostiles, o presentar de manera su oposición que se escapase a la vigilancia censoria; pero advertido el gobierno del daño que le hacía un periódico, tenía en su mano el remedio: suprimirlo. Entre las bárbaras restricciones ideadas por los enemigos de la libertad de imprenta, ninguna más terrible y funesta que la supresión, la muerte de un papel público. Como si una empresa de esta clase no mereciese respetos por la propiedad que representa, los capitales que pone en circulación, las familias que mantiene y la instrucción que promueve, de una plumada se daba en tierra con tantos intereses por virtud del famoso reglamento; y hubo ocasión en que se suprimieron cuatro periódicos en una sola real orden, como sucedió el 19 de mayo de 1834 al *Universal, Eco de la Opinión, Nacional* y *Tiempo*, atribuyéndoles doctrinas diametral-

mente opuestas a los principios conservadores sancionados en el *Estatuto Real.*[34]

(Those who consider the press as an estate in representative governments are talking about a free press. During the Estatuto ours was under the hard ferule of prior censorship, and it could hardly be called an estate. It brought immense benefits, because the continuous determination of the writer succeeded on occasion in disguising his hostile feelings, or in presenting his opposition in such a way that it escaped the vigilance of censorship. But once the government noticed the harm done to it by a newspaper, it possessed the remedy at hand: suppressing it. Among the barbarous restrictions thought up by the enemies of freedom of the press, none is more terrifying and dismal than the death of a public paper. Unmindful that an enterprise of this kind should have deserved some respect for the property it represented, the capital it put into circulation, the families it supported, and the instruction it promoted, one stroke of the pen would bring down all these interests by virtue of the famous regulation. And there was one occasion when four newspapers were suppressed by a single royal order, on May 19, 1834; namely, *El Universal, El Eco de la Opinión, El Nacional,* and *El Tiempo,* attributing to them doctrines diametrically opposed to the conservative principles sanctioned in the Estatuto Real.)

Let us note that this order was given only twenty-four days after the review of *La conjuración de Venecia.* Likewise, we should not deem a vain taunt the ironic banter aimed at the *Diario de Avisos* mentioned above.

There is an oft-quoted passage in this review that I would interpret, unlike some other students of Larra, as an ostentatious admission that the journalist is humoring Martínez. Let us not forget that the prime minister had the reputation of being easily beguiled. Would such an admission not mitigate the adulation? Let us examine the passage:

No acabaremos este juicio sin hacer una reflexión ventajosísima para el autor; ésta es la primera vez que vemos en España a un ministro honrándose con el cultivo de las letras, con la inspiración de las musas. ¿Y en qué circunstancias? ¡Un Estatuto Real, la primera piedra que ha de servir al edificio de la regeneración de España, y un drama lleno de mérito! ¡Y esto lo hemos visto todo en una semana! No sabemos si aun fuera de España se ha repetido esta circunstancia particular.

Sabemos que el señor Martínez, modesto en medio de su triunfo, se hallaba en el teatro, y que se escondía a los públicos aplausos en lo más recóndito del palco bajo número 6. Este mérito más. (1: 386)

(We cannot complete this judgment without making a comment most advantageous for the author. This is the first time that we see in Spain a minister honoring himself through the cultivation of letters, through the inspiration of the muses. And under what circumstances? A Royal Statute, the first stone which is to serve in the edifice of Spain's regeneration, and a play containing great merit! And we saw all this within one week! We do not know whether even outside Spain this particular circumstance has ever occurred.

We know that Mr. Martínez, modest in the midst of his triumph, was present in the theater, and that he concealed himself from public applause in the least exposed part of ground-floor box number 6. This is certainly one more merit.)

These lines do seem apt to flatter a man whom some may have considered, even at that time, "de espíritu aniñado." By announcing that he will make "una reflexión ventajosísima para el autor," Figaro appears to be calling our attention to his own compliments, thus hinting that he duly follows the dictates of caution by humoring the prime minister. Another phrase that should not escape scrutiny is "la primera piedra que ha de servir," which may be interpreted as a sort of notification. Such a hypothesis is corroborated by the attitude of the Progressive *procuradores* a few months later when they made excessive use of the prerogatives granted to them in the Estatuto. In pressing for additional rights, these representatives abused the "derecho de petición" provided by the charter. There is an even more patent indication of the relevance of Larra's phrase. In the speech of the Crown for the opening of the Cortes on July 24, Toreno, the most liberal minister in the government, managed to insert the famous "cimiento" paragraph:

El Estatuto Real ha echado ya el cimiento: a vosotros os corresponde, ilustres Próceres y Sres. Procuradores del reino, concurrir a que se levante la obra con aquella regularidad y concierto que son prendas de estabilidad y firmeza. (*Pr.*, Apéndice al núm. 3, p. 2)

(The Estatuto Real has already laid the foundation. It is up to you, Illustrious Próceres and Procuradores of the realm, to contribute to the erection of the structure with that regularity and order which is the virtue of stability and firmness.)

During the succeeding parliamentary sessions, the Progressives gave these words the broadest possible interpretation. In like manner, it is probable that Larra expected his attentive readers to construe "primera piedra que ha de servir" as freely as the procuradores would later construe "cimiento."

As for the "circunstancia particular," that it certainly was, when we consider that the liberals had been awaiting a constitution for almost three months. And then, we must not forget the short note that Larra sent to his newspaper immediately after the performance, and which appeared the day before the review. Its highest praise is not for the work itself:

Con los ojos arrasados aún, con el corazón henchido de contrapuestos sentimientos, sólo encontramos expresiones para proclamar esta representación como la primera de todas cuantas se han visto en Madrid, sobre todo con respecto a la perfección con que se ha puesto en escena. El público la ha coronado de aplausos. (1: 383, note 1)

(With eyes still inflamed, with a heart swollen by clashing sentiments, we only find expressions that will proclaim this performance as the first of all those seen in Madrid, especially with respect to the perfection of the staging. The public crowned it with applause.)

Here the critic extols the *mise-en-scène* "sobre todo" (we presume that Martínez paid a good amount for this out of his own pocket). The applause is the public's. Why is it that Larra's "sentimientos" are "contrapuestos," and which feelings are they? Does Figaro's admiration for the playwright clash with his disapproval of the statesman? Villa-Urrutia must have sensed the review's irony when he wrote:

Admiró Larra de Martínez de la Rosa que en una propia semana diese al público el *Estatuto Real* y un drama intitulado *La Conjuración de Venecia*, con lo que logró, según Cánovas del Castillo, acreditarse más de romántico con su drama que de liberal con su ley fundamental, para los revolucionarios literarios o políticos de la época.[35]

(Larra was amazed that in the same week Martínez de la Rosa could give to the public the Estatuto Real and *The Venetian Conspiracy*, whereby he succeeded, according to Cánovas del Castillo, in proving himself to the literary or political revolutionaries of that era, more of a Romantic with his drama than a liberal with his fundamental law.

It seems hasty to conclude that Larra was satisfied with the Estatuto Real. He may have rejoiced with his fellow-liberals because it was, after all, a significant step towards liberty. It meant the end of absolute monarchy; after the Calomarde era, this alone was cause for gladness. The Progressives and Isabelinos followed the cautious policy of cheering it for the sake of solidarity with the queen. Perhaps it was also the best way to allay the prime minister's fears, in the hope of catching him off his guard for a later coup.

When the Cortes did meet finally, it soon became clear that Progressive cooperation was a mere façade. Many *procuradores* adhered to the parliamentary rules prescribed in the Estatuto while doing all they could to stretch its interpretation. Their observance of the new legality was only superficial, however, for underneath it all, the Isabelina plotted to overthrow the government and establish a constitution written by Olavarría. The situation at the time was so complex that it is bold to assume that any person who moved in liberal political circles had any illusions about the Estatuto Real. Along with his prominent acquaintances, Larra in all likelihood decided to make a feigned gesture of thanks for "la primera piedra."

The next theatrical review, an unfavorable one, appears on April 28; it concerns *Ni el tío ni el sobrino* by Espronceda and Ros de Olano. The essay on *I Capuletti ed i Montechi* (May 3) is much more significant, since its first four paragraphs are partly political. The journalist begins by commending both the Estatuto and Giudita Grisi, the soprano.[36] This initiates a process that could be dubbed *laudatio ad absurdum*, whereby praise is bestowed upon one thing linked by analogy to something else; and the analogy is then carried to the point where it renders the initial encomium inconsequential. It should be noted also that the introductory tribute to the Estatuto gives an appearance of conventionality meant perhaps as a precaution, so that the censor might find what is to follow not too unpalatable:

> Cosa probada parece que han menester hacerse esperar las cosas en nuestro país para ser buenas; la experiencia ha hecho para nosotros un axioma de esta proposición, tanto en política como en música. Pocas cosas habrán ejercitado tanto nuestra paciencia como el Estatuto y la señorita Grissi; en cambio, sin embargo, muy pocas también nos han satisfecho más completamente. Si atendidos estos ejemplos puede dejar de ser paradójica nuestra inducción, debe servirnos de gran consuelo; porque, según ella, ¿qué esperanzas no podemos fundar de las cosas que en la actualidad nos tienen en expectativa? (1: 389)

> (It seems to be a certainty in our country that things have to become long-awaited in order to be good. Experience has made an axiom of this proposition for us, in politics as well as in music. Few things have exercised our patience as much as the Estatuto and Miss Grisi; on the other hand, nevertheless, very few have likewise satisfied us more completely. If, once these examples have been taken into account, our induction ceases to appear paradoxical, this will provide us with great consolation, because, accordingly, what hopes shall we then not be able to base on those things that keep us in expectancy at present?)

The first three words have a definite air of antithesis; to say about something that it appears proven is equivalent to doubting that it has been proven. Likewise, using "más" before "completamente" makes the latter word ambiguous, and Figaro would not be untruthful if he were to state that few things indeed have ever come near to satisfying him. There is also irony in the suggestion that his inductive reasoning is paradoxical.

Having compared the Estatuto to the excellent prima donna, Figaro now uses for a similar purpose the tenor Género, who is still "ese eterno mañana de los *dilettanti*"[37] (1: 389—"that eternal morrow of the dilettantes"). Then, shifting from the soprano to the tenor for the sake of analogy, Larra writes:

> ¿Qué no hemos de esperar de la ley Municipal, de la ley de Elecciones, de la de convocatoria; qué de nuestras Cortes, y qué, en fin, de nuestra completa libertad racional y de nuestra *próxima* felicidad? (1: 389)

> (What can we not expect from the Municipal law, from the Electoral law, from the law for summoning Cortes? And what shall we not expect from our Cortes, and what, finally, from our complete rational liberty and our *approaching* felicity?)

The reader is thus forced to conclude that all of this legislation will take too long to bring appreciable results. But the journalist does not drop the topic at this point; on the contrary, he insists on maintaining an analogy between politicians and musicians: "la medianía es insoportable en música; el justo medio es insufrible en circunstancias críticas" (1: 389—"mediocrity is unbearable in music; the just middle is unsufferable under critical circumstances"). The "juste milieu" is identified, of course, with Martínez's adoption of Victor Cousin's political theories, so that the final remark on ministerial indecision cannot but be construed as an attack on the prime minister himself: "Un tenor débil desluce una pieza concertante, un ministro blando desconcierta la máquina" (1: 390—"A weak tenor dulls a concert piece, a pliant minister disconcerts the whole set-up"). Though Larra never was a Doceañista, his prudence, his newspaper's policy, and, in any case, the censor would have put any open opposition to the Estatuto beyond the bounds of possibility. Nevertheless, the charter was but a creature of "justo medio" philosophy, so that, by suggesting the inadequacy of Martínez's principles and lawmaking, Larra has, in a way, put the Estatuto Real in a bad light.

"Las palabras," published on May 8, is also political, but it possesses the quality of universality to an apparently greater degree than the previous essays. Its first paragraph is pseudophilosophical, the type of exordium subsequently found in "El ministerial," though as a whole it is thematically akin to "Por ahora," written nine months later. In the latter, Figaro ridicules trite words of caution to eager reformers. In "Las palabras" he scoffs at verbiage without action, alluding to ministerialist newspapers that seek to maintain with vague hopes and platitudes the people's faith in governmental wisdom. By comparing the two essays, it becomes evident that the same politicians who once uttered "mañana" would later declare "por ahora no" ("not for now").

Larra does not fail to emit a jibe at the men in power whenever the opportunity arises. In his review of Ducange's *El verdugo de Amsterdam* (May 13), we find a pregnant vehicle:

> se forma causa al joven Federico. Las causas en Holanda deben de ir más de prisa que en Madrid, verdad es que no es difícil. A poco de estar preso, ya está sentenciado . . . (1: 395)

> (a lawsuit is drawn up against young Frederick. Lawsuits in Holland must be handled more quickly than in Madrid; of course, this should not be too difficult. He has hardly been imprisoned when he is sentenced . . .)

Three days later, while commenting on Beaumarchais' *Mariage de Figaro,* Larra implies that the public's hissing this play is proof that jacobinism has almost no following in Spain:

> Las mismas razones que han hecho su fortuna [in the rest of Europe] han debido causar en Madrid su desgracia; y a los que se empeñan en suponer que es de temer una semejanza de situación entre nuestro país y la Francia de la Revolución, ésta sería una de las pruebas que les daríamos para tranquilizarlos. . . . es imposible suponer en Beaumarchais la idea de predicar de buena fe la doctrina esparcida en su obra. Hay cosas tan atrevidas que llegan a estomagar. (1: 396)

> (The same reasons for its success [in the rest of Europe] must be those of its failure in Madrid; and this ought to be one of the proofs needed to tranquilize people who insist on supposing that a similarity is to be feared between our situation and that of France during the Revolution . . . one cannot possibly suppose that Beaumarchais thinks of preaching in good faith the doctrine dispersed throughout his work. Some things are so daring that they turn one's stomach.)

This passage should be examined in the light of other remarks supposedly meant to allay the government's fear of a coup, a fear resulting in its hesitancy to take liberal measures, such as the creation of a national guard.

The next theatrical—or rather, operatic—article, "*Ana Bolena*" (May 19), also contains a politically pregnant vehicle, used as an example in chapter 1. The remark that Judith Grisi seemed as much alone as the pretender in Portugal provides a theme for a subsequent essay, "El último adiós" (June 2), a low burlesque of Carlos's flight from the neighboring kingdom. More operatic and theatrical criticism also appeared at that time. The most politically significant one concerns a tragedy entitled *Numancia* (probably not the one by Cervantes); the review is mainly an attack on prior censorship, and, in describing the play and the acting, Larra cleverly adapts several phrases from the regulations decreed eight days previously. It ends on a bitterly ironic note, wittily but pathetically associating an aspect of Spain's cultural penury to the Progressives' disappointment in Martínez:

> El telón al caer se detuvo a la mitad del camino a tomar un ligero descanso; no parecía sino que caminaba por la senda de los progresos, según lo despacio que iba y los tropiezos que encontraba. Tardó más en bajar que han tardado las patrias libertades en levantarse. (1: 410)

> (Coming down, the curtain stopped halfway to take a little rest. It seemed to be journeying along the path of progress, judging from its slow pace and the snags it must have encountered. It took longer to drop than our country's freedoms to rise forth.)

The phrase, "la mitad del camino," is obviously a scornful reference to the "juste milieu." Larra also mocks the "ley del uno por ciento," described in the previous chapter, by stating that "un artículo de periódico ha de salir bien de primera vez, que en fin no es ningún *reglamento de milicia*" (1: 409—"a newspaper article must come out right the first time because, after all, it isn't a *militia regulation*").

The review of *Norma* (July 2) is even more daring. It refers to censorship through a theatrical simile: "Más breve, con algunas enmiendas, con menos todavía que las que suele hacer la censura en un artículo de oposición, el señor Género puede ir adelante" (1: 415—"If he were quicker, and with a few corrections, even less than those made by censorship in an opposition article, Mr. Género could make some progress"). Larra devotes his last paragraph to the question of Calomarde appointees in the civil service, which will be dealt with in chapter 9. One extremely significant sentence concerns another important topic, the government's fear:

> En el día no se puede vivir sin tener miedo: o a los revolucionarios que nadie ha visto y que nos llevan sin embargo a la anarquía, no se sabe por dónde, según ciertas gentes, o a las sociedades secretas que van a hacer un daño tremendo a la sordina, según la *Revista* y el *Eco*.[38] (1: 415)

> (It is impossible to live nowadays without being afraid, either of the revolutionaries whom no one has seen and who, according to certain folk, are nevertheless leading us into anarchy, though no one knows which way, or of the secret societies, who are going to bring tremendous harm on the quiet, according to *La Revista* and *El Eco*.)

It is noteworthy that a history attributed to Javier de Burgos reproduces an article from the *Eco del Comercio* attacking the secret societies. But the historian comments:

> Estos razonamientos eran una condenación explícita, terminante, no sólo de la sociedad de los *Isabelinos*, sino de todas las sociedades secretas sin excepción alguna. Y aquí debemos preguntar otra vez: ¿querían engañar a sus adversarios los que tales doctrinas predicaban, o se engañaban a sí propios? Lo que podemos decir es, que muchos de los admiradores de esas doctrinas fueron después inconsecuentes porque, o formaron parte de las sociedades secretas, o se unieron a ellas para derribar a los poderes legítimos del Estado.[39]

> (These arguments constituted an explicit, definitive condemnation, not only of the Isabelina, but of all secret societies without exception. And now we must again ask ourselves: did those who preached such doctrines wish to deceive their adversaries, or were they fooling themselves? What we can say is that many of the admirers of those doctrines were later inconsistent because, either they formed part of the secret societies, or they joined with them to tear down the legitimate powers of the State.)

Only three weeks later the Palafox conspiracy was unmasked. Is Larra therefore sincere when he appears to chide the ministry for being afraid of a supposedly nonexistent danger? His oxymoron, "daño tremendo a la sordina," is especially effective stylistically here. Yet we must remember that the government was indeed in trouble and perhaps the *Revista*, which represented the loyal opposition, was calling on Martínez to take liberal measures in the face of growing discontent and the threat of a leftist rebellion. Either Larra's remark is not ironic and accords with the newspaper's policy, or it really is ironic, making light of the government's justified alarm and thus counteracting any sympathy Martínez might gain for taking preventive measures. The latter is probably the case.

His next publication is a review of Rivas's comedy, *Tanto vales cuanto tienes*. Here Larra does not allude to politics except to mention Rothschild and Aguado. The same holds true with respect to two more reviews. Then comes an essay on the closing of theaters owing to poor attendance during the cholera epidemic. Larra grudgingly flatters the government but also tactfully blames it for not coming to their aid:

> Dirásenos, es verdad, que las graves atenciones que ocupan en el día al Gobierno han podido ser causa de esta fatalidad. No quisiéramos ofender a un Gobierno a quien tanto debemos; pero nosotros tenemos también nuestra opinión, y este punto no nos parecía de menos entidad que otros. Ésta no es ya una mera cuestión de teatros, sino de salud pública, de alta política; y no juzgamos equivocarnos al creer que no pueden desconocer estas verdades ministros ilustrados, y aun literatos y poetas, que miramos al frente de los negocios. (1: 421)

> (Truly enough, the reply will be that the attention the Government must devote to serious matters at this time may have been the cause of this calamity. We do not wish to offend a Government to which we owe so much; yet we also have our own opinion, and this point seemed to be of no less moment than the others. It is not a mere question of theater but of public weal, of statesmanship; and we do not feel we are mistaken in believing that enlightened ministers, even men of letters and poets whom we see in charge of the affairs of state, cannot be unaware of these truths.)

PROPERTY OF
UNIV. OF ALASKA LIBRARY

The last of the preparliamentary articles thus ends on a cautious but reproachful note. With the opening of a parliament, newspapers will obtain some protection from arbitrariness, through their connections with members of Cortes. Under these circumstances, Figaro's writing from now on appears bolder, as we shall see in the following chapters.

4

THE QUEEN OPENS
THE CORTES

THE nineteenth century in Spain has been called an oratorical era. Even novelists have admitted the influence of the declamatory art, which in itself possessed great masters as early as the first Cortes, where Agustín Argüelles acquired the epithet of "el divino orador." Hence, it should not be difficult to understand public enthusiasm for the reestablished Cortes after eleven years of parliamentary silence. By April 1836 Figaro could portray "un público más ocupado de los Estamentos que de los coliseos" (2: 203—"a public more occupied with Chambers than theaters"), and a month later he would comment:

> Dos cosas estamos esperando siempre para escribir en cuanto a redactores de teatros: que las sesiones de los Estamentos nos dejen meter baza en nuestro periódico, y que la empresa de este año nos dé alguna función buena . . . (2: 219)

> (In our capacity as theatrical editors, we are always waiting for two things: for the parliamentary sessions to make a little room

for us in our newspaper, and for this year's company to give us one good performance . . .)

All important speeches were reproduced or at least reported in the press, and the Cortes provided a popular conversational topic.[1] To be informed about the parliamentary goings-on seems to have been of paramount importance in social circles, and there is fair evidence that Larra attended the sessions regularly.[2] In "Buenas noches" (January 30, 1836) the journalist humorously advises his imaginary Parisian correspondent:

> por lo tanto te aconsejo que eches mano de las sesiones de Cortes y te las leas de cabo a rabo, y si llegas a entender claro en el asunto, te aconsejo también que te des la enhorabuena, y te tengas en lo sucesivo por hombre de talento. (2: 144)

> (therefore I advise you to take hold of the Cortes sessions and read them from head to tail, and if you get to understand anything clearly in the matter, then I also advise you to congratulate and look upon yourself henceforth as a man of talent.)

Fígaro's first article dealing with the Cortes, "Carta de Fígaro a un bachiller su corresponsal" (July 31, 1834), also contains a sentence that evinces the prominent treatment accorded by the press to parliamentary events:

> Además, aunque los partes oficiales y los relatos de las sesiones en sustancia no dicen nada, no dejan por eso de ser largos; nos ocupan por consiguiente las tres cuartas partes de nuestras columnas, y no nos dejan espacio para nada. (1: 423)

> (Moreover, even though the official dispatches and reports of the session say nothing substantial, nevertheless they are still long; accordingly they take up three quarters of our columns, and leave us space for nothing.)

Provision for public attendance is mentioned in a low burlesque manner. The magnificent aura of the upper house is dispelled through a nonce word made famous by Manuel Bretón de los Herreros's most popular comedy and through an implied comparison of grandiloquent oratory to the tenuity of traditional Spanish music:

Si viene a oír las discusiones estamentales, en buen hora, por lo que respecta al Estamento de Procuradores; pues en el de Próceres han encaramado al público en un camaranchón estrecho y *cortilargucho,* según dice *La Pata de Cabra,* como si no quisieran ser oídos. Se está allí tan mal como en el teatro de guitarra. (1: 424)

(If you come in order to hear parliamentary discussions, that's fine, with respect to Procuradores; because in Próceres they've stuck the public in a narrow drawn-out garret gallery, as if they didn't want to be heard. One is as uncomfortable there as at the guitar hall.)

Though humorous, the above passages may give the reader a notion of the importance of the preparations for the official opening on Thursday, July 24, the queen's saint's day. The Crown address read by her had been composed with all the rhetorical care of which Martínez de la Rosa was capable.[3] After much persuasion on his part, María Cristina had braved the cholera epidemic in order to make the event a genuine "sesión regia," and this act of courage allayed the unpopularity occasioned by her previous flight to San Ildefonso to avoid the disease. Unfortunately, the slaughter of the monks on July 17 added to the inauspiciousness of the circumstances. To make matters worse, the Isabelina conspiracy had been discovered and Palafox, whom the queen had just named a *prócer* for his role in the War of Independence, had been arrested on the eve of the solemn event. The final shock came when the queen rose to deliver the address and the audience saw she was pregnant. They assumed that the father-to-be was Fernando Muñoz, recently promoted from bodyguard to *gentilhombre.* This caused much consternation among those who had sought in María Cristina the strength of character and majesty needed for the task of ending the nation's devastating civil war.[4] The queen, moreover, read her speech too rapidly and without expression,[5] although it was its vagueness which especially displeased the Progressives.[6] Rather than suggest specific projects, it displayed generalities, giving the government margin for equivocation.

Figaro's comments are incisive:

¡Ah!, se me olvidaba: el discurso de la Corona ha gustado generalmente; es tan bueno, que es de aquellas cosas que no tienen contestación; a lo menos, hasta ahora nadie se la ha dado. Se asegura, sin embargo, que la están preparando a toda prisa. (1: 424)

(Oh! I almost forgot: the Crown speech was generally well received. It is so good that it is one of those things that cannot be contested. At least, up to now no one has replied to it; but we are being assured, however, that the reply is being prepared with all deliberate speed.)

The author's litotic feigned forgetfulness shows he held the address in small esteem, and the word "generalmente" implies that no one objected to its generalities. Consequently, it arouses no contestation, if we assume a pun on "contestación," which would hint likewise that delays in drafting a reply irritated the public. This was indeed the case, for a week had passed since the speech and no answer was forthcoming. In the upper house, the committee appointed on July 25 for this purpose (*Ilus.*, p. 9) had spent three days without coming up with anything (*Ilus.*, p. 12). For a document that finally proved to be of a formal and servile nature, the tardiness was indeed unwarranted. The final draft was not read until July 31, and it took considerable discussion before a favorable vote could be cast (*Ilus.*, p. 14 and appendix to no. 6). As for the lower house, no committee was appointed until Tuesday, July 29 (*Pr.*, p. 13); its projected reply was read on Friday, August 1.

The tenth paragraph of the "Carta de Fígaro" concerns another congressional matter, the excuses sent by delegates who chose to stay away from the cholera-infested capital. On July 22, two *procuradores* were heard from (*Pr.*, p. 4), on the 23rd three, and on the 26th and 29th seven, all alleging illness (pp. 6, 10, 12). Two members felt that military service justified their absence (*Pr.*, pp. 11–12), and another sent a doctor's certificate. Some resorted to documents purporting to prove their income was lower than that required by the electoral law for qualification. This situation explains Larra's remark: "Por acá no se encuentra un procurador; ni un cajista de imprenta, ni un médico, ni un limón, ni una sanguijuela por un ojo de la cara . . ." (1: 424—"around here you cannot find one *procurador*, or one typesetter, or one doctor, or one lemon, or one leech, even for your eyeteeth . . ."). Figaro's hyperbole about scarcity is therefore as applicable to congress as to the other items on the list, and it is stylistically balanced by his ensuing exaggeration of the number of absentees:

> No sé si me dejo algo a que contestar; si así fuese, en otra carta irá, pues a la hora que es ando de prisa por tener que formar una lista de los señores procuradores que no han llegado aún . . .(1: 424)

> (I don't know if I overlooked something to be answered. If so, it'll have to go in another letter because I have to rush to start drawing up a list of the honorable *procuradores* who have not arrived yet . . .)

As for the Próceres, the journalist is more concerned with the facilities available to the general public, as we saw above, and to the stenographers:

> Han arrinconado igualmente en un ángulo del techo a los taquígrafos, de tal suerte, que parecen telas de araña. Muy alto piensan hablar si desde allí les han de seguir la palabra. (1: 424)

> (The stenographers have likewise been pigeonholed in a corner of the ceiling, so that they look like cobwebs. The orators' words will have to be rather elevated in order to be heard and taken down up there.)

The Quevedesque simile[7] conveys a grotesque image of *próceres* having to speak loudly in order to be heard by the cobwebs; perhaps the trope insinuates Larra's contempt for their conservative orations, which are but dust caught up by another symbol of decay. In any case, Figaro's observation proved accurate, because the stenographers eventually had to be relocated after a speech was faultily transcribed (*Ilus.*, p. 25).

The uniform designed for the *próceres* by Martínez de la Rosa contributed to the spectacle. Its specifications are contained in the royal decree of July 26:

> Para los actos solemnes, . . . manto ducal, de terciopelo azul turquí con mangas anchas, como los usaron los Ricos homes de Castilla y de Aragón en los siglos XIV y XV, forrado de armiño, con la epitoga también de armiño, el cual arrastrará algo por detrás; por encima de la epitoga adornará el cuello del Prócer una gola, más subida por detrás que por delante. Bajo el manto llevará una

túnica de glacé o tisú de oro, que bajará hasta cubrir la rodilla, y cuyas mangas ajustarán en el puño, y estarán adornadas en este sitio por una guarnición estrecha de encaje; medias de seda blanca y zapatos de terciopelo azul con un lacito de cinta o galón de oro. En la cabeza llevará el gorro ducal, también de terciopelo azul, con vuelta de tisú de oro, y debajo del manto, la espada, pendiente de un cinturón de la misma tela que la túnica.[8]

(For solemn occasions, . . . ducal robe, of indigo blue velvet with wide sleeves, like those used by the peers of Castille and Aragon in the fourteenth and fifteenth centuries, lined with ermine, with the outer toga likewise of ermine. The robe should drag slightly behind. On top of the toga, a gorget, higher in the rear than in front, is to adorn the neck of the *prócer*. Under the robe he is to wear a tunic of silk glacé or gold tissue, which shall come down just below the knee, and whose sleeves will fit at the wrist, adorned at this point with a narrow lace flounce; white silk stockings and blue velvet shoes with ribbon or gold braid laces. On his head he will wear a ducal cap, likewise of blue velvet, with gold tissue facing, and under the robe his sword, hanging from a belt of the same material as the tunic.)

This description is sardonically ridiculed by Larra in the "Carta de Fígaro":

Por el pronto ya tenemos el uniforme de los señores próceres, que es manto azul rastrero, según las venerandas leyes del siglo XIV, exceptuando el terciopelo, que no alcanzaron aquellos Estamentos, si bien aquí entra el modificar aquellos venerandos usos según las necesidades del día; verdad igualmente aplicable al calzón de casimir, media de seda, hebilla y tahalí, de que nada dicen Pero López de Ayala, ni Zurita, ni el Centón, pero que constituyen con la gola altibaja y demás este nuevo antico-moderno. Tiene su correspondiente espada, su gorro y enagüilla de glacé. Dicen que cuesta mucho; pero más ha costado llegar a ese punto. Si vuesa merced tiene baraja, como es de suponer, mirando al rey de espadas podrá formar una idea aproximada, y por ende verá que es bonito; y que si bastan, como es de creer, para costearle los sesenta mil reales del procerazgo, ha de ser curioso el ver a esos señores vestidos y hablando, todo a un tiempo. (1: 423)

(For the time being we already have the uniform of the honorable *próceres*, a drag-blue robe, according to the venerable laws of the fifteenth century, except for the velvet, which the *Estamentos* of yore did not attain to, although here is where the modification of those venerable usages to suit the needs of the day comes in; a truth equally applicable to the cashmere breeches, silk stockings, buckle and shoulder belt, of which no mention is made by Pero López de Ayala, or Zurita, or the *Centón*, but which constitute, along with the high-'n-low wimple etc., this new antique modern. It has its corresponding sword, cap, and petticoat glacé. They say it costs a great deal; yet it has cost us even more to get to this point. If your grace hath a deck of cards, which I suppose you do, by looking at the king of spades you can get an approximate idea, and therewith you'll see it's pretty. And if the sixty thousand reales of peerage suffice, as we should believe, to pay for it, what a rare sight will be those gentlemen, dressed and speaking in unison!)

Certain humorous touches are especially subtle. The "manto ducal de terciopelo azul turquí . . . el cual arrastrará algo por detrás" becomes a "manto azul rastrero." This color must have been felt to differ sharply from "azul cristino," popularized in 1829 when the people saw their lovely new queen first set foot on Spanish soil. Figaro also insists on the high cost of the uniform, calling our attention to the financial qualifications for one category of *prócer* that we noted in chapter 2. Larra hints, of course, that the ideas expressed in the upper house would be as obsolete as the speakers' garments. Humor aside, it must be stated in all fairness that the archaic uniform was meant to impress wearers and foreign observers alike. If we are to believe Alcalá Galiano, Martínez must be given most of the credit for the sensation produced by the ceremonious vote in Próceres to exclude Don Carlos from the throne:

Oyóse a los hombres más ilustres de la nobleza española por sus timbres heredados y su considerable riqueza, a algunos prelados, a no pocos títulos de inferior esfera a los grandes, pero de alta y respetable todavía, y a multitud de personajes elevados a los empleos superiores y encanecidos en el servicio de su patria y de sus reyes, dar un voto que excluía del trono a quien se daba por representante de la monarquía antigua, así como por rey de derecho, faltando en aquella ocasión a D. Carlos todo cuanto da lustre y fuerza a la causa de los monarcas, y reduciéndole a ser rey de la plebe armada con calidades de tribuno, aunque con doctrinas de monarca. Admiró este paso a los extranjeros, y fue sabido con dolor y enojo por los nobles principales de otros países empeñados en sustentar los derechos del pretendiente al trono español, y en mirar su causa como una misma con la de otros tronos europeos cimentados en el poder de las clases superiores.[9]

(The most illustrious members of the Spanish nobility, for their inherited crests and considerable wealth, some prelates, not a few persons inferior to the grandees but yet bearing high and respectable titles, and a multitude of personages promoted to superior positions and grown gray in the service of the country and their monarchs, were all heard casting a vote which excluded from the throne the man who considered himself the representative of the old monarchy, as well as king by right. Everything that gives splendor and strength to the cause of monarchs slipped from Don Carlos on that occasion, and he was reduced to being king of an armed populace, with the qualifications of a tribune, though with the doctrines of a monarch. Foreigners looked upon this occurrence with amazement, and the news was learned with great chagrin and anger by the leading nobles of other nations who insisted on sustaining the rights of the pretender to the Spanish throne, and to look upon his cause as identical to that of other European thrones based on the power of the upper classes.)

Whether Larra was justified is therefore a moot point, and the prime minister must be given credit for what he accomplished. At the cost of resentment from the left, Martínez de la Rosa brought the Spanish nobility firmly over to the queen's camp. All the grandees except the Duke of Granada supported her, so that by December an observer could write: "These numerous classes are now too deeply compromised to hope for mercy from the Prince they have opposed, and who during the last four months has done little else than fulminate edicts of death and confiscation against them."[10]

The "Carta de Fígaro" also contains numerous allusions to other matters: inadequate measures against the cholera, the malfunction of public services, riots, the presence in government agencies of Calomarde appointees sympathetic to Carlism, interruption of the mails due to Carlist occupation of the main road from France, the ineffectuality of the Quadruple Alliance, and

Carlos's escape and reappearance in northeastern Spain on July 12. There are also caustic allusions to the flaws of a system where the ministers are not accountable to parliament, and therefore not too heedful of public opinion:

> Mis artículos en primer lugar no han de ser artículos de decreto que se fragüen a un dos por tres y a salga lo que saliere, sin perjuicio de enmendarlos luego o de que nadie se cure de obedecerlos. Al fin tengo mi poca o mucha reputación que perder. (1: 423)

> (In the first place my articles are not going to be like the articles of a decree, improvised in a wink and helter-skelter, taking it for granted that they can be emended later or that no one might take the trouble to obey them. After all, I have my reputation, great or small, at stake.)

This may possibly also refer to the militia decree of February 15, explained in chapter 2. Likewise, "al fin ni somos santos ni autoridades, que a todo el mundo oyen y a ninguno contestan" (1: 422 —"after all we are neither saints nor authorities, who hear everyone and answer no one"), where the mention of supplication to saints leads to an anecdote about the "cepillo de las ánimas." An Andalusian priest owes a peseta to a Catalan colleague, who collects the debt by removing a coin from an almsbox and advising the Andalusian to throw a peseta into the corresponding one in his church. The tale possesses a Cervantine flavor, remindful of the prologue to *Don Quixote*, part 2, and thus facilitates the transition to Figaro's salutation, which parodies the great novel's opening lines: "Mucho me huelgo, señor Bachiller de ese pueblo, de cuyo nombre mal pudiera acordarme, de haber recibido su carta benévola y preguntona" (1: 423—"It has been my great pleasure, dear Bachelor of that town whose name I could ill remember, to receive your benevolent and inquisitive letter"). The "letter" likewise shows Voltairian reminiscences. As a background for Martínez's policies, Larra ironically adopts a mock-Leibnitzian philosophy:

> Por lo demás, aquí, según usanza antigua, todo va como Dios quiere, y no puede haber cosa mejor, porque, al fin, Dios no puede querer nada malo. Nuestra patria camina a pasos agigantados hacia el fin para que aquel Señor la crió, que es su felicidad. (1: 423)

(As for the rest, here, following ancient usage, everything goes according to God's will, and nothing could be better, because, after all, God could not will anything evil. Our nation marches with giant steps toward the goal for which the Lord created her, which is its felicity.)

Of course, it is not literary influence that makes a masterpiece. What does constitute the stylistic excellence of this essay is in part the skillful joining of its various themes. One suggests the other in an ingenious epistolary chain. When two apparently unrelated topics are set down contiguously, the author endows the first with a feignedly casual capacity to introduce the second. For example, one such transition clearly illustrates Larra's opinion that the queen's speech should have encouraged an energetic initiation of measures for coping with Spain's numerous ills. A paragraph ends in this wise: "se encuentran mendigos a pedir de boca, basura en las calles a todas horas y una camilla al volver de cada esquina" (1: 424—"beggars can be found immediately on request, garbage in the streets at all hours, and a stretcher upon turning every corner"). The next one begins: "¡Ah!, se me olvidaba; el discurso de la corona ha gustado generalmente . . ." ("Oh! I almost forgot. People liked the Crown speech in general . . ."). The permeating realism of actual conditions looms thus over the jejune address of the Crown, making it appear even more insignificant. Another ironic touch is to communicate the most important piece of news, the arrival of Don Carlos, in a postscript, where it is mentioned in a palliative tone, with subtle ridicule for the ineffective Quadruple Alliance and the bad faith of Spain's allies.

5

A REPLY TO THE CROWN

AFTER seeing his first "letter" published, Figaro reviewed two plays, *Malvina* and *El casamiento por convicción,* and a concert. Only in the first theatrical article do we find a reference to politics, and a very vague one at that: "El público, sin embargo, no la ha silbado: él se sabrá por qué. ¿Es porque estamos en tiempos de paciencia y resignación?" (1: 425—"The public, however, did not hiss it. They probably have their reason. Is it because we live in times of patience and resignation?"). In the meantime, an answer to the address of the Crown had been drafted. This draft and its impending discussion were viewed by the left as an opportunity to urge liberal legislation, express opinions on the nation's plight, propose remedies, and force the hand of the ministry. Consequently, the Progressives were preparing a parliamentary campaign to press the government into passing prompt reforms, enacting constitutional guarantees of freedom, and creating an independent judiciary. The Moderate attitude, on the other hand, was to give lip service to liberty and the rights of the individual, but to concede so much to tradition that, after the Progressive draft was amended, human rights would be but a mere hope for years to come.

On August 13, 1834, the *Revista Española* published the "Segunda y última carta de Fígaro al bachiller, su corresponsal desconocido," whose opening lines may show the influence of Paul-Louis Courier de Méré's *Deuxième Lettre particulière:*

> Vous êtes babillard, et vous montrez mes lettres, ou bien vous les perdez; elles vont de main en main, et tombent dans les journaux. Le mal serait petit si je ne vous mandais que les nouvelles du Pont-Neuf; mais de cette façon tout le monde sait nos affaires. Et croyez-vous, je vous prie, moi qui ai toujours fui la mauvaise compagnie, que je prenne plaisir à me voir dans la Gazette?[1]

> (You're talkative and you show people my letters, or you lose them. They go from hand to hand and land in the newspapers. The harm would be small if I only sent news of Pont-Neuf [bridge at the center of Paris]; but this way everyone knows our business. And do you really believe that I, who have always fled bad company, take pleasure in seeing myself in the *Gazette?*)

Larra uses the same device as Courier; in addition, he manages to associate the problem of epistolary diffusion, so to speak, to the rhetorical diffuseness of the Moderates:

> ¿Querrá creer vuesa merced, señor Bachiller, que han encontrado malicia en la primera carta que le escribí, y cuya publicidad de ninguna manera he podido evitar en esta corte? De todo tiene la culpa el empeño que manifiesta de no tener nombre conocido, ni domicilio sabido, precisamente en unos tiempos en que las cosas todas se vuelven nombres. ¿No repara vuesa merced cómo una cosa se llama *regeneración*, otra *reformas*, ésta *Estamentos*, aquella de más allá *libertad*, esotra *representación nacional? ¿Qué más?* Cosa hay que se llama *seguridad individual*, y *ley*, y...
>
> ¿Qué le costaba a vuesa merced ponerse un nombre, y mas que vuesa merced no sea nada en sustancia tampoco? Así evitaríamos el que se anduviese todo el mundo leyendo lo que le escribo y murmurando de ello de corrillo en corrillo, ni más ni menos que si yo dijera todo lo que hay que decir, o todo cuanto en el caso me ocurre. (1: 428)

(Would you believe, my dear Bachelor, that they detected malice in the first letter I wrote you, whose notoriety I have been totally unable to prevent in this capital? The blame rests completely on the determination you show for not having a known name, or known residence, precisely in an era when all things turn into names. Haven't you noticed how one thing is called *regeneration*, another *reforms*, this one *Estamentos*, that one yonder *liberty*, that other one *national representation?* What more? There's even something called *individual security*, and *law*, and...

What would it cost you to put on a name, even though you are not anything substantial either? Thus we would avoid having everyone walking around reading what I write and whispering about it from one group to another, just as if I were saying everything that ought to be said, or everything that occurred to me under the circumstances.)

The seven abstractions set down by Figaro can be found in the debate on the proposed reply drafted by a Progressive committee:

La igualdad de derechos ante la ley y la libertad civil no pueden menos de ser consagrados en toda la extensión que reclaman la razón y la justicia: la seguridad personal debe ser protegida igualmente contra todo ataque del poder y de los abusos; y la inviolabilidad de la propiedad corresponde del propio modo sea anunciada como uno de los símbolos principales, o como la segunda cláusula del pacto social. (*Pr.*, appendix to no. 7, p. 2; August 1, 1834)

(Equality of rights under the law and civil liberty must not fail to be consecrated to the full extent demanded by reason and justice. Personal security must be protected likewise against all attacks from power and from abuses; and it is fitting that the inviolability of property be proclaimed in the proper manner as one of the principal symbols, or as the second article, of the social compact.)

Before passing the Estamento de Procuradores, the draft underwent several changes at the hands of the Moderates. The reasons for their objections should be evident. First of all, the Rousseau-inspired radicalism of the "pacto social" theory is incompatible with the Estatuto Real's status as a medieval *carta otorgada* (or *restablecida*, if one prefers). Moderate opinion would also have considered it a disquieting exaggeration for abstract reason and justice to claim the full extension of liberty. Is it any surprise,

then, that after five days the sentence in question was altered as follows?:

> Los procuradores del reino se lisonjean de que en el glorioso reinado de V.M. la igualdad de derechos ante la ley, la libertad civil, la seguridad personal y la inviolabilidad de la propiedad serán consagradas en toda su extensión contra los ataques del poder y de los abusos. (*Pr.*, appendix to no. 12, p. 2; August 7, 1834)

> (The Procuradores of the kingdom are greatly pleased that in the glorious reign of Your Majesty equality of rights before the law, civil liberty, personal security, and the inviolability of property will be consecrated in all their extent against attacks from power and from abuses.)

The amending process as well as Figaro's observations may be understood by leafing through the *Diario*, where we see Martínez making insinuations against the use of "pacto social":

> No parece sino que se trata de constituir una nación nueva, recién formada; mas no es ése el caso en que estamos, sino en el de reformar los abusos introducidos por el tiempo y los hombres en las leyes de una monarquía antigua, de una nación que a ellas debió en otro tiempo su prosperidad y su gloria. (*Pr.*, p. 47)

> (It seems as if one were trying to constitute a new nation, recently formed; yet this is not the situation in which we find ourselves, but rather in that of reforming abuses introduced by time and by men into the laws of an ancient monarchy, of a nation which to them owed in other times its prosperity and its glory.)

Martínez's concept of reform as a return to medieval institutions must have seemed ridiculous to Larra, because two words appearing here, "ley" and "reformar," are present in the passage previously quoted from the "Segunda carta." Another word in Figaro's list, "regeneración," appears in the reply to the Crown. Hence, it too must have lost its significance for Larra within the context of the less vigorous final draft.

During the debate Martínez de la Rosa used some qualifiers with "libertad," which also figures in the journalist's ironic list. The prime minister had uttered the phrase "una prudente libertad" (*Pr.*, p. 49) while assailing a Progressive motion to enact a bill of rights. In another instance, the committee which drafted the reply to the Crown wrote "razonable libertad," an expression kept in the final version. In one speech, Martínez resorted to "absoluta libertad de imprenta," "esta libertad ilimitada de la imprenta" (uttered disapprovingly, of course), and "grado de libertad" (a locution much to his liking) (*Pr.*, p. 42).

To communicate his derision, Larra invents a correspondent, but the fellow is a "corresponsal desconocido," a nameless being who supposedly exists but cannot be reached. The dubious existence of the "Bachiller" thus sets a tone of vagueness which, by analogy, the author can attribute to ideas such as freedom, thereby suggesting that they have lost their essence. "Las cosas todas se vuelven nombres," words of unclear connotation tossed about by orators. But while implying their insubstantiality, Figaro simultaneously assigns to these ideas certain demonstrative adjectives ("aquella de más allá," "esotra") that invest them with a spatial subsistence. Moreover, this antithetical play is heightened by the additional temporal interpretation of "más allá," which hints at the remoteness of true liberty under the present régime.

We should bear in mind that the freedom debated most specifically was that of the press, as reflected in the third paragraph of the "Segunda carta." I shall not quote it entirely, because this would not necessarily contribute to an appreciation of its conceptual complexity. Yet its perplexing succinctness assimilates it to the equally baffling first paragraph, thus initiating a process by which the mock letter acquires stylistically, through its very variety, a unity that it cannot fully possess thematically. But thematic devices do articulate the two passages. The third paragraph maintains and develops the epistolary tenor of the first while resuming the topic of the search for malice. Let us recall that the "Segunda carta" began thus: "¿Querrá creer vuesa merced, señor Bachiller, que han encontrado malicia en la primera carta . . . ?" In the third paragraph the theme of scrutiny is applied to the "Segunda carta" itself:

> si vuesa merced quiere divertirse con mis cartas, dígame quién es, y le escribiré en sesión secreta; pero entonces, ya, señor Bachiller, que la prohíban. Esta, pues, sobre ser la última, no encerrará re-

flexión ni broma alguna, tanto por las razones dichas, cuanto porque Dios sabe, y si no lo sé yo, que no tengo para gracias el humor;
en punto sobre todo a gobierno haré la del loco con el podenco.
"Quita allá que es gobierno." Hechos, no más, en adelante; y si a
los hechos lisa y llanamente contados les encuentra malicia, entonces dígole a vuesa merced que la malicia no estará en mí, sino en
los hechos o en el que los leyere; entonces malicia encontrarían
hasta en una fusión cordial del Estamento y del Ministerio. (1:
428)

(if you want to amuse yourself with my letters, tell me who you
are and I shall write you in secret session; but then, dear Bachelor,
let them prohibit it! The present letter, then, besides being the
last one, will contain no reflection or jest whatsoever, not only
for said reasons, but because God knows—and if not, I do—that
I am in no mood for pleasantries. With respect to government
especially, I'll act like the madman with the hound. "Careful, it's
governmental." Facts, nothing more from now on; and if they find
malice in the facts, smoothly and plainly related, then I can tell
you that the malice won't be in me but in the facts or in the eye of
the reader. Then they might find malice even in a cordial fusion
of the Estamento and the Ministry.)

The above reference to a private letter as "sesión secreta" is
more than just an ingenious metaphor. We can perceive this on
examining the discussion that ensued when Pedro Manuel Velluti
y Navarro, the Marquess de Falces, implied on August 3 that public debate was improper for so delicate a matter as human rights:

Nadie negará que los que la comisión propone no son otra cosa
que la libertad de imprenta, la igualdad ante la ley, establecimiento
del jurado, etc., etc.: esto se debía haber discutido en el Estamento
después de haberse votado si debía ser en sesión pública o secreta:
entonces sería cuando el Estamento, lleno de madurez, podría pre-
sentarlas [viz., peticiones] a la Reina. (Pr., p. 28)

(No one will deny that those things proposed by the committee
are none other than freedom of the press, equality before the law,
establishment of the jury system, and so forth. This should have
been discussed in the Chamber after a vote on whether it should
be in public or secret session. This would be when the Chamber,
full of maturity, could present petitions to the Queen.)

No closed meetings of the Estamento took place until August 20, seven days after the "Segunda carta's" publication; hence Larra must be satirizing Falces's speech. His implication is that the proceedings of a secret session would transpire immediately, since the Progressive representatives were evidently willing to divulge them.

As for the sentence, "Quita allá que es gobierno," also appearing in the above passage from the "Second letter," it is an adaptation of a famous phrase in the prologue to the 1615 *Quixote*, telling of a madman who dropped stones on every canine that crossed his path. One day an infuriated dogowner thoroughly drubbed him for hurting his *podenco*. After this incident, every time he felt the desire to hurt an animal, hound or not, the madman would hesitate and desist, muttering to himself, "Este es podenco, guarda." Figaro's adaptation is quite appropriate.[2] After enough encounters with the censor, a journalist will ultimately resign himself to inhibiting his criticism of the government, automatically, instinctively. Then, irrational fear begets more fear, and an author may refrain altogether from criticism; did such a fate not befall Spanish letters during the Calomarde era? More specifically, Larra's mot burlesques the legalism inherent in the Moderates' demand for a very formal reply, as evidenced by Latorre's speech of August 3: "Todo lo que no sea, como he dicho, ceñirse al discurso de la Corona, lo tengo por intempestivo, así como el prevenir medidas que el Gobierno prevendrá en su día" (*Pr.*, p. 28—"Everything which, as I have said, does not limit itself to the speech of the Crown I deem inopportune, as well as preparing measures that the government will prepare in their time"). As we can see, there are two levels of analogy, whereby Larra has found yet another way to join the particular to the universal, the parliamentary detail at hand to the great problem of freedom, the symptom to the malady.

In the next passage the journalist chides the upper chamber for the inanity of its reply to the Crown:

En el Estamento de Próceres ya sabrá vuesa merced que la contestación al discurso del trono fue cosa muy bien escrita; fue un modelo de lenguaje y de elegancia castellana; es uno de los trozos más correctos que posee la lengua. (1: 429)

(In the Estamento de Próceres, as you know, the reply to the speech of the throne was something very well written. It was a model of language and Castilian elegance; it is one of the most correct passages in the Spanish tongue.)

Such documents are expected as a matter of course to have a fixed style; moreover, the tone of the present reply is quite servile toward the monarch. Figaro, therefore, while extolling it for being what it is supposed to be, leads up to the word "correcto," which has a *double entendre;* politically as well as stylistically, the document is correct, and nothing more, for it repeats the ideas of the royal address paragraph by paragraph.

We should note, however, that the upper house contained a small minority who argued for a more assertive and specific reply to the Crown. These Progressives opposed the draft prepared by a conservative committee made up of the Marquess de Santafé, Manuel José Quintana, Javier de Burgos, the Archbishop of Mexico, the Marquess de las Amarillas, the Marquess de la Candelaria, the Count de Monterrón, the Duke of Veragua, and Eusebio Bardají y Azara (see *Ilus.,* p. 9). The draft was finally read to the members on July 31 and debated August 2. During debate, the partisans of the committee, principally the prime minister and Javier de Burgos (*Ilus.,* p. 18), wished the reply to remain as general in scope as the queen's speech; to be, in other words, merely formal. Martínez de la Rosa managed to establish a similarity between his own opinions and certain principles that could supposedly be deduced from ancient Spanish parliamentary tradition. In this way, the Progressives might be portrayed as deviates from this national tradition (*Ilus.,* p. 17). Those who spoke against the draft were Gil de la Cuadra, Antonio Cano Manuel, and, above all, the Duke of Rivas, who wanted the reply to list projects of specific reforms, viz., a bill of rights, a law regulating police power, one to determine the organization of the Milicia Urbana, one to guarantee freedom of the press, laws clarifying Spain's relations with her colonies, and means of putting an end to political parties.[8] By their efforts in this instance, the three leftist *próceres* initiated Progressive parliamentary tactics. Dissatisfied with the limited power given to the Cortes, they would now seize upon every occasion to force legislation. Their attempts were always frustrated in the upper house. In the lower house the Progressives were more successful. They managed to introduce into their reply to the Crown, presented on August 1, all but the last two of the projects mentioned by Rivas in Próceres (*Pr.*, appendix to no. 7, p. 2).

This was possible because, for the moment, the lower chamber found itself in the opposite situation from that of Próceres. The committee was Progressive and its proposal underwent opposition from the Moderates. These proceedings are the topic of Figaro's sixth paragraph, where we sense his concern with a subject that affected him professionally, the discussion on whether freedom of the press should be mentioned in the reply to the Crown. The initial draft read as follows:

> La libertad de imprenta, esa centinela y puesto avanzado de las demás garantías, necesita entre nosotros verse exenta de las restricciones que hoy la reducen casi a la nulidad. Las buenas leyes pueden prevenir los abusos o castigarlos cuando tengan efecto, de un modo que haga muy difícil su repetición; mas nunca es justo ni prudente sacrificar positivas ventajas a los temores de un riesgo acaso imaginario, ni la facultad de propalar el pensamiento por este medio existe cuando la reprimen la censura previa o la arbitrariedad. (*Pr.*, appendix to no. 7, p. 2; August 1, 1834)

> (Freedom of the press, that sentinel and outpost of the other guarantees, needs to be relieved among us of restrictions which at this time almost reduce it to a nullity. Good laws can forestall abuses or punish them when they occur, in a manner that would make their repetition very difficult; but it is never just or prudent to sacrifice positive advantages to fears of a risk which is perhaps imaginary. The ability to spread ideas by this means does not exist when prior censorship or arbitrariness repress it.)

For the final version, the above had been changed to:

> La libertad de imprenta, esa centinela y puesto avanzado de las demás garantías, es de desear obtenga entre nosotros toda la amplitud que sea compatible con la moral y con un sistema de política bien entendido: amplitud por la que, sin incurrir en el riesgo de que se minen u ofendan las costumbres ni las bases y principios de la sociedad, se logre la más fácil extensión de los conocimientos y

de las verdades útiles al Gobierno y a la nación. (*Pr.*, first appendix to no. 12, p. 2)

(It is to be desired that freedom of the press, that sentinel and out-post of the other guarantees, will attain among us all the extension compatible with morality and with a well understood political system; an extension by means of which, without incurring the risk of undermining or offending the customs or the foundations and principles of society, the easiest spread of knowledge and truths useful to the Government and the nation may be brought about.)

This alteration did not occur without heated debate. Worthy of note is Toreno's speech of August 3:

La libertad de imprenta es una de las grandes cuestiones, y acaso la más delicada de tratar, y sobre todo por un Ministerio, porque al instante se cree que no se quiere que se examine su conducta. Esta creencia, habiendo Representación nacional [one of the terms which Larra treats so ironically in his first paragraph], es errónea, pues todo Diputado tiene derecho de censurar las operaciones del Ministerio. Este no puede huir de semejante censura: de lo con-trario no habría libertad [another word in Larra's list!]. El Go-bierno en abstracto adora, es idólatra de la libertad de imprenta; pero la cuestión es si cuando hay una guerra civil será conveniente establecerla. Entro con franqueza en la cuestión, aunque podía evi-tarla, porque es preciso se sepan los principios del Gobierno. En el día las obras voluminosas y de instrucción sólida, excepto de polí-tica y religión, tienen libertad; y el Ministerio probablemente no se opondrá a que todas las obras voluminosas y de instrucción sólida, aun políticas, corran libremente, porque el país necesita esa in-strucción; pero tal vez por ahora podrá poner restricción para los periódicos, que al lado de mucho bien pueden derramar un veneno mortífero . . . (*Pr.*, p. 24)

(Freedom of the press is one of those great questions, perhaps the most delicate to bring up, and especially by a Ministry, because at this instant it is believed that an examination of its conduct is not wanted. This belief is erroneous when there is national representa-tion, since every Deputy has the right to censure the operations of the Ministry. The latter cannot escape such censure; otherwise there would be no liberty. In the abstract, the Government adores, it is an idolater of, freedom of the press. But the question is this:

when there is a civil war on, whether it is convenient to establish it. I am broaching the question with frankness, even though I could avoid it, because it is imperative that the Government's principles be known. Nowadays voluminous works of solid learning, save those about politics and religion, enjoy freedom; and the Ministry will perhaps not be opposed to having all voluminous works of solid learning, even political, be freely accepted, because the nation needs this instruction. But perhaps for the time being it ought to impose a restriction on newspapers, which, though they can do much good, can also spill forth deadly venom . . .)

Besides the use of the phrases "representación nacional" and "libertad," which in Larra's opinion are a sham, we also find "por ahora," a term very frequently used by the Moderates, taken up by Larra in the paragraph in question, and later made the title of another article in the *Revista Española* (February 10, 1835). Toreno's words did not remain unanswered, for we find in López's subsequent remarks the following:

Sus ideas en este punto no concuerdan con las de la comisión; precisamente las obras voluminosas no se hallan al alcance de muchos, al paso que los periódicos y obras sueltas pueden circular mejor y llevar a todas partes esa misma instrucción que se reconoce ser tan necesaria. (*Pr.*, p. 35)

(His ideas on this point do not agree with those of the committee. It is precisely voluminous works that are not within the means of many, while newspapers and single works can circulate better and bring to every part that very instruction which is recognized to be so necessary.)

Santafé, in his speech of August 4, was even more explicit than Toreno about the inopportuneness of freedom of the press:

Efectivamente, es muy esencial tener presente que para dar una ley no basta la circunstancia de que sea justa; es menester que sea tal que se acomode a los hábitos de aquellos a quienes se dirige; es menester que éstos estén preparados, digámoslo así, para recibirla. (*Pr.*, p. 33)

(In fact, it is quite essential to keep in mind that in order to issue a law the circumstance of its being just is not sufficient. It must be able to accomodate itself to the habits of those for whom it is meant. It is necessary that these people be prepared, so to speak, to receive it.)

Joaquín Abargues immediately answered him on this point, and later López answered Toreno:

> Por último, se ha dicho que la libertad de imprenta podía reclamarse para obras grandes, y dejando la previa censura para las demás. Esto no era hacer nada nuevo, porque en el día tenemos de hecho semejante libertad. (*Pr.*, p. 35)

(Finally, it was stated that freedom of the press could be claimed for large works, leaving prior censorship for other kinds. To do this is nothing new, because we now have such freedom.)

The debate lasted until August 6, when Martínez de la Rosa made another speech on the subject, and Fermín Caballero dwelt on the inconsistencies of censorship policies (*Pr.*, p. 42).

Larra's comments display a pathetic irony:

> De la [contestación] de Procuradores, nada tengo que contar a vuesa merced, si no es que en este momento no es oportuno que use el hombre del don de la palabra con que le distinguió Su Divina Majestad de los demás animales. Lo que urge por ahora es que cada uno calle lo que sepa, si es que no lo quiere decir en un tomo voluminoso, que entonces, como nadie lo ha de leer, debe el hombre ser libre; pero decirlo todas las mañanas en un periódico, eso no. El don de la palabra es como todas las cosas: repetido diariamente, cansa. (1:428–429)

(About Procuradores' reply, I have nothing to report, except that at this moment it is inopportune for man to make use of the gift of speech with which His Divine Majesty distinguished him from the other animals. What is urgent for the time being is that everyone should keep to himself what he knows, unless he wants to say it in a voluminous tome, because, then, since no one will read it, man must be free. But to say it every morning in a newspaper, no. The gift of speech is like all things. Repeated daily, it becomes tiresome.)

In the first place, we should note that at a time when all eyes were fixed on the proceedings, the phrase "nada tengo que contar" shows a certain contempt for the chamber, owing to what the journalist must have considered the obsequiousness of the majority toward the government. Stylistically, the paragraph is masterful. The transformation of Toreno's "las obras voluminosas" into "un tomo voluminoso" exhibits great sensitivity for the poetic value of alliteration. The "vocales graves" (*o* and *u*⁴) add sonic vividness to the image of a heavy book and the burden of censorship. The last word, "cansa," so obviously related to the idea of heaviness that in this context we associate it with heavy tomes, is ironically applied by Larra to the lightweight newspapers. Yet the word "cansa" could also constitute a literal hint that people are growing weary of reading in their newspapers the oratorical brilliance of Martínez, who does possess "el don de la palabra." Another clever device, found in the discussion of God's gift of speech to man, is to use "Su Divina Majestad" to signify Him, thus insinuating that, unlike God, S.M. la Reina Gobernadora, the other majesty, hardly believes in bestowing the same privilege.

The journalist's seventh paragraph concerns the establishment of the jury system, referred to by the committee's draft as "el oportuno establecimiento del jurado, esencial salvaguardia de la inocencia" (*Pr.*, appendix to no. 7, p. 2), a passage which the Moderates managed to excise. The parliamentary debates leading to its omission from the final reply begin on August 3 with López's defense of its inclusion:

> Se ha añadido además que debía establecerse el jurado, y acaso sea ésta la proposición que ha alarmado más a los Sres. Procuradores que se han propuesto impugnar a la comisión. Para deshacer cualquiera equivocación que les pueda ofuscar, es necesario acudir a los conocimientos filológicos. La comisión no pide el *inmediato* establecimiento, sino el *oportuno* establecimiento del jurado. Modifica la idea por la palabra *oportuno*. No fija tiempo ni ocasión de hacerlo; tampoco lo niega. Ha prescindido absolutamente de esta segunda cuestión, que podrá ser motivo, bien de una petición del Estamento, o bien de una invitación de parte del Gobierno; pero se expresa de un modo explícito y sin reserva. (*Pr.*, p. 21)

> (It was also added that the jury system should be established. This was perhaps the proposal which most alarmed the *procuradores* who intend to impugn the committee's statement. In order to undo any equivocation that might obfuscate them, it is necessary to re-

sort to philological knowledge. The committee does not ask for the *immediate* establishment, but the *opportune* establishment of the jury system. It modifies the idea with the word *opportune*. It fixes no time or occasion for carrying it out; neither does it deny it. It has dispensed absolutely with this second question, which could become an occasion for either a petition from the Chamber or an invitation on the Government's part. Yet it expresses itself in an explicit manner and without reservation.)

The same day, Diego Medrano opposed it:

Hay otra razón muy importante sobre otro punto, fundado en el mismo principio [that is, of not attempting any reforms until one is certain that they will work in practice]. Hablo del jurado; y a pesar de las observaciones del señor preopinante, creo que sería mejor omitir el párrafo relativo a él, porque en España, según mi opinión, no puede establecerse por ahora, ni en mucho tiempo, hasta mejorar la educación política. Un ensayo que se hizo [viz., in the Cortes of 1820–1823 by none other than Martínez de la Rosa; see his speech, *Pr.*, p. 27] sobre este particular probó no estar la nación en disposición de recibir una institución tan nueva. (*Pr.*, p. 22)

(There is another very important argument on another point, based on the same principle. I am speaking of the jury system, and in spite of the observations of the previous speaker, I believe it would be better to omit the paragraph relating to it, because in Spain, in my opinion, it cannot be established for the time being, or for a long time to come, until the political situation has improved. An attempt that was made once on this very subject proved that the nation was not properly disposed to receive such a new institution.)

López answered Medrano thus:

La comisión no entra en la cuestión de si es o no tiempo de establecerlo: habla sí de que es útil; y como el Estamento dura tres años, nada tiene de particular que exprese ahora esta idea, reservándose entrar en la discusión de su oportunidad cuando llegue el caso. (*Pr.*, p. 22)

(The committee does not go into the question of whether it is time or not to establish it. It does speak of its utility; and since the

Estamento is to last three years, there is nothing unusual about expressing this idea, reserving the matter of entering into the discussion of its opportuneness when the occasion arises.)

Following López's speech, Toreno again was called upon to argue the Moderate side, and pointed out that, as for the words "esencial salvaguardia de la inocencia," "esto no es exacto," for which opinion he proceeded to cite examples from European history, such as the times of Alfred the Great and the Reign of Terror of the French revolution.

> Malas son siempre las generalidades. Cuando la educación sea otra; cuando la juventud y las masas hayan tenido enseñanza que hasta ahora no tienen, entonces podrán plantearse estas y otras instituciones cuya utilidad no desconoce el Gobierno. La comisión bien pudiera haber imitado en esto la reserva que ha tenido en otros puntos; por ejemplo, nada habla de libertad religiosa: ¿y por qué la comisión no la toca, sin embargo que sabe los males que ha producido en España la intolerancia? Porque sabía que era inoportuno e imprudentísimo. (*Pr.*, p. 25)

> (Generalities are always bad. When education has changed, when youth and the masses have had the kind of teaching that they now lack, then these and other institutions whose usefulness the Government does not ignore can be set up. The committee might have imitated in this matter the reserve which it exercised on other points. For example, it says nothing of religious freedom. And why does the committee not touch upon it, even though it knows the evils that intolerance has produced in Spain? Because it knew that it was inopportune and extremely imprudent.)

Though there was more discussion on this point, by López (*Pr.*, p. 26), Martínez de la Rosa (p. 27), Santafé (p. 33), López again,[5] and Martínez de la Rosa (p. 48), the object of Larra's humor seems to be Toreno's speech. The latter, as we can see, compares the supposed inopportuneness of establishing the jury system to that of granting religious freedom, while holding that Spanish youth is politically unprepared for liberal institutions. In his satire of Toreno's opinions, Larra succeeds in closely connecting all these ideas. He starts by relating the word "jurado" with the decalogue according to Jerónimo Martínez de Ripalda:[6]

> Los jurados no son para este momento; no hay cosa peor que jurar, y si es en vano, peor que peor. En eso va de acuerdo el partido ministerial con el padre Ripalda. Se ha convenido, por ahora, en que los españoles somos muy brutos para decir lo que pensamos, y más para que nos juzguen en regla. (1: 429)

> (Sworn juries are out for the time being; there is nothing worse than swearing, and if it is in vain, horrors! On this point the ministerialist party is in agreement with Fr. Ripalda. It has been decided, for the time being, that we Spaniards are too brutish to say what we think, and even more so to be judged in due form.)

Larra thereby connects Spain's political immaturity to a religious immaturity exemplified by distortions effected for the sake of catechistic simplicity.[7] Let us note that it was Toreno himself who broached the subject of religious liberty. Another significant locution used by the journalist here is "en vano," which reflects the ministerialist' objection to giving even token lip service to the possible establishment of a jury system. Likewise, by inserting the phrase "por ahora," the author parodies Toreno. The last sentence of Larra's paragraph is especially forceful, since the writer appears to speak for all the people ("los españoles somos"), whose destiny is fixed by a fiat of undetermined origin—a pathetic impression imparted by the impersonal reflexive "se ha convenido."

Figaro now turns his attention to the first sentence in the proposed reply, and to the debate it brought about. The sentence thanks the sovereign for having pronounced

> principios y deseos cuya ejecución bastará a hacer la prosperidad de esta nación heroica; prosperidad a que es llamada por un concurso de circunstancias felices, pero de que porfiadamente la alejaron por mucho tiempo los vicios de una legislación absurda. (Pr., appendix to no. 7, p. 1)

> (principles and desires whose execution will suffice to bring about the prosperity of this heroic nation, a prosperity to which it is called through a convergence of happy circumstances, but from which the evils of an absurd legislation obstinately kept it away.)

The latter expression was impugned by Toreno on August 33:

> Hay otras expresiones en el mismo párrafo que debían omitirse. Tal es la que dice una *legislación absurda:* esto es demasiado gene-

ral, demasiado vago o inexacto: en España no ha habido legislación absurda; sí ha habido a veces *administración absurda.* Se llama *legislación absurda* con poca razón a la que sirvió a nuestros abuelos, cuyo estudioso y profundo saber elevó a esta nación a un grado de grandeza y prosperidad en que quisiéramos volverla a ver. En el siglo XVI en que la libertad estaba floreciente, regía esa legislación, cuyo desuso y olvido produjo infinitos males: en esto estuvo el absurdo, no en la legislación, y es una acriminación demasiado infundada sobre todas las generaciones anteriores, la que pone la comisión, que no debe pasar aquí. No la debemos hacer nosotros, que somos generación más joven, y que anhelamos volver a nuestra patria al estado floreciente en que ellos la tuvieron. Es preciso que miremos por el honor de la nación para no ofenderle con una frase indiscreta; es preciso estudiar mucho esas frases para no estamparlas en un documento público, y por eso repito que no hay dificultad en las cosas, sino en el modo de decirlas. (*Pr.,* p. 23)

(There are other expressions in the same paragraph which should have been omitted. Such a one is *absurd legislation;* this is too general, too vague or inexact. In Spain there has never been absurd legislation; there has been at times, though, *absurd administration.* With little reason can the term *absurd legislation* be applied to what served our grandfathers well, whose studious and profound knowledge raised this nation to a level of greatness and prosperity at which we should like to see her again. In the sixteenth century, when liberty was in flower, this legislation, whose disuse and oblivion produced infinite evils, still held sway. The absurdity consisted in the disuse, not in the legislation. What the committee has written is an overly unfounded crimination for all previous generations, and it must not pass judgment here. Let us not accuse, for we are a younger generation who yearn to take our country back to the flourishing state in which they had it. It is necessary to look after the nation's honor so as not to offend it with an indiscreet phrase; it is necessary to study these phrases carefully so as not to set them down in a public document, and therefore I repeat that there is no difficulty in the things themselves but in the manner of saying them.)

This appeal to tradition and national honor did not deter López from defending the original phrasing:

La comisión está exactamente en los mismos principios que S.E. [Toreno] en punto a la reseña de los males de la nación; pero cree que sin faltar a la verdad y al decoro puede emplear la expresión *legislación absurda.* La comisión ha mirado esto como el resultado de los abusos enunciados por S.E., pues el período largo que ha trascurrido desde que cesó de haber Cortes en España hasta los sucesos actuales, bien puede decirse han creado una legislación absurda, sobre las ruinas de la antigua, grandiosa, memorable, excelente, qua había. (*Pr.*, p. 25)

(The committee stands on exactly the same principles as His Excellency with respect to the review of the nation's ills, but it believes that it can use the expression *absurd legislation* without abandoning truthfulness and decorum. The committee has looked upon this as the result of the abuses set forth by Your Excellency, because it can indeed be stated that during the long period from the time there ceased to be Cortes in Spain until the present events an absurd legislation has been created on the ruins of the old, grandiose, memorable, and excellent one that existed.)

Martínez de la Rosa's oration, delivered immediately after López's, contains a lengthy passage about the phrase in question. It must be quoted in full for the simple reason that Larra laconically assumes his "corresponsal desconocido" is informed, as we shall see. Martínez spoke as follows:

La comisión habla sobre los males producidos por una *legislación absurda:* ni es exacta ni decorosa la expresión, ni la idea es verdadera; adolece de cuantos vicios puede adolecer.

No es fácil, cuando se trata de la decadencia de una nación, señalar causa única a que deba atribuirse. Es un principio cierto que cuando decae un imperio no es sólo por una causa; es por un gran concurso de ellas: y en un Congreso de legisladores sienta mal el aventurar que esta causa es sólo la *legislación absurda.* Más me atreveré a decir: si se hubiera querido designar una causa única, había otra más exacta, cual era el haberse abolido la institución de las Cortes, poco frecuentadas desde la entrada de la dinastía austriaca. Esto era mucho más exacto, porque habiendo habido Cortes, no hubiera habido esos errores en la administración que hoy se lamentan: no hubiera habido esos códigos que ahora se califican de absurdos; no hubiera sido la política de España ni la que siguió bajo los principios de la dinastía austriaca, ni la que siguió después durante el curso del siglo pasado, sino la natural y propia que la convenía; no hubiera habido Ministros arbitrarios que no cumpliesen con sus deberes, ni hubieran sucedido esos males que ahora enumera la comisión.

No es esto decir que no sea verdad hasta cierto punto lo que dice la comisión, sino que está poco meditada su expresión. Otra palabra hubiera podido expresar mejor la idea. Los Ministros están lejos de hacer la apología de la legislación española, cuando se ocupan en revisar los códigos para reformarlos, y cuando en esta misma legislatura van a presentar uno, y los demás seguirán después. Prueba de que están convencidos de su incoherencia y defectos, pero cuando tratan de esto, no deben los Ministros consentir en silencio que se diga por los legisladores mismos esa expresión poco meditada de *legislación absurda;* porque mientras no haya otras leyes, esas mismas tienen que seguir rigiendo en el país, y sería impolítico, y sobre todo en tiempo de agitaciones intestinas, privarlas del prestigio de esa especie de obediencia habitual que necesitan para ser respetadas. (*Pr.,* p. 26)

(The committee speaks only of the ills caused by an *absurd legislation:* the expression is neither exact nor decorous, nor is the idea itself true. It embodies as many flaws as it possibly could.

When dealing with the decadence of a nation, it is not easy to point out a unique cause to which it must be attributed. It is a sure principle that when an empire wanes this is not from one cause alone, but from a sum of many. In a congress of legislators it is ill befitting to venture the opinion that this cause is merely the *absurd legislation.* And I shall even make bold to say more: if a unique cause had to be designated, another could have been chosen, a more exact one, namely, the abolition of the institution of the Cortes, too infrequently resorted to since the entry of the Austrian dynasty. This is much more exact, because if there had been Cortes, those errors that are so regretted in the administration would not have been made, those codes that are now qualified as absurd would not have existed; the policies of Spain, those followed under the principles of the Austrian dynasty as well as those followed during the course of the last century, would have been instead the natural and proper ones suitable to the nation. There would not have been arbitrary Ministers who did not fulfill their duties, and the ills which the committee now enumerates would not have occurred.

This is not to say that what the committee states is not true to a point, but rather that its expression has not been sufficiently meditated upon. Another word would have expressed the idea better. The Ministers are far from propounding an apology for Spanish legislation, since they are occupied with revising its codes in order to reform them, and since in this very legislature they will soon present one, to be followed by others. Here is proof, then, that they are convinced of its incoherence and defects; but when such a matter is being taken up, the Ministers must not allow through their silence this insufficiently pondered expression, *absurd legislation*, to be spoken by the legislators themselves; because while there exist no other laws, those still have to be in force in the land, and it would be impolitic, especially in a time of internal disturbances, to deprive them of the prestige of that kind of habitual obedience that they need in order to be respected.)

The next day Santafé expressed a similar opinion in much stronger language:

Cuando la comisión habla de las causas que han motivado la decadencia de España, atribuye ésta principalmente a su legislación absurda. En esta expresión entiendo que se ataca directamente a la gloria de nuestros mayores. La legislación no ha sido absurda en España; lo que ha habido es que se ha faltado en el modo de ejecutarla; su ejecución no ha estado acompañada de todos los caracteres esenciales que debían acompañarla. (*Pr.*, p. 32)

(When the committee speaks of the causes that have brought on the decadence of Spain, it attributes it chiefly to its absurd legislation. With this expression I feel that it attacks directly the glory of our forefathers. Legislation in Spain has not been absurd. What happened was a failure to execute it properly. Its execution was not accompanied by all those essential characteristics that should have attended it.)

In view of an impending defeat, the members of the committee suggested the compromise, "administración absurda," in the belief that the ministerial party could not find as powerful an argument against it as against the original locution. It is apparent that they were anxious to keep the word "absurd," even if it had to qualify "administration" rather than "legislation," thereby weakening its effect considerably. It must be kept in mind that Martínez de la Rosa attempted to give his system a semblance of tradition, and was accordingly wary of any criticism of the laws of the land as a whole, though not adverse to anyone's alleging that they had been disregarded by tyrannical and absolutist governments. It is evident, therefore, that the compromise involved a vital concession on the part of the Progressives, who probably had hoped to use the phrase "legislación absurda" as a pretext for a future proposal to overhaul the corpus of Spanish law, which at the time still consisted of the Novísima recopilación, a haphazard rearrangement of the Hapsburg Nueva recopilación, in turn a revision of the Partidas and other medieval statutes.[8] The prime minister's cautiousness, it must be admitted, forces him to show some hypocrisy. He concedes that, had it not been for the Austrian dynasty, those codes that are now called absurd would not exist ("no hubiera esos códigos que ahora se califican de absurdos") and mentions their incoherence and defects ("su incoherencia y defectos"). Yet, rather than casting them aside and building anew, he would revise the codes in order to reform them ("revisar los códigos para reformarlos").

Notwithstanding the retreat of the Progressive committee members from their original position by acquiescing to the substitution of "administration" for "legislation," in keeping with Martínez's suggestion, the prime minister was still unhappy about the wording. His next oration, a model of casuistry—and rhetoric also—seems to be the special target of Larra's laconic sentence; hence the speech is quoted at length:

> Las principales reflexiones que iba a hacer para impugnar este párrafo giraban sobre el supuesto de que la comisión hubiera permanecido en el dictamen de sostener las palabras "legislación absurda." Pero supuesto que la comisión ha variado esta expresión, sustituyendo por ella la de "administración absurda," ya estamos en otra posición, y estrechando las distancias nos entenderemos mejor, porque no era fácil decir hasta qué punto había influido esa legislación llamada absurda en la decadencia de España. (*Pr.*, p. 38)

> (The principal observations I was going to make to impugn this paragraph revolved on the supposition that the committee would maintain its opinion in upholding the words, "absurd legislation." But seeing that the committee has altered this expression, replacing it with "absurd administration," I feel we are now in another situation, and by narrowing down the distance between us we shall understand each other better, because it was not easy to specify up to what point this so-called absurd legislation had contributed to the decadence of Spain.)

The orator now proceeds to dislodge his opponents from the position to which they have retreated at his own suggestion. Is it right, he asks, to attribute the decadence of Spain to one cause only? To answer his rhetorical question, Martínez de la Rosa compares the nation to a human body, whose diseases we do not understand sufficiently to ascribe them to any one cause. Likewise, it is not incumbent on Cortes to examine matters of historical causality:

> Sobre este punto yo haré una simple pregunta a la comisión: ¿es lo mismo legislación absurda que administración absurda, o son cosas diferentes? Si es lo mismo, o la comisión se equivocó ayer, o se equivoca hoy. Si ayer la causa de la decadencia de España era la legislación absurda, ¿cómo hoy lo es la administración absurda? Tan aventurado es, señores, querer con una sola palabra expresar con generalidades decisiones capitales. (*Pr.*, p. 38)

> (On this point I shall ask the committee a simple question: is absurd legislation the same thing as absurd administration, or are they different? If they are the same, then there should be no alteration. If they are not, then either the committee was in error yesterday, or it is in error today. If yesterday the cause of Spain's decadence was absurd legislation, how can it be today absurd administration? This is why it is so risky, gentlemen, to want to generalize by means of one word about such capital decisions.)

Now that Martínez has implied that it may be as difficult to defend one phrase as the other, he proceeds to attack once more the "legislación absurda" argument, knowing full well that it is the more vulnerable of the two. Every nation possesses some absurd laws, even England, model of enlightened and free countries. Moreover, to speak of absurd legislation in Spain is an insult to our ancestors and predecessors, whose Partidas are a monument of wisdom;

> y si la comisión se hubiera obstinado en sostener su primera palabra, hubiera tenido necesidad de fijar desde qué tiempo esa legislación que llama absurda había contribuido a la decadencia del esplendor y prosperidad de España. (*Pr.*, p. 38)

> (And if the committee had persisted in maintaining its first word, it would have been necessary to determine since when this legislation which it calls absurd contributed to the decadence of the splendor and prosperity of Spain.)

As for the administration, no one in his senses, of course, can deny that it has been absurd; least of all the present ministers themselves, who have done so much to reform it. Here the prime minister enumerates what his régime has done already to remedy the situation. Nevertheless, the nation's ills have a thousand causes. And now Martínez begins an oratorical feint by shifting to a defense of what he has just finished attacking, the legislative argument:

> los males de España provienen de mil causas; . . . provienen de la sustitución de leyes absurdas a otras excelentes y supresión de éstas. ¿Ignoran acaso los señores de la comisión que la decadencia no ha consistido tanto en las leyes absurdas cuanto en la supresión de otras saludables antiguas? ¿Hay quien haya olvidado que en la última edición de la Novísima Recopilación se arrancaron por manos pérfidas las dos leyes más ventajosas para la felicidad de esta nación; las dos leyes que S.M. la Reina Gobernadora acaba de tener la gloria de restablecer; las dos leyes relativas a no poderse imponer contribuciones sin la intervención de las Cortes, y a reunir éstas en los casos arduos y graves? Estas dos leyes se suprimieron de nuestros códigos; están en la nueva Recopilación, pero no en la Novísima. (*Pr.*, p. 39)

> (Spain's ills spring from a thousand causes; . . . they ensue from the substitution of absurd laws for excellent ones, with suppression of the former. Are the members of the committee perhaps unaware that our decadence has consisted not so much in absurd laws as in the suppression of others, ancient and sound? Is there anyone here who has forgotten that in the last edition of the Novísima Recopilación the two laws most advantageous to the felicity of this nation were ripped out by perfidious hands, those two laws that Her Majesty the Queen Regent has just had the glory to restore, the two laws against imposing taxes without the participation of the Cortes, and to summon the latter together in arduous and serious cases? These two laws were suppressed from our codes. They are in the Nueva Recopilación but not in the Novísima.)

And now the orator turns again to the other argument, asserting that "la administración ha sido viciosa" while praising the Estatuto Real, allowing him to conclude at last that "la idea de la comisión puede ser verdadera; pero un Cuerpo legislativo no debe aventurar frases que puedan ser censuradas con fundamento"

(*Pr.*, p. 39—"the committee's idea may be true, but a legislative body must not venture phrases that could be censured with good reason"). After this oration, López felt that he was defeated, and it cost Toreno little effort to persuade the Estamento to vote for the words "el olvido de sus antiguas instituciones" ("forgetting its ancient institutions") instead of the phrasing originally proposed (*Pr.*, p. 39). But all this debate, this Ciceronian brilliance, these anatomical and historical analogies, this casuistry, rather than inciting Larra to lengthy criticism, evokes but one laconic sentence: "Sabrá vuesa merced cómo se ha determinado que la legislación nuestra no es absurda" (1: 429—"You probably know how it has been determined that our legislation is not absurd"). Only Larra can produce litotes which have the impact of sarcasm.

Figaro's next paragraph deals with the excuses sent by Catalan delegates who did not show up for the sessions. Concerning this matter, the *Diario* contains one entry for August 9:

Lo mismo quedó [enterado el Estamento] de una exposición de los Sres. Fina, Martí, Palaudarias, Plandolid y Siscar, Procuradores por Gerona, Tarragona, Barcelona y Lérida, manifestando hallarse detenidos en Martorell por motivo del cólera.[9] (*Pr.*, p. 53)

(The Chamber was also informed of a declaration from Messers. Fina, Martí, Palaudarias, Plandolid, and Siscar, *procuradores* for Gerona, Tarragona, Barcelona and Lérida, stating that they had interrupted their journey at Martorell owing to the cholera.)

Martorell is less than twenty-five kilometers from Barcelona. Larra's raillery of the Catalans includes the following sentence: "Eso de representar ha de ser donde a uno le coja, porque andarse de ceca en meca para dar *representaciones nacionales*, eso fuera ser procurador de la legua" (1: 429—"This business of representing has to take place wherever it may come upon you, because the country will have to get used to the Cortes disbanding into travelling troupes to give oratorical performances"). The use of the word "representación"—enhanced by playing on the phrase "cómico de la legua"—sets the stage for a pun that connects stylistically this paragraph to the next, which concerns the aftermath of the Isabelina conspiracy:

Ya sabe vuesa merced cómo estaban presos dos individuos sobre lo de aquella grandísima conspiración que dicen que ha habido; como no les han encontrado delito, los han desterrado uno a Badajoz y otro a Zaragoza; parece que han representado, pero sus representaciones son como las de Cataluña, que nadie las oye.[10] (1: 429)

(You already know how two persons were imprisoned as a result of that great conspiracy which, rumor has it, was going on. Being found not guilty, they were exiled, one to Badajoz and the other to Saragossa. It seems they petitioned, but their petitions are like those of Catalonia, heard by no one.)

The last paragraph of the "Segunda carta," moreover, suggests that the fate of the Isabelinos, with whom Larra obviously sympathizes, may likewise befall the writer: "Perdonará vuesa merced, porque he oído llamar a mi puerta. Acaso vengan a prenderme o a llevarme a Zaragoza" (1: 430—"Please excuse me; I heard a knock at my door. Perhaps they've come to arrest me or take me to Saragossa"). The idea that someone is coming to arrest Figaro finally explains the title, "última carta." It also links the topic of press freedom to the fate of the conspirators, thus giving the "epistolary" essay maximum unity.

Before passing to Larra's next article, let us go back to two passages of considerable importance for an understanding of Figaro's position. The first touches upon the political alignment of the press:

¡Ah! ¿Sabe vuesa merced quién es ministerial?... *La Abeja*. Aquella *Abeja*... En una palabra, la *Abeja*. ¿Sabe vuesa merced quién es el periódico de la oposición? *La Revista*. Ello nos cuesta un ojo de la cara. (1: 429)

(Well! Do you know who's ministerialist now?... The *Bee*. That *Bee*... In a word, the *Bee*. Do you know which one is the opposition paper? *La Revista*. And does it cost us our eyeteeth!)

Let us remember that *La Revista* was not a far-left paper but represented rather the loyal opposition. Hence it appears from Larra's quip that this newspaper now opposed the government more than had been expected. As for *La Abeja*, fortunately there is an extant letter dated March 5, 1835, written by Tomás Quintero to Domingo Delmonte. It provides sufficient background information for Figaro's comment:

> También me acuerdo de otra [carta perdida], aunque no de su fecha, en que hablaba a V. larguísimamente de cosas políticas y entraba en explicaciones sobre el fenómeno de hallarme dirigiendo un periódico ministerial, cuando tantos años he vivido oliéndome el cuello a cáñamo
> > "Por seguir la sublime locura
> > De Washington y Bruto y Catón."
> Pero debe advertirse que yo soy el fundador de ese periódico que ahora lleva la librea ministerial y antes con el título de Universal que yo le di, era el más exaltado de los diarios de la oposición. Un artículo del número 42 produjo la supresión del papel; y después de más de veinte días de suspensión, obtuvo el empresario permiso para continuarle con el título de la *Abeja*. Mas habiendo perdido considerable cantidad de dinero, y no habiendo entrado en esta especulación sino por ganar, se resolvió a seguir el camino diametralmente opuesto al que le había atraído tanta pérdida, y aquí tiene V. al periódico convertido en ministerial. Yo desde luego me hubiera separado: pero me rogaron que continuase dirigiendo la empresa, a lo menos hasta encontrar quien de ella se encargase: mas no habiéndose logrado esto hasta el mes de enero último, entonces fue cuando logré retirarme, y desde entonces me tiene V. retirado de toda empresa periodística.
> Pero no me fue posible retirarme sin gravísimos altercados con el empresario, quedando los dos desde aquel día como enemigos, de modo que no nos hemos visto más; y de esto proviene que ni siquiera me ha continuado remitiendo la abeja . . .[11]

(I also remember another lost letter, but not its date, where I spoke to you at length on political matters and went into explanations about the phenomenon of finding myself editor-in-chief of a ministerialist newspaper, I who have been living for years with my neck smelling of hemp [too close to the noose], "For following the sublime folly / Of Washington, Brutus, and Cato." But you should know that I am the founder of this newspaper, which now wears ministerialist livery. Beforehand, with the title *El Universal*, which I gave it, it was the most *exaltado* of the opposition dailies. An article in number 42 brought about the suppression of the paper, and after more than twenty days of suspension the manager obtained permission to have it continue with the title of *La Abeja*. But, having lost a considerable amount of money, and having gotten into this speculation only for profit, he decided to follow a path diametrically opposed to the one that brought him so much loss, and so now you've got this paper converted to ministerialism. I would have taken leave immediately, but they begged me to stay at the head, at least until they might find someone to take charge. But as this was not accomplished until last January, it was only then that I managed to quit, and since that time you have me retired from journalism.

But it was not possible for me to quit without serious altercations with the manager, so that from that day the two of us have been as enemies and have not seen each other. As a result he has not even sent me a single copy of *La Abeja* . . .)

The other noteworthy passage in Figaro's essay mentions the possible resignation of a minister:

Corren voces de que un ministro va a hacer dimisión; pero no lo crea vuesa merced; éstas son bromas; lo mismo están diciendo hace meses de otro, y pasa un día, y pasa otro día, y, en resumidas cuentas, no pasan días por él. (1: 428)

(There are rumors that a minister is going to resign, but don't believe it. These things are jokes; they've been saying this for months about another one, and one day goes by, then another, and, in sum, his days are not numbered.)

Alcalá Galiano appears to refer to Larra's remarks when he notes in his *Historia*, with a dozen years' hindsight:

Cantaron, pues, los periodistas victoria al ver derrotados a los ministros, y aun de ellos hubo quien algo se dejase decir tímida y rebozadamente sobre que debían hacer renuncia; pero tal insinuación, lejos de encontrar aprobadores, apenas fue entendida. . . . Semejante revés en otro tiempo y lugar habría acabado con el ministerio; pero en España y entonces no era posible que así fuese, pues de haber renunciado sus cargos Martínez de la Rosa y Toreno, se habría experimentado grande embarazo en punto a nombrarles sucesores . . .[12]

(The newspapermen sang to victory when the ministers were defeated, and there was even one among them who allowed himself to say timidly and hazily something about their having to resign. But such an insinuation, far from meeting with approval, was hardly understood. . . . Such a defeat in another time and place would have brought the ministry to an end, but in Spain and at that period it was impossible, because if Martínez de la Rosa and Toreno had resigned, great obstacles would have arisen concerning appointment of successors for them . . .)

6

ABSENTEEISM AND
INACTION

T HE next known article by Larra is unsigned and appeared
in the *Revista Española* of August 24, 1834, nine days after
the "Segunda carta." Entitled "Modas," its scheme is totally metaphorical, the events of the times being presented in the
language of clothing and hair-styling. This essay bears some
thematic resemblance to a chapter entitled "Modes d'aujourd'hui"
in Pigault-Lebrun's first novel, *L'Enfant du Carnaval*, with which
Larra may have been acquainted, since he mentions Pigault-
Lebrun in "El casarse pronto y mal" (November 30, 1832). Moreover, working on *El Correo de las Damas* the previous year had
made Larra familiar with fashion editing, for he made similar
puns then (cf. 2: 16). Hence, we might not expect to find parliamentary expressions here. Nevertheless, the essay contains references to the proceedings in Cortes, chiefly where Figaro predicts
pessimistically that the fashion of being amazed at the inaction of
the Estamentos ("asombrarse de la inacción de los Estamentos") is

one which will probably last longer than the low hemline ("probablemente más que el talle largo") (1: 431).

The third and last paragraphs also fall within this category, since they bear upon the excuses of delegates who were failing to show up for the sessions. Larra's comments must be viewed against the background of a rather shameful state of affairs. The Cortes were then spending an inordinate amount of time hearing explanatory letters from absent members, whose justifications were sometimes quite flimsy. Three possible reasons could be surmised for falsely excused absences. A delegate could be afraid of the cholera; if a *prócer*, he might not want to be involved with a liberal government; or he might hesitate to commit himself by voting on the resolution condemning Don Carlos. (See chapter 4 for a resumé of the absentee situation up to July 31.) On August 1 three *procuradores* sent word that they were ill, and a long discussion took place on the validity of the medical excuse of a fourth (*Pr.*, pp. 16, 18). A fifth informed the chamber by mail that his income fell short by one thousand reales of the sixty thousand minimum (*Pr.*, p. 16). On August 9 five Catalan representatives sent their excuses, as we noted in the last chapter, as well as another delegate, "manifestando estar tomando baños para restablecer su salud" (*Pr.*, pp. 51–53—"sending notification that they were taking the baths to recover their health"). One *procurador*-elect wrote the chamber that he could not come "por estar enfermo de un achaque que padece habitualmente dos veces al año, y del que espera restablecerse pronto" (*Pr.*, p. 60—"as he is going through a chronic illness from which he suffers twice a year and hopes to recover soon"); another "por estarse restableciendo de una enfermedad en Archidona, y que así que lo esté se presentará" (p. 62—"because he is recuperating from illness in Archidona, and as soon as it is over he will present himself"); and a third "a causa de la enfermedad habitual de la vista que hace mucho padece" (p. 59—"because of the usual eye disease from which he has been suffering for a long time"). In the last case, the committee "opinaba no ser bastante causa para privarse el Estamento de su cooperación, dispensándole en lo posible del trabajo de comisiones" (*Pr.*, p. 62—"deemed that it was not a sufficient reason for the Chamber to deprive itself of his cooperation, and would excuse him whenever possible from committee work"). Two members-elect requested permission to give up their posts in order to attend to their business and were excused four days later (*Pr.*, p. 74). One wrote that he believed he could not be a *procurador* because part of his income came from his wife's estate. He was advised that this made no difference and directed to come (*Pr.*, p. 62). In addition, between August 16 and 22, ten representatives notified the Estamento that illness kept them home.

In the upper house the situation was worse because, after all, its members did not seek to be elected but were automatically named for their qualifications. A *prócer* who declined the honor would incur the queen's wrath; yet, once in his post, it was incumbent on him to vote on the resolution condemning Don Carlos. Between August 2 and 20, forty *próceres* sent letters explaining their inability to attend. Some were justified, such as Palafox, who had been placed under surveillance at home as a result of the plot (*Ilus.*, pp. 15, 16, 27). One member was on duty with the palace guard (*Ilus.*, p. 26). Several alleged illness: headaches and fever; "tenaz indisposición"; "sus males"; "absoluta imposibilidad de asistir por enfermedad"; "una erupción en la pierna"; "larga y grave enfermedad"; convalescing from the cholera; taking the baths in Paris; taking the baths in Spain; an attack of rheumatism on the way to Madrid (*Ilus.*, p. 38). One excuse was patently flimsy, and another member had the gall to refuse the post. The Marquess de Camarasa, who declined to come even though he lived in Madrid,[1] became the subject of indignation and a special motion (*Ilus.*, pp. 36, 44).

In two instances the matter of a *prócer*'s attendance aroused some controversy with respect to a possible encroachment by the Crown on the prerogatives of the chamber. On August 11 the Estamento learned that the queen had given the Archbishop of Valladolid permission to return to his diocese. The reaction to this announcement can be inferred from the committee's report: "La opinión de la comisión es que sólo al Estamento le corresponde examinar las excusas de los señores Próceres que han prestado su juramento o puedan considerarse como tales Próceres" (*Ilus.*, p. 33—"The opinion of the committee is that the examination of the excuses of Próceres who have sworn an oath or who can be considered as such pertains only to the Chamber"). A week later the Archbishop of Burgos, having obtained the queen's leave, absented himself allegedly for the same reason as his colleague from Valladolid and was severely criticized in the chamber. Some of his peers felt he had no right to depart without the Estamento's permission; the frankness of one *prócer* is indeed revealing:

> Preguntó el señor Álvarez Guerra si el Arzobispo de Burgos había solicitado su licencia después de ser nombrado individuo de la comisión especial para el examen de la exposición relativa a la conducta de don Carlos. (*Ilus.* p. 44)

> (Mr. Álvarez Guerra asked if the Archbishop of Burgos had requested his excuse after being named to the special committee to examine the report on Don Carlos's conduct.)

It should be pointed out that the Marquess de Camarasa had also been appointed to this committee, and that consequently it could not meet for lack of a quorum.

Faced with these untoward occurrences, several *próceres* proposed on August 16 a resolution making attendance compulsory, under penalty of losing the *procerazgo* within two weeks.

> El Sr. Duque de Castroterreño observó que cuando había una necesidad imperiosa de que la mayor parte de los Próceres acudiesen a sostener los derechos de la nación y del Trono, era doloroso que procurasen algunos evadirse de llenar este deber tan sagrado . . ." (*Ilus.*, p. 40)

> (The Duke of Castroterreño observed that when there was an urgent necessity for most Próceres to come in order to sustain the rights of the nation and the Throne, it was regrettable that some should attempt to avoid fulfilling this sacred duty . . .)

Cano Manuel defended the proposal, saying that

> hay muchos Próceres pasivos que no vienen a tomar parte en las cuestiones importantes . . . Exímase en buen hora de venir al Estamento a los que sus circunstancias particulares no se lo permitan; pero ¿habrá de mostrarse el Estamento indiferente con aquellos que tanta facilidad tienen para presentar sus pruebas, y no lo hacen cuando basta un mero ofrecimiento de exhibirlas luego que las circunstancias se lo permitan?

Sobre éstos es sobre quien debe recaer una censura severa aunque sus operaciones sean arregladas, puesto que se excusan a asistir de [sic] la deliberación de un negocio en que la nación unida con S. M. y con su Gobierno va a ejercer un acto de los más grandes. (*Ilus.*, p. 40)

(there are many inactive Próceres who are not coming to take part in the important questions . . . Let those whose particular circumstances prevent them be exempted. But should the Chamber show itself indifferent to those who could so easily present their proofs [of eligibility] but fail to do so even when a mere offer to show them as soon as conditions allow suffices?

It is the latter who should undergo severe censure, even if their finances have been put in order, because they avoid attending the deliberation of a matter in which the nation, together with Her Majesty and its Government, will perform an act of great import.)

The speaker even went so far as to utter the word "deserción," and the Marqués de las Amarillas, who followed him, used no reticence in mentioning the real reason for the absences:

No está tampoco en el orden que algunos Sres. Próceres pasados dos o tres meses después de haber presentado sus papeles, vengan a sentarse entre nosotros después de pasado el compromiso. (*Ilus.*, p. 41)

(Neither is it in order that some Próceres, two or three months after having presented their papers, should come to sit among us once the obligation to commit themselves has passed.)

After this, the secretary of the interior, José María Moscoso de Altamira, put a damper on the project by pointing out that

el Estamento debe tomar en consideración que S. M. es quien nombra los Próceres, y que el disminuir o anular este nombramiento es peculiar e inherente de las prerrogativas del Trono. (*Ilus.*, p. 41)

(the Chamber must take into consideration that it is Her Majesty who names the Próceres, and that diminishing or annulling this appointment is peculiar to and inherent in the prerogatives of the Throne.)

Nevertheless, a committee was created to investigate the matter. Two days later it issued a statement condemning

> la indisculpable morosidad de los que sin justa excusa parece [sic] querer evadirse de cumplir tan sagrado deber . . . Se dé cuenta a S. M. de la falta de cumplimiento de los Ilustres Próceres que pudiendo no se han presentado hasta ahora en el Estamento . . . (*Ilus.*, p. 48)

> (the unpardonable tardiness of those who without valid excuse seem to want to avoid fulfilling such a sacred duty . . . Remissness on the part of those Illustrious Peers who, even though they could, have not yet appeared in the Chamber should be reported to Her Majesty . . .)

There was discussion on this, but nothing was settled, and the Próceres adjourned for ten days (*Ilus.*, p. 49).

The whole problem is taken up humorously in the last paragraph of "Modas," where the author mocks those who fear to commit themselves:

> De colores, en fin, estamos poco más o menos como estábamos; si bien el *blanco* y *negro* son los fundamentales, aquél más caído, éste más subido; lo más común, especialmente en personas de calidad, son los colores *indecisos, tornasolados,* partícipes de negro y blanco, como gris o entre dos luces; en una palabra, colores que apenas son colores; es de esperar que pronto se habrán de admitir, sin embargo, de grado o por fuerza, colores más fuertes y decididos, puros y sin mezcla alguna. En el ínterin chocan tanto estos últimos que hay personas nerviosas que sólo al considerar que habrá que entrar en ellos, padecen y ofician, y guardan la cama.[2] (1: 432)

> (As for colors we are more or less as we were before, although *white* and *black* are still basic [these symbolize absolutist and liberal], the former somewhat faded, the latter brighter. The usual thing, especially with persons of higher rank, are the undecided, *changeable* colors of *shot fabrics* containing both black and white, such as grey, or in the twilight; in short, colors that are hardly colors. It is to be hoped that soon, however, stronger and more daring colors, pure and unmixed, will be accepted, freely or by force. In the meantime they are so shocking that there are nervous souls who, at the thought of putting them on, get ill, send messages, and stay in bed.)

The many phrases giving an impression of vacillation exemplify Larra's cleverness at combining the ideological and stylistic effects of political and linguistic "shuffles": "en una palabra," "es de esperar que pronto se habrán de admitir," "sin embargo," "en el ínterin." These are all pat phrases frequently and inordinately encountered in the prevaricating arguments of the ministers.

The last paragraph is not the only one which touches upon the absences of *procuradores*. The author had already demonstrated his concern earlier in the essay:

> Hacen furor los oficios de próceres y procuradores imposibilitados: es por cierto cosa furibunda. Al cabo de algún tiempo sucederá con estas *imposibilidades* de asistir, lo que sucedía el invierno pasado con los capotes forrados de encarnado, que no había barbero sin capote; a este paso, dentro de poco no habrá representante sin *imposibilidad*. Es de esperar, sin embargo, que esta moda de poco gusto y de menos *patria* se proscriba, como se proscribió para siempre el escote exagerado de las mujeres, al cual se parece demasiado en presentar desnudas cosas que deben siempre estar tapadas. (1: 431)

> (The communications of *próceres* and *procuradores* who find themselves incapacitated are the latest rage; in fact, it's outrageous. After a while the same thing will happen with these *incapacities* as with the red-lined capes last winter, when there wasn't a barber in town without one. At this rate it won't be long before every representative has his *incapacity*. Let us hope, nevertheless, that this fashion, in poor taste and un-Spanish, will be proscribed, just like women's exaggerated necklines, which it resembles in baring things that should always be covered up.)

Figaro's fourth paragraph, still maintaining the "fashion" metaphor, touches upon the reaction of the newspapers to the goings-on in Cortes. Throughout the passage we can discern Larra's constancy to the ideal of freedom of the press, manifest in the implication that criticism is good for legislative bodies: "Empiezan a estilarse mucho los *artículos de oposición:* se asegura que hacen bien a todos los cuerpos" (1: 431—"Articles of opposition are coming into style; people say that they are beneficial to all bodies"). This pun on "articles," journalistic and vestmental, is maintained over two paragraphs. First the author mentions the possi-

bility of secret sessions as a means of avoiding bad publicity, which issued from what some might consider the counter-productive press:

> Algunos [artículos] se ven, sin embargo, que hacen tan mala cara al Estamento, como las *ferronières* de metal a las señoras, que las desfiguran todas y *hacen traición* a su hermosura; en este caso están los de hechura llamada a la *sesión secreta*. (1: 431)

> (Some articles, however, give the Estamento a rather sour look, like steel *corsets* to ladies, disfiguring them and *treacherously undermining* their beauty. In this category are those fashioned à la *secret session.*)

(The phrase "a la" obviously parodies the gallicisms of the world of fashion. A pun may possibly be intended on "hechura"; the government's henchmen would be called to participate in the sessions.) Unfortunately, secret sessions would have been an ineffectual solution, since several columnists were also members of parliament (for example, Fermín Caballero): "Lo más raro es que, según parece, esos artículos salen fabricados del mismo Estamento . . ." (1: 431—"The most amazing thing is that it seems these articles are turned out in the Chamber itself . . .").

The fifth paragraph portrays the other camp, which turns out the ministerial articles. Puns also abound here, including the one on "flores" that will be found again in "Un periódico nuevo" (January 26, 1835).[3] Next comes a passage concerning the shortness of the sessions, a matter that Larra must have found frustrating, considering the pressing need for action. The Procuradores' record, which notes the starting and adjourning times of the meeting, attests to their brevity:

Wednesday, August 6	3	hours
Thursday, August 7	1 ¼	
Saturday, August 9	2 ½	
Monday, August 11	1 ¾	
Tuesday, August 12	3	
Wednesday, August 13	2 ¾	
Thursday, August 14	3	
Saturday, August 16	3 ¼	
Monday, August 18	1 ½	

Wednesday, August 20   ½ hours
    (in public session, plus a short secret
    session)
Thursday, August 22   1

At the conclusion of the August 22 session, the president of the
chamber made an annoucement that also bears out the problem:

> No teniendo ningún asunto de que podamos ocuparnos mañana,
> nos reuniremos el lunes a las diez de la suya, para continuar los
> asuntos pendientes, y si acaso las comisiones en este intermedio nos
> han presentado ya sus trabajos, se principiará a tratar de ellos. Yo
> no tengo que excitar el celo de los individuos que las componen,
> pues que de ellos depende que tengamos en que ocuparnos, siendo
> así que ahora no tenemos materia alguna de que tratar. (*Pr.*, p. 80)

> (Since there is no business that we can take up tomorrow, we shall
> meet on Monday at ten in the morning in order to continue with
> pending matter, and if by chance the committees in the meantime
> have already presented their reports, we shall begin by dealing
> with these. I need not spur the zeal of the individuals serving on
> these committees, since we depend on them for something to be
> engaged in, it being the case now that we have nothing to deal
> with.)

Figaro's comment is short but incisive:

> Se siguen estilando las *sesiones cortas*, como si dijéramos a media
> pierna; en esto se dan la mano con los vestidos de maja; así es que
> suelen dejar lo mejor en descubierto. (1: 432)

> (Fashion still favors *short sessions*, as if we said mid-calf; so they
> can give a friendly handshake to majas' dresses. In doing this they
> are wont to leave the best part uncovered.)

In his opinion, the really important matters were never taken up by
the Estamento. To put it in banking terms, the account it gave of
itself did not have much in its favor (this is, of course, the meaning of the pun on "descubierto"). A comical effect is also obtained by the purposely clumsy "pierna-mano" antithesis, where
the inappropriate expression "darse la mano" assimilates the parliamentary proceedings to the *majas'* skirts. The grotesqueness of

the whole paragraph justifies the "bad" pun on "descubierto."[4] As Larra fully knew, however, the Cortes could not initiate legislation. Nevertheless, the Progressives strove to circumvent this limitation by drafting proposals for petitions. The ministers then maneuvered deftly to prevent their discussion, resulting in parliamentary inaction. Indeed, "dejar lo mejor en descubierto" refers to unsuccessful attempts to debate the Carlist menace, the *indultos*, and the supposedly disloyal government employees (*Pr.*, pp. 63–67).

The Moderates, on the other hand, averred that their idleness was motivated by caution, as we can see by Moscoso de Altamira's rejoinder to Rufino García Carrasco: "Harto tiempo, señor, hemos sacrificado a la locura y a la extravagancia; sacrifiquemos alguna vez a la circunspección y a la prudencia, y seremos verdaderamente libres" (*Pr.*, p. 66—"We have sacrificed long enough, gentlemen, to folly and extravagance. Let us sacrifice at some time to circumspection and prudence, and we shall be truly free"). Larra sees the problem otherwise:

En punto a calzado, sólo podemos decir que lo más común es andarse *con pies de plomo*. Con respecto a talle, la gran moda es estar *muy oprimido*, tan estrecho que apenas se pueda respirar; por ahora a lo menos éste es el uso; podrá pasar pronto, si no nos ahogamos antes. (1: 432)

(In footwear, the usual thing seems to be to walk around with *lead in one's shoes*. As for waistlines, the style is to be held as in a *tight grip*, and one can hardly breathe. For the time being at least this is in fashion. Soon, however, we may stop choking on it, unless we sink first.)

7

A BILL OF RIGHTS

AFTER "Modas" (August 24, 1834), we have nothing by Larra until September 1, when the *Revista* published a straightforward criticism of a performance of Gaetano Donizetti's *Parisina*. On September 5, "La gran verdad descubierta" appeared, along with a column of five journalistic quips dubbed "Rehiletes." In the meantime, the Próceres had met twice (Saturday, August 30,[1] and Wednesday, September 3), and the Procuradores nine times (August 25, 26, 28, 29, 30, and 31, and September 1, 2, and 4). Some important issues were discussed. In the Próceres, one session was devoted to those members who had presented as an excuse for their absence the long period necessary to gather proof of sufficient income (*Ilus.*, pp. 53–55). The meeting of September 3 consisted of speeches by Martínez de la Rosa, the Duke of Rivas, Toreno, Cano Manuel, and Manuel García Herreros about the conduct of Don Carlos. Rivas romantically depicted the latter's supporters as "un partido que quiere fundar un trono bárbaro y un altar sacrílego y furibundo, rodeado de

149

lagunas de sangre y montañas de cadáveres, sobre la tumba de la civilización moderna" (*Ilus.*, p. 66—"a party that wants to establish a barbarous throne and a sacrilegious and enraged altar, surrounded by lakes of blood and mountains of cadavers, on the tomb of modern civilization"). Then the chamber, without delay, approved a decree excluding Carlos and his lineage from the Spanish throne.

In the lower house a petition was presented on August 25 for a sanitation law enabling the country to prepare for epidemics. The Progressives used it to utter a veiled criticism of the government's inefficiency in coping with the cholera. The same day the president of the chamber approved the printing of a petition to revise its procedural rules, and the ministry presented a projected law on the responsibility of judges.[2] Meanwhile, a new criminal code recommended by Garelly was in committee, but its deliberations were so protracted that another committee had to be appointed to examine the second half of the document.

That afternoon, the Progressives put before the chamber a petition to the Crown to abrogate the famous Voto de Santiago, a special tax with a glorious name, paid by certain districts to the ecclesiastical authorities of Saint James of Compostela. Since the rate of taxation was based on the number of draft animals used in plowing, the highest amounts were often levied on the worst terrain. The Oath of Saint James and its repeal has considerable historical importance, for it began to be challenged in the nineteenth century. Juan Antonio Melón, appointed *Juez de Imprentas* at Godoy's behest, allowed the publication in 1805 of Antonio del Camino's *Memoria*, which demonstrated the falsity of the evidence offered to justify this tax.[3] That opened the way for its abolition, championed by Calatrava in the Cortes of Cádiz. It was again debated during the Triennium, but reinstated in 1823. Consequently, the Progressives now considered it one of the first items of business. Martínez de la Rosa, however, managed to prevent their petition from coming to a vote. The next day he placed before the Estamento his own project for repealing the Voto, thus foiling the Procuradores' attempt to take the initiative away from the government. The debate lasted two days, Saturday and Sunday, August 30 and 31, because the Progressive and Moderate views diverged considerably. The former, especially Joaquín María López and Luis Pizarro, Conde de las Navas, wanted to rescind the levy outright, and even demanded the cancellation of back taxes. The Moderates, however, succeeded in putting through a milder law, out of regard for firms that were at the time creditors of the Chapter of St. James, and for the charitable institutions it administered, such as hospitals.

Though Larra mentions the Oath of St. James in later essays, the subject does not come up in "La gran verdad descubierta," which deals solely with a petition to the Crown for a bill of rights. These *derechos fundamentales* consisted of twelve articles, much of whose wording was taken from the French constitution of 1790. After being examined by three committees, in accordance with requisite procedure, the projected petition was read to the chamber on August 28. The session of September 1 was devoted to a debate of the project *in toto*, and the next day's meeting to a discussion of its first article: "La libertad individual es protegida y garantida; por consecuencia ningún español puede ser obligado a hacer lo que la ley no ordena" (*Pr.*, p. 96—"Individual freedom is protected and guaranteed; consequently, no Spaniard can be forced to do anything not ordered by law"). The debate resulted in a compromise: "Las leyes protegen y aseguran la libertad individual" (*Pr.*, p. 158—"Laws protect and insure individual freedom"), which Larra ridiculed for its inanity.

It stands to reason that discussion of a fundamental principle would elicit intellectual, abstract arguments. Such was the case during the bill of rights debate, where probaby more historical and scientific knowledge was displayed than in any other session of this legislature. The Progressives called upon English, French, and even United States history, Jeremy Bentham, Benjamin Constant, and the law of habeas corpus in England. Telesforo Trueba y Cosío felt that since Portugal possessed such guarantees, Spain was ready for them too. "¿Quién habrá aquí que quiera sostener que la España está más atrasada que el Portugal?" (*Pr.*, p. 135—"Is there possibly anyone here who would maintain that Spain is more backwards than Portugal?"). Fermín Caballero argued that Spain had indeed progressed in twenty years, because the same law which had been passed by a two-thirds vote in 1812 was unanimously approved in 1834 (*Pr.*, pp. 150–152). He was probably referring to the Oath of Saint James, but the argument seems

somewhat specious because in 1834 the reactionaries, having rebelled, were not present in the Cortes to defend their interests.
Moderate oratory, on the other hand, included analogies from the
physical sciences and a refutation of Rousseau. One ministerialist,
Pablo Santafé, asserted that the Estatuto Real contained sufficient
guarantees, but the Progressives answered that only under a well-
intentioned ministry could the Estatuto Real protect individual
liberty. What would happen after a change of ministers?

One aspect of the discussion bore on the tense and mood of the
verb in the first half of the article; this necessarily brought up embarrassing questions relating to Spain's readiness and the possibility that proclaiming such a principle in the present indicative
would entail its immediate application. Martínez de la Rosa took
it upon himself to impugn the article on these grounds:

> Dice el Sr. López que es preciso consignar el principio, dejando
> suspensa su aplicación, o según la imagen de un escritor que al
> efecto ha citado, echar un velo a la estatua de la ley. Pero, señores,
> ¿es tan sencillo como se supone establecer un principio para deci-
> dir al momento que se suspende su aplicación? Reflexiónese bien
> que esto es más peligroso y perjudicial que no establecerse. Desde
> el punto en que se declara un principio o derecho, es preciso po-
> nerle en práctica, porque si se le dice al pueblo: *esta ley te con-
> viene; pero no puede dársete,* ¿no es lo mismo que decirle: *el
> Gobierno te usurpa lo que de derecho te corresponde?* Dejo a la
> sabiduría del Estamento el calcular las consecuencias. (*Pr.,* p.
> 140)

> (Mr. López says we must set down principle, leaving its applica-
> tion in abeyance, or, according to the trope of a writer whom he
> quoted for the purpose, place a veil over the statue of the law.
> But, gentlemen, is it so easy to establish a principle and in that very
> moment decide to suspend its application? Think and you will
> realize this is more dangerous and harmful than not establishing it.
> From the moment a principle or right is declared, it must be put
> into practice, because if the people are told, *This law suits you,
> but it cannot be given to you,* is this not like telling it, *the Govern-
> ment usurps from you what is rightfully yours?* I shall leave it up
> to the wisdom of the Chamber to calculate the consequences.)

Toreno likewise proposed a change in the verb:

No me parece que este primer artículo en los términos en que está concebido pueda considerarse como una verdad exenta de oposición, y por lo mismo me parece que en vez de expresarse como hace la petición, diciendo: "la libertad individual es protegida y garantida," estaría mucho mejor dicho así: "La ley protegerá y asegurará la libertad individual." (*Pr.*, p. 149)

(It does not seem to me that this first article, in the terms in which it has been conceived, can be considered a truth not subject to opposition, and thus, instead of being expressed as in the petition, namely, "individual freedom is protected and guaranteed," it would be much better if it read, "The law shall protect and insure individual freedom.")

These arguments were answered by Joaquín María López:

Se dijo también que la redacción era inexacta, pues que se hablaba del tiempo presente al decirse *la libertad individual es protegida*, suponiéndose que no existía tal protección. Me parece que semejante lenguaje está al nivel de los principios o bases fundamentales establecidos en las Constituciones de otras monarquías. . . . El Sr. Conde de Toreno, en el hecho de querer sustituir a las palabras del artículo las de que *la ley protegerá la libertad individual*, manifiesta que no es una especie de sistema el que le mueve a combatir el principio, sino que considera que sería más conveniente al estado de la nación hacer mañana lo que se pide hoy. A mí sin embargo no me satisface este modo de pensar. En semejante caso no habremos hecho más que una promesa estéril a la nación. Decir que las leyes protegerán la libertad civil, no es consagrar este principio como se necesita. Las leyes civiles son posteriores a la ley fundamental, y antes de levantar la obra es necesario poner los cimientos; antes es necesario que la ley fundamental proclame este principio como imprescriptible, y luego los códigos civiles sabrán garantirle. (*Pr.*, p. 154)

(It was also stated that the redaction was inexact, because the present tense was used in saying *individual freedom is protected*, it being supposed that such protection did not exist. It seems to me that such language is on a par with principles and fundamental bases established in the Constitutions of other monarchies. . . . The Count of Toreno, in wanting to replace the words of the article by *the law shall protect individual freedom*, makes it evident that what moves him to oppose the principle is not a kind of system, but rather that it would suit the state of the nation better to do tomorrow what is requested today. In such a case we would have done no more than make a barren promise to the nation. Stating that the laws shall protect civil liberty is not like consecrating this principle as it needs to be. Civil laws come after the fundamental law, and before the edifice rises it is necessary to put in the foundations. This principle must first be proclaimed by the fundamental law as imprescriptible, and then the civil codes will be able to guarantee it.)

Another Progressive rejoinder was delivered by Telesforo de Trueba y Cosío, who, in asserting the importance of faithfulness to ideals, seems to have paraphrased Jeremy Bentham:

Un principio no se puede establecer ni sancionar poco a poco: un principio como la verdad se admite desde el momento que se conoce; porque la luz de la verdad aparece desde el instante que se abren los ojos para verla. Además, señores, la libertad no es una ciencia que se aprende; es un instinto natural impreso en el corazón humano; y desde el momento en que conoce puede servirle, el hombre tiene derecho a satisfacerlo, y para conseguirlo tiene que buscar los medios más cortos y eficaces. (*Pr.*, pp. 134–135)

(A principle cannot be established or sanctioned little by little. A principle such as truth itself is admitted from the moment it is known, because the light of truth appears from the instant the eyes are opened to see it. Moreover, gentlemen, liberty is not a branch of knowledge that is learned; it is a natural instinct stamped on the human heart, and from the moment he knows that it can serve him, man has a right to satisfy it; and in order to obtain it he must seek the shortest and most efficacious means.)

It is sad to note that Trueba's words exemplify perfectly the idealism demolished in the 1840s by the same men who had so enthusiastically embraced it in the 1830s (cf. chapter 1, note 18).

The most pertinent arguments touched on the definition of law and on extralegal obligations. The Marquess de Falces, for one, brought up the subject of martial law. Toreno criticized the second part of the proposed article, pointing out that it could be interpreted in such a way that grounds would be found for not heeding the *bandos de policía* or the *reglamentos*, under the pretext that, strictly speaking, they were not laws. It was Martínez de la Rosa, however, who presented this argument most cogently:

"La libertad individual es protegida." Querrá decir: "debe ser protegida"; porque si, como dice, lo es, ¿a qué hacer esta petición? "por consecuencia ningún español puede ser obligado a hacer lo que la ley no ordena." Este principio está exactamente copiado de la Constitución francesa del año de 91. Pero ¿es exacto?.... Yo me atrevo a decir que no sólo no es exacto, sino que no hay nación en donde haya existido ni podido existir. Parece natural a primera vista el decir que un hombre puede hacer todo aquello que no le prohiba la ley. Pero ¿no se funda la sociedad en una cadena de obediencias que no están consignadas en las leyes? El niño manifiesta obediencia a la autoridad paterna, el discípulo a su maestro; y empezando por el último escalón de la sociedad, hasta llegar al primero, todos se hallan con obligación de obedecer a sus jefes y superiores; y ni los mandatos de su padre, ni los preceptos de su maestro y otros de esta clase son leyes; como no lo son las órdenes de policía, ni los decretos del Gobierno, a menos que quieran confundirse todos bajo el nombre impropio de ley. Por consiguiente carece de exactitud esta petición en los términos en que está redactada. (*Pr.*, pp. 140–141)

("Individual freedom is protected." What is probably meant is, "must be protected"; because if, as is stated, it *is*, then why make this petition? "Consequently no Spaniard can be forced to do what is not ordered by law." This principle is copied verbatim from the French Constitution of the year 1791. But is it precise?.... I make bold to say that not only is it not precise, but that there is no nation where it has existed or where it could have existed. It seems natural at first glance to say that a man can do everything not forbidden by law. However, is society not founded on a chain of command not set down in the laws? The child shows obedience to paternal authority, the student to his teacher; and beginning with the bottom rung of society, all the way to the top, we all find ourselves obliged to obey our chiefs and superiors. Yet neither his father's orders nor the precepts of his teacher, and others of this type, are laws. The same applies to police regulations, Government decrees, unless all are to be confused under the inappropriate name of law. Therefore this petition lacks exactness in the terms in which it is redacted.)

The above was delivered during the discussion of the bill of rights *in toto*, on September 1. The next day, at the session devoted to article 1, the prime minister argued this point more explicitly:

Senté ayer, y repito hoy, que el artículo (cual está) es inexacto, es vago, es falso. No es cierto que el hombre no pueda hacer solamente lo que la ley le prohíbe; ni ha existido una sociedad en que se haya establecido en la práctica este principio. A no ser que los señores que sostienen el artículo den el nombre de ley a toda especie de mandato, a una ordenanza de policía o a cualquier orden del último funcionario público. La del centinela por ejemplo, que no permite pasar por un punto; la del sereno que impide pernoctar en la calle; la del alcalde de un pueblo que exige el cumplimiento de aquellas medidas de buen orden que se ha tenido por conveniente tomar. Si se entienden por leyes estos mandatos, enhorabuena; pero si se entiende aquella palabra en sentido rigoroso, no ha existido ninguna nación en que no se prohiba hacer cosas que no están vedadas por la ley.

Dije, sí, que en la sociedad hay una escala de obediencia, una serie de subordinación establecida para el buen régimen de la sociedad, no dependiente de esta u otra forma de gobierno, y que no es exacto decir que sea lícito hacer todo aquello que la ley no prohibe, porque hay muchas cosas que no las prohíben las leyes, sino reglamentos, órdenes, mandatos de la autoridad, y es preciso obedecerlas. Una de dos: o este principio es inexacto, o es menester entenderlo así; y la prueba de que el Ministerio no se opone a lo que el artículo tenga de verdadero, es que el Sr. Secretario de Hacienda ha dicho que la prudencia exigía que se variase, manifestando que las leyes deben garantir la libertad individual. Éste es un axioma; pero como está concebido el artículo, no es exacto. *La seguridad individual es protegida y garantida* (dice el artículo). ¿Lo es o no? Si se quiere decir que lo es, dígase: "lo es actualmente." Si se quiere decir que las leyes deben proteger la libertad individual, exprésese de esta manera. (*Pr.*, pp. 155–156)

(Yesterday I established, and today I repeat, that the article—as it now is—is imprecise, vague, and false. It is not true that man can do only what the law does not forbid him, and never has there existed a society where this principle was established, unless the gentlemen who uphold the article give the name of law to every kind of rule, to a police regulation or any order from the lowest public functionary. For example, that of the sentinel, not permitting passage through a certain point; that of the night watchman, which forbids spending the night in the street; that of a town mayor, requiring that certain measures suitable to orderly conduct be taken. If these rules are understood to be laws, well and good;

but if the word is understood in its strict sense, no nation has ever existed where doing anything not prohibited by law is not forbidden.

I did say that in society there is a chain of command, a series of subordination established for the good management of society, not depending on this or that form of government, and that to say that it is lawful to do everything not forbidden by law is not precise, because there are many things not prohibited by the laws, even not by regulations, orders, rules of authorities, and they must be obeyed. One or the other: either this principle is imprecise, or it must be understood thus. And the proof that the Ministry is not opposed to any truth the article may contain, is that the Secretary of the Treasury stated that prudence demanded its alteration, declaring that the laws must guarantee individual freedom. This is an axiom; but it is not precise in the form in which it now stands. *Individual security is protected and guaranteed*, the article states. Is it or is it not? If what is meant is that it is, then say, "it is presently." If what is meant is that the laws must protect individual freedom, let it be expressed thus.)

Toreno also had something to say on the matter: "Tendríamos que entrar en la gran cuestión de qué es lo que se entiende por ley, y por consiguiente qué leyes deben formar la base de la libertad civil" (*Pr.*, p. 149—"We would have to go into the great question of what is understood by law, and therefore of which laws must form the basis of civil liberty"). It was now Fermín Caballero's turn to answer the ministers on this point. We should note how it follows from his argument that the passage of article 1 would increase the power of the Cortes:

El Sr. Conde de Toreno en su discurso ha presentado los graves inconvenientes que se seguirían de adoptar el artículo tal como está redactado; ha dicho, entre otras cosas, que si su segunda parte se aprobase en los términos en que está concebida, acaso se desentenderían algunos de la observancia de los reglamentos de policía y otros que puedan establecerse; esto nos metería en la gran cuestión de definir qué es ley y qué es reglamento; cuestión que convendría mucho ventilar, porque si las leyes no pueden hacerse sin el concurso de los poderes del Estado, sería muy útil marcar los límites de la ley y los del reglamento; pues con el nombre de tales reglamentos se pueden hacer leyes, y al contrario.

Como en los mismos principios del artículo (*Lo leyó*) se alude a las leyes fundamentales, es claro que en él no se comprenden las puramente reglamentarias y civiles. Por todas estas razones creo que el Estamento hará un bien al país, y estoy íntimamente convencido de ello, si aprueba el artículo tal como está redactado. (*Pr.*, p. 152)

(In his speech the Count of Toreno set forth the serious consequences encountered in the adoption of the article as it is now redacted. He said, among other things, that if its second part were approved in the terms in which it is now written, then perhaps some persons will disregard police and other regulations that might be established. This might bring us to the great question of defining what is a law and what is a regulation, a question which it would indeed behoove us to ventilate, because if laws may not be created without the concurrence of the estates, it would be useful to denote the limitations of law and of regulations, since under the name of regulations laws can be created, and vice-versa.

In the very bases of the article there is an allusion to the fundamental laws; thus purely regulatory and civil ones are clearly not comprised in it. For all these reasons I believe the Chamber will perform good and great service to the country, and I am deeply convinced of it, if it approves the article as redacted.)

Caballero's speech, inadvertently or not, makes it obvious that article 1 in its original form was a threat to the validity of royal decrees.

When at last a vote was taken, a tie of 52–52 resulted. Because such a case had not been foreseen in the rules of the Estamento, a debate on procedure arose, with some ensuing disturbance. Finally, the article was passed in the form proposed by Antonio González, "Las leyes protegen y aseguran la libertad individual," 95 to 2 with 4 abstentions (José Rosendo de la Vega y Río, Santafé, López, and Moscoso de Altamira). The latter was, as the reader will recall, one of the ministers; it is about him that Larra inserted in his "Rehiletes" the following paronomasia:

El señor Secretario de lo Interior no ha querido votar en pro ni en contra del primer artículo de la famosa petición. Es decir, que el señor Secretario de lo Interior ha dejado su opinión *secreta* en su *interior*. Esto es llevar al extremo la escrupulosidad de su ministerio. (1: 435–436)

(The honorable Secretary of the Interior has desisted from voting for or against the first article of the famous petition. In other words, the Secretary of the Interior has left his opinion *secret* in his *interior*. This is certainly carrying to extremes the scrupulousness of his office.)

Another *rehilete* seems to echo Toreno's words quoted above from *Pr.*, p. 149. It reads:

Adoptando el Estamento el primer artículo de la gran petición, ya sabemos que *la ley protege y asegura la libertad individual.* Ya no nos falta más que saber qué acogida hará el trono a la petición, qué es libertad individual, cómo protege la ley, qué ley es ésa, y quién es el encargado de cumplirla. (1: 436)

(With the adoption by the Chamber of the first article of the great petition, we now know that *the law protects and insures individual freedom.* Now all we need to know is what kind of reception the petition will get from the throne, what is individual freedom, in what way the law protects, what law this is, and who is in charge of putting it into effect.)

Larra's and Toreno's motives, however, are different. The minister draws attention to the uselessness and untimeliness of the article's first draft, whereas the journalist points up the unsubstantiality of the final version, the importance of the Cortes, the disregard for fundamental rights, and Spain's jurisprudential muddle. Toreno displays his usual flippancy by calling a basic problem "la gran cuestión," thereby implying a pragmatic attitude on his own part. Larra, on the other hand, by using the phrase "la gran petición," ironically hints at the meaninglessness of the article's final redaction.

"La gran verdad descubierta" refers humorously to the physical sciences. It is not, however, a mock-naturalist allegory like "La planta nueva" (November 10, 1833); hence we should look elsewhere for his sources or inspiration. The most plausible origin of his pseudoscientific allusions is perhaps parliamentary oratory itself. Let us keep in mind the decadent state of Spanish universities with their scholastic orientation, and the superstitious suspicion surrounding scientific knowledge. Some *procuradores* could compensate for their political moderation by displaying, through

physical theory and terminology, their emancipation from scholasticism and their championship of modern ideas. Accordingly, there was no place for scholastic thought in this parliament.

"La gran verdad descubierta" provides an excellent example of Larra's skill at turning pseudoscientific argumentation against those who introduce it. He accomplishes this through irony, of course. In the present instance, Larra may have had in mind the following words from a speech by the Marquess of Falces:

> Si me es permitido emplear un símil del orden físico para aplicarle al orden moral, diré que en España e Inglaterra son iguales, lo mismo que en todas partes, los principios físicos. Desde Bails hasta Vallejo, lo mismo que Bezout, Lacroix y Newton, todos han sentado y reconocido los mismos principios físicos, que los cuerpos son graves, que la reacción es siempre igual y contraria a la acción, etc.; y sin embargo, vemos muy desiguales aplicaciones de estos principios exactísimos en ambos países. En España no vemos una máquina de vapor, al paso que en Londres y Manchester hay fábricas dilatadísimas en que se ve la continua aplicación de estos principios. En Londres y Madrid el mismo es el efecto de la palanca, del vapor, etc.; pero en la aplicación es donde está el defecto.
>
> En vano pues se proclamarán los principios si no se puede hacer inmediatamente su aplicación . . .[4] (Pr., p. 137)

(If I may be allowed a simile from the physical realm to apply it to the moral realm, I shall state that physical principles are equal in Spain and England, just as everywhere else. From Bails to Vallejo, as well as Bezout, Lacroix, and Newton, all have asserted and recognized the same physical principles, that bodies have weight, that reaction is always equal and opposite to action, and so forth. Nevertheless, we can see in both countries very unequal applications of these most precise principles. In Spain we see no steam engines, while in London and Manchester there are huge factories where we can witness the continuous application of these principles. In London and Madrid the effect of levers, steam, and so forth, are the same, but it is in their application that we find the defect.

Thus, principles are proclaimed in vain if their application cannot be made immediately . . .)

Figaro's comments parody Falces's style, but they are also ideologically informed by Progressive opinion. Though he expressed

it through irony, in this case Larra's thought seems very close to that of Trueba y Cosío, quoted above. The satirist writes:

> ¡Que nos quiten esa ventaja! A un dos por tres descubrió Copér-
> nico que la Tierra es la que gira; en un abrir y cerrar de ojos descu-
> brió Gassendi la gravedad de los cuerpos; Newton halló su prisma
> en un mal vidrio; Linneo encontró los sexos de las plantas entre
> rama y rama. Pero han sido necesarios siglos de opresión y una
> corrección ministerial para descubrir que la ley protege y asegura
> algo. He aquí la diferencia que hay de las verdades físicas a las ver-
> dades políticas: aquéllas suelen encontrarse detrás de una mata;
> éstas están siglos enteros agazapadas detrás de una corrección mi-
> nisterial. (1: 435)

> (Let them try to take this advantage away from us! In a flash
> Copernicus discovered that what revolves is the earth; in a twin-
> kling of the eye Gassendi found the gravity of bodies; Newton
> encountered his prism in a mere piece of glass; in the bushes Lin-
> naeus came upon the sexes of plants. But centuries of oppression
> and a ministerialist correction were needed for the discovery that
> the law protects and insures something. This is the difference be-
> tween physical truths and political verities: the former are usually
> found in a clump of foliage, while the latter have been crouching
> for centuries behind a ministerialist correction.)

Falces, as we can see, finds an analogy between physical and moral law but denies the universality of their applicability. Fígaro burlesques the analogy by ironically refuting it. We may notice that Larra develops two levels of irony simultaneously; one is litotic, because there are innumerable differences between the laws of the moral and physical realms, not just one; the other con-sists in reversing the amounts of time needed to make a great dis-covery and to find the obvious. Yet there is pathos in this humor-ous reversal, since it does take centuries for Spain to open its eyes to reality; and now the reality is but a mirage, a mere truism!:

> Dirán que los grandes trastornos políticos no sirven para nada.
> ¡Mentira! ¡Atroz mentira! Del choque de las opiniones nace la ver-
> dad. De dos días de discusión nace un principio nuevo y luminoso.
> ¿Saben ustedes lo que se ha descubierto en España, en Madrid,
> ahora, hace poco, hace dos días no más? Se ha descubierto, se ha
> decidido, se ha determinado que *la ley protege y asegura la liber-*

tad individual. Cosa recóndita, de nadie sabida, ni nunca sospechada. Han sido precisos todos los sucesos de La Granja, la caída de tres ministerios, una amnistía, la vuelta de todos los emigrados, la rebelion de un *mal aconsejado príncipe,* una Cuádruple Alianza, una guerra en Vizcaya, una jura, una proclamación, un Estatuto, unas leyes fundamentales resucitadas en traje de Próceres, una representación nacional, dos Estamentos, dos discusiones, una corrección ministerial, un empate y la reserva de un voto importante, que no hacía falta, para sacar del fondo del arca política la gran verdad de que *la ley protege y asegura la libertad individual.* (1: 435)

(People will say that great political upheavals serve no end. What a lie! An atrocious lie! Truth is born of the clashing of diverse opinions. From two days of discussion a new and luminous principle arises. Do you know what was discovered in Madrid, now, just a while back, a mere two days ago? It was discovered, it was decided, it was determined that *the law protects and insures individual freedom.* Oh recondite verity, known to no one, nor ever suspected! All the events of La Granja, the fall of three ministries, an amnesty, the return of all the exiles, the rebellion of an *ill-advised prince,* a Quadruple Alliance, a war in Biscay, an oath, a proclamation, an Estatuto, fundamental laws resurrected in Próceres's clothing, a national representation, two Estamentos, two discussions, a ministerial correction, a tie, and the tabling of an important vote, unneeded of course, were necessary to dig out of the bottom of the political treasure-chest the great truth that *the law protects and insures individual freedom.*)

We can sense here a possible hint that Procuradores has betrayed a sort of revolution, that it has not given the Spanish people their due after so much turmoil and suffering. Nevertheless, it is not all the *procuradores* who are to blame, but the fifty-two ministerialists who brought on the tie. Rather than establish a fundamental principle for the protection of the people, their representatives have enounced a truism stating what the law is. And this is just what the ministers wanted! It is clear from Toreno's speech that only "una verdad exenta de oposición" would be acceptable to him. Martínez de la Rosa himself might have called it "un axioma" (see above).

Now let us analyze Larra's literary reaction to these events. We might note beforehand the possible influence, conscious or not, of Courier's *Simple Discours.*[5] Yet Larra's irony is much more complex than Courier's. And if we are to better understand Figaro's talent, we must first surmise how a less witty person, likewise sympathetic to the Progressive cause, might enunciate on a literal level his reaction to these proceedings. Such a person would state the case this way: after ages of oppression the nation sought a principle expressing ideals of freedom, but the ministers whittled down the principle to a triviality. Now the reader of this study will note that the foregoing sentence contains the adversative conjunction "but." Larra, however, uses the copulative conjunction "y": "Pero han sido necesarios siglos de opresión y una corrección ministerial para descubrir que la ley protege y asegura algo." To coordinate in this manner the centuries of tyranny and the anticlimactic correction is typical of Larra's magnificent wit. The grammatical equivalence insinuates ideological parity; yet the thought of equating these two utterly disproportionate ideas appears so monstrous that the result is ludicrous rather than sarcastic, pathetic rather than aggressive humor.

It should be emphasized that the target of Larra's banter is mainly the ministers, whom he blames for debilitating the article through a "corrección ministerial." This expression is used three times in the essay, besides the variant "modificación ministerial" found in the following passage:

> Ábrase la discusión, discútase el punto, pronúnciese la modificación ministerial, *et voilà la vérité*, que salta como un chorro, y salpica a los circunstantes. ¡Uf! *La ley protege y asegura la libertad individual.* Luego que esto esté escrito y sancionado, ya quisiera yo saber quién es el que no anda derecho. ¿Qué ladrón vuelve a robar, qué asesino mata, qué faccioso vuelve a levantar cabeza, y qué carlista, en fin, no se apea de su destino? (1: 435)

> (Open the discussion, debate the point, let the ministerial modification be pronounced, and *voilà!*, the truth, gushing forth and sprinkling the gathering! *The law protects and insures individual freedom.* After this is written up and sanctioned, I'd like to know who'll dare not to go straight. What thief will rob again, what assassin kill, what rebel will raise his head, and what Carlist, finally, will get off his high job?)

Larra's metaphor of the sudden sprinkling jet seems very much in keeping stylistically with the preceding pseudoscientific burlesque, since it reminds the reader of a chemistry laboratory demonstration. Moreover, the author has broached another topic, the government employees problem, though without impairing the unity of his piece; quite the contrary, the new themes are masterfully woven into the main fabric. The figurative use of "apea" in this context does not obviate its literal connotation; on the contrary, it brings to mind a scene of mounted rebel raiders, thus faintly assimilating the Carlist-sympathizing employees with criminals. We might note that the expressions "encontrarse detrás de una mata" and "agazapadas detrás de una corrección ministerial" also smack of the metaphorical portrayal first given in "La planta nueva"—the factious bandit about to ambush the mail coach, for example. Thus, by means of the dismal prevalent conditions, Larra provides a background for the newly revealed grand abstraction and combines concurrently the "truth" motif of Martínez's and Toreno's speeches with the "discovery" motif of Falces's.

The debate on the petition for a bill of rights ended on September 10. Six days later an article by Larra, berating the ministerialists for their stand, appeared in the columns of the *Revista Española.* "El ministerial" (September 16, 1834) must be viewed in terms of the few modifications that the government party was able to effect, and likewise of its failure to alter the committee's draft as broadly as it hoped to.

Articles 2 and 3 were passed unaltered:

> 2°. Todos los españoles pueden publicar sus pensamientos sin previa censura. Art. 3°. Ningún español puede ser perseguido, preso, arrestado ni separado de su domicilio, sino en los casos previstos por la ley y en la forma que ella prescriba. (*Pr.,* p. 96)

> (2. All Spaniards may publish their thoughts without prior censorship. Art. 3. No Spaniard may be pursued, imprisoned, arrested, or taken away from his residence except in cases anticipated by law and in the manner prescribed therein.)

Article 4 prohibits ex post facto laws: "La ley no tiene efecto retroactivo; y ningún español será juzgado por comisiones, sino por los tribunales establecidos por ella antes de la perpetración del delito" (*Pr.,* p. 96—"The law has no retroactive effect, and no

Spaniard shall be judged by committees, but by the tribunals established by law before the perpetration of the crime"). The chamber passed this and even voted for an additional sentence: "Lo mismo se entiende en los negocios civiles" (*Pr.*, p. 224—"The same applies to civil affairs"). Article 5 as originally proposed was worded thus: "La casa de todos los españoles es un asilo que no puede ser allanado, sino en los casos y forma que ordena la ley" (*Pr.*, p. 96—"The house of every Spaniard is an asylum that may not be broken into, except in the cases and form that the law allows"). It was changed to: "No puede ser allanada la casa de ningún español sino en la forma y en los casos que ordena u ordenare la ley" (*Pr.*, p. 207—"No Spaniard's house may be broken into except in the form and cases that the law allows or might allow"). The new version, we must admit, is clearer and less ambiguous, especially without the emotional word "asilo," which could lend itself to embarrassing interpretation. The same can be said of article 6, drafted by the committee as: "La ley es igual para todos los españoles; por lo mismo ella protege, premia y castiga igualmente" (*Pr.*, p. 96—"The law is equal for all Spaniards; hence it protects, rewards, and punishes equally"). Its final form reads: "Todos los españoles son iguales ante la ley" (*Pr.*, pp. 209–210—"All Spaniards are equal before the law"). Article 7, after undergoing some changes, was voted in as follows: "Los españoles son igualmente admisibles a todos los empleos del Estado, y todos deben prestarse con igualdad a las cargas del servicio público" (*Pr.*, p. 219—"All Spaniards are equally admissible to all employ, and all must offer themselves with equality to the duties of public service"). Article 8 was presented as: "Todos los españoles tienen igual obligación de pagar las contribuciones votadas libremente por las Cortes en proporción de sus haberes" (*Pr.*, p. 96—"All Spaniards are equally obligated to pay the taxes freely voted by Cortes in proportion to their estate"), but the Moderates managed to exscind the words "igual," "libremente," and "en proporción de sus haberes" (*Pr.*, p. 222), which would have brought on innumerable problems. Article 9, dealing with property rights, was passed in its original form, save for a change in word order and the omission of a redundant phrase. Articles 10 and 11 were passed intact, a significant moral victory for the Progressives because they both implied control over the government:

"Art. 10°. La autoridad o funcionario público que atacase la libertad individual, la seguridad personal o la propiedad, comete un crimen, y es responsable con arreglo a las leyes. Art. 11°. Los Secretarios del Despacho son responsables por las infracciones de las leyes fundamentales, por los delitos de traición y concusión, y por los atentados contra la libertad individual, seguridad personal y derecho de propiedad. (*Pr.*, p. 96)

(Art. 10. An authority or public functionary that attacks individual freedom, personal security, or property commits a crime, and is responsible pursuant to the laws. Art. 11. The Secretaries of the Cabinet may be held responsible for infractions of fundamental laws, for crimes of treason and exaction, and for violations of individual freedom, personal security, and right of property.)

One of the most hotly debated was the last: "La Milicia urbana se organizará en toda la nación en conformidad de los reglamentos y ordenanzas que discutieren y aprobaren las Cortes" (*Pr.*, p. 96—"The Urban Militia shall be organized throughout the nation in conformity with the regulations and ordinances discussed and approved by Cortes"). The final version reads: "Art. 12°. Habrá una institución de Guarda nacional para la conservación del orden público y defensa de las leyes. Su organización será objeto de una ley" (*Pr.*, p. 225—"Art. 12. There shall be an institution of national guard for the conservation of public order and defense of the laws. Its organization shall be the object of a law"). The original draft, of course, would have given the parliament considerable authority over the militia. Finally, it must be pointed out that despite all this activity the petition was never heeded by the Crown.

Before we pass to the parts of the debate that prompted Figaro's satire, let us review some pertinent political realities. One article especially, the second, would evoke Larra's adamant concern, since its purpose was to guarantee a press free from censorship. If the situation is analyzed dispassionately, we may perceive the reasons for Moderate wariness. During the Triennium, freedom of the press had been abused. Newspapers turned provocative and irresponsible, like the infamous *Zurriago*, which insulted the king, coined nasty epithets for honorable citizens, and spread rumors about their private life; the best-known epithet is, of course, "Rosita la Pastelera" for Martínez de la Rosa. The libel laws were

good, but the will to respect them lacking. In addition, the manner of prosecuting abuses left much to be desired. Many liberals had sought to solve national problems by emulating foreign institutions, especially the jury system, which they considered a desideratum of all free societies. Their efforts resulted in the application of the jury system to libel cases, where condemnation required a two-thirds vote (eight of the eleven jurors). According to Eguizábal,

> la mayor parte de las veces se han absuelto los escritos aunque fuesen subversivos, aunque de la manera más abierta excitasen a la sedición y a la desobediencia, aunque contuvieran grandes calumnias y groseras injurias.[6]

> (most of the time, writings were absolved even though they were subversive, even though in the most overt manner they incited to sedition and disobedience, even though they contained calumnies and rude insults.)

As several historians have stated, the French invasion of 1823, led by the Duc d'Angoulême, was provoked in large measure by the injudiciousness of the press; hence the Moderates feared a repetition of this situation in 1834. Larra, however, disagreed with the Moderates because he felt that the circumstances were different from those of ten years previously. This is evident in the caricature of the ministerialist: "le suena siempre en los oídos el cañoneo del año 23. No ve más que el *Zurriago*, no oye más que a Angulema" (1: 439—"the cannonade of 1823 is constantly ringing in his ears. He sees only *El Zurriago;* he hears only Angoulême").

Now let us go back to the essay's beginning, a mock-philosophical exordium of the kind used earlier in "Las palabras" (see chapter 3), which portrays the ministerialist by means of a pseudo-naturalist technique found also in "La planta nueva" and "El hombre pone y Dios dispone." One of the similes is the parrot, of course. Others are the lobster, mine, bee, reptile, reed, water, thorn, compass needle, sunflower, camel, and madman.[7] Scientists are mentioned (Buffon, Valmont de Bomare, Jussieu, Tournefort, de Candolle, Cuvier, Humboldt, and Gall), but this is done to parody Moderate oratory, as we shall see.

Larra may have borrowed some of the ideas he travestied in his

first paragraph from a speech by Sebastián de Ochoa against the immediate establishment of freedom of the press:

No soy enemigo de la libertad de imprenta; para mí ésta es un astro radiante que ilumina y vivifica las sociedades. La defendí con cuanto calor pude en otra época; pero ahora, más cauto, he modificado mi modo de pensar por la experiencia que tengo de once años y lo que he visto en el año 23 . . .

. . . En España para saber ciertos principios no ha sido necesario recurrir a Voltaire, a Holbach, a Milton ni a otros extranjeros; esos principios de obligaciones de los Monarcas con los pueblos están consignados en una porción de libros de que nadie hace caso en el día . . . en Quevedo . . . en sus tratados de la *Vida de Cristo*, la de *Marco Bruto* y otros, he visto esos mismos principios . . .

. . . Cuando en España se hizo la guerra al despotismo, creyeron los autócratas que se iba a extender aquí el jacobinismo, y no a pararse en una justa libertad, sino que, unidos los jacobinos de España con los de Francia, iban a encender otra vez las luchas del terrorismo, e inundar al mundo de sangre. Por eso destruyeron la libertad en España, y después del año 14 se trató de estancar todas las luces. Vino el año 20, y todas las clases de la sociedad, sin distinción, nombraron por sus representantes a personas amantes de la libertad; cosa que se repitió en las elecciones del 22.

Las medidas tomadas del año 23 acá todas han tendido a apagar la instrucción . . . Sentado esto, creo que podríamos comparar la libertad de imprenta . . . al agua . . . Ninguna cosa hay más indispensable, repito, y menos costosa que el agua; con todo, ese verano se nos ha prohibido beberla por consejo de los médicos, porque podía hacernos daño. Pues lo mismo sucede con la libertad de imprenta . . . (*Pr.*, p. 172)

(I am not an enemy of press freedom. For me it is a radiant star, illuminating and giving life to societies. I defended it as heatedly as possible in another epoch; but now, being more cautious, I have modified my way of thinking through an experience of eleven years and what I saw in the year 1823 . . .

. . . In Spain, to know certain principles we never had to have recourse to Voltaire, Holbach, Milton, or other foreigners. These principles of obligations of Monarchs to their peoples are consigned to a number of books that no one pays attention to nowadays . . . in Quevedo . . . in his treatises, the *Life of Christ*, of *Marcus Brutus*, and others, I have seen these same principles . . .

. . . When war was waged in Spain against despotism, autocrats believed that jacobinism would begin to spread here, not merely stopping at a just liberty, but that Spanish jacobins united with those of France would again spark the strifes of terrorism, and bathe the world in blood. Therefore they destroyed liberty in Spain, and after the year 1814 there was an attempt to extinguish all enlightenment. Came the year 1820, and all classes of society, without distinction, named as their representatives persons who loved freedom; this was repeated in the elections of 1822.

The measures taken since 1823 have all tended to destroy education . . . Now that these premises have been established, I believe we could compare freedom of the press . . . with water . . . Nothing is more indispensable, I repeat, and less expensive than water. Nevertheless, last summer we were warned not to drink it by doctors' orders, because it could have harmed us. Well, the same thing applies to freedom of the press . . .)

Certain themes are broached here which we should note before turning to Figaro's burlesque: the comparison of press freedom to an enlightening star; a recapitulation of political upheavals since the Napoleonic invasion, with the Triennium and Ominous Decade considered as sobering experiences; foreign thinkers such as Voltaire, Holbach, and Milton, to whose socio-philosophical principles we need not have recourse, since similar ones can be found within the Spanish tradition; an analogy from the natural world—liberty compared with water, which is necessary to maintain life but not potable during an epidemic. Such themes also find a place in Larra's essay. The political upheavals are here, but whereas Ochoa deals with them socio-ideologically, Figaro, as a "humanist," treats them in the light of personal vicissitudes. Ironic dismissal of a philosophical tenet because its author has never been in Spain is here likewise, and so are several analogies to the natural world. Let us examine its beginning:

¿Qué me importa a mí que Locke exprima su exquisito ingenio para defender que no hay ideas innatas, ni que sea la divisa de su escuela: *Nihil est in intellectu quod prius non fuerit in sensu?* Nada. Locke pudiera muy bien ser un visionario, y en ese caso ni sería el primero ni el último. En efecto, no debía de andar Locke muy derecho: ¡figúrese el lector que siempre ha sido autor prohibido en nuestra patria!... Y no se me diga que ha sido mal mirado,

como cosa revolucionaria, porque, sea dicho entre nosotros, ni fue
nunca Locke emigrado, ni tuvo parte en la Constitución del año 12,
ni empleo el año 20, ni fue nunca periodista, ni tampoco urbano.
Ni menos fue perseguido por liberal; porque en sus tiempos no se
sabía lo que era haber en España ministros liberales. Sin embargo,
por más que él no escribiese de ideas para España, en lo cual anduvo acertado, y por más que se le hubiese dado un bledo de que
todos los padres censores de la Merced y de la Victoria condenasen
al fuego sus peregrinos silogismos, bien empleado le estuvo. Yo
quisiera ver al señor Locke en Madrid en el día, y entonces veríamos si seguía sosteniendo que porque un hombre sea ciego y sordo
desde que nació, no ha de tener por eso ideas de cosa alguna que a
esos sentidos ataña y pertenezca. Es cosa probada que el que no ve
ni oye claro a cierta edad, ni ha visto nunca, ni verá. Pues bien,
hombres conozco yo en Madrid de cierta edad, y no uno ni dos,
sino lo menos cinco, que así ven y oyen claro como yo vuelo. Hábleles usted, sin embargo, de ideas; no sólo no las tienen sino que
¡ojalá no las tuvieran! Y de que estas ideas son innatas, así me queda
la menor duda como pienso en ser nunca ministerial; porque si no
nacen precisamente con el hombre, nacen con el empleo, y sabido
se está que el hombre, en tanto es hombre en cuanto tiene empleo.
(1: 437)

(What do I care if Locke gives expression to his exquisite mind to
defend the proposition that there are no innate ideas, or if the
motto of his school is, *Nothing is in the intellect that was not first
in the senses?* Not a whit. Locke may very well have been a vision-
ary, and in such a case he would neither be the first nor the last.
In fact, Locke couldn't have been walking a very straight line.
Just think, dear reader: he has always been a forbidden author in
our country!... And don't tell me that they looked askance at him,
like something revolutionary, because, between you and me,
Locke was never an exile, he had no part in the Constitution of
1812, or a job in 1820, nor was he ever a newspaperman, nor did
he belong to the Urban Militia. He was not even persecuted as a
liberal, because in his day no one knew what having liberal ministers in Spain would be like. Nevertheless, notwithstanding his not
writing ideas for Spain—and he was right not to do it—and notwithstanding his not giving a hoot about the Father censors of La
Merced and La Victoria condemning to the flames his magnificent
syllogisms, he certainly had it coming to him. I'd like to see Mr.
Locke in Madrid now, and then we'd see if he'd keep on maintain-

ing that because a man is deaf-mute from birth, he doesn't have any ideas about anything concerning and appertaining to the aforementioned senses. It's been proven that whoever neither sees nor hears plainly by a certain age, has never seen and never shall. Well now, I know in Madrid men of a certain age, and not just one or two but at least five, who see and hear plainly *like I can fly*. Speak to them, however, about ideas. Not only don't they have any, but would that they hadn't! And about these ideas being innate, as little doubt remains in my mind as the desire to ever be a ministerialist; because if they are not necessarily born with the man, they are born with the job, and it is a well-known fact that man is a man insofar as he has a job.)

Several themes underlie the above satire. The principal one is the ironic repudiation of a foreign philosopher, ultimately meant to ridicule intellectual isolationism. By correctly portraying Locke as an "autor prohibido" who (unlike Bentham, I might add) never wrote "ideas para España, en lo cual anduvo acertado," Larra parodies Ochoa's assertion that "en España para saber ciertos principios no ha sido necesario recurrir a Voltaire, a Holbach, a Milton ni a otros extranjeros." In this manner, Figaro unveils the myth-laden opinions of the ministerialists, of whom it can be said: "Hábleles usted, sin embargo, de ideas; no sólo no las tienen sino que ¡ojalá no las tuvieran!" As the journalist knows too well, tyrannically imposed obscurantism has prevented the country from developing. Is it not pathetic that even a *procurador*, owing to his own intellectual deprivation and the subtle xenophobic influence of his environment, should be incapable of thinking clearly about the intellectual deprivation of the environment itself? It is glaringly false to state, as Ochoa did, that Spaniards had no need to resort to foreign sources; the truth is that they were simply not allowed to study or use them, at the risk of being severely punished for heresy.

Another topic can be perceived by examining the difference between Ochoa and Larra in reciting important dates and making comparisons to nature. The *procurador* is candid, whereas the journalist is mock-serious. Figaro, having assimilated the devices of oratorical argumentation, parodies its travesty of philosophy, not the philosophy itself. It is not the philosopher who is ridiculed but the ministerialist, guilty of misapplying philosophy. By using

a principle of Locke's to introduce his burlesque argument, Figaro implies that philosophers can be cited to advocate any political opinion. Moreover, the principle is Locke's only insofar as it
is understood in an innatist manner; this apophthegm was, after
all, quite acceptable to most scholastics, as long as the intellect
was conceived of according to Aristotle or Aquinas. Therefore,
Larra's use of an apophthegm acceptable to several schools is
doubly clever, since it reinforces his primary implication that a
Moderate politician will justify his notions by means of any convenient philosophy.[8] Larra, to be sure, really feels that the ministerialists neither see nor hear, provided these two verbs are understood figuratively. On the other hand, his remarks purport to
negate the practical application of Locke's principle in Madrid,
with the ironic assumption that the two verbs be understood literally. Thus, Larra's disquisition refutes a philosophical tenet by
jestingly using for a premise evidence that is fallacious in its literal
acceptation, but valid for the author when taken figuratively.
Furthermore, when orators venture to compare the practical application of philosophical principles to that of scientific ones, they
open themselves to Figaro's wily imitation. Indeed, Ochoa was
not the only delegate to give the example. The Marquess of Falces, who had used such analogies in a previous discussion,[9] repeated his tactics on September 4:

> Aunque lo que el Estamento aprobó antes de ayer no tiene analo-
> gía con lo que se discute, recordaré que en ello sancionó un gran
> principio, cual es que las leyes deben proteger y asegurar la liber-
> tad, axioma eterno que en el orden moral puede compararse al
> físico de que el sol alumbra, y sólo falta deducir las consecuencias
> que en el mismo orden se puede decir análogas a la facultad de ca-
> lentar, iluminar y no quemar. (*Pr.*, p. 167)

> (Although what the Chamber approved the day before yesterday
> bears no resemblance to what is being discussed now, let me re-
> mind you that in doing so it sanctioned a great principle, namely,
> that laws must protect and insure liberty. This is an eternal axiom,
> comparable in the moral realm to the physical one that the sun
> gives light, and we need only deduce the consequences which in
> that same realm may be said to be analogous to the faculty of heat-
> ing, illuminating, and not burning.)

Perhaps Larra still had Falces's previous speech as well as this one in mind when, to explain the relation between ministerialist and minister, he used a botanical analogy, describing the ministerialist as "girasol en mirar al que alumbra"[10] (1: 439—"a sunflower, since it looks to the one that shines").

Martínez de la Rosa himself was not beyond using scientific analogies:

> Por lo mismo que el pensamiento es tan libre, tan indefinido, tan vago, que sus delitos no tienen cuerpo, y que la fuerza de la opinión, semejante a la de los vapores, es grandísima, inmensa, pero no se tocan ni se palpan; por lo mismo en esta materia es tan difícil conciliar el orden con la libertad. Este problema, que es el problema del siglo, que tiene en conmoción a toda Europa, en esa especie de enfermedad que padecen las naciones (porque tal puede llamarse la agitación, ese malestar que les roba su felicidad y sosiego, hasta que encuentran su aplomo y su nivel) . . . (Pr., p. 175)

> (For the very reason that thought is so free, so indefinite, so vague that its transgressions are bodiless, and that the force of opinion, like the force of gases, is great, immense, though they cannot be touched or handled; for this reason, then, it is so difficult to reconcile order with freedom in the present topic. This problem, which is the problem of our century, which has shaken all Europe, is a kind of illness suffered by nations—because their agitation, this malaise robbing them of their happiness and rest until they find their poise and levelness, must be given such a name . . .)

Of considerable significance here is Toreno's reply to Joaquín María López, who, in defending freedom of the press, had exalted the faculty of writing for its antiquity. The count made a show of rebutting López by asserting with his typical casualness that the faculty of speech is inherent in mankind:

> Ha dicho [el Sr. López] que según [la razón] el pensamiento es un don natural; no hay duda, es un don que debemos al Criador; pero de esta base, que es incontestable, ha sacado consecuencias que no lo son. Ha sentado que el pensamiento es anterior al habla; como si ésta pudiera dejar de existir en el hombre, siendo tan inherente a ser como el canto a los pájaros y el ladrido a los perros.

La escritura viene tras del habla, y así como ésta comunica los pensamientos por medio de sonidos fugitivos, lo hace la escritura por medio de signos permanentes; y he aquí la diferencia de estos dos medios de comunicarlos. El arte de escribir, pues, no es sino el ejercicio y desarrollo de la facultad de pensar. Por tanto, el señor preopinante se ha equivocado . . . al decir que los jeroglíficos eran anteriores al habla . . .[11]

(Mr. López said that, according to reason, thought is a natural gift. It is without doubt a gift we owe the Creator. But from this incontestable basis he drew consequences that are not so. He asserted that thought is previous to speech, as if the latter could cease to exist in man, when it is indeed so inherent to his being as song to birds and barking to dogs.

Writing comes after speaking, and just as the latter communicates thoughts by means of fleeting sounds, writing does it through permanent signs. This is the difference between the two means of communicating them. The art of writing, then, is but the exercise and development of the faculty of thought. Consequently, the previous speaker erred . . . in saying that hieroglyphics were prior to speech . . .)

A good many people may have taken this aspect of the debate seriously, and, in all likelihood, Toreno's words about the inherence of language became a topic for *tertulias*, while Locke was introduced to support empiricism against epistemological rationalism and innatism.[12] Perhaps a disquisition on the subject appeared in a newspaper. This, in addition to Ochoa's speech, could have suggested to Larra the topic of his first paragraph, where innatism is ironically travestied: "Y de que estas ideas son innatas, así me queda la menor duda . . . porque si no nacen precisamente con el hombre, nacen con el empleo . . ." The theme is developed later:

La materia, que en forma sólo de procurador producía un discurso racional, unas ideas intérpretes de su provincia, se seca, se adultera en forma ministerial; y aquí entran las ideas innatas, esto es, las que nacen con el empleo, que son las que yo sostengo, pese a los ideólogos. (1: 438)

(Matter, which in the form merely of *procurador* produced a rational discourse, some ideas interpretive of its province, dries up, becomes adulterated in ministerialist form. And here is where innate ideas come in, that is, those born along with the government job, which are the ones I maintain, ideologists to the contrary.)

There is another passage in Toreno's speech that Larra might have found suggestive:

En fin, citar ahora estos autores es lo mismo que si para hablar de las aplicaciones portentosas del vapor, o de los descubrimientos en el sistema sideral, se mentasen mecánicos o astrónomos anteriores a Watt y a Herschell; y ahora que me acuerdo de estos hombres célebres en las ciencias físicas, diré que no sé por qué el señor López, impugnando el axioma que ha sentado el Sr. Martínez de la Rosa, que la reacción es igual a la acción, ha asegurado que esto era antiguamente, y que ahora ya no es así. Ignoro qué autores digan esto y cuáles puedan decirlo, pues la inercia que ha alegado en su favor es una propiedad de los cuerpos conocida mucho ha, y que se ha tomado en cuenta para aquel axioma. (*Pr.*, p. 181)

(In sum, to quote such authors now would be as if, in order to speak about the portentous applications of steam power or discoveries in sidereal systems, we were to mention mechanics or astronomers prior to Watt and Herschel. And speaking of these famous men of science, may I say I wonder why Mr. López, impugning the axiom stated by Mr. Martínez de la Rosa that the reaction is equal to the action, asseverated that it was so of yore, but not so now? I am ignorant of what authors say this or which ones could say it, as the inertia alleged by him in his favor is a property of bodies known for a long time and taken into account for the axiom.)

Toreno, as we can see, compares some philosophers supposedly cited by López to scientists whose theories are considered obsolete, thereby implying the irrelevance of these authors to the problem at hand. This argumentation by analogy may have prompted Larra to assert jestingly that he cannot find any writer whatsoever whose work contains the slightest information relevant to a study of the ministerialist, since this creature appears completely new:

Podría haber algo de confusión en lo que llevo dicho, porque los ideólogos más famosos, los Condillac y Destutt-Tracy, hablan sólo del hombre, de ese animal privilegiado de la creación, y yo me ciño a hablar del *ministerial*, ese ser privilegiado de la gobernación. Saber ahora lo que va de ministerial a hombre es cuestión para más despacio, sobre todo cuando creo ser el primer naturalista que se ocupa de este ente, en ninguna zoología clasificado. Los antiguos, por supuesto, no le conocieron; así es que ninguno de sus autores le mienta para nada entre las curiosidades del mundo antiguo, ni se ha descubierto ninguno en las excavaciones de Herculano, ni Colón encontró uno solo entre todos los indios que descubrió; y entre los modernos, ni Buffon le echó de ver entre los racionales, ni Valmont de Baumare lo reconoce . . . (1: 437)

(There might be some confusion in what I said, because the most famous ideologists, the Condillacs, the Destutt-Tracies, speak only of man, this animal privileged by Creation, and I limit myself to speaking of the *ministerialist*, this being privileged by Administration. Now, to find out the difference between man and ministerialist is a question that needs much further deliberation, especially since I believe I am the first naturalist to devote himself to this creature, as yet unclassified in any zoological treatise. The ancients, to be sure, were unacquainted with him, so that none of their authors mentions him at all amid the curiosities of the ancient world, and none has been discovered in the excavations of Herculaneum. Neither did Columbus come across a single one in the midst of all the Indians he discovered. As for the moderns, Buffon did not notice him among the rational beings, and Valmont de Bomare does not recognize his existence . . .)

Perhaps Toreno's speech, from which two passages were quoted above, did not suggest directly to Larra the pseudonaturalist theme, but it cannot be doubted that the analogical argumentation indulged in by the *procuradores* exacerbated his critical sensitivity. In any case, his fabric of mock similes is more persuasive than the potpourri of supposedly serious ones uttered in the chamber. A pregnant and neat burlesque arises from a miscellany of slipshod and false analogies.

Some of Figaro's rhetorical devices are quite remarkable. An antithetical parison with homoeoteleuton introduces the dominant contrast between man and his artificially bred subspecies: "hablan sólo del hombre, de ese animal privilegiado de la creación, y yo me ciño a hablar del *ministerial*, ese ser privilegiado de la gobernación." This verbal play sets the tone for all that follows it. Larra also displays exceptional virtuosity toward the end of the first paragraph: "Pues bien, hombres conozco yo en Madrid de cierta edad, y no uno ni dos, sino lo menos cinco, que así ven y oyen como yo vuelo." The adynaton-simile that concludes the sentence is effective despite its triteness because it bears upon activities within its own category, the faculties of the body; it also vivifies through parallelism the ensuing simile, invented by the author, "así me queda la menor duda como pienso nunca en ser ministerial," which involves the faculties of the mind.

There are some witty puns in the latter part of the essay; for example, the ministerialist is "muy buen cristiano en no votar" (1: 439), where his unwillingness to vote for Progressive measures is coupled to cultural inhibitions engendered by Ripalda's catechism.[18] Likewise, a pun on "urbano," ironically followed by an anticlimax, brings to mind the debate on article 12: "Con respecto al reino animal, somos harto urbanos, sea dicho con terror suyo, para colocar al ministerial en él. En realidad el ministerial tiene más de artefacto que de otra cosa" (1: 438—"With respect to the animal kingdom, we are too urbane to place the ministerialist in it. In truth, the ministerialist is closer to artifacts than anything else").

Up to now we have examined parts of the essay that merely allude to the debates. In "El ministerial" there is, however, one paragraph that openly satirizes Moderate oratory. The ministerialists' equivocal self-justification of their stand against press freedom becomes the special target of Larra's banter. The following extracts from speeches intended to vitiate the petition are all directed at article 2, save for the last example, which bears on article 8:

Medrano:

> Aunque he pedido la palabra en contra de la petición, no es para hablar en sentido contrario al en que ha hablado el señor preopinante, y a las sólidas razones que ha expuesto; antes por el contrario estoy conforme en lo sustancial de ellas . . . (*Pr.*, p. 109)

> (Although I asked for the floor in order to oppose the petition, I did not do so to speak in a manner contrary to the previous orator's, or against the solid arguments expounded by him. Rather, on the contrary, I am in agreement with them in substance . . .)

Santafé:

> He pedido la palabra, no para hablar en contra de . . . , sino con
> el vivo deseo de que se ilustre más y más la materia tan importante
> . . . Para entrar en la cuestión diré que nos debemos ceñir en el
> caso presente a tratar tan sólo de si . . . No trato ahora de si se
> debe establecer esto o aquello . . . Bajo este principio es preciso
> confesar que . . . (*Pr.*, p. 136)

> (I asked for the floor, not to speak against . . . but with the fer-
> vent desire that such an important matter be illuminated further
> . . . In order to enter into the question I must say that the present
> case should not be limited only to dealing about whether . . . I
> am not treating now of whether this or that should be established
> . . . Under this principle it is necessary to confess that . . .)

Agustín López del Baño:

> Hablaré del 2°. artículo de la petición, no porque me
> oponga . . . , ni a que se conceda . . . , ni mucho menos a que se
> amplíe . . . ; sino porque creo . . . Es necesario tener presente
> que . . . (*Pr.*, p. 160)

> (I am going to speak about the second article of the petition, not
> because I am opposed. . . , or for the purpose of conceding . . . ,
> or much less so that we might broaden . . . ; but rather because
> I believe . . . It is necessary to keep in mind that . . .)

Vega y Río:

> Convengo en que la libertad de imprenta . . . , pero también es
> cierto que . . . Soy amigo de la ilustración que produce la libertad
> de imprenta, pero me parece que atendiendo a que la experiencia
> nos dicta . . . (*Pr.*, p. 164)

> (I am in agreement about the fact that press freedom . . . , but it
> is also certain that . . . I am a partisan of the enlightenment pro-
> duced by freedom of the press, but it seems to me that if we take
> cognizance of what experience dictates . . .)

Marqués de Falces: "Conozco que es embarazoso y resbaladizo el
terreno en que se coloca un Procurador del reino cuando parece
que quiere poner corrección a los principios de eterna ver-

dad. . . ." (*Pr.*, p. 167—"I realize that the grounds on which a Procurador of the realm places himself when he appears to want to emend principles of eternal truth are awkward and slippery . . ."). El marqués de la Gándara Real: "He pedido la palabra, no contra el fondo del artículo, sino sólo para hacer algunas observaciones sobre su redacción . . ." (*Pr.*, p. 220—"I have asked for the floor, not against the substance of the article, but only to make a few observations about its redaction . . .").

Gándara's apophasis is parodied by one sentence of Figaro's fifth paragraph, which follows:

> Es papagayo por otra parte; palabra soltada por el que le enseña, palabra repetida. Sucédele así lo que a aquel loro, de quien cuenta Jouy que habiendo escapado con vida de una batalla naval, a que se halló casualmente, quedó para toda su vida repitiendo, lleno de terror, el cañoneo que había oído: "¡Pum! ¡pum! ¡pum!" sin nunca salir de esto. El ministerial no sabe más que este cañoneo. *La España no está madura.—No es oportuno.—Pido la palabra en contra.—No se crea que al tomar la palabra lo hago para impugnar la petición, sino sólo sí para hacer algunas observaciones, etc., etc.* Y todo ¿por qué? Porque le suena siempre en los oídos el cañoneo del año 23. No ve más que el *Zurriago*, no oye más que a Angulema. (1: 438–439)

> (He is, on the other hand, a parrot. A word let forth by his trainer is a word repeated. The same thing occurs with him as with the bird Jouy speaks about, who, having gotten out alive from a naval battle where he happened to find himself by chance, kept repeating for the rest of his life, terror-stricken, the cannonade he had heard, "Boom, boom, boom!" without ever getting off the subject. The ministerialist knows only this cannonade. *Spain is not ripe.— It is not opportune.—I request the floor in opposition.—Let it not be thought that on taking the floor I do so to impugn the petition, but indeed merely to make some observations, and on and on.* And all this, why? Because the cannonade of the year 1823 is constantly ringing in his ears. He sees only *El Zurriago*, he hears only Angoulême.)

The comparison of the ministerialist to Jouy's frightened parrot is a truly genial tour de force. Of course, the parroting of the orators' propitiatory initial remarks gives rise to the obvious simile. But Larra has gone further by developing an analogy between the bird's idée fixe and the ministerialist's caution. There are four cannonades, that of the naval battle, its imitation by the parrot, that of Angoulême's army, and the repetitive evidence of its latency in Moderate political theory. They are inseparably blended, since the last cannonade is implicitly compared to all the rest. The concepts of fright, fear, and obsession are so subtly intermixed that the reader is hardly aware of the paragraph's extraordinary structure. In addition, its conclusion assimilates it to the first paragraph: "Yo quisiera ver al señor Locke en Madrid en el día, y entonces veríamos si seguía sosteniendo que porque un hombre sea ciego y sordo desde que nació, no ha de tener por eso ideas de cosa alguna que a esos sentidos ataña y pertenezca" (1: 437). For mockingly inconsequential reasons Locke would have had to recant his philosophy; out of unfounded caution the ministerialist disavows his liberalism.

This similar treatment of heterogeneous topics is a hallmark of Larra's artistry. It leads the reader's mind subtly back to the disarray of the ambience. And then, it is imperative for the journalist to be subtle at a time when those whom he would parody seem to be treating their own opinions ironically. The following extract from a speech by Santafé bears this out:

> Puesto que los Sres. Procuradores han citado la libertad de imprenta como necesaria para sostener las libertades sociales, se hace preciso rectificar sus ideas en esta parte, y a este fin sólo haré una ligera observación que probará no ser exacto su raciocinio. No creo que trataremos de disfrutar, o por lo menos no lo conseguiremos nunca, más libertad que los romanos y los atenienses. Pues bien: entre ellos hubo una libertad ilimitada, y no conocieron la imprenta. (*Risas y murmullos*). La imprenta se inventó en 1440, más de dos mil años después de la existencia de la libertad entre griegos y romanos. Esto solo basta para hacer ver que no es esencial la libertad de imprenta para los derechos sociales. (*Murmullos*). (*Pr.*, p. 152)

> (Since the honorable Procuradores have referred to freedom of the press as necessary to sustain social liberties, their ideas must be rectified on that score, and to this end I shall make only a slight observation that will prove their reasoning to be imprecise. I cannot believe that we shall ever attempt to enjoy—or at least we shall never obtain it—more liberty than the Romans and Atheni-

ans. Well then: unlimited liberty existed among them, and they did not know the printing press. [*Laughter and whispering.*] Printing was invented in 1440, more than two thousand years after the existence of liberty among Greeks and Romans. This alone is enough to demonstrate that freedom of the press is not essential to social liberties. [*Whispering.*])

Santafé's clownish discourse, whether sincere or not, is an excellent example of a phenomenon due in large part to the spirit of disillusionment latent in Moderate ideology.

8

THE GUEBHARD LOAN

L ARRA'S journalistic production abated after "El ministerial"
    (September 16, 1834). During a period of one month, the
    papers printed only three pieces bearing his signature, an
operatic article, "*La Straniera*" (September 20), "Segunda carta
de un liberal de acá a un liberal de allá" (October 7), and "Primera contestación de un liberal de allá" (October 15). Of the
three reasons that may be adduced for this scarcity, censorship is
always one possibility. Another is that Larra's activities as a playwright may have taken precedence over those of the journalist;
Macías, we must note, made its first appearance at the Príncipe
on September 24. Yet this second possible explanation cannot be
applied to the twelve-day halt in production from September 24
to October 7. As for the third reason, it needs considerable elucidation because a change of newspapers is involved.

The opera review was the last piece done by Figaro for *La Revista Española* until he rejoined its staff to publish "La sociedad"
on January 16, 1835; both the "Segunda carta" and the "Primera

contestación" appeared in *El Observador*. Larra's switch has not really been explained satisfactorily.[1] We do know that detractors spread false rumors about his motives, which he answered in a letter to *La Abeja* on October 8.[2] A theory I should like to put forward is that these two articles were written several days before they were published; that Larra submitted them to *La Revista*, which rejected them; and that *El Observador* then accepted them in revised form. Let us see how this may have occurred.

In his "Segunda carta" the "liberal de acá" writes:

has de saber que mi primera carta fue malamente interceptada; y no es decir que te la enviase por Vizcaya, lo cual hubiera sido grave error geográfico, sino por el conducto de este malhadado periódico, que perdone la censura. (2: 17)

(You should know that my first letter was foully intercepted. This is not to say that I sent it by way of Biscay, which would have been a serious geographical error, but through the channels of this ill-fated newspaper—censorship have mercy upon it!)

Sánchez Estevan comments on the above that "esto de la *segunda* carta sin haber aparecido la primera, como Fígaro remacha, bien pudiera relacionarse con la salida de la *Revista Española;* aunque más parece cosa de la censura."[3] ("this business of a *second* letter without a first one being issued could possibly be connected to his leaving *La Revista;* still, it seems likelier to be related to censorship"). But the last phrase in the above quotation from Larra is just another sally against censorship, a humorously stated wish that its heavy hand will spare the newspaper. Hence, we should not dismiss Sánchez Estevan's first hypothesis, which then leads us to seek an indication of Figaro's dissatisfaction with *La Revista*. Can we find such a clue in the "Segunda carta"? Although at first it seems logical that the phrase "este malhadado periódico" should refer to the paper in which the article appears, *El Observador*, this is not necessarily the case. Perhaps Larra ingeniously pretends to blame his present newspaper in order to avoid a useless quarrel with his former publisher; those in the know would understand that he really refers to *La Revista*.

This latter hypothesis is corroborated by the somewhat dated content of the articles in question, both of which could just as well have been published immediately after the debate on the foreign debt, which had begun on September 16 and ended on October 2. The obsoleteness of the two essays can be deduced from the folowing summary of parliamentary events:

1. September 20–24   "Continuity" polemic ("vencedores y venci-dos").
2. September 25   "Errar y enmendar" oration of Trueba y Cosío.
3. September 30   Martínez's speech belittling the effect of Car-los's arrival ("un faccioso más").
4. September 30   "Descarte" pronouncements on the Gueb-hard loan.
5. October 4   Meeting of Próceres.

References to the above events are distributed as follows in Figaro's essays: the "Segunda carta" (October 7) alludes to (2) and refers directly to (5); and the "Primera contestación" (October 15) refers to (1) and alludes to (3) and (4).

It should be noted that the "Segunda carta's" reference to Próceres (2: 18) is a parenthetical remark bearing no relation to the principal topics of the essay. This remark may possibly have been added before the essay went to press in order to give the "Carta" the appearance of being up to date. In sum, it is quite possible that Larra tried in vain to have a "Carta" and its "Contestación" published in *La Revista* before he went over to the more progressive *Observador*, now edited by his mentor Alcalá Galiano,[4] where they were refashioned for belated printing.

All three articles make general allusions to the political situation. In "Representación de *La Straniera*" Figaro uses Giudita Grisi's poor performance as an opportunity to fling an apophasis at the government:

El saber dejar el campo oportunamente es hacer eterna e inviola-ble para siempre la fama adquirida; el querer consolidarla cuando no puede ir más allá en guerra, en política, en literatura, en artes, es el cuento del que estando bueno se murió por querer estar mejor; es el jugador gananancioso doblando siempre. La carta mala viene por fin, y un solo revés echa por tierra todos los triunfos anteriores. Creerá acaso el lector, acostumbrado a vernos dirigir nuestros tiros al Poder, que queremos hacer aplicación de estas reflexiones a algún ministro, que pudiera haber dejado con gloria

antes el teatro hoy de su derrota. Dios nos perdone. Por hoy no
era ésa nuestra intención. Somos harto respetuosos para no dejar
descansar siquiera en un artículo a los pilotos de nuestra generación. Vaya la nave como pueda; en buen hora por hoy, no seremos
nosotros los que tratemos de echarla a pique con una nueva anda-
nada o un arriesgado abordaje. Hablemos sólo de la ópera . . .
(1: 440)

(Knowing how to make a timely withdrawal from the field is to
render acquired fame eternal and inviolable. To want to consoli-
date it when no more can be done, in war, in politics, in literature,
in the arts, is like the healthy man who dies from having tried to
be even healthier, or the winning gambler who always has to keep
on betting. The bad card is dealt at last, and one change of luck
strikes down all previous triumphs. Perhaps the reader, accustomed to seeing us aim our shots at authority, is thinking that we
wish to apply these reflexions to some minister who could beforehand with glory have stepped off the present boards of his defeat.
May God forgive us. We are too respectful to prevent the pilots
of our regeneration from resting in peace at least in one article.
Let the ship sail as it may. For the time being, we shall not be the
ones who try to sink it with a new broadside or by boldly attacking the subject. Let us speak of opera only . . .)

In the "Segunda carta" and the "Primera contestación" Larra mentions just about every newsworthy item in Madrid, even the cholera (2: 18), in his usual manner, cleverly linking all the topics in
such a way that their relation to each other reveals Spain's underlying ills. Yet most of the subjects Fígaro lists have already been
touched upon in the parliamentary debates, as we shall see.

Now for the first time Larra concerns himself with the piteous
state of the exchequer. While Spaniards begin to discern a civil
war looming longer and fiercer than they have ever imagined,
they are also faced with the grim fact of their country's bankruptcy. The government is not only expected to provide for ordinary administrative needs but also to defray the increasing cost of
an unwieldy army on a war footing and to repay a mounting ac-
cretion of debts.

Fair terms for the huge loan that was needed could be obtained
only from the house of Rothschild, the sole firm desirous and
capable of handling such amounts, but it would lend nothing un-

til the Cortes recognized Spain's foreign debt. The debt had become an international issue because, when the absolutists regained power in 1823, Ferdinand declared null and void all the acts of the preceding constitutional government, including every financial liability it had incurred. The contracts for the Triennium loans were rescinded by this decree but the money was not returned. On the other hand, the absolutist régime validated the loan that had been obtained for the Urgel Regency and always paid the interest promptly.

In all fairness it should be pointed out that the Urgel Regency, whose rôle in destroying the Triennium was discussed in chapter 1, did not benefit from this loan, since the first installment was delivered not to it but to the regency established in Madrid by the Duc d'Angoulême. Hence, the funds were never applied in any direct way against the Liberal régime of the Triennium. On the contrary, they became from the first an integral part of the national budget, as the Moderates pointed out during the debate. Nevertheless, the Progressives, who stood pat on their principles, could not be swayed by such considerations and insisted on the loan's treacherous origin as sufficient reason for not reimbursing it. Europe had to be shown once and for all that no Spanish monetary legislation could ever be considered valid without parliamentary ratification.

On September 11 the committee which had been appointed to study the government's proposal on the foreign debt delivered two reports to the chamber. The majority report expressed the Progressive view:

> Como la deuda extranjera no tiene toda ni el mismo origen, ni la misma legalidad, la comisión ha creído deber dividirla en dos clases, a saber, la contraída y reconocida por las Cortes, y la no contraída ni reconocida por ellas. . . .
>   . . . Si hay una deuda que ofrezca pocas razones para ser sostenida, muchas sí para ser combatida, es la deuda que empezó el 16 de Julio de 1823 y tuvo origen en el préstamo que con la casa de Guebhard contrató una junta de rebeldes, que sublevándose contra su país y su Rey, fue uno de los instrumentos con que se valió la Santa Alianza para destruir en España el Gobierno legítimo, arrancar al Monarca del seno de la Representación nacional,

y someterle a una facción que usurpando el augusto nombre de S.M., consiguió, con el auxilio de fuerzas extranjeras, entronizar la tiranía en nuestra amada patria. . . .

. . . Contratos celebrados con personas que carecen de autorización legal, son por su esencia nulos . . . Reconocer estipulaciones de esta especie sería autorizar transacciones liberticidas, alentar locas esperanzas y provocar los esfuerzos del partido del Pretendiente. La España libre no se mancillará con el reconocimiento de una deuda contraída para imponerla las cadenas. (*Pr.*, pp. 233–234)

(Since the whole foreign debt does not have the same origin or the same legality, the committee has felt it necessary to divide it into two categories, to wit, the part contracted and recognized by Cortes, and the other neither contracted nor recognized by them. . . .

. . . If there is one debt that provides few reasons to uphold it, and many indeed to contest it, it is the one initiated on July 16, 1823, and originating with the loan contracted with the house of Guebhard by a junta of rebels, which, rising up against their nation and their King, became an instrument used by the Holy Alliance to destroy Legitimate Government in Spain, tear the Monarch from the bosom of National Representation, and subject him to a faction that, usurping the august name of His Majesty, managed with the aid of foreign armies to enthrone tyranny in our beloved land. . . .

. . . Contracts transacted by persons lacking legal authorization are by their very essence null and void . . . Recognizing stipulations of this sort would be to authorize liberticidal transactions, encourage insensate hopes and foment the efforts of the Pretender's party. Free Spain shall not blemish herself with the recognition of a debt contracted to put her in chains.)

The minority, on the other hand, supported the government's proposal that "todas las deudas contraídas por el Gobierno en el extranjero en diversas épocas, y señaladamente los empréstitos tanto anteriores como posteriores al año 1823, son *deuda del Estado*" (*Pr.*, Apéndice 2 al núm. 12, p. 3, and Apéndice al núm. 36, p. 3—"all debts contracted abroad by the Government in diverse periods, and especially the loans previous as well as subsequent to the year 1823, are *debts of the State*"). Consequently, the minority report of the committee asserted that:

En concepto de los que suscriben, son igualmente sagradas las deudas contraídas desde 1823 a 1831, sin desconocer por eso los vicios de aquel Gobierno.

Éstos varían, pero las naciones subsisten. En el día no pueden existir sin crédito, y no hay crédito sin buena fe: falta cuando se busca pretextos o excusas para no reconocer lo que se debe, cuando se rompen los pactos, se desatienden las obligaciones o dilatan los pagos . . . (*Pr.*, Apéndice al núm. 36, p. 2)

(In the opinion of the undersigned, debts contracted from 1823 to 1831 are equally sacred, notwithstanding the faults of that Government.

Governments change, but nations subsist. Nowadays they cannot exist without credit, and there is no credit without good faith. When pretexts or excuses are found to avoid recognizing an indebtedness, when pacts are broken, obligations neglected or payments deferred, then credit is lacking . . .)

Here, then, in the diverging views of the majority report of the Progressives and the minority report of the ministerialists, we can clearly find the basis of a hard-fought polemic over the principles underlying the validity of Spanish governments and their responsibility for the acts of their predecessors. Moreover, the debate laid bare the nation's financial straits; government spokesmen pointed out that the amount they hoped to borrow would merely provide for monies already owed. It was evident that under such circumstances the debt could multiply indefinitely, and, to be sure, this prognostication found expression in Progressive oratory. The first to give vent to these feelings was Trueba y Cosío, on September 16, while he impugned the financial machinations engaged in by Burgos and Aguado eleven years previously:

Hemos visto que la renta perpetua no sale del empréstito Real como sale la luz de la vela para irla consumiendo poco a poco hasta que queda extinguida, pero sale cual de una bellota sale la soberbia encina para crecer espantosamente y reproducirse hasta el infinito . . . (*Pr.*, p. 251)

(We have seen that the perpetual annuity does not come out of the Royal loan as light issues from a candle to consume it little by little until it has disappeared, but rather as the proud oak comes from an acorn in order to grow frightfully and reproduce ad infinitum . . .)

Another picturesque simile was employed with like intent by Alberto Felipe Valdrich, Marqués de Torremejía, on September 24:

Además, estos empréstitos que adolecen de los vicios que el de Guebhard, son como la hidra de la fábula, que cortada una cabeza renacen más, y es menester restañarlas con fuego. (Pr., p. 362)[5]

(Moreover, loans with flaws like that of Guebhard are as the hydra of fable, on which more heads are born every time one is cut off, so that it is necessary to staunch them with fire.)

On September 9 Martínez de la Rosa reproached the Procuradores for the delay in voting for the Rothschild loan, which he said was urgently needed in the war effort; but his admonition was soon rebutted by José Vigil de Quiñones, Marqués de Montevirgen:

Así pues, se ve que no es por falta de dinero por lo que se prolonga la guerra de Navarra. Y pregunto: ¿será por falta de dinero por lo que algunos de nuestros generales son sorprendidos y comprometen las tropas más valientes? ¿Será por falta de dinero por lo que se dan esos decretos escandalosos por el Ministro de la Guerra imponiendo penas y castigos a los oficiales que no quieren ir a batirse? . . . ¿Será por falta de dinero que la milicia urbana no está todavía en disposición de hacer el servicio interior, a fin de poder dejar en libertad al ejército para operar? (Pr., p. 245)

(Accordingly, we can see that it is not for lack of funds that the war in Navarre goes on. Let me ask then if it is from lack of funds that some of our generals are ambushed and endanger the most valiant troops. Is it through lack of funds that the War Minister puts out those scandalous decrees imposing penalties and punishments on officers who don't want to go and fight? . . . Is it for lack of funds that the urban militia is still not in condition for internal service, in order to leave the army free for its operations?)

The Progressives, then, refuted the government's contention of a necessary connection between Carlist growth and lack of funds. Figaro combines the two factors rhetorically, thereby ironically reflecting their opinion that the blame lay elsewhere: "la facción parece deuda del Estado, según crece" (2: 18—"the way it's

growing, the faction looks like a State debt"). This pregnant vehicle must have struck a sympathetic chord amidst the despair
brought about by national bankruptcy and news of military defeats.

As for Montevirgen's charges concerning the militia, Figaro
echoes them also, as we shall see below, because they developed
into a major topic. Remón Zarco del Valle, the secretary of war,
replied to the marquess; then García Carrasco spoke for the Progressives:

> Hoy mismo, hoy mismo se desconfía de esta Milicia urbana; se ha
> prohibido que se reúnan los batallones de la capital, donde otras
> veces os ha dado pruebas de valor y disciplina, y se ha cubierto
> de laureles; no está lejano el día 7 de julio del año 22. Se quejan
> de esta Milicia porque se teme más a los hombres de bien armados,
> que a los facciosos; ni aun por compañías, que era como se les
> había dado la orden para reunirse y recibir la instrucción, se les
> permite ya hacerlo... ¿Con qué objeto se tiene aquí este ejército?
> No puedo adivinarlo, señor. (Pr., p. 260)

> (Today, even today, the Urban Militia is mistrusted. The battal-
> ions of the capital, where at other times it proved its bravery and
> discipline, covering itself with laurels, have been forbidden to
> assemble. The seventh of July, 1822, is not so distant. This militia
> is resented because decent men in arms are feared more than the
> rebels. Not even in companies, which is how the order had been
> given for assembly and training, are they permitted to do so... For
> what purpose is this army here? Sir, I can't possibly guess.)

Joaquín María López also had his say on the matter:

> La Milicia urbana en su principio fue la explosión, si cabe decirlo
> así, del entusiasmo general; y hubiera contado la mayor fuerza
> posible, si los reglamentos del Gobierno, su viciosa aplicación y las
> disposiciones que sucesivamente se han dictado para este benemé-
> rito cuerpo, no hubieran paralizado su movimiento y su tendencia.
> Aun ahora mismo se ha estado a pique de desorganizarla a pretexto
> de darle nueva forma; se ha sembrado un descontento general en
> todas las clases, y acaso hubieran tenido peores resultas si no se
> hubieran prevenido con nuevas disposiciones, o con suspensión
> de las que se habían dictado, lo que es la mejor prueba de su in-
> oportunidad. (Pr., p. 326)

(In its beginnings the Urban Militia was the explosion, if the expression be allowed, of general enthusiasm, and it would have been numbered as the greatest possible force if Government regulations, their faulty application, and the provisions prescribed for this worthy body had not paralyzed its movement and tendency. Even now it was just in danger of being disorganized under pretext of giving it a new form. General discontent has been sown among all ranks, and perhaps worse results would have ensued if they had not been forestalled with new dispositions or the cessation of the ones formerly drawn up, the greatest proof indeed of their inopportuneness.)

Both García Carrasco and López had repeated Montevirgen's allegations against the ineptitude of the generals engaged in fighting the Carlists. These, as well as the militia problem, are reflected in the meiosis of the "liberal de acá":

La milicia urbana ya se ha reunido, no sólo una vez, sino que creo que ha sido hasta dos. Se dice que si dará o no dará un poquito de servicio las tardes de los días de fiesta en el teatro. Con esto ya verás qué paso lleva Zumalacárregui. (2: 18)

(The urban militia has assembled, not just once, but, I believe, as much as twice. There's some rumor about whether or not it might help out a bit at the theater in the afternoon on holidays. Now we'll see how Zumalacárregui watches his step.)

The "liberal de allá" asks in the return mail: "¿Cómo va de milicia urbana? Ya inspirará confianza a todo el mundo; ya estará toda organizada y armada; doylo por supuesto" (2: 20—"How are things militiawise? It must be inspiring confidence in everybody. It's completely armed and organized by now, I guess. I just assume it"). The questions of the imaginary Portuguese are the more ironic when we note that only 100,000 of the 220,000 urbanos were armed.[6]

Let us now turn to the theme of "vencedores y vencidos" which is, to be sure, the most salient feature of the fictitious correspondent's "letter." His ironic remarks constitute variations on this theme, stemming from a part of the debate about governmental continuity. Should the present régime be considered a prolongation of the Ominous Decade, a resumption of the Triennium, both, or neither? It was Toreno who initiated this line of argument. Defending the recognition of the Guebhard loan, which, as he pointed out, had been legitimized by Ferdinand VII, he implored:

> Ha dicho el señor preopinante [Montevirgen] que todos estos empréstitos fueron hechos en medio de la fuerza extranjera: es cierto que en un principio fue así; pero aun entonces los extranjeros no se mezclaron en ello; y después, libre la nación de su presencia, libre ya, continuó sumisa presenciando las operaciones sin que nadie se opusiera a ellas antes de ahora; y ahora, ¿cuándo? Cuando no ha variado la forma de aquel Gobierno por un sacudimiento popular, sino cuando se ha modificado por las concesiones que ha tenido a bien hacer la excelsa Reina Gobernadora. Y entonces ¿dónde vamos a parar? No nos olvidemos de nuestro origen. (*Pr.*, p. 249)

> (The previous speaker said that all these loans were made in the midst of foreign forces. It is true that it was so at the beginning, but even then the foreigners did not take part in the matter. Later, when the nation was free of their presence, it submissively kept witnessing the financial operations without anyone showing his opposition to them until now. And to do so now? When the form of that Government has not been altered through uprising, but modified by concessions that our excellent Queen Regent deemed worthy to make? And then, what would we be coming to? Let us not forget our origin.)

Toreno implied in addition that all nations have to pay nolens volens for the political aberrations imposed upon them, and that to estrange French sympathies by unwisely repudiating the loan would be uselessly foolhardy ("echar bravatas vanas"). The Marqués de Torremejía later rebutted his conclusion:

> el empréstito de Guebhard . . . no puede ser reconocido, en mi concepto, sin un contrasentido . . . Nosotros, que entramos nuevos en la palestra, que heredamos a uno y otro Gobierno, ¿llevaremos a tal punto la legalidad y pundonor, que reconozcamos los dos? (*Pr.*, p. 253)

> (The Guebhard loan . . . , in my opinion, cannot be recognized without a self-contradiction . . . We who newly enter the con-

troversy, who inherit both governments, are we to carry legality and point of honor so far that we must recognize the two?)

As the debate progressed, many speakers, seeking precedents for their opinions, roamed through the history of national finance since the Middle Ages. Still, the main line of discussion always lay close to the question of recognizing the nation's legislative inheritance. Miguel Polo, a ministerialist, asserted that if the bondholders of the Decade loans saw them invalidated, they would then turn to supporting the Pretender.[7]

Up to this point the orators had merely skirted the issue of governmental continuity. On September 18 the problem began to be attacked directly when García Carrasco broached the concept of systems:

> me ha causado tanta extrañeza como la doctrina sentada por un Sr. Secretario del Despacho y repetida por algún Sr. Procurador, que me propongo rebatir. Señores: cuando entramos en un sistema de libertad; cuando principian a establecerse garantías, creo que es un absurdo decir que este sistema de libertad es una continuación del de la Inquisición y los cadalsos. (*Pr.*, p. 274)

> (it has amazed me as much as the doctrine set forth by one of the cabinet ministers and repeated by a Procurador, and I aim to impugn it. Gentlemen: when we enter into a system of freedom, when guarantees begin to be established, I feel it is absurd to say this system of liberty is a continuation of that of the Inquisition and the gallows.)

The speaker then went on to say that the ten-year régime was imposed and at first maintained with the aid of foreign bayonets, but that

> En estos once años hemos visto infinitas pruebas de querer recobrar los derechos perdidos: hablen las víctimas de Torrijos, Bazán, Miyar, etc. Me ha parecido útil hacer esta vindicación; y repito que no creía a la nación española merecedora de tanta injusticia.[8] (*Pr.*, p. 274)

> (During the last eleven years we have seen innumerable attempts to recover the lost rights. Let their victims, Torrijos, Bazán, Miyar, speak! I deemed it useful to make this vindication, and I repeat I did not feel the Spanish nation deserved such injustice.)

By mentioning Calomarde's martyrs, who lost their lives opposing the régime that benefited from the Guebhard loan, García Carrasco gave the lie to Toreno. Yet this is tantamount to stating that the government of 1834 was in no way a continuation of the ten-year régime; that on the contrary its roots lay in the ideals of those who were executed for treason on the king's orders. Deeming these comments still not sufficient, Carrasco hinted at the ministry's supposed pusillanimity:

> Es necesario que no olvidemos que la marcha que se ha propuesto seguir el Gobierno francés es intimidar a la España y a los Procuradores para que no ejerzan un acto de justicia. Yo lo digo a los Señores Procuradores del reino, que no bastarían ni esas amenazas ni otra porción de medios para corromper sus almas patriotas. (*Pr.*, p. 278)

> (We must not forget that the course of action decided upon by the French Government is to intimidate Spain and the Procuradores to prevent them from performing an act of justice. I will say it to the Procuradores of the realm, that those threats and a few other means would not suffice to corrupt their patriotic souls.)

The next day the Conde de las Navas, in the midst of a brilliant philosophical oration, made another caustic comment about the ministers, as we shall see below. These attacks began to wear down Martínez de la Rosa's equanimity. He defended the policy by which his administration had negotiated with Rothschild and Ardoin. If the government had wanted a ruinous loan, he asseverated, it could have found it easily, "y aun diré más: si hubiera querido retardar la reunión de las Cortes, pudiera haberlo hecho" (*Pr.*, p. 280—"and I shall say even more: if it had wanted to delay the meeting of Cortes, it could have done so").

No one replied immediately to the prime minister but, two days later, Fermín Caballero uttered for the first time the famous phrase "vencedor ni vencido," used to describe Spain's political heritage:

> Ha dicho también uno de los Señores Secretarios del Despacho que entre nosotros no hay partido vencedor ni vencido. Si por partido se entiende los que luchan a viva fuerza en el campo de batalla, convendré con S.S. en que hasta que se levantó la facción

de Navarra no le había. Pero qué, todos los partidos vencedores o vencidos ¿se reducen a los que pelean con las armas en la mano? Pues qué, ¿no hay partidos de opinión? ¿Y éste no ha triunfado del otro? ¿No ha triunfado la razón, la libertad y la justicia?

El tercer principio es que el orden de cosas en que nos hallamos es de un género que ni es continuación del Gobierno representativo ni del de los once años. Yo creo es continuación de las dos épocas. Examinados los principios y el orden legal de que hoy dependemos, y al que hemos sido restituidos, diré que esta Representación nacional es continuación de las anteriores. Si examinamos el Trono de nuestra tierna Reina Isabel II, hija heredera y legítima sucesora de Fernando VII, creo es continuación de los once años. (*Pr.*, p. 311)

(One of the Secretaries of the Cabinet also said that among us there is neither a vanquishing nor a vanquished party. If by party we are to understand those who fight with brute force on the field of battle, then I agree with His Lordship that until the Navarre faction arose there was none. But are all winning and losing parties to be defined as those which fight with weapons in hand? Are there not parties of opinion? And did the present one not triumph over the other? Did reason, freedom, and justice not triumph?

The other principle is that the state of affairs we find ourselves in is of a type which is neither a continuation of the representative Government nor of that of the eleven years. I believe it is a continuation of both epochs. The principles and legal order on which we now depend and to which we have been restored having been examined, I conclude that this National Representation is a continuation of former ones. If we examine the Throne of our tender Queen Isabel II, daughter, heiress, and legitimate successor of Ferdinand VII, it is a continuation, I believe, of the eleven years.)

Caballero then said that the choice in such a vital theoretical matter could not be left up to two or three individuals. In other words, Martínez was treading on dangerous ground if he continued this line of argument. Now we should note that Caballero declares the contemporary administration to be a continuation of both periods. But since the periods are totally opposed in principle, such an assertion implies the unavoidability of choices among existing contradictory legislation. At the same time, Caballero attributes to Martínez the opinion that his régime is a continuation of neither.

With the debate now hinging on such fine distinctions, the prime minister had to be extremely careful in charting a course for his arguments. Indeed, it seems that throughout the discussion, Progressive orators attempted to exacerbate Martínez into making a blunder, very subtly to be sure. On September 21, for instance, Joaquín María López said:

> Nos ha dicho por último el Sr. Ministro que aquí no hay vence-dores ni vencidos, y preguntándose si el actual Gobierno era una continuación del constitucional, se ha contestado a sí mismo: *no, no y mil veces no.* Pero prescindiendo de la inoportunidad de la re-flexión, porque no se trata de anular todos los actos de un de-terminado sistema, ¿es el actual, el de la justicia y el de una libertad razonable; es el del decoro y dignidad nacional, para que no pase-mos por un empréstito violento, injusto y ruinoso, sellando nuestro desacierto con las lágrimas y la miseria de tantas familias? Yo con-testaré usando del mismo giro de expresión del Sr. Ministro: *sí, sí y mil veces sí.* (*Pr.*, p. 326)

> (The Honorable Minister told us lastly that there are neither van-quishers nor vanquished here and, having asked if the present Government were a continuation of the constitutional one, he answered himself: *no, no, a thousand times no.* But, dispensing with the inopportuneness of this remark, because there is no en-deavor to annul all the acts of a specific system, let me ask: can the present one be considered that of justice and reasonable lib-erty, that of national decorum and dignity, if we allow a violent, unjust, and ruinous loan to pass, putting as a seal on our blunder the tears and misery of so many families? Let me answer using the same turn of phrase as the Honorable Minister's: *yes, yes, a thou-sand times yes.*)

When it came his turn to speak, Martínez must have felt com-pelled to take up these theoretical arguments, almost as if the Progressives had drawn him into them against his will. He deftly met the challenge by elaborating upon the very theme that Ca-ballero had expounded to describe the ministry's position, the "vencedores ni vencidos" concept, words that neither he nor To-reno had actually spoken, but which constituted nonetheless an epigrammatization of Martínez's ideas:

El segundo principio que se nos atribuye es el de que no hay partido vencedor ni vencido. Esto lo han dicho y lo repiten los Secretarios del Despacho. En España no hay ahora partido político vencedor ni vencido: no, señores: ¿cuál es el partido vencedor? ¿Dónde está? ¿Quién ha salvado la patria? ¿Dónde están los libertadores para que les distribuyamos coronas?... En la España no hay más que la potestad regia que no ha concedido mercedes, sino que ha restituido derechos, que ha levantado la nación abatida para colocarla en el punto que le corresponde, para enlazar su libertad y gloria con la firmeza y esplendor del Trono.

Tercer principio: Que el Gobierno actual era una especie de género neutro (si no he entendido mal), y que no era ni continuación del régimen de la Constitución ni del Gobierno absoluto. Esto es cierto. El Gobierno actual se ha propuesto el restablecimiento de las antiguas leyes fundamentales de nuestra nación, amoldadas a lo que exige ahora la mudanza de tiempos y de circunstancias. (*Pr.*, p. 313)

(The second principle attributed to us is that there is no conquering or conquered party. The Secretaries of the Cabinet have said this and repeat it. In Spain there is now no vanquishing or vanquished political party. No, gentlemen. What is the vanquishing party? Where is it? Who saved the nation? Where are the liberators, so we may distribute crowns to them?... In Spain there is only the royal power, which has bestowed no favors but has restituted rights, which has raised an abject nation in order to place it at its suitable level, to join its freedom and glory with the firmness and splendor of the Throne.

Now the third principle: that the present Government was a kind of neutral gender—if I understood correctly—and that it was neither a continuation of the Constitutional régime nor of the absolute Government. That is correct. The present Government has aimed at the reinstatement of the ancient fundamental laws of our nation, molded to what the change of times and circumstances demand.)

Perhaps the reader will now sense, despite Larra's ridicule, the great utility of Martínez's neomedieval concept of government and how well it served him to confound his opponents.

The next day's session began with a speech by Francisco Belda, a Progressive who decided to employ a strong counter-argument. Hinting at the spurious origin of the Ominous Decade, he hit upon an analogous phrase to describe the results of Angoulême's intervention: "No hubo entonces en España más que perseguidores y perseguidos, víctimas y verdugos" (*Pr.*, p. 318—"There were then only persecutors and persecuted, victims and executioners"). Then Joaquín María López followed with the lengthy speech attacking the ministry, from which a paragraph was quoted above. Later in the session the Marqués de Montevirgen dwelt on this point even more explicitly:

> Ha dicho S.S. que aquí no hay vencedores ni vencidos; perdóneseme que diga que no puede en manera alguna adoptarse esta proposición tan absolutamente, y que S. S. ha sacrificado, por decirlo así, un principio a una brillante imagen. Aquí hay un principio vencedor y otro vencido; y no hay ni puede haber cambio político sin que esto suceda.
>
> Se ha cambiado el principio de un Gobierno absoluto por . . . la augusta Reina Gobernadora, que se ha puesto al frente del principio que ha triunfado . . . (*Pr.*, p. 337)

> (His Lordship said that there are here neither vanquishers nor vanquished. Pardon my saying that this proposition cannot in any way be adopted so absolutely, and that His Lordship has sacrificed, so to speak, a principle to a brilliant trope. Here there is a vanquishing principle and a vanquished one; there neither is nor can there be political change without the occurrence of this.
>
> The principle of an absolute government has been changed by . . . our august Queen Regent, who has placed herself at the head of the principle that has triumphed . . .)

An interesting variation on the theme is found in a speech by the Marqués de Torremejía, who, though he spoke against the loan, did so in a conciliatory manner by obfuscating the issue:

> No se diga que aquí hay un partido que dé la ley, como sucede en ciertas circunstancias. En balde se pregunta: ¿cuál es el vencedor y cuál el vencido? Cuando se hacen semejantes preguntas, es porque no hay vencidos ni vencedores, sino en los campos de batalla. En 1823 y 24 nadie preguntaba si había vencidos; claro estaba que los había, y harto dura era su suerte y el yugo del vencedor. Pero ahora no sucede así; recuérdense los sucesos con imparcialidad: ellos hablan . . . (*Pr.*, p. 361)

(Let it not be said that there is here a party which makes the law, as happens in certain circumstances. In vain do we ask who are the conqueror and the conquered. When such questions are asked, it is because there are no vanquishers and vanquished save on battlefields. In 1823 and '24 no one asked if there were some vanquished. Of course there were, and their luck and the vanquisher's yoke were hard. But this does not happen now; let us recall the events impartially: they speak for themselves . . .)

The marquess likewise reminded his audience that upon Fernando's death the queen had called on the Voluntarios Realistas to protect her daughters, and with similar arguments he concluded that "en nuestro campo no hay más que vencedores" (*Pr.*, p. 361 —"in our camp there are only vanquishers"). As for the Guebhard loan, "en cuanto a reconocer me es indiferente, con tal que no se pague" ("as for recognizing it, this is immaterial to me, as long as it is not paid"). But this equivocal remark was followed by an admonition:

Sepan esos prestamistas clandestinos que si hacen sus operaciones con un partido, no basta que venza éste por un corto espacio de tiempo, sino que es preciso que siga vencedor todo cuanto necesiten para reintegrarse, y que de lo contrario así que se restablezca el orden y el imperio de las leyes son nulos de todo punto, y pierden lo que dieron." (*Pr.*, p. 362)

(Let it be known to these clandestine moneylenders that if they carry on their transactions with one party, it will not avail them if the latter is the winner for a short time. The party must remain the vanquisher long enough for them to get repaid. Otherwise, as soon as order and the rule of law are restored, the contracts are null and void, and they lose what they gave.)

The same day, Damián de Lasanta and the Conde de las Navas, who opposed the loan, were answered by two ministerialists; and then the "vencedores ni vencidos" topic was heard in the chamber for the last time when García Carrasco reminded his audience of the turmoils that had brought fast change only a few months before:

Aunque no es precisamente de la cuestión presente, como se ha dejado oír en este lugar esa frase de vencedores y vencidos, me permitirá el Estamento que conteste a ella. Yo no hubiera creído jamás que semejante idea se hubiese pronunciado aquí; pero yo afirmaré que hay vencedores y vencidos, pues sin haberlos no hubiera habido el cambio inmediato y decidido que hemos visto. Además de lo ocurrido en la Granja, todo el mundo sabe que el deplorable Ministerio de Cea Bermúdez no dejó el campo sino después de una batalla, en la que aunque no se peleó con las armas, hubo contienda, y moralmente existieron vencedores y vencidos. Posteriormente los enemigos del Trono de Isabel II, los enemigos de las libertades patrias han tratado de conspirar; y por todas partes, y en especial en Navarra y provincias Vascongadas, han sido vencidos. La excelsa Reina Gobernadora se gloria de estar a la cabeza de estos vencedores, de estos sostenedores de la libertad; y siendo así, no sé por qué el Sr. Secretario del Despacho de Estado se desdora de pertenecer a ellos. (*Pr.*, p. 365)

(Though it may not concern the present question, since the phrase "vanquishers and vanquished" has been mentioned in this hall, I beg the Chamber to let me reply. I would never have believed that such an idea might find expression here; but I will affirm that there are vanquishers and vanquished, because without their existence the immediate and decisive change seen by us would not have taken place. Besides the Granja events, everyone knows that the deplorable Zea Ministry left the field only after a battle, where strife occurred even though people did not fight with weapons, and morally there were vanquishers and vanquished. Afterwards the enemies of the Throne of Isabel II, the enemies of our liberties, attempted to conspire, and everywhere, especially in Navarre and the Basque provinces, they were vanquished. Our excellent Queen Regent proudly heads these vanquishers, these sustainers of freedom. This being so, I cannot understand how the Honorable Secretary of State can become tarnished by belonging to them.)

García Carrasco, as we can see, shrewdly changed the concept of "vencedores y vencidos" from what Martínez had taken it to mean. Anticipated in this argumentative deviation by the Marqués de Torremejía, he was thus enabled to place the prime minister's sincerity at issue. It seems as though the whole debate went according to plans carefully laid by the Progressives, who may have agreed to trap the minister into focusing the discussion on an elu-

sive concept upon which the Progressives could embroider more
fruitfully than he.

The finishing touch was executed by Larra, who twisted the
significance of the expression by treating it as Voltaire would
have a Leibnitzian maxim. For Figaro, the phrase "vencedores y
vencidos" is like Pangloss's "tout est au mieu" in *Candide:*

> Convengamos en que es un gran consuelo para uno que lo pasa
> mal decirle al oído: *Lo pasa usted mal, pero hágase usted cargo de
> que no hay vencedores ni vencidos.* En no habiendo vencedores ni
> vencidos, que te roben al volver de una esquina, que te salga una
> lupia en medio de la frente, o una joroba en medio de las espaldas,
> nada te debe importar; porque sin esos *vencedores* y *vencidos* no
> hay felicidad posible en la tierra, como lo hallarás escrito en todos
> los filósofos. Despachaos, pues, los liberales casteçaos a vencer a
> alguien y si los carlistas no se dejan vencer, venceos por el pronto
> a vosotros mismos, que ése será el vencimiento que esos señores
> querrán dar a entender como necesario para que todo entre en
> caja, sobre ser esa clase de victoria la más agradable a los ojos de
> Dios. (2: 19)

> (Let us agree that it's a great consolation to anyone for whom
> things are going badly to whisper in his ear: *You're having a hard
> time, but take into consideration that there are no vanquishers or
> vanquished.* Since there are no vanquishers or vanquished, then if
> you get held up while you're turning the corner, or a tumor starts
> growing in the middle of your forehead, or a hump on your back,
> don't mind a bit. Because without those *vanquishers* and *van-
> quished* there's no possible happiness on earth, as you will find
> written down in all the philosophers. Make haste then, you Baeti-
> can and Tarraconensian liberals, to vanquish someone, and if the
> Carlists don't let themselves be conquered, overcome in yourselves
> the devil, the world, and the flesh, for this will be the final con-
> quest, as those gentlemen give us to understand, necessary for ev-
> erything to fit neatly into little boxes and coffers, especially since
> this kind of victory is the most pleasing in the eyes of God.)

We may perceive that Figaro goes beyond Voltairian transformation, for after the words "todos los filósofos," he takes up the
political issue again. If the Spanish liberal follows ministerialist
policy, he will have to "vencerse a sí mismo," he will have to
dominate, or worse yet, repudiate his ideals for a new Spain and

become a Moderate, compromising and static. At the root of Larra's Progressive opinion, then, is the feeling that progress is impossible in Spain at the time without a clear recognition that there are indeed victors and vanquished. And, of course, the apparent ease with which Figaro can establish a connection between a specific problem and the general problem of Spain, as in this paragraph, is due in large measure to the strength of his convictions. This may help us understand the esteem in which the Generation of '98 held him. They too were wont to examine each situation in the light of Spain's general problem. Larra, however, accomplished his literary purpose through pathetic wit, whereas his modern admirers sought theirs in a philosophical or poetic vein.

The 'Segunda carta" contains another theme inspired by the debate. This is the ironic notion that it is advantageous to undertake anything by beginning with the end. During the discussions much controversy arose over the order of procedure for dealing with the budget, of which the national debt was an inseparable part. Toreno, who was preparing this budget, had assumed that the Guebhard loan would be recognized by the Cortes. Hence the interest on the loan is included in the budget, swelling the latter, and thus requiring in turn a larger loan from Rothschild. Consequently, Toreno felt compelled to point out the difficulties the government would encounter as a result of the committee's change in its proposal:

> El plan, como lo ha presentado la comisión (perdónenme los señores que la componen), tiene un grandísimo defecto, y es haber invertido el orden de las ideas; porque hablar de lo que se necesita, y fijar la suma sin que se sepa antes si el déficit será mayor o menor, parece no muy oportuno. (*Pr.*, p. 248)

> (The plan as presented by the committee—with my apologies to its members—contains a great defect, namely, inverting the order of the ideas; because to speak of what is needed, and to fix a sum without knowing beforehand whether the deficit will be greater or less, does not appear very timely.)

The secretary of the treasury presumes, of course, that it is his ideas which follow a natural order. But the opposition could argue just as well that Toreno should not have presumed that recognition would be forthcoming, and that it was now his fault if a new budget had to be presented with the Guebhard interest payments eliminated. For clarity's sake, let us review the problem: the ministers had first determined the national debt (1), then made a request for a loan (2), and would later present the budget (3). The Progressives contended that (1) had not been properly determined (because recognition of the Guebhard loan had been assumed); hence, owing to the elimination of repayments, (3) should really be less than the government anticipated. And, as a consequence, they could make no judgment about (2).

Toreno's point of view was defended on September 18 by the Marqués de Falces, a ministerialist, who compared national finances to a private inheritance:

> Por algunos señores se ha indicado que no tiene relación inmediata el reconocimiento de la deuda extranjera con el empréstito; pero a mí me parece al contrario. Nosotros nos hallamos en el mismo caso que aquel que hereda unos bienes que han estado mal administrados y se encuentran casi destruidos. Lo primero que debe hacer es arreglar su conducta y sus gastos para volver aquéllos a su primitivo ser, y por consiguiente conseguir un crédito que le facilite las anticipaciones que necesite. (*Pr.*, p. 284)

> (A few gentlemen have indicated that recognition of the foreign debt has no immediate relation to the loan. But to me, it seems to be the contrary. We find ourselves in the same situation as a person who inherits an estate that has been ill administered and is almost destroyed. The first thing he must do is regulate his conduct and expenses to bring his possessions back to their original state, and thereby obtain the credit that will get him the loans he needs.)

Two days later Fermín Caballero replied by claiming that it was the government, not the commitee, which had failed to do first things first:

> ¿Se ha de poner a las Cortes en el conflicto en que nos ha puesto este proyecto de ley, cuando apenas están enteradas de ningún ramo de cuantos componen la administración; cuando no se les ha presentado la Memoria de Hacienda, que les ha sido prometida; y cuando no se trata de las exposiciones de los demás Secretarios del

Despacho, ni aun se ha concedido a los Procuradores del reino el derecho de preguntar?[9] (*Pr.*, p. 306)

(Must the Cortes be thrown into the conflict this projected law has brought us to, when we have hardly received information from any of the several branches of the administration, when the promised Treasury report has not been presented, when the reports of the other Secretaries of the Cabinet are not being considered, and when the right to ask questions has not even been conceded to the Procuradores of the realm?)

A variant on this theme is found in the speech of Trueba y Cosío, who dwells on the possibility of amending after erring:

Hay otra alternativa; si no reconocemos [the Guebhard loan], podemos errar; pero estamos a tiempo de enmendar nuestro yerro: si reconocemos, ¿qué haremos luego? Si vemos que hemos hecho mal, ¿tendremos tiempo de enmendarlo? Yo llamo la atención del Estamento sobre esto, y deseo que los Sres. Procuradores del reino reflexionen bien si después de votar que se reconozca toda la deuda desde el año 23 acá, habrá modo de enmendar el yerro; y que no reconociéndolo, si nos equivocamos, podremos enmendarlo dentro de un mes o un año. (*Pr.*, p. 371)

(There is another alternative. We could err by not recognizing the Guebhard loan, but we still have time to correct our error. If we recognize it, what can we do then? If we see we have done wrong, shall we have time to change it? I call the attention of the Chamber to this point, and wish the Procuradores of the realm might reflect on this: if, after voting that the whole debt from 1823 on be recognized, there will be any way to emend the error; and, in case we did not recognize it, if, should we be in error, we could emend it within a month or a year.)

Since Larra states ironically that in Spain last things are done first, he must obviously hold to the Progressive point of view. We might also note how he manages to connect the theme of consecution with that of error and emendation:

Sin duda será cosa que te asombre, querido Silva Carvalho d'Alburquerque, recibir mi segunda carta antes que la primera. Ya se ve, acostumbrados ahí en Portugal a proceder lógicamente y a empezar siempre por el principio, me tratarás de loco, si es que no me tratas de ministerial. Pero te has de hacer varios cargos. En primer lugar, no en todas partes hay las mismas costumbres. En España solemos empezar por lo último, dejándonos lo principal en el tintero, y pensar que yo solo me he de salir del camino trillado es pedir peras al olmo, o, lo que es lo mismo, libertad a un Ministerio; es buscar cotufas en el golfo; más claro, por si no entiendes este refrán, es buscar una sentencia de muerte en causa carlista.

Ni yo veo la necesidad de empezar siempre por el principio: sobre ser esto cosa que a cualquiera le ocurriría, y aquí no somos cualquiera, el empezar por lo último tiene la singular ventaja, que a ti no te habrá ocurrido, de aparecer las cosas acabadas desde luego. Las naciones se manejan como los sonetos; los cuales, si han de ser buenos, no hay poeta mediano que no los empiece por el último verso. Agrega a esto que de hacer las cosas mal resulta otro beneficio, cual es el de poderlas enmendar, y así lo que no va en el libro va en la fe de erratas. A cuyo propósito viene de perilla recordarte el cuento de nuestro don Bartolomé, acerca del mal pintor que quería blanquear, y luego pintar su casa, y a quien un inteligente aconsejaba que mejor le estaría para su gloria pintarla primero y después blanquearla. (2: 17)

(Doubtless you will be amazed, my dear Silva Carvalho d'Alburquerque, to receive my second letter before the first. Of course, accustomed as you are in Lusitania to proceed logically and always begin at the beginning, you'll probably call me mad, unless you call me a ministerialist. Nevertheless, several things must be taken into consideration. First of all, not in all places does one find the same customs. In Spain we are wont to begin at the end, leaving the main part in the inkpot. To think that I alone among my countrymen should get off the beaten track is asking for pears from the elm tree, or in other words, liberty from a Ministry. It's like getting figs from thistles; to put it more clearly, in case you don't get this proverb, it's like seeking the death sentence for the Carlist cause.

Anyway, I don't see the need for always starting at the beginning. Besides the fact that this is the sort of thing anybody could think up—and here we're just not anybody—to begin at the end has the singular advantage, which probably never occurred to you, of making things appear finished right away. Nations must be handled like sonnets. If they're going to be good, they get written beginning with the last verse, as any mediocre poet can tell you. Add to this that doing things badly yields another benefit, to wit, being able to emend them, so that what doesn't go in the book can go in the list of errata. Apropos of this, perhaps you recall our dear don Bartolomé's story about the bad painter who wanted to white-wash and then paint his house, and who was advised by a wit that for the sake of his reputation it would be better if he painted first and whitewashed afterwards.)

We could possibly surmise that Larra's remark, "otro beneficio, cual es el de poderlas enmendar," parodies Trueba's speech. Yet Trueba was definitely Progressive, especially since he expressed his intention to vote against the loan. How is it then that Figaro directly satirizes him? The explanation is quite simple, I believe, because it should be evident that most Progressives would have been utterly displeased with Trueba for even suggesting the possi-bility that the Cortes could err by not recognizing the loan. The true Progressive considered it axiomatic that recognition would be an error; the matter was for him a question of ideology, not of immediate financial necessity. We can assume that Larra's friends were not ready to sacrifice their principles to political or eco-nomic expediency; the world had to know that the Guebhard loan would never be recognized.

The "Primera contestación" touches on the same theme of order of precedence. Here the author's humor, however, is based on a pun on *cartas* which may possibly allude to the use of the words "descarte" and "descartar" in references to the Guebhard loan after it failed to be recognized. See *Pr.*, pp. 392, 397, 399, 402, 413, and especially Díez González on September 30: "Ha-biéndonos descartado del empréstito de Guebhard, ha resultado por esta razón un descargo de 40 millones a favor de la nación, aunque yo saco solamente 37 millones" (*Pr.*, p. 411—"Discarding the Guebhard loan has resulted in a forty million acquittance in favor of the nation, although [according to my calculations] I get only thirty-seven million"). Although *descartar* is a dead metaphor, its reflexive use in conjunction with *sacar* could sug-gest a card game. The imaginary correspondent's reply begins:

Dices, querido liberal casteçao, que me asombrará el recibir tu segunda carta antes que la primera. Te equivocaste, amigo, como es estrella vuestra en todas ocasiones: a mí en hablándoseme de ese país no me asombra nada. Hubiérame antes parecido cosa rara haber recibido tus cartas por su orden. Ya por acá sabemos que en punto a *cartas* no jugáis muy limpio.

Pero en fin, he recibido la segunda, a propósito de lo cual te diré que vengan ellas, y vengan como y cuando puedan, que yo luego las ordenaré, como Dios me diese a entender, a semejanza de aquel que, no sabiendo más de ortografía que muchos gobernantes de gobierno, enviaba juntos en la postdata gran número de comas y signos de puntuación, añadiendo a su corresponsal: "Por lo que hace a los puntos y las comas, ahí van todos juntos para que usted se entretenga en ponerlos en su lugar, que yo ando de prisa." (2: 19).

(Dear Castilian liberal, you say that I'll be amazed to receive your second letter before the first. You were wrong, my friend, as you Spaniards are on every occasion. When anyone talks to me about Spain, nothing amazes me. On the contrary, it would have seemed strange to receive your letters in the right order. We already know here that you people don't play a straight *card game*.

Anyhow, I've received the second one, apropos of which I'll just say: let them come, whenever and however they can, and I'll put them in order myself, in whatever way God allows me to figure it out, like the fellow who, not knowing how to spell much better than many government officials, used to send his correspondent a great number of commas and punctuation marks in the postscript, adding: "As for the periods and commas, here they are all in one bunch so you can entertain yourself by putting them in their places; I'm in a hurry.")

It seems that there is here much more than an obvious pun on the safety and efficiency of the mails, censorship, and the Spaniards' reputation among the Portuguese for being card sharks. Allusion to the debate is a possibility, corroborated by Larra's italicizing of "cartas." Perhaps he is also chaffing the Moderates for having been fooled, by mooting over a technicality, into switching the order of the foreign debt and the public employees debates, as we shall see in the next chapter.

Another theme occurring in the "Segunda carta" involves the image of roads and paths. It may possibly reflect the dead metaphor "camino," frequently heard during the debates, which made its first appearance on September 17 in the Conde de las Navas's caustic remark about the ministers:

no porque yo desconfíe de ninguno de los Sres. Secretarios del Despacho en particular, sino porque con la mejor buena voluntad pueden equivocar el camino, cuyos resultados serían desgraciadamente los mismos que si se hubiese hecho con intención. (*Pr.*, p. 271)

(not because I distrust any of the Secretaries of the Cabinet in particular, but because, even with the best of intentions, they can take the wrong path, which would unfortunately have the same results as if it had been done on purpose.)

The day after Navas's speech, government policy found a champion in Ángel Polo y Monje, who felt that "no habiendo otro camino" ("there being no other path to follow"), the legislators had to find "la felicidad que consiste en la unión del Gobierno con las Cortes" (*Pr.*, p. 273—"the felicity which consists in the union of the Government with the Cortes"). Also on September 18 Martínez de la Rosa defended his honesty against the insinuations of García Carrasco, upholding the negotiations that his government had made with Rothschild and Ardoin: "Se entró en el camino legal, el camino opuesto a las tramas clandestinas" (*Pr.*, p. 280—"a legal path was followed, a path contrary to clandestine deals"). On September 30 the quixotic Ramón Llano Chavarri, speaking out against all loans and proposing wild schemes for raising money, announced: "Creo que se debe abandonar ese camino ruinoso que hasta ahora ha llevado a esta desgraciada nación a hacer empréstito sobre empréstito para pagar solamente los intereses de ellos"[10] (*Pr.*, p. 416—"I think we must abandon this ruinous path that up to now has taken this unfortunate nation to get loan after loan in order to pay only their interests"). The use of this ordinary, half-dead metaphor by the orators may have inspired Larra to play on the word:

Con respecto a caminos no hay otra novedad, si es que eso se puede llamar novedad, que el seguir los más de ellos interceptados, incluso el de las reformas. A bien que siempre nos queda expedito el del cielo, que es el gran camino, y por el cual caminamos a pasos agigantados con toda la paciencia de buenos cristianos; los demás en realidad más son veredas que caminos.

A propósito de veredas, ya sabrás que han nombrado a Mina para la guerra de Vizcaya. Mina hará una carrera rápida con este

Gobierno. Un año ha tardado no más en ser empleado. Otro año más, y sabe Dios adónde llegará.[11] (2: 18)

(With respect to paths there's nothing new except the fact, if it can be called new, that most of them are still intercepted, including that of reforms. At least we can be thankful that the path to heaven is still open to us. This is of course the great way, on which we are travelling with giant steps and all the patience of good Christians. The others are really trails rather than paths.

Speaking of trails, you probably already know that they named Mina for the Biscay war. Mina will have a promising career in this Government. It took him no more than a year to get the job. In another year, God knows how far he'll get!)

With his usual skill, Figaro again takes one word to unite several ideas. The main point of the first paragraph quoted above is that the only possible road toward national regeneration had to be paved with reforms—including press freedom—and that loans and taxes were but stopgap measures, "veredas." This last word helps to link the two paragraphs stylistically, for in the second it takes on additional meaning. *Vereda* is usually applied to narrow mountain paths rather than those on flat land; hence it may well suggest to the reader the guerrilla terrain of the Basque country,[12] as well as the government's slowness in bringing to an end the war against the elusive mountaineers. Furthermore, the word "empleado" provides a thread for the introduction of the next passage, as we shall see.

The Próceres met only once between September 18 and October 13. During that session, held on October 4, there was little business, except that the question of government employees came up, as evidenced by the following entry in the *Diario:*

Leída otra comunicación del Sr. Presidente del Consejo de Ministros, en que participaba un Real decreto por el que queda a voluntad del Estamento la provisión de las vacantes de la Secretaría y demás dependencias del mismo, se acordó que se contestase quedar enterado, y haber recibido con agrado esta nueva prueba de la bondad de S.M. (*Ilus.*, p. 94)

(A communication from the Prime Minister was read, announcing a royal decree placing at the disposition of the Chamber vacant positions in the ministry and its dependencies. It was agreed to send the acknowledgment, expressing the pleasure of receiving this new proof of Her Majesty's kindness.)

This should easily explain Larra's next paragraph, linked to the previous one by the word "emplean." It contains two remarks, one about the infrequency of meetings, the other about the topic discussed in the lone session:

> El Estamento de Próceres tuvo anteayer una sesión: es probable que tenga otras. —Sabrás cómo ya se emplean por todas partes los hombres de talento. No se da un solo destino que no sea al mérito.[13]

(The Estamento de Próceres held a session yesterday; it may probably hold more. You must know how men of talent are already being employed everywhere. Not a single position is given for anything but merit.)

The concession of civil service appointments to the upper house in cases of vacancy was certainly no solution of the problem. It gives an appearance of cunningly sidestepping the issue by making a gesture to the Cortes' "rubber-stamp" chamber. In the lower house the question had been broached forthrightly. On September 17 García Carrasco had attacked the faults of the judicial system, where magistrates appointed during the former régime predominated. He charged that two-thirds of the *corregidores* were Carlists. Carrasco, moreover, ironically connected the civil servant problem to the military situation: "¿Con qué objeto se tiene aquí este ejército? No puedo adivinarlo, señor. ¿Habría tantos facciosos, si los empleados de Calomarde no continuaran en sus destinos?" (*Pr.*, p. 260—"For what purpose is this army kept here? Sir, I cannot guess. Would there be so many rebels if Calomarde's employees did not stay in their jobs?"). This may have provided a topic for Larra, who also links the two themes of the employees and the war when he speaks of Mina, as we saw above.

Along with that of the vanquishers and vanquished, there is another important central idea in the "Primera contestación de un liberal de allá." It emanates from the famous remark commonly attributed to Martínez de la Rosa that the pretender, who had succeeded in returnng to Spain clandestinely, was merely one more rebel ("un faccioso más"). Nevertheless, my search for this particular locution in the *Diario* of each house has proven fruitless. I am inclined to think that Martínez, who shortly before had used the phrase "mal aconsejado príncipe" ("ill-advised prince"), would not have inserted such a blunt comment in his meticulously prepared speeches. In any case, though his use of the phrase itself cannot be ascertained, the ideas that would have inspired it do appear in the prime minister's oratory:

> cuando el ejército de Portugal [i.e., Rodil's observation army] llegó a las provincias [of the Northeast], casi al mismo tiempo apareció el Pretendiente, y esto reanimó el entusiasmo de sus partidarios. Afortunadamente el Gobierno no se equivocó en su pronóstico cuando dijo que a pesar de la espectativa de toda Europa, la venida del Pretendiente no agravaría nuestra situación: fuera de España se contaban los días que tardaría en llegar a Burgos, a Madrid; pero a pesar de que su venida causó una sorpresa notable en todas partes, *no produjo*, como habíamos pronosticado, *casi ningún efecto*. El Pretendiente ha tratado de contratar empréstitos y no lo ha logrado; ha tratado de armar barcos que están paralizados. No dirá el Gobierno hasta qué punto ha contribuido a ello. (*Pr.*, p. 431; italics mine)

> (when the army that had been stationed along the Portuguese border got to the Northeast provinces, the Pretender appeared at almost the same time, and this revived his partisans' enthusiasm. Fortunately the Government did not err in its prognosis when it said that, in spite of the expectations of all Europe, the Pretender's arrival would not aggravate our situation. Outside Spain people were counting how many days he would take to get to Burgos, then to Madrid. But although his arrival caused noticeable surprise everywhere, *it produced*, as we had predicted, *almost no effect*. The Pretender has tried to obtain loans without success; and to fit out ships that are immobilized. The Government will not say to what extent it contributed to this.)

Martínez seems to have appraised the situation erroneously, however, for Carlos's presence gave his partisans more fighting courage; and besides, his foreign supporters sent money and supplies with greater assurance.[14] Larra perceived the falsity of the prime minister's reasoning and restated it ironically:

> Que está el pretendiente en Vizcaya..., y bien, ¿y qué es el pretendiente? Según una feliz expresión de un diputado francés, traducida y arreglada para vosotros por un amigo tuyo y mío, nada: *un faccioso más*. (2: 20)

> (The pretender is in Biscay?... So what? What is the pretender? According to the felicitous phrase of a French deputy, translated and arranged for you by a friend of yours and mine, nothing: *just another rebel*.)

Augusto Conte asserts that Martínez was really imitating Louis XVIII, who, upon returning to France after the Napoleonic era, declared that he was just another Frenchman.[15] If this is the case, then Figaro's remark is a subtle bit of low burlesque. Martínez, who was *procurador* for Granada, spoke for the Spanish Crown; Louis XVIII spoke for himself, but that does not really make him a deputy.[16]

Now Figaro sets about to employ the phrase in all sorts of ways. Carlist growth, often mentioned in the debates, becomes "Bien contado, nada: diez y ocho mil facciosos más" ("correctly counted, nothing: eighteen thousand more rebels"). The defeat of Luis Ángel Carondelet is "Nada: una sorpresa más" ("nothing: another surprise attack"). The ten-year period can be dismissed as "Nada: diez años más de despotismo" ("nothing: ten more years of despotism"). The Panglossian note makes itself felt especially in the sentence: "y que te ahorcasen a ti, por ejemplo. ¿Y qué sería esto comparado con la inmensidad del universo? Nada: un ahorcado más en el mundo" ("and if they should hang you, for example. What would that be compared to the immensity of the universe? Nothing: just another man in the gallows"). In the meantime the national debt adds up to nothing but "una miseria más . . . una deuda más . . . un empréstito más" ("just one more pittance . . . just another loan"). Finally, the cholera, not unlike the Lisbon earthquake in *Candide*, is "una calamidad más" (2: 20—"just another calamity").

We should note especially the stylistic balance provided by the process; the latter half of the essay evolves from the phrase "un faccioso más" in the same way that the first half develops from "vencedores y vencidos."

9

❦❦❦❦❦❦❦❦❦❦❦❦❦❦❦❦❦

CIVIL SERVANTS

Recognition of the Guebhard loan, as we can gather from the foregoing chapter, necessarily involved the paramount question of governmental continuity. If the acts of the Triennium and the Ominous Decade were to be considered equally valid in determining the present régime's responsibility, would not some fundamental contradictions arise? The next issue to come up in Cortes plainly demonstrated the inevitability of legal disparities. And because this issue, the status of the presently unemployed Triennium functionaries, dealt more directly with particular livelihoods than with public funds, it elicited considerably more vehemence than the Guebhard loan. Within a fixed number of civil service positions available, which appointments were valid, those of Calomarde or of the constitutional régime? Larra, like every Liberal, was deeply interested in the question and voiced his opinion in several essays, beginning with "Los tres no son más que dos." In this early piece (February 18, 1834) the *comparsa blanca* blurts out at the *negros* that their real motive is, among others, to snap up "los empleos, en fin, que por tantos años tuvimos nosotros" (1: 349—"in short, the jobs we had for so many years"). Figaro's sympathy for jobless Liberals is manifest also in the letter to the "Bachiller" (July 31):

> Díceme que viene vuesa merced a Madrid. Si está pronto a presentar sus cuentas a Dios, venga cuanto antes. Si viene a pretender, o ha tenido empleo y ha sido emigrado en tiempo de la Constitución, no hay para qué. Si es carlista puede venir seguro de adelantar algo, que carlistas, y muchos, encontramos en buenos destinos, que le favorezcan; preguntaráme tal vez si no los quitan: ¿para qué, si andando el tiempo ellos se irán muriendo? (1: 424)

> (You say you're coming to Madrid. If it's for the purpose of presenting an accounting to Saint Peter, then come immediately. If it's to solicit employment, or you had a job in the days of the Constitution and were exiled, there's no reason to. If you're a Carlist you can come certain to make progress, because there are Carlists, and many, in good jobs who would favor you. You'll probably ask me why they aren't dismissed. Why should they be, since they'll die off with time?)

Another indication of Larra's position on the matter is an incisive statement in the "Segunda carta" about Mina's appointment, as we saw in chapter 8.

"La cuestión transparente" (2: 21–23), published in *El Observador* on October 19, treats the subject more profoundly than the other essays. We should likewise pay close attention to the barbs of the "Tercera carta de un liberal de acá a un liberal de allá" (2: 46–47). However, unlike "La cuestión transparente," which was probably written before it, the "Tercera carta" remained unpublished until Larra brought it out in his *Colección.*[1] "La cuestión transparente" consists in a witty commentary on a detail of the crucial discussion about government employees. The three-day debate (October 15–17) centered on the "Proyecto de petición sobre revalidación de los empleos concedidos por Real nombramiento en los años de 1820 a 1823." The first two articles of the projected petition, which had been read to the Procuradores over a month earlier, on September 8 (*Pr.*, p. 202), are as follows:

Artículo 1°. Se declaran válidos todos los empleos, grados, honores civiles, militares y eclesiásticos, conferidos por título Real desde 7 de Marzo de 1820 hasta 30 de Setiembre de 1823.

Artículo 2°. Los funcionarios públicos de todas clases que obtuvieron título Real, gozarán de la antigüedad que les corresponda por su nombramiento en la época constitucional. (*Pr.*, Apéndice al núm. 33, p. 2)

(Article 1. All positions, ranks, and civilian, military, and ecclesiastical honors conferred by Royal letters patent March 7, 1820, to September 30, 1823, are declared valid.

Article 2. Public functionaries of all classes who obtained Royal letters patent shall enjoy the seniority corresponding to them through their appointment during the constitutional period.)

The "employees" debate had been scheduled to begin on September 13, which happened to be the final session on the "bill of rights." Five days had therefore elapsed since presentation of the proposal. But when the chamber was ready to start discussion, its president announced that the petitioners had combined the first two articles into one sentence:

Se declaran legítimos todos los nombramientos civiles, militares y eclesiásticos hechos por S.M. desde 7 de Marzo de 1820 hasta 30 de Setiembre de 1823; y en su consecuencia los que los obtuvieron recobrarán sus grados, honores, condecoraciones, antigüedad y rango correspondientes a dichos nombramientos Reales. (*Pr.*, p. 239)

(All civilian, military, and ecclesiastical appointments made by His Majesty from March 7, 1820, to September 30, 1823, are declared legitimate; consequently those who obtained their ranks, honors, decorations, seniority, and the category corresponding to said Royal appointments will regain them.)

Let us now pause to examine how the two versions vary. Their main difference is the word "empleos," appearing only in the first. Since there is a more or less fixed number of government positions, use of the term "empleos" implies that Calomarde's men should be removed in order to give their jobs back to the former civil servants. The second version, on the other hand, would have its conditions satisfied by the distribution of pensions to the Triennium employees; the Ominous Decade jobholders would accordingly retain their posts. Yet there is another important difference between the two versions. The second affected many more people, because the term "nombramientos" includes jobs that can be given out by *jefes de oficina*, whereas only the monarch or his ministers can bestow *títulos Reales*. The Moderates immediately objected to this last-minute change, and obtained postponement of debate until the proposal could be resubmitted through proper channels.

Consequently, action on this matter had to await the conclusion of the foreign debt debate. We should ask ourselves at this point whether the sudden change in the proposal's wording did not constitute a Progressive stratagem. The Progressives had initially drafted a petition strong in one respect and mild in another, and at the last hour substituted for it another proposal, strong and mild in inverse order. It is not improbable that the Progressives themselves planned the postponement on purpose, perhaps making the Moderates appear responsible. Since the latter were acquiring a reputation for their delaying tactics, blame would not fall upon the Progressives at first. But of course, laying blame on the Moderates could not be the sole reason for the Progressives' maneuver, and we should scrutinize the ensuing parliamentary proceedings for a clue.

The clue can be easily found in the intervening foreign debt discussion, which provided the Progressives with the type of argument they did not yet have on September 16. Some new considerations now aided the cause of the former civil servants. Let us recall that the government's proposal for a loan from Rothschild had involved recognition of all previous foreign debts, including those of the Triennium. Hence, by the time the "employees" debate began, as rescheduled, the government had already recognized the legality of some of the Triennium's financial legislation. It stands to reason that recognition of one piece of legislation effected between 1820 and 1823 was bound to open the door to the possibility of recognizing other measures taken during the constitutional period. Consequently, the efficacy of Martínez's arguments in countering Progressive advocacy of the present applicability of these other Triennium acts was considerably weaker than it had been before the foreign debt debates.

This is evidenced in the very first speech dealing with the employees question, delivered by Trueba on October 15: "Tratándose de una cuestión de grande cuantía, se ha repetido en este Estamento que no podrían dejar de reconocerse los actos emanados de un Gobierno legítimamente constituido" (*Pr.*, p. 531—"In dealing with a question of great importance, it was repeated in this Chamber that acts emanating from a legitimately constituted government could not fail to be recognized"). As we can see, the Progressives had strengthened their case by postponing the "employees" debate until the foreign debt discussions were over.

We have observed so far that the proposal had two versions, that of September 8, and that of September 13, which altered and combined the previous one's first two articles. We can assume, therefore, that the drafting committee expected some debate on the wording. This is probably why, when the proposal was again presented to the chamber on October 15, it came in the form of a third version that reflected a compromise between the first two. Rather than use "título Real" or merely "nombramientos," it introduced the term "Reales nombramientos" (*Pr.*, p. 530). Moreover, even this third redaction was altered during debate as a result of Argüelles's[2] apprehensions about its wording (*Pr.*, p. 554), and the petition was finally drafted in a language conveying the presupposed legality of Triennium legislation:

> Siendo legítimos todos los Reales nombramientos civiles, militares y eclesiásticos hechos por S.M. desde 7 de Marzo de 1820 hasta el 30 de Setiembre de 1823, los que los obtuvieron y se hallaban en el goce de ellos en esta última fecha, recobrarán sus grados, honores, condecoraciones y antigüedad correspondientes a dichos nombramientos Reales. (*Pr.*, p. 565)

> (Since all civilian, military, and ecclesiastical Royal appointments made by His Majesty from March 7, 1820, to September 30, 1823, are legitimate, those who obtained them and were in possession of them on the latter date shall regain their ranks, honors, decorations, and seniority corresponding to said Royal appointments.)

This fourth redaction, introduced on the last day of discussion (*Pr.*, p. 558), immediately attracted the obvious Moderate opposition, here championed by Medrano:

No creo necesario en primer lugar entrar en la cuestión de si son legítimos o no los actos del Gobierno que rigió desde el año 1820 al 1823. Digo más: los doy por supuestos. El resultado es que para ponerlos en planta en la actualidad se necesita una rehabilitación; por manera que en la forma en que se ha redactado el artículo 1º., me parece que no es exacto. Porque empezando por la expresión *siendo legítimos,* parece que todo lo que se hizo entonces se debe practicar ahora; lo cual está en contradicción con lo que se ha manifestado relativo a que de aquel sistema debemos tomar lo que nos convenga. (*Pr.,* p. 558)

(First of all I believe it unnecessary to go into the question of whether or not the acts of the Government which ruled from 1820 to 1823 are legitimate. I shall say even more: I take them for granted. The result is that a rehabilitation is needed in order to work them into the organizational structure at present. Thus article 1 in the form in which it has been drawn up seems imprecise. Because, starting with the expression, *are legitimate,* it appears that everything done at the time should be practiced now, which is in contradiction to what was stated relative to having to take from that system whatever suits us.)

It is obvious that the last sentence quoted above reflects the opinions of the prime minister himself. In fact, the debate came close to degenerating into another "vencedores y vencidos" repartee, for Martínez de la Rosa stated again that his government was not a continuation of either of the two preceding regimes, and that the nation had to accept the inheritance of both. The present epoch, he added, could not be called "constitucional, en la acepción que comúnmente solemos dar a esta palabra" ("constitutional, in the acceptation we usually give to the word") because

Esto sería querer anudar aquella época con ésta, y hacer una especie de paréntesis de los diez años pasados, y ya hemos dicho repetidas veces los inconvenientes que de esto resultarían al Trono y al Estado. (*Pr.,* p. 545)

(This would be like wanting to unite that epoch with the present one, and make a sort of parenthesis out of the past ten years, and we have already stated several times the difficulties for the Throne and the State that would result from such a thing.)

Yet such abstractions failed to convince those who beheld with compassion the Liberal civil servants, jobless and impoverished, beside Calomarde's henchmen still in government employ. Trueba was the first to portray their plight. Although he admitted "en honor de la verdad" that "el Gobierno, siguiendo el impulso de sus sentimientos patrióticos y de sus ideas liberales, ha colocado ya a muchos emigrados" (*Pr.*, p. 531—"the Government, acting on the impulse of its patriotic feelings and liberal ideas, has already placed many former exiles"), a great injustice was being committed toward the Liberal repatriates, for they were being treated worse than any other group:

hálláronse como pobres amnistiados; no encontraron abiertos los brazos fraternales que esperaban; hallaron sólo miradas de recelo y de sospecha; se les consideraba como hombres contaminados de una lepra política, incapaces de corrección a quienes ni la experiencia ni las desgracias podrían jamás curar; hombres que fraguaban dentro de su pecho planes constantes de trastorno y de conspiración. ¿Cuál ha sido la conducta que se observó con los emigrados de América? Es cierto que el señor que fue intendente de Cuba goza ahora de 40,000 rs. sólo por la afanosa tarea de pasearse por Madrid, y por el mérito relevante de haber pertenecido a los persas. (*Pr.*, p. 531)

(they found themselves poor amnestied persons. They did not encounter the open fraternal arms they expected. They found only looks of misgiving and suspicion. They were considered men contaminated by a political leprosy, incapable of correction, whom neither experience nor misfortunes could ever cure; men who must have been constantly forging in their bosoms plans for upheaval and conspiracy. But what attitude was taken toward the exiles from America? It is true that the gentleman who was administrator of Cuba is now earning 40,000 reales just for the arduous task of taking walks through Madrid, and for the outstanding merit of having belonged to the Persians [coalition of absolutists which in 1814 helped Ferdinand abrogate the constitution and return as absolute monarch].)

The speaker cited further examples, and the audience likewise could recall some mentioned by Francisco Serrano a month before, during the foreign debt debate: Calomardine *cesantes* who were contributing half their pensions to the Carlist cause (*Pr.*, p. 268). The difference between the treatments accorded Liberal repatriates and former absolutists was indeed shocking, and the audience must have been especially impressed with the bold comparisons uttered by Juan Palarea:

¿Y sería conveniente a la política, sería obrar conforme a los principios de rectitud, tener siempre separados con una mancha, con un sambenito, a estos individuos por haber prestado su juramento a las leyes que existían, que regían y gobernaban en la época del año 1820 al 23? . . . ¿No se les ha de considerar siquiera en la clase de cesantes, como a todos los demás? Los empleados nombrados por el Gobierno anterior que no tiene por conveniente el actual que continúen en el desempeño de sus funciones, los separa, y pasan a clase de cesantes, para disfrutar el sueldo con arreglo a los reglamentos vigentes; ¿y por qué han de ser de peor condición los beneméritos españoles que fieles a sus principios no faltaron a su juramento? (*Pr.*, p. 534)

(And would it be politically suitable, would it be acting in conformity with upright principles, to keep these individuals always separated by means of a taint, a sanbenito, for having made their oath to the laws that existed, that were in force in the epoch from 1820 to 1823? . . . Can't they be considered at least in the retired category, like all others? When the present Government finds it inconvenient that certain employees appointed by the former one continue exercising their functions, it dismisses them and they go into the retired category, benefiting from a salary or pension in accordance with regulations in force. And why must the meritorious Spaniards who, faithful to their principles, did not break their oath, have an inferior status?)

The ministerialists appeared rather inhuman and inconsiderate when they contested such principles. In fact, Palarea's speech was meant as a rejoinder to the ultra-Moderate discourse of the ill-informed Francisco Javier de León Bendicho. Another conservative, the Marqués de Falces, even had the callousness to suggest that the proposed measure would be too costly; to this Antonio González adroitly replied by comparing the expense of proposals that the marquess had defended:

El Sr. Falces, que fue uno de los abogados que defendieron los empréstitos extranjeros, y uno de los que proclamaron que debía reconocerse lo hecho en los diez años; el Sr. Falces, que no tenía entonces en consideración los gravámenes que la nación padecía,
ahora se lastima y llora porque se trata de la remuneración de estos
infelices. Entonces se trataba de millones, y el Sr. Falces con el
mayor calor decía que se pagasen todos los réditos, que montaban
a una gran suma, y ahora se lastima del estado en que se encuentra
la nación para pagar esta cantidad. (*Pr.*, p. 540)

(Mr. Falces, one of the advocates of the defense of foreign loans,
one of those who proclaimed that what was done during the ten
years had to be recognized, who did not then take into consideration the liens and burdens suffered by the nation, now complains
and weeps because the remuneration of these unfortunate persons
has been taken up. We were then dealing with millions, and Mr.
Falces heatedly said that all the payments, which came to a considerable sum, should be made, and now he grieves at the state of
the nation for having to pay this quantity.)

This speech was so convincing that no more members dared pronounce against the petition; whereupon Alcalá Galiano, who
spoke next, remarked: "observo con placer que el Gobierno no se
ha opuesto, ni espero que se oponga a la petición, pues es notoria
su justicia" (*Pr.*, p. 543—"I note with pleasure that the Government has not opposed the petition, and I hope it will not, for its
justice is notorious"). Nevertheless, he added, the wrongs had
not abated, especially the quasi-official discrimination against
amnistiados.

Extreme views were voiced by Joaquín María López, who,
rather than advocate pensions for the Triennium employees, proposed to oust the Calomardines from their jobs:

Enemigos naturalmente de nuestras libertades, si no hay contra
ellos pruebas convincentes de su criminal conducta, al menos son
altamente sospechosos, y por consiguiente deben ser separados de
sus destinos. (*Pr.*, p. 548)

(Being natural enemies of our freedoms, even if there are against
them no convincing proofs of their criminal conduct, at least they
are highly suspicious, and therefore must be discharged from their
posts.)

It speaks well for the other Progressives that they were not so vengefully arbitrary. Toreno replied to López that many functionaries of the constitutional government had also been allowed to serve during the absolutist period, and that in most cases they had conformed to the retention of their posts for reasons of economic survival. Moreover, there were many employees of the ten-year period "que en lugar de servirse de sus empleos para molestar y perseguir, no hicieron sino lo opuesto" (*Pr.*, p. 551— "who instead of using their positions to vex and persecute, did the very opposite"). Though the misfortunes of the exiles should not be forgotten, he added, we should not judge the compromising behavior of those who stayed behind as if it were a crime rather than a sign of weakness. The secretary of the treasury stood for balance and tolerance, citing as an example the cases of Llauder and Mina, once enemies, now fighting side-by-side (*Pr.*, p. 551).

This was as far as the Moderates could go ideologically. On the practical side, Sebastián Cuesta, who said frankly, "Yo soy ministerial," suggested that the petition be redacted in the mild form of: "Se suplica a S.M. tome bajo su protección a los que . . ." (*Pr.*, p. 552—"Your Majesty is implored to take under her protection those who . . ."). But Argüelles impugned this proposed emasculation, and the petition was approved for detailed discussion (*Pr.*, p. 555).

Many of the arguments used in discussing the petition as a whole were repeated the next day when it was considered article by article. Figaro's editor-in-chief, Alcalá Galiano, participated in the session, starting with a pithy remark about his opponents' tactics:

Los que tienen alguna experiencia de la marcha que se sigue en los cuerpos representativos, o por mejor decir en toda reunión de hombres, saben que es cosa muy común el admitir los principios para después rechazar las consecuencias . . ." (*Pr.*, p. 561)

(Those who have any experience of procedures followed in representative bodies, or rather, in any assembly of men, know that it is quite common to admit principles and later reject the consequences . . .)

Then, referring to the former employees' plight, he cleverly embraced the opinion "que no hay vencedores ni vencidos," to which he gave his own interpretation:

> Los vencidos hasta ahora no son los que armados pelean contra la legítima e inocente Reina Isabel II, sino los que lo fueron cuando lo fue la independencia y libertad de la patria. (*Pr.*, p. 562)

> (The vanquished up to now are not those who are in arms, fighting against the legitimate and innocent Queen Isabel II, but those who were [vanquished] when the independence and liberty of the country was.)

Alcalá Galiano had learned perhaps two days before from "Silva Carvalho d'Alburquerque," Figaro's imaginary Portuguese correspondent, that this phrase, like others, could be applied at will to any situation and interpreted in the way which best suited the speaker.

If orators like Galiano could perchance be influenced by the imaginary "liberal de allá," there is little doubt, on the other hand, that their oratory was diligently examined by the other liberal, the "liberal de acá," the flesh-and-blood Figaro. His "Tercera carta" contains an obvious allusion to the debates.

> Así es, que cuando yo digo que somos libres, no quiero yo decir que . . . podemos dar en tierra con los empleados de Calomarde que quedan en su destino, lo cual tampoco sería justo, porque yo no creo que porque los haya empleado éste o aquél dejen por eso de necesitar un sueldo. ¡Pobrecillos! (2: 47)

> (So, when I say we're free, I don't mean we can . . . overthrow the Calomarde employees who are still in their jobs, which wouldn't be fair, because I can't believe that they don't need a salary just because this person or that person employed them. Poor fellows!)

Hence Larra's opinion, though expressed ironically, coincides with Joaquín María López's advocacy of the ouster of Calomarde appointees (see above). In fact, the journalist had uttered this view much earlier, on July 2, in the ironic last paragraph of "Representación de *Norma*":

Una cosa nos queda advertir a la dirección de escena. En la decoración del templo última del segundo acto, se quedaron rezagados
cuatro árboles corpulentos y frondosos de la anterior. Pero ¡qué
arraigados! Parecían cuatro abusos. Hacían la misma figura, en medio de los adornos de la nueva decoración, que algunos empleados
del año 23 en las oficinas del año 34. (1: 415)

(One more piece of advice for the stage management. In the temple scene, the last in act II, four luxuriant and sturdy trees from
the previous one were left behind. But, oh how well rooted! They
cut the same figure, among the adornments of the new decoration,
as some employees from 1823 in the offices of the year 1834.)

Now we might ask ourselves if Alcalá Galiano, Larra's superior
on *El Observador*, would have approved for publication in his
newspaper opinions as extreme as López's, the editor-in-chief of
the more aggressive *Eco del Comercio*.[3] Could it have been Galiano, rather than the censor, who averted publication of the "Tercera carta," deeming it counter-productive? This hypothesis is
unprovable, of course, but nebulous indications lure us toward it.
Figaro aims some subtle hints against the Calomardine appointees
in addition to the remarks quoted above. These hints appear connected with ambiguous allusions to conspiracies, which in turn
make the essay smack of a call to revolt, as I shall attempt to show.

But to get back to the essay's more evident aspects, we should
note that the sessions had served as a reminder of the Decade
functionaries' privileged position in contrast to the injustices perpetrated upon Liberals. This disparity may have inspired Figaro
to develop in the "Tercera carta" an antithesis based on two types
of conspirators, in the hope that his readers might sense an analogy:

Suponte por un momento, aunque te pese hasta el figurártelo, que
eres español. No te aflijas, que esto no es más que una suposición.
Que eres español, y que dices para tu capote, por ejemplo: "Yo
quiero ser carlista." Enhorabuena: coges tu fusil y tu canana, y
ancha Castilla; nadie te lo estorba; que te cansas de la facción y que
te vas a tu casa: nadie te dice una palabra, con tal que tantas cuantas veces lo hagas, uses de la fórmula de decir que te acoges a algún
indulto de los últimos que hayan salido, o de los primeros que han
de salir. Ya ves tú que esto no cuesta trabajo. Que te levantas un día

de mal humor, y que conspiras como carlista, o que te defiendes en tu cuartel a balazos o con cualquiera otro medio inocente: vas a Filipinas y ves tierras, y siempre aprendes geografía.

Verdad es, que si como te había de dar por conspirar en favor de los diez años, te da por conspirar en favor de los tres, hay una diferencia, y es que entonces no necesitas salir al campo ni tirar un tiro para que te prendan, sino que te vienen a prender a tu misma casa, que es gran comodidad; pero, amigo, no se cogen truchas a bragas enjutas, y algo le ha de costar a uno ser liberal. Y luego que eso te sucederá si eres tonto, porque nadie te manda ser liberal; tú puedes ser lo que te dé la gana. Añade a eso que libertad completa no la hay en el mundo, que eso es un disparate. Así es que cuando yo digo que somos libres, no quiero decir por eso que podemos ser liberales a banderas desplegadas y salir diciendo por las calles "¡Viva la libertad!" u otros despropósitos de esta especie; ni que podemos dar en tierra con los empleados de Calomarde que quedan en su destino, lo cual tampoco sería justo, porque yo no creo que porque los haya empleado éste o aquél dejen por eso de necesitar un sueldo. ¡Pobrecillos! (2: 46–47)

(Suppose for a moment, though even imagining it may weigh upon you, that you are Spanish—don't grieve, this is a mere supposition—that you are Spanish and tell yourself, for example: "I want to be a Carlist." Fine. You get your gun and cartridge belt, and . . . broad as you please are the plains of Castille! No one stops you. Say you get tired of the rebel faction and go home. No one says a word, provided that every time you do it you make use of the formula stating that you invoke for protection one of the latest dispensations issued recently, or of the first that are going to come out. So you see this can be done without any bother. If one day you get up in a bad mood and conspire as a Carlist, or defend yourself inside your barracks with bullets or some other innocent means, you can go to the Philippines and see the world; this way you can always learn geography.

It's true that, if instead of conspiring for the ten years, you take it into your head to conspire for the three, there's one difference. In this case you don't need to go out in the country or fire any shots in order to be captured. They'll come to get you in your own house, a great convenience indeed. But, my friend, trout isn't caught in dry breeches, and it has to cost something to be a liberal. And besides, this'll happen to you if you're stupid, because no one's telling you to be a liberal; you can be whatever you please.

Add to this that there's no such thing as complete freedom in this world—the idea is absurd. So when I say we're free I don't mean we can be liberals with flags unfurled and go out into the street saying, "Long live freedom!" or other such nonsense; or that we can overthrow the Calomarde employees who are still in their jobs, which wouldn't be fair, because I can't believe that they don't need a salary just because this person or that person employed them. Poor dears!)

The last sentence above has been quoted anew in order to show the possibility of analogy between Carlist rebels and Calomarde appointees, as well as between Isabelina conspirators and unemployed civil servants. Use of the words "diez años" and "tres años" in conjunction with conspiracies facilitates recognition of the affinity. It should be pointed out, nevertheless, that during the Ominous Decade the Carlinos and Calomarde's henchmen had little liking for each other. Hence, the journalist's hint at a comparison is as thought-provoking as Serrano's remark, quoted above from *Pr.*, p. 268, about *cesantes* who contribute to the Carlist cause. The "Tercera carta," moreover, exudes an air of disgust toward the régime, a deeper revulsion than has been apparent heretofore, and prognosticates an imminent coup:

> Desengáñate de una vez y acaba de creer a pies juntillas, no sólo que vivimos bajo un régimen representativo, aunque te engañen las apariencias, sino que todo esto no es más que una pura representación, a la cual, para ser de todo punto igual a una del teatro, no le faltan más que los silbidos, los cuales, si se ha de creer en corazonadas y en síntomas y señales anteriores, no deben andar muy lejos, ni de hacerse esperar mucho, según la mareta sorda que se empieza ya a sentir. (2: 46)

(Open your eyes once and for all and stop believing on bended knee, not only that we live under a representative régime, even though appearances may deceive you, but that this whole thing is nothing more than a mere representation, which, in order to be totally like a theatrical performance, merely lacks but the hisses. But these, if we are to believe in heartbeats and external symptoms and signs, couldn't be too far off and aren't making themselves scarce much longer, according to the muffled surge starting to be felt.)

The revolt predicted by Larra turned out to be the abortive Correos mutiny of January 17. Figaro displays only contempt in his "Third letter," not merely for the régime's domestic program, viz., the employee question, but also for the supposed ineffectiveness of its foreign policy; his postscript reads: "La Cuádrupla Alianza sigue produciendo saludables efectos" (2: 47—"The Quadruple Alliance still produces salutary effects").

In fact, the government's ineffectuality is brought out by almost every detail of the "Tercera carta." Larra's remark about the "Memoria de Marina," for example, is fully corroborated when we compare the navy's report to those of other ministries. Despite its lamentable state, the Spanish fleet was the least pressing issue at the time; but of course a report had to be read to the Cortes for this just as for every other branch of government. It is ironic, however, that the secretary of the almost nonexistent navy should have delivered the longest one.[4] Figaro's opinion on the matter is inserted among related commentary:

Tiénela [contestación], sí, la segunda [carta tuya, Silva], y larga; tanto que pudiera ocupar con ella más pliegos que ocupó la Memoria de Marina presentada en las Cortes, más tiempo que dura una facción, y más terreno que el que reconoce cuando y como quiere Zumalacárregui, sin darte por eso más fruto ni más sustancia que el que pueden dar de sí todas esas cosas juntas. (2: 46)

(Your second letter, dear Silva, could indeed be answered, and at length; so much so, in fact, that it could occupy more pages than the Navy report recently presented in Cortes, more time than a rebellion lasts, and more terrain than Zumalacárregui covers on reconnaissance when and how he wishes, but, despite that, without giving you any more profit or substance than all those things put together.)

The "Memoria de Marina" is evidently considered to have no productive value and is therefore tossed among other pregnant vehicles.

The foregoing explanation of the employees debate has been given primarily to shed light on the "Tercera carta." It can likewise serve as an introduction to "La cuestión transparente." Such an introduction, however, does not suffice. To understand the latter essay, we should be acquainted with more than the general topic of the sessions, because "La cuestión transparente" hinges on polemic terminology developed by the orators. The terms used in this debate have a history of their own and in themselves contain the seeds of controversy. Consequently, we must comprehend their implication. To study them, let us first examine an argument the Progressives turned to most persistently; namely, that reinstatement of the civil servants was more a question of principle than of people. Trueba, in speaking about the good fortune of the few former exiles who found government posts upon their return, took up this line of reasoning at the very beginning of the deliberations:

> Pero varios de éstos por sus méritos anteriores, y por los servicios que podían prestar, era no sólo justo haberles colocado, sino que hubiera sido imprudente haberse hecho lo contrario: yo, señores, no debo contentarme con esto; lo que deseo es que se admita el principio; aquellos altos personajes que llevan en su nombre el prestigio y la fuerza, llevan también consigo su recomendación; yo quisiera que el principio se hiciese extensivo hasta a aquellos infelices que no pueden presentar más títulos que su lealtad y padecimientos. (*Pr.*, p. 531)

> (But not only was it fair to place several of these, owing to their prior distinction and the services they could render, but it would have been imprudent to do otherwise. I, gentlemen, must not allow myself to be satisfied with this. What I want is to see the principle admitted. The names of important persons carries prestige and power, and thus likewise their recommendations. I should like the principle extended to those unfortunate persons whose only titles are their loyalty and sufferings.)

Palarea expressed the same opinion; it was not only "una cuestión puramente de personas, sino de cosas" (*Pr.*, p. 553—"purely a question of persons but of things"); it should also be considered from the standpoint of "conveniencia pública" (p. 534).

The next day's session began with a speech by the Marqués de Falces. Although he attacked the proposal on several counts, especially from an economic point of view, the marquess did not shun petty reasoning. He doubted the good faith and aptitude of many of the unemployed functionaries and added that losing one's job was like sustaining property damage through an act of war, for which no one is ever compensated. To this argument Antonio González replied:

> Es muy sensible que se diga por el Sr. Falces, o por otro, que ésta es una cuestión de personas: yo la voy a considerar bajo el punto de vista de cuestión de principios, añadiendo que es una cuestión de honor nacional. (*Pr.*, p. 540)

> (It is quite regrettable that Mr. Falces, or anyone else, should say that this is a question of persons. I am going to consider it from the viewpoint of a question of principles, adding that it is a question of national honor.)

By designating it as a question of national honor, González could then claim that he was advocating a "principio conservador," and hence analogies could be made with the ministerial defense of the Guebhard loan:

> Los Sres. Secretarios del Despacho, cuando se han ventilado las grandes cuestiones del reconocimiento de la deuda extranjera, y todos los que han votado con ellos han invocado, no sólo el principio conservador, sino el de la equidad; y yo pregunto: ¿qué principio de equidad y conservación habría en que se respete todo lo hecho en los diez años, y no se respete todo lo hecho anterior y posteriormente? Podremos presentar este precioso ejemplo de distinguir las épocas, cuando nosotros debemos ser los primeros en hacer una franca fusión de principios, para que no haya desunión entre los españoles? (*Pr.*, p. 540)

> (When the great questions pertaining to recognition of the foreign debt were ventilated, the Secretaries of the Cabinet and all those who voted with them invoked not only the conservative principle but that of equity. Let me ask: what principle of equity and conservation could there be in respecting everything done during the ten years, and not what was done before and after? Can we give such an example of nicely distinguishing between epochs, when we should be the first ones to bring about a sincere fusion of principles, in order to avoid disunity among Spaniards?)

Alcalá Galiano reiterated these ideas, but with a different emphasis, because he sought to answer the sardonic Marqués de

Falces, who implied that he, the marquess, was merely protecting his friends the same way the Progressives were looking after theirs. Falces had said:

> No creo que en el ánimo de ninguno de los Sres. Procuradores influya la consideración del interés o perjuicio que resulte de la votación, para no hacerla con la imparcialidad debida; pero conociendo su delicadeza, me parece que muchos se abstendrán de votar en este negocio. Y yo, si personalmente no tengo un interés particular, ¿cómo podré olvidar el que tengo como español y amante de mi patria al considerar que la suerte de amigo míos, compañeros de opinión, y con quien me unen lazos sagrados de amistad, pende de la aprobación de esta petición? Sin embargo, haciéndome superior a todo, miraré esta cuestión sólo como Procurador del reino y defensor de los intereses de mis comitentes. (*Pr.*, p. 538)

> (I do not think that considerations of personal interest or detriment influence the opinion of any *procurador* to the point of not voting with due impartiality. But knowing the delicacy of the question, it appears to me that many will abstain from voting on the matter. As for me, if personally I have no particular interest in this, how can I forget the interest I have as a Spaniard who loves his country when I consider that the fate of friends of mine, companions who share my views, with whom I am united by the sacred bonds of friendship, depends on the approval of this petition? Nevertheless, placing myself above all this, I shall view this question only as a Procurador of the realm and defender of my constituents' interests.)

Galiano replied unflinchingly to Falces's wily innuendos and insincere disinterestedness, in spite of

> los embarazos . . . que de suyo me ofrece la cuestión, para no renunciar la palabra, ni seguir el consejo de un Sr. Procurador, que no por ser mi adversario político será mirado por mí como enemigo. Se ha dicho en efecto que todos los que estamos interesados en la cuestión, debíamos abstenernos de hablar o votar: no sé si se nos ha dicho como reconvención o como consejo; pero por si hay quien lo ignore, diré a mis compañeros, a los que me escuchan en general y a la opinión pública, . . . que fui empleado del Gobierno constitucional, y como tal me hallo interesado personalmente en este asunto . . . Cuando mi provincia me ha honrado

con el cargo de su Representante, me supuso un terrible deber, que estoy obligado a desempeñar hasta exponerme al riesgo de ser vituperado por abogar en favor de lo que crea ser justo. Por esto repito, señores, que me hallo interesado personalmente en esta cuestión, y no me avergüenzo de ello; pero no están sólo comprometidas en este asunto las personas, ni son únicamente éstas las que me obligan a tomar la palabra en él; están comprometidos además de las personas, los principios; está comprometida la causa más noble, más justa y más nacional que hubo nunca; la causa de una época célebre, que triunfante o vencida, siempre vivirá en la memoria y en el afecto de todos cuantos tengan sentimientos nobles y generosos. . . .

Se trata asimismo de cuestiones y principios sobre manera importantes; principios que versan sobre las doctrinas fundamentales de la sociedad, y sobre el respeto que mutuamente se deben todos los Gobiernos; y digo mutuamente, porque un Gobierno que sucede a otro, por lo mismo debe respetar lo hecho por éste, si quiere que se respete lo que él haga. . . .

Un señor preopinante ha hablado de que deben aquí reinar sentimientos de unión [of the two periods, the three-year and the ten-year]: en esto convengo enteramente con S.S., y eso mismo es lo que se pretende con la petición: igualar a los perseguidos y despojados con los demás. (*Pr.*, pp. 542–543, 545)

(the impediments . . . which this question offers by its very nature, in order not to relinquish the floor and follow the advice of a Procurador, whom I shall not consider my enemy just because he is my political adversary. It was said indeed that all those of us who had an interest in the question should abstain from speaking or voting. I do not know whether we were told this as a reproach or as advice. In case anyone does not know it, I shall now tell my companions, all my listeners, the public opinion, . . . that I was employed by the constitutional Government, and as such I have a personal interest in the matter . . . When my province honored me with a call to be its Representative, this implied for me an awesome obligation which I am duty-bound to carry out to the point of exposing myself to the risk of being reviled for advocating what I believe to be right. Therefore I repeat, gentlemen, that I find myself personally interested in the question, and I am not ashamed of it. But it is not just persons that are involved in the matter; and it is not just by persons that I am obliged to take the stand. Besides persons, principles are involved. What is involved is the most noble, most just, most patriotic cause ever to exist, the cause of a famous epoch which, triumphant or vanquished, will always live in the memory of all who possess noble and generous feelings. . . .

We are also dealing with questions and principles of the greatest importance, principles bearing on the fundamental doctrines of society, and on the mutual respect governments owe one another. And I say "mutual," because a Government that succeeds another, if it wants its actions to be respected, must by that token respect those of its predecessor. . . .

A previous speaker said that feelings of unity [of the two periods] should reign here. I agree entirely with His Lordship on the matter, and this is precisely what the petition attempts to do: to render the persecuted and despoiled equal to the others.)

Now when he saw how Galiano turned supposedly ministerial arguments to Progressive ends, the prime minister must have realized that his opponents' strategy was gaining the day. They had managed to reverse the order of the foreign debt and employees debates, and could consequently make use of principles uttered by the Moderates during the previous sessions. No matter how much Martínez might claim his régime to be a Medieval Revival, his desire to recognize all foreign debts despite their cost was undeniably founded on a principle of continuity. And now it was this very principle of continuity that the Progressives championed in order to vitiate the Moderates' economic objections to the reinstatement of employees. This ironic reversal of theoretical grounds, coincident with a change in the objects to which they were practically applied, attests to the brilliance of the Progressives' maneuvers. Yet the prime minister made a last attempt to rebut his adversaries, even though he understood that any objection on ideological grounds would make his position untenable. He appealed once more to his stock arguments, caution and reserve in effecting reforms, the dual political heritage, the restoration of medieval checks on the Crown, and the eclectic wisdom of choosing the best from previous régimes. But Martínez must have known that such notions were not really to the point, because he ventured to reason from more practical considerations. And because these arguments are the very ones that Larra later derided, it behooves us to examine them at length. First of all, the prime minister, while making claims about his own impartiality, asserted that it would be "inexpedient" to inject into the deliberations the issue of the present legality of Triennium measures; moreover, his opponents' feelings "obfuscated" their reason:

Imparciales y desinteresados en esta cuestión, ya personalmente, y ya como Ministros, tampoco desearíamos que se tratase como una *cuestión de principios*, porque juzgamos más bien inoportuno que conveniente desentrañar la legalidad y validez de los actos del régimen constitucional o del Gobierno que le ha sucedido. El Ministerio no entra en esas cuestiones, de suyo delicadas, y aun tal vez peligrosas; pero como encargado de la aplicación de cuantas reformas y medidas se adopten, tiene que calcular los obstáculos, los inconvenientes, los efectos que han de producir en la práctica. El Gobierno puede apreciar más de cerca sus consecuencias probables; pues francamente parece muy sencillo y muy fácil todo aquello que se mira bajo el aspecto de la generosidad, que cautiva los sentimientos, y aun ofusca hasta la razón de los Sres. Procuradores a Cortes; y cuando llega el Ministerio y éste tiene que hacer *la aplicación*, tropieza con mil dificultades que tal vez no se habían previsto. (*Pr.*, p. 546)

(Being impartial and disinterested in this question, both personally and as Ministers, we wish also that it not be treated as a *question of principle*, because we deem it inopportune rather than convenient to dig into and pick apart the legality and validity of the acts of the constitutional regime or of the Government succeeding it. The Cabinet does not go into these questions, delicate by their nature and perhaps dangerous; but charged with the application of all reforms and measures that are adopted, it must calculate the obstacles, the inconveniences, the effects which they bring about in practice. The Government can appraise its probable consequences from a closer vantage point. Frankly, everything seems quite simple and easy when looked at from the viewpoint of generosity, which captivates the feelings and even obfuscates the reason of the Procuradores of the realm; but when the Ministry comes on the scene and has to *apply it*, it meets up with a thousand difficulties which perhaps had not been foreseen.)

The prime minister also felt obligated to answer Galiano, who had questioned the validity of one of Martínez's favorite equivocal catchwords, "restaurar." Galiano had said:

El Sr. Presidente del Consejo de Ministros, en una ocasión en que aun no tenía yo la honra de ocupar este asiento, dijo que el Gobierno actual no era ni el constitucional ni el absoluto, sino el restaurador de las leyes fundamentales [of the pre-Hapsburg Spanish monarchy]. No puedo menos de observar que restaurar es cosa de tiempo, y absoluto o constitucional es de índole o esencia: puede restaurarse el absolutismo o el constitucionalismo. (*Pr.*, p. 544)

(The President of the Council of Ministers, on an occasion at which I did not yet have the honor of occupying this desk, said that the present Government was neither the constitutional nor the absolute one, but rather the restorer of the fundamental laws [of medieval times]. I must observe that restoring is a question of time, and absoluteness or constitutionality one of nature or essence. Absolutism, or constitutionalism, can be restored.)

In his answer, quoted below, the prime minister counters Galiano's phrase, "cosa de tiempo," with the notion that to heal dissensions in the body politic "también es cosa de tiempo." But the most significant aspect of Martínez's discourse is, to be sure, the innovation of the term "cuestiones transparentes":

Si tal ha sido el plan seguido por el Ministerio [of avoiding political systems or partialities], así respecto de *principios políticos* como de reformas, ¿no podremos decir también cuál ha sido su conducta respecto de personas? Con respecto a personas (puesto que esta cuestión, aunque se ha dicho que es de principios y no de personas, es de uno y otro, y siempre que se trate de empleos, son estas cuestiones transparentes, y se ve por detrás a las personas), ¿cuál ha sido en este punto la conducta del Ministerio? La de evitar todo lo que pueda aparecer o llevar el aspecto de clases y categorías, y tratar de borrar, en cuanto es posible, los vestigios de partidos y disensiones. Mas esto también es obra de tiempo; están muy recientes los sucesos; aún brotan sangre las heridas; y sólo el tiempo y la acción del Gobierno pueden cicatrizarlas. (*Pr.*, p. 547)

(If the plan [of avoiding political systems or partialities] has been the one followed by the Cabinet, with regard to both *political principles* and reforms, can we not likewise state what its conduct has been with regard to persons? With respect to persons—since this question, even though it was said to be of principles and not persons, is of both; every time employment is dealt with, these are transparent issues, and the persons are seen in the background—

what then has been the Ministry's conduct? It has been to avoid
everything that might seem to carry with it any appearance of
classes and categories, and try to efface wherever possible vestiges
of parties and dissensions. But this is also the work of time. Events
are very recent. The wounds are still gushing blood, and only time
and the Government's action can staunch them.)

Assuredly, the prime minister's parenthetical asseveration that the
question is one of persons rather than principles directly contra-
dicts Trueba and Palarea.

In the body of Larra's essay, the titular phrase, "cuestión transparente," is accompanied by the expressions "mal aconsejado,"
"cimiento," and "rama podrida." These terms can likewise be
traced to the Cortes and are found mostly in ministerial oratory
advocating the exclusion of Don Carlos and his descendants from
the Throne. During the sessions devoted to the motion on the Pretender, all delegates concurred in barring the Carlist line from
kingship, but the Moderates founded their arguments on medieval law, specifically the Partida dealing with treason, while the
Progressives emphasized the common good and the will of the
governed. Hence, for principle's sake, politicians made a bone of
contention out of something they agreed upon. The ministry
sought a reaffirmation of the Medieval Revival supposedly embodied in the Estatuto Real, while the Progressives took the opportunity to reassert ideas bordering on the dangerous doctrine
of national sovereignty. In Próceres, the only one to express the
latter beliefs was the Duque de Rivas (*Ilus.*, p. 65). The ministerial view was expounded by Martínez himself in the first oration
of that memorable day, September 23, when Don Carlos was
repudiated by the Spanish nobility. The prime minister expressed
straightway his conservative opinion, linking the exclusion of the
pretender with his own political system. The terms "cimiento"
and "mal aconsejado" are used by him to this effect:

> Ilustres Próceres: En 4 de Abril próximo pasado, cuando los
> Secretarios del Despacho tuvieron la honra de proponer a S.M.
> la Reina Gobernadora la restauración de las antiguas leyes de la
> Monarquía, como el cimiento más firme para asegurar el Trono y
> hermanar la causa de éste con la libertad y derechos de la nación,
> expusieron a S.M. las poderosas razones que había para la convo-

cación de las Cortes generales del reino, con arreglo a nuestras antiguas instituciones, y con sólo aquellas reformas y variaciones que exigía la mudanza de tiempos y circunstancias.

Entre las varias razones que expusieron, fueron unas de las principales las siguientes: "Ante las Cortes generales del reino, con el libro de la ley en la mano, de la manera más solemne de que se halle ejemplo en los fastos de la Monarquía, se expondrá a la faz de la nación y del mundo la conducta del mal aconsejado Príncipe . . ." (*Ilus.*, p. 59)

(Illustrious Próceres: On April 4 of this year, when the Secretaries of the Cabinet had the honor of proposing to Her Majesty the Queen Regent the restoration of the ancient laws of the Monarchy as the firmest foundation on which to secure the Throne and unite its cause with liberty and the rights of the nation, they expounded to Her Majesty the strong reasons prevailing for convoking the general Cortes of the realm, in accordance with our ancient institutions, and with only those reforms and variations that the change of times and circumstances demanded.

Among the several arguments, some of the main ones were the following: "Before the general Cortes of the realm, with the book of the law in hand, in the most solemn manner of which an example can be found in the annals of the Monarchy, the conduct of the ill-advised Prince shall be revealed to the face of the nation and the world . . .")

The Duque de Rivas replied that Don Carlos should be excluded

porque está en oposición directa con los intereses nacionales. Este último es el solo punto de vista bajo el cual nosotros debemos examinar esta cuestión escabrosa: examinar la de los otros dos [the hereditary and the criminal] sería traspasar nuestras atribuciones . . . el envolver esta cuestión en textos de la ley escrita, es darle cierto aire de proceso que no conviene de ninguna manera a este Estamento . . . Nosotros no somos jueces; somos legisladores: no juzgamos; hacemos leyes: los que juzgan deben hacerlo con arreglo a las leyes establecidas de antemano: los que hacen leyes no lo pueden hacer apoyándose en otra ley, sino siguiendo únicamente el norte de todas ellas, la conveniencia pública y el interés nacional. (*Ilus.*, p. 65)

(because it is in direct opposition to the national interest. This is the only point of view from which we should examine this scabrous question. To examine the other two [the hereditary and criminal] would be going beyond our attributes . . . To wrap up this question in texts from written law is to give it a certain air of a lawsuit in no way befitting this Chamber . . . We are not judges; we are legislators. We do not cast judgment; we make laws. Those who do the judging must do so in accordance with laws previously established. Those who make laws cannot do so by resting on another law, but only by following the direction of them all, public convenience and national interest.)

In this speech Rivas made one of his most famous pronouncements, romantically describing the Carlists as "un partido que quiere fundar un Trono bárbaro y un altar sacrílego y furibundo, rodeado de lagunas de sangre y de montañas de cadáveres, sobre la tumba de la civilización moderna" (*Ilus.*, p. 66; translated above).

As we can see, the Progressives wanted to forgo the traditional aspect and to break with medieval law. Martínez replied that it was imperative to consider all legal facets. Two weeks later, when the motion concerning the pretender came up in the lower house, these arguments were repeated and the prime minister used the third expression in Larra's list:

Siglos enteros se recorren sin encontrar un caso semejante por fortuna de las naciones. Por fortuna digo, pues que no se corta nunca una rama sin que se resienta el árbol del Estado; y para hacerlo se necesita tanto tino, tanta destreza como la que usa el buen agricultor cuando cortando una rama podrida procura no herir el tronco ni dejar al descubierto las raíces. (*Pr.*, p. 489)

(Fortunately for nations, entire centuries can be gone over without coming across a similar case. I say fortunately, because a branch can never be cut without afflicting the tree of State; and to do this, as much skill and deftness must be used as the good husbandman's, who, when cutting a rotten branch, tries not to harm the trunk or leave the roots exposed to injury.)

The day was bound to come when Martínez's opponents would employ his rustic metaphor against him. They found their opportunity during the employees debate, in which, conversely to the discussion on the pretender's exclusion, it was the Progressives who espoused legalistic principles; the Moderates in this instance appealed merely to economic and administrative convenience. Thus it was that on October 16 Alcalá Galiano, advocating repeal of the 1823 decree which had declared null and void the Triennium legislation, purposely transferred the metaphor from the royal family tree to the unjust law, thereby undoing the trope's subtle ambiguity:

> El Sr. Secretario del Estado dijo también con su natural elocuencia que no se puede tocar a un árbol ni aun podrá cortarle las ramas podridas sin que se resienta el tronco y aun las raíces; y en otra ocasión, valiéndose de un símil análogo, dijo igualmente que era arriesgado tocar a los cimientos del Trono, aun cuando fuese para fortalecerlos o robustecerlos. En la primera de estas comparaciones no creo que estuvo muy feliz S. S.; pues cabalmente la poda o tala de las ramas muertas de un árbol, lejos de dañar al tronco, y mucho menos a las raíces, los robustecen y dan lozanía y frondosidad al árbol.
>
> En cuanto a los cimientos del Trono, los miro, y me complazco en ello, como tan indestructibles, que no creo tengan peligro alguno; tanto más, cuanto que la experiencia ha demonstrado que el Gobierno no sólo más conveniente para esta nación, sino el único posible, es el monárquico constitucional o representativo. (*Pr.*, p. 544)
>
> (The Secretary of State said also with his natural eloquence that a tree cannot be worked on, or even its rotten branches be cut off, without afflicting the trunk and even the roots. On another occasion, making use of an analogous simile, he said likewise that it was risky to work on the foundations of the Throne, even for the purpose of strengthening or fortifying them. I do not feel that the first of these comparisons was quite felicitous for His Lordship, precisely because the pruning or lopping of a tree's dead branches, far from damaging the trunk, and even less the roots, strengthen the latter and make the tree luxuriant and vigorous.
>
> As for the foundations of the Throne, I see them, and enjoy doing so, as so indestructible that I do not think they run any risk at all; the more so, because experience has shown that not only the most suitable Government for this nation, but the only one possible, is a constitutional or representative monarchy.)

Besides urging the repeal of a decree that took away so many jobs, Galiano, as we can see, defended constitutional monarchy, an extremely bold stance because the Estatuto was not a constitution. Was he thus hinting that a revolt might occur if the ministry did not acquiesce? Perhaps Galiano also meant to have the figure of the rotten branch apply to those of Calomarde's henchmen who still enjoyed government employ, as well as to the insidious law of 1823. As for the foundations of the Throne, they would not necessarily be shaken by a shake-up in the ministry.

Faced with all these possible insinuations, Martínez stuck to his guns by defending his tropes on "cimientos" and "rama podrida," while injecting "inoportunidad"[5] into the discourse:

> S.S. ha tenido la bondad de recordar algunas imágenes usadas por mí, que no entraré a defender por su oportunidad o inoportunidad, pero S.S. debe saber que en las imágenes no se requiere una exactitud rigurosa, como en las demostraciones matemáticas. No trato de defender la exactitud de la alegoría de que me valí en un discurso (me parece fue cuando se trató de la exclusión de Don Carlos y de su línea); dije que era necesario proceder en esta materia con mucho pulso y esmero, como el que emplea un hábil agricultor, cuando al cortar una rama podrida cuida mucho de no herir el tronco, ni dejar a descubierto las raíces; porque su intención y deseo es cortar la rama perjudicial, y conservar el árbol. Si es exacta o no la alegoría, lo dejo al juicio del Estamento.
>
> Dije en otra ocasión (y me parece fue en el Estamento de Ilustres Próceres) que tal era la condición de la Monarquía, que aun cuando fuese para robustecerla era preciso tocar con sumo cuidado los cimientos del Trono, para no conmover al Estado. Este principio es exacto; y la experiencia ha mostrado que todas las naciones, al llegar a estas cuestiones, no menos graves que espinosas, las han mirado con muchísimo pulso. (*Pr.*, p. 545)

(His Lordship has had the kindness to recall some tropes used by me, which I shall not defend with respect to their opportuneness or inopportuneness, but His Lordship must know that rigorous precision is not required for tropes, as it is for mathematical proofs. I shall not attempt to defend the exactness of the allegory to which I had recourse in a speech—it seems to me it was when we were dealing with the exclusion of Don Carlos and his line. I said it was necessary to proceed in this matter with painstaking care, like that used by a skillful husbandman when, while cutting a rotten branch, he takes heed not to injure the trunk or expose the roots, because his intent and desire is to cut the harmful branch and save the tree. I leave to the judgment of the Chamber whether the allegory is precise or not.

I said on another occasion—and it seems to me it was in the Estamento de Próceres—that the state of the Monarchy was such that, even in order to strengthen it, it was necessary to touch with extreme care the foundations of the Throne, in order not to disturb the State. This principle is exact, and experience has shown that all nations, when they come to such serious and thorny issues, have viewed them with great tact.)

The weakness of his vindication is ample evidence of the Progressives' success in turning against Martínez not only his political abstractions but also the very figures that adorn them.[6]

Figaro could accordingly remind the prime minister of his quandary. Not only does Larra list the moot mots, but he uses Martínez's own dictum, "cuestión transparente," as the title of the journalistic repartee, thereby ironically reflecting the Progressives' ideological transposition of ministerial abstractions:

No ha dos días que un señor orador apellidó en el Estamento de Procuradores a la cuestión de los empleos *cuestión transparente*, porque detrás de ella, por más que se quiera evitar, siempre se ven las personas. Nosotros pensamos lo mismo. Hay expresiones felices que nunca quedarán, en nuestro entender, bastante grabadas en la memoria. Cuánto sea el valor de estas expresiones, dichas en tiempo y lugar, no necesitamos inculcárselo al lector. Felices son por lo bien ocurridas; felices por el apropósito, y felices, en fin, porque hacen fortuna. Estas expresiones, de tal suerte dispuestas y colocadas, suelen ser el cachetero de las discusiones, la última mano, la razón, en fin, sin réplica ni respuesta. Después que un orador ha dicho en clara y distinta voz que el Pretendiente *es un faccioso más*, ya quisiera yo saber qué se le contesta. Cuando un orador suelta el *mal aconsejado*, el *inoportuno*, el *cimiento* y la *rama podrida*, ya quisiera yo que me dijeran hasta qué punto puede llevarse la cuestión en cuestión; y si hay oradores, si hay epítetos y adjetivos, si hay expresiones felices, hay cuestiones que no lo son menos. (2: 21)

(Only two days ago in the Estamento de Procuradores an orator called the employees question a *transparent* issue, because behind it persons are always seen, no matter how much one tries to avoid it. We also think so. There are, in our opinion, certain felicitous expressions that will always be etched on our memory. We need not impress the reader with the value of these expressions, when uttered at the right time and place. They are felicitous because they are striking, to the point, and make a hit. In fact, handled in a particular way, they become the coup-de-grâce of discussions, the last stroke, without reply or response. After an orator has said in a plain and clear voice that the Pretender is *one more rebel*, what can we answer, I'd like to know? When an orator lets forth with that *ill-advised*, that *inopportune*, the *foundation*, and the *rotten branch*, I'd like someone to tell me how far we can make an issue of the issue. If there are felicitous orators, epithets, adjectives, and expressions, there are issues that are no less so.)

The above passage constitutes the beginning of Larra's article. When the reader reaches the end, the notions evolved in the first sentence have been developed to their limit. The author has explained why his ideas coincide with Martínez's; but of course they disagree in one particular, which is the crux of the question. By "persons" the satirist means the incumbents, whereas the minister had denoted the unemployed. Hence, the process of terminological reversal that began in Cortes is consummated by Figaro's irony:

¡Qué no se divisa detrás de ciertos empleos, y no a ojos vistas precisamente, sino aun a cierra ojos! Se ven los empleados; verdad es que apenas se ven los de los tres; pero, en fin, se ve, en una palabra, se ve que se ve algo; se ve que se verá más; y se verá, digámoslo de una vez, lo que siempre se ha visto; se ven los compromisos, los amigos, los parientes... es el gran punto de vista; todo se ve. ¡Fatalidad de las cosas humanas! En las otras cuestiones anhelaríamos la transparencia. Y en esta que se ve, nos hallamos precisados a exclamar: *¡Ojalá no se viera!* (2: 21–22)

(Oh the things we can see behind certain positions, right under our noses, even while holding them! We can see the employees. To be sure, we can hardly see those of the three years, but, after all, we can see something. In a word, we see that something can be seen, that more will be seen. And what will be seen, let's say it once and for all, is what has always been seen: deals, friends, relatives... We've found the great point of view: everything can be seen. Oh fatality of human affairs! In other issues we might yearn for transparency. And in this one in which one can see, we are compelled to exclaim: *If we could only shut our eyes!*)

Let us examine carefully the style of "La cuestión transparente." After an expository exordium, the author develops his irony, subtle at first but progressively evident, until it is finally broken by a blaring note of pathos, a desperate inculpation of the political system for its rottenness and of the ministry for its procrastination.

The satirist, in fact, develops a gloss on the minister's words: "siempre que se trate de empleos, son estas cuestiones transparentes, y se ve por detrás a las personas." At the essay's end, he conjugates "se ve" in a repetitious present, a future that merely reflects the ever-present past of conservative reticence, and a contrary-to-fact subjunctive of exasperation. A cursory reading, moreover, will show how the satirical process sweeps beyond parliamentary references, lampooning all the political realities of the day. Reminiscences of previous congressional sessions (on Carlos's exclusion, the bill of rights, press freedom, the militia) punctuate a flow of humor, a flow which remains unified through the unrelenting theme of the obstruction of progress by entrenched interests and through a gamut of visual terms linked to the "transparente" topic: "oscuro," "trasluz," "espeso," "negro," "tupido," "de pura gasa," "claro," "lente," "divisarse," "verse," "ojos," "vista," "transparencia." All political issues on the Spanish scene are transparent, Larra hints ironically. The reader can let his imagination wander, because the contention that there are "persons" rather than "principles" behind political viewpoints should apply to the ministry just as well as to the Progressives (Martínez's conservatism, say, is what keeps him in office; those in power maintain themselves there by denying the Spanish people civil rights that might protect them if they expressed their objections; lack of press freedom likewise protects the ministry from attack; the militia's weakness assures its inability to participate in a coup). There are no persons behind such issues as denial of a bill of rights, press freedom, or weapons for the militia, says Figaro ironically. The implication is, of course, that there are persons, or at least one, the prime minister himself: "Semejante al retablo de maese Pedro, las pocas figuras que hay, todas están delante. Detrás, ni aun Ginesillo de Parapilla y Pasamonte, que las mueve, se distingue" (2: 21—"As in Maese Pedro's puppet-show, its few figures are in front. Behind, not even Ginesillo, who moves them, can be made out"). Martínez, who like Ginesillo had once been a prisoner, also ran a puppet show.

"La cuestión transparente" is one of the best articles written by Larra during this period. The author, while examining the several applications of Martínez's mot, "cuestión transparente," enumerates other phrases of his, which happen to have been turned against him in parliament. Larra convincingly adds this one to the list. Like "Hernán Pérez del Pulgar" in its ironic progression and assertive ending, and like "La gran verdad descubierta" in conciseness, thematic arrangement, and careful combination of ideological and verbal play, "La cuestión transparente" should be ranked among Figaro's finest pieces.

10

THE EXPULSION
OF BURGOS

Although he wrote no more parodies of oratory until February 1835, Figaro kept up his commentary on parliamentary affairs. His next essay, "La calamidad europea," though initially published in the *Colección*,[1] must have been composed shortly after October 18, 1834. On that date the Próceres had expelled from their midst Javier de Burgos, accused of profiting improperly from governmental transactions during the Ominous Decade. Larra's article, not printed at the time for reasons beyond the author's control ("por circunstancias ajenas a la voluntad del autor"), burlesques an exculpatory letter sent to the newspapers by the ostracized *prócer*. Burgos's message had predicted dire results from the action of his peers, and it is the magnified import ascribed to the expulsion that the journalist ridicules. Perhaps Figaro even parodies the letter's style.[2] As for the speeches delivered on that supposedly fateful day, it will be helpful to summarize and quote them even though they were not used by Larra to compose his essay.

Turning to the *Diario de las sesiones*, we find Burgos's name in an unflattering context as much as a month before the proceedings against him. This occurred during the foreign debt debates in Procuradores, when Trueba impugned his role in the conversion of the Guebhard loan into perpetual annuities (*Pr.*, p. 251). Then on September 17, while arguing that a foreign loan could be avoided by curtailing administrative expenses, Francisco Serrano spoke of the former minister in highly critical terms: "El Ministro que había del Fomento, con su natural atrevimiento, planteó las subdelegaciones de dicho ramo con tanto lujo, que había secretario de dichas oficinas que tenía más sueldo que yo" (*Pr.*, pp. 267–268—"The then interior minister, with his natural boldness, set up the subdelegations of this branch with such luxury, that there were secretaries in these offices who had higher salaries than I did"). Serrano was a general. This criticism notwithstanding, it should be pointed out that during that crucial period the political allegiance of the provinces needed to be maintained at all costs, and hence the *subdelegados* had to exhibit their importance. Nevertheless, Serrano opened the door for further onslaughts; the next day García Carrasco took it upon himself to besmirch the *prócer*'s reputation:

Sin que conste por ninguna otra Real orden, se autorizó por el Ministro de Hacienda y el director de la caja de amortización a D. Javier de Burgos para que pasase a París, como comisionado regio, nueve días después de haberse anulado el empréstito. El Estamento encontrará una contradicción, cual es la de a qué iba un comisionado para una cosa que no existía. Llegó a París, y se celebró un convenio entre Guebhard y Carrères, Aguado y Burgos, sin que el Gobierno español tuviese ningún conocimiento de él. A pesar de todo, y sin autorización ninguna para ello, firmó Burgos un contrato con esta compañía, para que no sufriesen tanto retraso las remesas, el cual no se cumplió como se debía, sin embargo de lo estipulado.

Soret, que era entonces el director del Tesoro, dijo que era nulo lo hecho. (*Pr.*, p. 276)

(Without its being put in writing by means of any other Royal order, Don Javier de Burgos was authorized by the secretary of the treasury and the director of the amortization office to go to Paris, as royal commissioner, nine days after the loan was annulled.

The Chamber will notice a contradiction; to wit, why a commissioner was designated for something that did not exist. He arrived in Paris, and an agreement was made between Guebhard and Carrères, Aguado, and Burgos, without the Spanish government's knowledge. Despite all this, and without any authorization whatsoever, Burgos signed a contract with this company so that remittances would not undergo so much delay; but, notwithstanding what was stipulated, the contract was not carried out as it should have been.

Soret, who was then director of the treasury, said that what had been done was null and void.)

On the day following García Carrasco's speech, the attack was renewed by Palarea, but in general terms, through metaphorical hints at Burgos's guilt. Then, on September 24, the dreaded Conde de las Navas entered the fray:

El Conde de la Alcudia en el año de 1831, deseoso de saber los agios que se fomentaban con la deuda de Guebhard y sus emanaciones, se irritó hasta tal punto, que trató de formar un expediente sobre el empréstito de Guebhard, incluso hasta el de Holanda. Halló tales iniquidades, robos y perfidias, que se vio en la precisión de manifestárselo al Rey, y éste, no pudiendo desconocer la verdad de su Ministro, mandó que se formase la causa al Ministro Ballesteros y a Burgos. Estos documentos no aparecerán en el Ministerio: ¿por qué? A la penetración de todos puede estar. Si a mí me mandaran formar una causa, y luego me entregaran los medios de hacerla desaparecer, lo haría para siempre. (Pr., pp. 358–359)

(In the year 1831 the Count of La Alcudia, wishing to know what speculations were being promoted through the Guebhard loan and its outgrowth, became so angry that he tried to start an investigation of the Guebhard loan, and even that of Holland. He discovered so many inequities, thefts, and perfidies that he found himself compelled to inform the King. The latter, who could not fail to recognize the truth his Minister showed him, ordered a suit against Ballesteros [the treasury minister] and Burgos. These documents will probably not be found at the Ministry. Why not? This must be evident to everyone. If I had a suit brought against me, and later were given the means to make it disappear, I would do it once and for all.)

This was the final and most virulent assault heard in Procuradores against Burgos. The polemic then passed to the newspapers. On September 26 *La Abeja* and *La Revista Española* published a letter from the *prócer* stating that at the proper time he would reply to "las injurias que, abusando deplorablemente de la inviolabilidad parlamentaria, había articulado contra mí el Conde de las Navas en 24 de setiembre"[3] ("the insults which the Count of Las Navas, abusing deplorably his parliamentary inviolability, has uttered against me on September 24"). Burgos had planned to put off his vindication until the foreign debt proposal reached his own chamber, but when the Próceres postponed debate, he decided to defend himself in writing. His *Observaciones sobre el empréstito Guebhard*,[4] organized around eight points of argumenation, came off the press on October 6. This pamphlet, however, did not still the waters; they bestirred themselves anew, because the issue again came to the surface in no. 93 of *El Observador*, which contains a communication from Javier de Burgos replying to the accusations of the Conde de las Navas.[5]

At last the moment of truth arrived—or of falsehood, as the case may be. On October 18, the Estamento de Ilustres Próceres started its discussion of the foreign debt. Burgos had been warned not to attend but, feeling unjustly slandered and hence impelled to defend his honor by facing the charges, he went to the session anyway. As soon as the government's proposal was read, General Miguel Ricardo de Alava rose to express his chagrin because a certain *prócer* had dared to show himself:

> Este ilustre Prócer, acusado de este modo, no debe el Estamento permitir que se presente en este lugar hasta que por una justificación legal haga ver que está libre de toda mancha, poniendo de este modo a cubierto su honor.
>
> Señor: el Estamento de ilustres Próceres es una corporación muy antigua en esta nación; pero el desuso ha hecho que aparezca hoy como una planta exótica, que por nuestra fortuna ha venido a aclimatarse. El espíritu de igualdad hace que se le mire con cierta desconfianza, y ahora más que nunca es necesario que se haga acreedor por la conducta de sus individuos a la respetabilidad pública,
>
> Lejos de mí la idea de que el ilustre Prócer sea culpable; pero mi opinión es que mientras no vindique competentemente su conducta, no debe asistir a las sesiones. (*Ilus.*, pp. 103–104)

(The Chamber must not allow this illustrious Prócer, thus accused, to show himself here until he demonstrates by a legal justification that he is free of any taint, thereby safeguarding his honor.

Sir: The Estamento de Próceres is a very ancient body in this nation, but disuse makes it appear today like an exotic plant, which is providentially becoming acclimatized. Owing to the spirit of equality, it is looked upon with distrust, and now more than ever it needs to make itself worthy of public respect through the conduct of its members.

Far from me to think that the illustrious Prócer is guilty; but it is my opinion that until he vindicates his conduct competently, he must not attend the sessions.)

General Francisco Javier Castaños, hero of Bailén, who was president of the chamber, agreed, adding that "es práctica constante en los tribunales y corporaciones el no estar presentes sus individuos siempre que se trata de sus personas o conducta" ("it is a constant practice in courts of law and public bodies that a member not be present whenever his person or conduct is being discussed").

It thus appears that Burgos's right to be considered innocent until proven guilty was expediently sacrificed to the repute of the chamber, some of whose other members, incidentally, may also have been involved in the disreputable loan transactions. Since the *prócer* was prepared to answer accusations, it is probable that airing the matter might have divulged information incriminating to a fair number of persons. Perhaps the hindrance of Burgos's exculpation attempt was a self-protective measure.[6]

When the Duque de Bailén gave his approval to Alava's suggestion, Burgos was expelled in the manner recorded as follows in the *Diario de las sesiones:*

El Sr. Presidente: Se pondrá a votación la moción hecha por el ilustre Prócer. Entre tanto, sírvase el Sr. Burgos salir del salón hasta que éste resuelve.

El Sr. Burgos: Yo protesto.

El Sr. Presidente: Proteste V.E. cuanto guste; pero retírese.

El Sr. Burgos: Yo me retiraré; pero protesto. (*Ilus.*, p. 104)

(The president: The motion made by the illustrious Prócer will be put to a vote. In the meantime, Mr. Burgos will kindly leave the

Chamber until it has come to a decision.

Mr. Burgos: I protest.

The president: Your Excellency may protest as much as you want; but leave.

Mr. Burgos: I shall leave; but I protest.)

The ostracized member then sent his peers a letter of protest, read to the chamber on October 25 (*Ilus.*, p. 114). Burgos was finally exonerated in November, but in the meantime he had left for Paris in disgust and indignation, after sending an article to the Madrid papers.[7] This article is the object of Larra's banter. He begins by listing seven calamities, the Trojan War, the Persian wars, the expansion of the Roman Empire, the Barbarian invasions, religious wars, wars of succession, and the French revolution with the ensuing Napoleonic wars. Then he concludes:

Hemos llegado a la octava calamidad europea. ¿Pues cuál otra horrible calamidad nos amenaza? ¿Otro cólera? Si el hombre nació para morir, la peste es una muerte cualquiera. Mayor es la calamidad que nos amaga; más terrible la prueba a que nos sujeta la Providencia. ¿Algún reglamento? Eso sería una gota más en el mar. ¿Algún empréstito? El deber es calamidad sólo para quien ha de pagar, o para quien presta. ¿Otra invasión de rusos? Más todavía. ¿Qué sería una invasión de rusos? Algunos años de despotismo. Para pueblos tan acostumbrados, para pueblos donde hay aún quien pelee por él, nada. Es volver la tortilla. No faltaría quien la comiera.

La gran calamidad europea, la calamidad de las calamidades, he aquí cómo la hallamos consignada en un communicado que en un periódico leemos.

"Que conmigo se haga una injusticia—nos dice un personaje, un tanto cuanto atropellado en las formas—puede ser un triunfo para mis enemigos; pero en el caso presente, la violencia usada hacia mí es un desastre para todos, es una brecha abierta en el corazón de nuestras instituciones, es una calamidad nacional; y ¿quién sabe si no podrá hacerse una calamidad europea? Los trastornos que podrían resultar de tan evidente violación de los principios conservadores de nuestro régimen, podrían ir más allá de los Pirineos."

He aquí bien clara la gran calamidad, que entretanto que lo es para la Europa, lo es indudablemente para el que escribe. La cosa en verdad no es insignificante como muchos creen; bien pudiera ser trascendental; pero lo que ni nosotros habíamos presumido, ni nuestros lectores tampoco, es que esto podría trastornar el mundo. Curiosos por demás de lo que nos podría acontecer, hemos recorrido, como ha visto el lector, la historia del mundo y de sus calamidades. Hemos temblado por nosotros y por la Europa. ¿Obrará este accidente como el robo de Elena? ¿Será Troya nuestra patria? ¿Tendrá los resultados del levantamiento de Remo y Rómulo? ¿Será la voz del destituido el grito de Lutero? ¿Imperará a los mares como el *quos ego* de Virgilio? ¿Será su desgracia, justa o injusta, legal o ilegalmente llevada a cabo, el Waterloo de nuestra pequeña libertad? ¿Qué parte del mundo se hundirá? ¿Obrará como un diluvio, como un castigo del cielo, o como una calamidad puramente humana?

¡Ah! ¡Plegue al cielo apartar de nosotros tan terribles infortunios! *¡Lejos, pobre España, lejos de nosotros el profeta y la profecía!!!* (2: 44–45)

(We now come to the eighth European calamity. What other horrid calamity threatens us? Another cholera? If man was born to die, then this plague is just one more way of going. The calamity menacing us is bigger; the test to which Providence now subjects us is greater. Some new regulation? This would be another drop in the sea. A new loan? Indebtedness is a calamity only for the one who has to pay, or for the lender. Another Russian invasion? No, worse yet. What, after all, would a Russian invasion be? A few years of despotism, nothing for a people so accustomed to it, where there are men still fighting on its behalf. It's like turning over a pancake; there'll always be someone around to eat it.

The great European calamity, the calamity of calamities, can be found in a letter to the editor of a newspaper, worded as follows:

"That injustice has been done to me—we are told by a personage who, from a formalistic point of view, has been roughed up a bit—can be considered a triumph for my enemies. But in the present case the violence used against me is a disaster for all; it is an open breach in the heart of our institutions, a national calamity. And who knows if it might not become a European calamity? The disorders that could result from so evident a violation of the conservative principles of our régime might become felt beyond the Pyrenees."

So here is, clearly stated, the great calamity, which, while drawing near for Europe, undoubtedly exists for the writer of the above. In truth, the matter is not insignificant, as many believe. It could well be transcendental; but what neither we nor our readers should ever have presumed is that it might disarrange the world. Curious as we were, besides, to know what may happen, we went over the history of the world and its calamities, as the reader noticed. We trembled for our sake and Europe's. Will this incident have an effect similar to the rape of Helen? Is our land another Troy? Will it have the same results as the uprising of Romulus and Remus? Will the voice of the expelled individual be like the challenge of Luther? Will it rule the seas like Virgil's *quos ego?* Will his mishap, whether just or unjust, legally or illegally brought on, be the Waterloo of our feeble liberty? What part of the world is to be swallowed up? Will it act as a flood, a punishment from heaven, or a purely human calamity?

May heaven preserve us from such terrible misfortunes! *Poor Spain! Away, away with the prophet and the prophecy!!!*)

After reading the above, we may question Larra's purpose. What did Figaro hope to accomplish by deriding the exaggerated pleas of a man unjustly disgraced? This problem requires careful investigation, and even then we cannot be certain of documents that will throw light on Larra's stand. But at least a viable hypothesis can be put forward. Larra opposed recognition of the Guebhard loan and allied himself with those politicians who prevented its effective defense in the upper house by expelling its champion from the Cortes. For Larra, disavowal of legislation not ratified by Cortes was more important than the honor of Javier de Burgos. The former *Secretario de Fomento,* let us not forget, had initiated a severe and arbitrary method pf prior censorship,[8] which was not likely to win the journalist's sympathy with his plight a year later. If Burgos's pamphlet, letters, and article could spark among legal-minded citizens any guilt or alarm over the expedient but arbitrary ouster, Figaro's essay would allay their scruples by showing that the accused was making mountains out of molehills.

The rejection of "La calamidad europea" for publication did not deter its author from another attempt to broach the subject. In his next articles, however, he merely hints at the topic, even though precedents for overt criticism abounded in parliamentary oratory. On September 19, for example, Palarea asserted in Procuradores that national bonds were in the hands of tres o cuatro agiotistas, acostumbrados a chupar la sangre española, porque hay una porción de hombres que se mantienen a costa de la sangre de los pueblos, y son los que han mojado las manos en los empréstitos del año 23 acá. (*Pr.*, p. 291)

(three or four speculators, accustomed to sucking Spain's life-blood, because there are men who support themselves at the cost of the blood of nations, and they are the ones who got their hands wet in the loans from 1823 on.)

On the same day, speaking of Burgos, Serrano used the phrase, "su natural atrevimiento," quoted at the beginning of this chapter. Larra may have been directly influenced by these speeches because a month and a half later, the title of a comedy played at the Teatro de la Cruz, *El vampiro*, gave him an excuse to remind his readers that in Spain

sea dicho con permiso de la censura, si un vampiro es una persona que regresa de luengos sitios a chupar la sangre de los hombres, aquí tenemos uno a la vuelta de cada esquina. Toda la diferencia está en que, más sesudos los alemanes, conservan un miedo muy natural a los que les chupan la sangre, al paso que aquí, más acostumbrados, los vemos andar entre nosotros, y aun hacémosles agasajos. En cambio, nuestros vampiros, más domesticados que los alemanes, no se andan espantando las comarcas ni chupando a salto de mata, sino que chupan a pie firme, van al teatro, van a paseo, viven sanos y colorados, y es preciso estar tan seguros como lo está uno de que murieron efectivamente en otro tiempo para no persuadirse de que son inmortales.

Por lo demás, parécese bastante el *Vampiro* puesto en la Cruz a los vampiros que nos ponen la cruz a nosotros. Va y viene, es arrogante y atrevido; quiérenlo echar, y él no se quiere ir, y por fin se escabulle y se esconde... Gasta coche y cara feroz...; enteramente lo mismo. (2: 23)

(—provided we may say so with the censorship office's permission—, if a vampire is a person who returns from faraway places in order to suck human blood, then here there is one at every street corner. The difference is that the Germans, who have more brains, retain a very natural fear of those who suck their blood, while we, being more accustomed, see them walk among us and even show them friendly consideration. Our vampires, on the other hand, more domesticated than the Germans', don't go around terrifying the countryside by furtively pouncing on their prey. They do their sucking with their feet on the ground; they go to the theater, take walks, live healthy and comfortable lives. In fact, one of them is so sure of himself that we have to be pretty sure ourselves that they did die off in past ages in order not to be convinced that they are immortal.

Aside from this, the *Vampire* put on at the Cruz bears some resemblance to the one who is crucifying us. He comes and goes, arrogant and bold. People try to get rid of him, and he won't go; finally he sneaks off and hides... He has a carriage and a ferocious expression...; entirely alike.)

The hypothesis that this passage is a characterization of Burgos is by no means unfounded. We should note how the description of the vampire as "atrevido" accords with Serrano's phrase above. And the words "quiérenlo echar, y él no se quiere ir, y por fin se escabulle" probably refer to the expulsion scene of October 18.

From a stylistic point of view, the excellence of this theatrical review consists primarily in the fortunate combination of politics and drama, a frequent technique of Larra's. Antimetaboles, such as the one on *cruz*, evince likewise Figaro's facility for utilizing every particular. The Burgos affair is not the only political allusion in Larra's article, which discusses, besides *El vampiro*, Ventura de la Vega's translation of Scribe's *La Grande Aventure*. Figaro says inter alia:

Arreglada a nuestra escena por mano maestra, comenzaremos por hacer justicia al traductor, quien no sólo la ha adaptado bien, sino que la ha salpimentado de gracias propias y picantes, entre las cuales no es la menor ni la menos oportuna la coplita alusiva al Estatuto, que dice en las primeras escenas Retascón. Alabar en esta parte al señor Vega no es más que dar a Dios lo que es de Dios, y al César lo que es del César. (2: 23)

(Let us first do justice to the translator, who adjusted it to our stage with a masterful hand, not only adapting it well, but also spicing it with his own piquant wit, not the least amusing or opportune example of which is the jingle alluding to the Estatuto, spoken by Retascón in the first act. To praise Mr. Vega for this is merely to render unto God what is God's and unto Caesar what is Caesar's.)

On pondering this passage, we might conclude that, while "no es la menor" applies to Vega's muse, "oportuna" may be an apt word for Martínez de la Rosa's political creed; and that the two are as distinct as God and Caesar.

The other Larra essays of this period bear little relation to the Burgos affair. The first is "Lo que no se puede decir no se debe decir," apparently contemporaneous with "La calamidad europea." Though political, it does not touch on parliamentary events but is instead a satire of the newspaper censorship regulation issued by Moscoso de Altamira on June 1, which Larra quotes extensively.[9] Not published at the time, this essay was first printed in the *Colección* and bears the date October 1834.[10] Nevertheless, since verifiably erroneous dates appear on other unpublished articles, we cannot assume reliability in this case; and besides, it is difficult to determine time of writing because of a total absence in the essay of any reference to historical events.

There are, however, political echoes in essays written shortly afterwards. A review of Scribe's *El diplomático* (November 2) alludes to diplomatic problems:

> Concluiremos deseando a nuestros Chavignys tanta fortuna como el de Scribe, puesto que sería una incongruencia exigirles más habilidad, ya que las armas no tienen la mejor fortuna. ¡Pluguiera al cielo y a Scribe llover tantas casualidades felices, que no se echase de menos en ellas el talento! ¡Pluguiera al cielo que nuestra Cuádrupla Alianza, cuyo objeto sigue desgraciadamente en pie, nos mereciese tantos aplausos como monsieur Chavigny, desembarazándonos, a imitación suya, y aunque fuese por casualidad, de nuestros dos importunos pretendientes! (2: 31)

> (Let us conclude by wishing our Chavignys as much luck as Scribe's, since it would be incongruous to expect of them more ability when we consider that arms aren't having the best of luck. May it please heaven and Scribe to rain upon us so many happy chance events that talent will not be missed! May it please heaven that our Quadruple Alliance, whose goal still stands firm unfortunately, will deserve from us as much applause as Monsieur Chavigny, getting rid, as he does, and even if through sheer luck, of our two vexatious pretenders!)

This passage demonstrates Larra's cleverness at comparing the theater and politics. While taking Scribe to task for abusing the deus ex machina, he implies that letters (one branch of the state) will need that kind of luck, since arms (the other branch) has not had much success either.

In the two-part essay entitled "Dos liberales o lo que es entenderse," published on November 13 and 16, the author again gives his opinion on the employees problem in pseudoautobiographical form. What was pointed out in the chapter on civil servants suffices as an explanation of its content. It is noteworthy that the essay's second installment contains a rather nasty allusion to Burgos:

A saber yo hurtar, otro gallo me cantara, y no tendría en el día necesidad de ser hoy en el día liberal, que antes pudiera ser lo que me diese la gana; y así podría irme a Francia con el dinero y la maldición del público, como tomar a mi cargo un buen destino de donde pudiera seguir haciendo de las mías, que el dinero llama dinero. (2: 35)

(If I knew how to steal, I'd certainly be better off and wouldn't have to be a liberal right now. I could be whatever I wanted; I could go to France with the public's money and curses, or get myself a nice position where I could be up to my old tricks, because it takes money to make money.)

Larra's next known work is a translation of a Scribe play staged on November 26, after which there is nothing from his pen until December 12 when the pessimistic *artículo de costumbres* entitled "La vida de Madrid" appears in *El Observador*.[11] One more piece of Larra's is known to have been printed in 1834, an attack on the abuse of special privilege by the members of the city council ("Bailes de máscaras," December 17). This was apparently a very difficult period for Figaro;[12] he may have been quite ill. In the meantime several important parliamentary debates took place, none of which are reflected in his signed articles. The first debate concerned some new bylaws Martínez had prescribed for Cortes, one of which required that twelve members sign a petition before it could go to committee; many *procuradores* felt that it was the prerogative of a congress to prescribe bylaws for itself. Another debate touched upon the proposed publication of a *Diario de Cortes* giving full and faithful transcriptions of the deliberations, so that Spaniards would not have to rely for information solely on the unreliable précis and incorrect quotations of the press. The Moderates in this instance felt that *La Gaceta,* a government publication, was sufficient, though admitting its inaccuracy in "unofficial" reporting. The most important sessions lasted from November 10 to 25 in Procuradores and from December 15 to 16 in Próceres. They dealt with the government's proposed law to determine membership and organization of the militia, which, as we know, posed a threat to the ministers, who feared its use in a coup. Yet there is no mention by Larra of these parliamentary happenings until much later, a state of affairs for which we have no substantiated explanation.

11

MACHINATIONS IN
THE CABINET

W E shall now deal with three articles, "Revista del año 1834," "Atrás," and "Adelante," of which, whether through censorship or through caution on the editor's part, not one was published at the time. "Revista del año 1834" first appeared in the *Colección;* the other two were not even published during the author's life.[1] The only possible way of dating these essays is through their content, careful analysis of which unavoidably leads to the conclusion that "Atrás" was written in late December 1834, "Revista" on December 31, and "Adelante" between January 4 and 17, 1835.[2] The period that concerns us here, the month preceding the Post-Office Mutiny of January 17, does not present itself clearly to the historian, owing to its troubled nature. Much information is lacking on political affairs as well as Larra's life; but this should not surprise us because many persons who were then plotting against the government attained power a year or two later, at which time they felt embarrassed about their former conspiratorial role and saw to it that the historiography of the period would suffer several lacunae. With respect to Larra we can surmise, nevertheless, that in the course of that month he was probably ill and possibly had to be bled.[3]

The dominant factor in this month-long period was the machinations of the secretary of war, Manuel Llauder, whose rise to power was facilitated by his predecessor's blunders. Zarco del Valle's failure had become evident as the conflict worsened, with Christinist troops suffering humiliating defeats at the hands of Zumalacárregui. As one might expect, the Progressives blamed the whole cabinet, whose political attitude, they emphasized, was the ultimate cause of these military reverses. And they pointed to an obvious example, the policy of barring liberal generals from command. Increasingly railed at for its inefficiency, the government finally decided to give the left its chance to improve the situation. Altering its policy, the ministry on November 3 gave command of the Army of the North to Espoz y Mina, guerrilla hero of the War of Independence and leader of an ill-fated Liberal incursion from France in 1830.

Mina did not obtain better results than his conservative predecessors. Though well-acquainted with the Basque country, he was old, sick, lacking in strategic knowledge, and inclined to retaliate unscrupulously. All this was bound to have political repercussions. Zarco del Valle, realizing that the Progressives were not about to place the blame on their hero, resigned rather than face their ire. The Progressives, of course, would fain have made a scapegoat out of any minister, especially to cover up the errors of a general they did not want discredited. According to one historian, Zarco's remarks to the queen about her morganatic marriage, whose first fruit was born in secrecy on November 7, 1834, were another reason for his resignation.[4]

On December 13 Manuel Llauder assumed the vacant post. Though not Martínez's choice, he was favored by María Cristina; hence, the prime minister did not stand in the way of his nomination. Llauder, it will be remembered, had been an instrument of Ferdinand's policy in pursuing the reactionary Agraviados and, later, Mina. During the last days of the Zea régime, however, he had joined the liberal camp by his famous exposition to the regent (see chapter 2). Because of this opportunist inconsistency, the Progressives still looked upon him with suspicion, and Mina had to swallow his pride on seeing an old persecutor appointed his superior. It did not take long, however, for the Progressives to start badgering Llauder in Cortes. The daily debates on the war ministry budget, lasting from December 27 to 31, served as an occasion to criticize him for some administrative changes he had effected in his ministry, the attack coming from the Conde de las Navas (*Pr.*, pp. 1032, 1041), Manuel Arango (p. 1033), and Antonio González (p. 1035). Llauder must have sensed from the beginning that the more liberal the government, the worse he would fare, for there was too much bitterness against him from the left. Not even his statement in Procuradores that "he repuesto a centenares y aun millares de oficiales que habían sido destituidos por la reacción de 1823" (*Pr.*, p. 1003—"I have reinstated hundreds, thousands of officers who had been dismissed through the reaction of 1823") could help him win much sympathy. Furthermore, he was ambitious. He took advantage of the government's weakness to bring himself to the fore and thus incurred the suspicion and rivalry of his colleagues, who could plainly see that he was attempting to form his own ministry.[5] Contemporary observers correctly predicted that Llauder's behavior would lead to a coup, caused by "la división del Ministerio desde la llegada de Llauder, que se propone formar uno de su cuenta para salvar la patria, cuya situación es cada día más complicada"[6] ("the division in the cabinet since the arrival of Llauder, who plans to form one of his own in order to save the country, whose situation becomes more complicated every day"). It goes without saying that the prospective régime would have been even more conservative than Martínez de la Rosa's. And this is precisely what Larra means by the word "Atrás" and the phrases,

> un Ministerio que sea el justo medio entre Cea y *el justo medio;* que se coloque entre setiembre del año pasado y setiembre de éste, si cabe en tan corto trecho. (4: 325)

> (a ministry that will be the middle road between Cea and *the middle road;* which will fit halfway between September of last year and September of the present one, a rather short period within which to snuggle, if you ask me.)

It was to help avert the threat of a swerve to the right that Larra wrote "Atrás," in which he ironically attributes the danger of a sudden swing of the pendulum to Spain's having gone too far to the left and lists litotically the few measures that have been taken by the government in that direction:

> He aquí el inconveniente de andar demasiado: en un año, nada más que en un año, nos veíamos libres, como quien dice; ya se habían hecho dos o tres ejemplares, lo menos, con carlistas; se habían convocado Cortes; se había echado abajo, no sin dificultad, el voto de Santiago: todo el voto de Santiago; se había discutido largamente, muy largamente, la tabla de derechos; no se habían prohibido en todo el año más que cuatro o cinco periódicos, de Real Orden; se había mudado el nombre de Ministerio de Fomento en Ministerio de lo Interior, y el de subdelegado en gobernador; se había protegido tanto a la Milicia Urbana, que ya la teníamos dividida por cuarteles; y se había animado tanto el espíritu público, que ya había cuatro batallones, cuatro, en Madrid—en todo Madrid—. ¡Cuidado si habíamos adelantado! Se podía imprimir todo lo que permitían los censores regios; y en fin, asómbrense VV. de lo que habíamos andado. Ya varias veces había prometido el Gobierno dar la ley de Ayuntamientos. (4: 325)

> (This is the disadvantage of going too fast: in one year, no more than one year, we found ourselves free, as one might say. At least two or three examples had been set with Carlists; Cortes had been convoked; the Oath of Saint James, the entire Oath of Saint James, had been done away with, though not easily; the bill of rights had been discussed at length, at great length; not more than four or five newspapers in the whole year had been prohibited by royal order; the name of Ministry of Development had been changed to Ministry of the Interior, and its subdelegates renamed governors; the Urban Militia had been so well protected that it was already quartered; and popular enthusiasm had been so encouraged that there were four battalions, four, in Madrid—in all of Madrid—. You can bet we had made progress! You could print everything permitted by the royal censors; and so, just be astonished at how far we'd gone. The Government had promised several times a new electoral district law.)

It must be emphasized that the above should in no way be construed as criticism of Cortes. It is plainly an attack on the cabinet. The Procuradores had in fact kept busy, not only debating the budget since December 11, but, before that date, drafting, discussing, and passing several petitions. Most of the petitions went virtually unanswered by the Crown, which explains why Larra makes light of whatever has been accomplished. Exaggeration or, in this case, understatement, is usual fare in satirical writing, especially when progress is measured in the glare of frustration. It ought to be pointed out that the regent had replied to some of the petitions with the mere formula, "mandaré examinarlas y resolveré lo conveniente" (*Pr.*, p. 705—"I shall have them examined and shall determine what is convenient"). Such heedlessness would eventually break the patience of virulent deputies like the Conde de las Navas, who expostulated the government on October 20 during the debate on bylaws:

> Se ha dicho que el derecho de petición es bastante extenso y que no lo hay tanto en Francia. Pues aquí, con tanta latitud como tiene es nulo, porque con un *visto bueno y al Archivo* está despachado . . . Ha hablado S.S. [Argüelles] del veto absoluto; pero no ha hecho mérito de este *visto bueno y al Archivo*, y que disimulen hasta la legislatura que viene." (*Pr.*, p. 581)

> (It was said that the right of petition is sufficiently broad and that in France it is not as much so. But here, with all its latitude, it is worthless, because with an *acknowledged and to the Archives* the matter is settled . . . His Lordship spoke about the absolute veto, but did not mention this *acknowledged and to the Archives* by means of which the matter is dissembled until the next legislature.)

In order to understand the gravity of the situation, we should note in passing that, besides those already mentioned in the preceding chapters, fifteen petitions had been presented to the Crown by Cortes, including one for the redemption of mortgages held through mortmain, by means of government bonds; several on local taxation; one to abolish the special privileges of the inhabitants of Sierra Morena; another to prohibit the importation of foreign grain; one on the salaries of consular employees; and the controversial petition on electoral district assemblies (*ayuntamientos*). Among the tasks performed by the Cortes, we should also note several proposals discussed in Procuradores but put aside or defeated before reaching the Crown: among them one on the raisin tax; another on entailed estates (*mayorazgos*); and one for renewal of friendly relations with the former American colonies (the matter was dropped after the government had been bitterly attacked). Furthermore, ever since December 11 the chamber had been occupied with the budget. And just before that, three days were spent debating and passing a law on property of undetermined ownership (*bienes mostrencos*). It is therefore evident that the parliament had not been idle. Neither had the ministers, whose time was taken up drafting their budgets and defending their programs in Cortes. Figaro's satire obviously cannot be directed at indolence—as some critics have erroneously believed—but rather at political stagnation; and not at the representatives but, as usual, at the ministry.

"Revista del año 1834" corroborates with its direct assertions the ironic nature of statements in "Atrás." The sentence, "He visto abolido el voto de Santiago, pequeño paso, y como éste otros tan menudos que ni los recuerdo" (2: 51—"I saw the Oath of Saint James abolished, a small step, and, like this one, others so tiny that I can't even recall them"), spoken by the old year, echoes "se había echado abajo, no sin dificultad, el voto de Santiago: todo el voto de Santiago" (4: 325) of "Atrás." The phrase, "todo el voto," refers to Martínez's attempt, discussed in chapter 7, to put through a halfway measure. Likewise, the dying year utters with respect to censorship: "Debo advertir que he vivido amordazado, y que muero todavía sin voz" (2: 51—"I should note that I have lived with a gag on, and die still voiceless"). This is equivalent to the meiosis of "Atrás": "Se podía imprimir todo lo que permitían los censores regios" (4: 325). "Revista del año 1834," because of its recapitulative nature, is bound to repeat the mots of previous essays. Such is the case with the locution "naturaleza antico-moderna" applied to Cortes, and the witty pun, "En mis primeros momentos de vida, en tiempo de máscaras por más señas, llamé al poder a un hombre todo esperanzas, de estos de quienes se dice simplemente que prometen" (2: 51—"In the first moments of my life, during the mascarade ball season—as a further indication—, I called to power a man who was all hopes, the kind about whom it is said simply that they promise"). There is, moreover, one sentence in this article that may be inspired by parliamentary oratory. Alcalá Galiano, during the October 20 debate on by-laws, had exclaimed: "la desconfianza, esa desconfianza en el poder popular; ese temor a la anarquía, el cual, sin ver el verdadero peligro que nos amenaza, nos hace recelar otro enteramente ilusorio" (*Pr.*, p. 576—"distrust, this distrust of popular power; this fear of anarchy, which causes us, without perceiving the real threat, to beware of another, a totally illusory one"). These words of his friend and editor may have been in Larra's mind when he wrote: "Durante mi tiempo ha nacido un monstruo, el *miedo a la anarquía;* monstruo como el terror, pánico; él ha perseguido a mis hijos predilectos, él ha alargado la vida a los hijos de mis diez antepasados..." (2: 51—"During my time was born a monster, the *fear of anarchy;* a monster like terror, like panic; it persecuted my favorite children and prolonged the life of the children of my ten predecessors...").

Let us now turn to Figaro's next piece, "Adelante," which is addressed to his old friend Silva Carvalho d'Alburquerque, the imaginary Portuguese. Several ideas already expressed in "Atrás" are taken up again, especially the infighting ensuing from Llauder's machinations. One of Larra's sentences on the subject is noteworthy: "El resultado fue que se levantó una nube, que hubo listas de ministros nuevos que era lo que había que leer, y aun yo te dijera sus nombres, no más que por distraerte" (4: 326—"What happened was that it raised up a storm; there were lists of ministers, and they were something to read! I might even tell you their names, just to amuse you"). The journalist, nonetheless, is merely echoing the Progressives' consternation, later expressed, for example, by García Carrasco on January 19 during the debate following the Correos incident:

> Se ha dicho que un individuo del Gobierno trataba de presentar nuevos candidatos que reemplazasen a sus compañeros; y causa horror el decir los sujetos que designaba la opinión pública como tales. (*Pr.*, p. 1243)

> (It was said that a member of the Government was trying to present new candidates to replace his colleagues; and mere mention of the individuals indicated as such by public opinion causes horror.)

Larra, in addition, uses such references to national events in order to reiterate his distress over censorship, though not directly but through apophasis:

quien perdió en la refriega fue el artículo ["Atrás"], que no vio la
luz; no vayas a entender que se prohibió, nada de eso; ni yo lo dijera si hubiera sido así, ni me lo dejaran imprimir tampoco.[7] (4:
326)

(in the struggle, the one that lost was the article, which did not
see the light. Don't get it into your head that it was prohibited,
nothing of that sort. If this had been the case, I wouldn't say so,
and they wouldn't let me print it either.)

Figaro also mentions the troubles he underwent owing to his article of December 17, "Bailes de máscaras. Billetes por embargo,"
which exposed incipient graft in the municipal government.

It is only halfway through "Adelante" that Larra begins to discuss parliamentary events, namely the debates on the budget, the
ayuntamientos, and judgeships. The ministers had presented their
budgets to Cortes several weeks previously, and, as committees
pored over them, it became evident that heated discussions would
take place before the chamber gave its approval. The expected
antagonism came to the surface on December 5 when the Conde
de las Navas accused the ministry of "morosidad" for some delay
in providing the budget committees with pertinent financial information (*Pr.*, p. 832). First on the list was the royal household
budget. The government's request, presented to the lower house
on October 11, 1834, had amounted originally to 56,300,000
reales, divided as follows: 35,000,000 for Isabel; 12,000,000 for
María Cristina; 5,760,000 for Don Francisco; 3,000,000 for Don
Sebastián; and 540,000 for the Princess of Saxony (*Pr.*, appendix
to no. 60, p. 2, and pp. 864–866). On December 4, the committee
appointed to examine this budget announced its judgment to reduce it to 46,650,000 reales, divided as follows: 30,000,000 for Isabel; 12,000,000 for María Cristina; 3,500,000 for Don Francisco;
and 1,150,000 for Don Sebastián (*Pr.*, pp. 830, 866). It also advocated the cancellation of the Princess of Saxony's pension. A
minority report was delivered by Ignacio Samponts, who recommended an even more austere budget of 36,650,000, giving 24,-
000,000 to Isabel, 8,000,000 to María Cristina, but not diverging
from the majority with respect to Don Francisco and Don Sebastián. It was pointed out that the Princess of Saxony's allowance
had amounted to the contribution of a whole province.

A vehement debate began on December 11. Istúriz, one of the first to speak, went back to the subject of the national debt and suggested that it be paid "con tal cosa (cosa que aunque yo sepa cuál es no la diré, porque al Gobierno es a quien toca proponerla al Estamento)" (*Pr.*, p. 868—"with something—something I won't say even though I know what it is, because it's up to the Government to propose it to the Chamber"). He probably meant the appropriation of Church property. There followed a long discussion on procedure. According to Joaquín José de Muro, Marqués de Someruelos, this budget was hard to determine because, whereas in others "partimos ya de datos y necesidades positivas, . . . en el presupuesto de la casa Real por el contrario todas las consideraciones son morales" (*Pr.*, 870—"we can begin to reckon from positive data and needs, . . . in the Royal Household budget, on the contrary, all considerations are moral"). Trueba y Cosío, on the other hand, felt that the Estamento should examine the budget with the same thoroughness as customs inspectors looking for contraband (*Pr.*, p. 887). When Toreno attempted to damp the intensity of the debate by hinting that it would lead to distrust of Spanish credit abroad, Argüelles answered that all Europe already knew of Spain's financial situation (*Pr.*, p. 870). In any event, the *procuradores* had to proceed with great delicacy, for they did not want to offend María Cristina. Even the fiery Joaquín María López, though he approved of a further reduction in Isabel's allowance, had scruples about altering the regent's 12,000,000 (*Pr.*, p. 886). (This was, of course, a mere formality; Isabel's allowance was in her mother's hands.) López was also first in proposing cancellation of Don Sebastián's allowance, the result being that this Infante received nothing. Perhaps the matter was badly handled by the Progressives. Sebastián had not sworn allegiance to Isabel as queen because he was in Italy at the time of the ceremony. Nevertheless he had earlier attended her proclamation as Princess of Asturias. Thus, the decision of the Procuradores may have become the decisive factor in his subsequent trip to the Basque provinces to join Carlos.

The question of the regent's and the queen's budget was, to be sure, a matter of great delicacy. The Procuradores began treating it in a roundabout way, but soon the Progressives put aside their reticence lest they lose the argument. Thus, a comparison with the French and English royal budgets (*Pr.*, p. 887) paved the way for a comparison between the needs of presidents and kings (p. 893). Lofty words about gratitude to the regent were soon replaced by mention of the blood shed to maintain the Bourbons on the throne (*Pr.*, p. 901), about whose splendor the Progressives were not as concerned as the Moderates. One of the latter was worried lest the royal family have to sell its stables and rent its horses and carriages. He was answered by a Progressive who emphasized the burden on the nation and suggested that the queen could stay at La Granja, where the common people could not gaze upon her. Other points of argument were royal protection of the arts and sciences, upkeep of historical monuments and palaces, and the shame of forcing Isabel to dismiss her father's servants. Someone felt that a female child should receive less than a king. Caballero threw back at Martínez de la Rosa his favorite point of departure, the Middle Ages, by speaking of the medieval Cortes' limitations on the king's budget of yore. Navas brought Joseph Bonaparte's budget into the debate, which led to some sharp repartee (*Pr.*, pp. 931, 934).

Apparently the ministers had informally sent word to the pertinent committee that they would not oppose its curtailment of the royal household budget. Alcalá Galiano, having learned of this, callously stated in the debate that he would like to know "el secreto de por qué habiéndola fijado el Gobierno en 35 millones, después se había convenido en rebajarla a 30, para ver si podía aplicarse el mismo secreto a otra rebaja mayor" (*Pr.*, p. 913—"the secret about why, after fixing it at 35 million, the Government agreed to lower it to 30, so I might see whether the same secret could be applied to another, bigger reduction"). This brought on some sharp replies, because it constituted an accusation that the committee majority's five-million reduction was a pretense to avoid giving an appearance of staunch ministerialism. When the time came to decide on its 30,000,000 proposal for Isabel, the Procuradores rejected it by 74 to 56 votes, with two abstentions.

On December 16 the minority proposal, Samponts's 24 million, was likewise defeated, by a vote of 80 to 64. Then debate began anew, resulting in a compromise proposal of 28 million being sent to committee (*Pr.*, p. 920). This, along with a new minority report by Samponts, came up for discussion on December 17. Samponts's proposal was upheld by the Conde de las Navas, who showed that 27, and not 28, was the mean of 24 and 30 (*Pr.*, p. 930). Persevering in arithmetical reasoning, he argued that since a reduction from 35 to 30 million had been deemed feasible, then one from 30 to 24 was just as workable (*Pr.*, p. 932). Navas also objected to the 6,000,000 reales assigned to the royal stables alone, and felt that care of historical monuments should be temporarily discontinued (*Pr.*, p. 931). As a final blow, in trying to convince his hearers that the royal household appropriation should be in proportion to the nation's resources and not to its general expenditures (Francisco Domecq y Victor's opinion), Navas compared it to servants' wages (*Pr.*, p. 930).

But the discussion had degenerated to the Progressives' disadvantage, and the 28 million were approved by 78 votes against 43, with two abstaining. On December 18 María Cristina's 12,-000,000 reales were voted by 115 to 14 opposed, the latter including Samponts, Istúriz, Navas, and Caballero, who wanted to reduce the regent's budget further. Joaquín María López, Antonio González, and Argüelles sided with the majority, one of the few instances where the Progressive core was divided.[8]

Next came Don Francisco's allowance. Joaquín Fleix, who advocated the government's proposal, pointed out that Francisco and Luisa Carlota had eight children to support, as well as "la importancia del servicio que a la causa de la libertad hizo su augusta esposa, volando desde las columnas de Hércules a la Granja a desbaratar los planes de los amantes del absolutismo" (*Pr.*, p. 942 —"the importance of the service rendered to the cause of liberty by his august spouse, who hastened from the Pillars of Hercules to La Granja in order to thwart the plans of the lovers of absolutism"), a reference to the events described in chapter 8. But Fleix was no match for the Conde de las Navas, who argued that since the queen's apportionment had been reduced the same fate might as well befall this one, in the same proportion. Finally, the government's proposal was rejected by 97 against 23, and the curtailed allowance specified by the committee approved.

When they came to Don Sebastián, the Progressives, who wanted to cut him off from the budget, criticized him in a way approaching slander. Navas, for example, declaimed that "no se

debe dar ni un cuarto al Infante Don Sebastián" (*Pr.*, p. 947—
"not even a penny must be given to Don Sebastian"). Martínez
de la Rosa had to rebuke these speakers by stating that

> debe estar prohibido y vedado descender a una especie de arena,
> para entablar una lucha personal, a fin de que tratándose de rebajar
> las cantidades propuestas, se entre a hacer inculpaciones que por
> vagas e indeterminadas deberían omitirse, aun con respeto al último
> de los ciudadanos, cuanto más aludiéndose a personas colocadas
> en tan alta clase y categoría. (*Pr.*, p. 948)

> (descending to a kind of arena to start a personal contention for
> the purpose of lowering the proposed quantities should be for-
> bidden, in order to avoid inculpations which ought to be omitted
> owing to their vagueness and uncertainty, not only with respect
> to the last of our citizens, but the more so when alluding to persons
> situated at such high rank and category.)

In any case, the Progressives got their point across, and the chamber determined by 65 against 22 votes to give nothing to Sebastián. The same fate befell the Princess of Saxony, the last person
in the royal family for whom an allowance had been requested.
In view of this last development, I should like to put forward a
hypothesis that might elucidate a passage in "Adelante."

It does not require much imagination to surmise that soon after
the public learned about the fate accorded Don Sebastián, some
wag, or wags, uttered the well-known proverb, "El último mono
es el que se ahoga," which means that in a time of crisis those at
the bottom come to grief.[9] It fits the situation perfectly and must
soon have been on everyone's lips. I shall attempt to explain below how this may tie in with Larra's essay.

We have seen how, in the case of the royal household budget,
the Progressives achieved their purpose by reducing not only the
amounts proposed by the government but also those proposed by
the committee's majority. This indicates a triumph on the floor as
well as in committee. On the other hand, they did not fare so well
in the debates on the state and war budgets, which lasted respectively from December 19 to 23 and 27 to 31. The chamber, in voting funds for the administration of these two departments, did not
reduce the committee's proposed amounts. Hence, any success
the Progressives had must have been in the committees. In some

cases the government's higher figures were actually preferred by the Procuradores to their committee's recommendations.[10]

It is understandable that after these goings-on Larra should write in "Adelante":

> Ahora estamos con los presupuestos: el primer día todo era sacar de una parte y sacar de otra; y como el de Casa Real fue el primero, y pilló a la gente caliente y con ganas de ahorrar, sucedió lo contrario de lo que dice el refrán, es a saber, que aquí fue el primer mono el que se ahogó: pero luego ha sucedido como en todas las cosas; con que *adelante*. Se están haciendo unas economías, que no hay para qué elogiarlas; y esto van ta de prisa, que bien se puede decir que ya el presupuesto va de capa caída. (4: 326)

> (Now we've gotten to the budgets. On the first day it was all removing from this part and picking from that; and since the Royal Household came first, and this budget caught people in an excited mood and with the desire to save, what happened was the contrary of what the proverb says; to wit, here the first monkey was the one that drowned. But later on things happened as they always do. So, *let's go on*. You just can't praise the economies that are being made. The whole business is going so rapidly, you could say that whatever the budget is cloaked in droops down.)

Here Figaro makes use of a pun on *pillar*, for which he prepares the way with *sacar*, so that by semantic assimilation the reader will think of its primary acceptation. But "caliente" is predicate to "gente"; consequently, *pillar* must be understood in its familiar acceptation of "sorprender a uno en un descuido." The author's meaning is that the opening of the debates found the delegates in an animated state and with a desire to economize; many Moderates at this critical moment were "caught" voting with the Progressives, thus relinquishing ministerialist tendencies when it came to saving their constituents some tax payments. On the other hand, we are reminded of the literal meaning of *pilló*. Anything used as the subject of such a verb would be automatically personified; hence we imagine the budget "pillaging" the taxpayers' assets, or, for that matter, the Progressives "pillaging" the royal household budget by removing appropriations here and there.

Furthermore, the royal household budget, which came first, was considerably slashed, but not the two that followed it. In this case, consequently, the first monkey is the one who drowned. This remark may not seem very witty *per se*. Yet when we consider that people were probably saying (about the royal household budget alone) that the last monkey drowned (referring to the Princess of Saxony), then we realize how cleverly Larra turned the concept around, applying to this situation, by a linguistic tour-de-force, the opposite of the characterization used by everyone else.

Yet the flow of humor has not stopped. The image we have of the budget is still a boatload of monkeys, so that the personification, or rather "simification," reinforces the combination of punning and irony in the next sentence. Although the debates on the state and war budgets took ten days, very few economies resulted. Consequently, "esto va tan de prisa" is ironic in two ways: no one is in any hurry to reduce the budget and the discussions have been going on too long. Combining this punned irony with "va de capa caída" is a stroke of genius: to write that the budget is crestfallen is merely ironic, for in fact few curtailments have been made in it; but to imply moreover that its cape hangs down straight because it is walking slowly is to restore its literal meaning to a trite expression, the hallmark of great wit.

In "Adelante" Larra also criticizes governmental inaction on a *ley de ayuntamientos*, thereby reflecting the reaction of Progressive *procuradores* to Martínez's equivocation. A petition on the matter had been approved by three committees, whose reports were read on October 9. At this point the *Diario* evinces a pretty piece of political strategy on the government's part:

Concluida la lectura, el Sr. Secretario del Despacho de Estado expuso que, lejos de oponerse el Gobierno a esta petición, había por su parte trabajado largo tiempo sobre tan interesante y complicada materia, y que por resultado de sus trabajos tenía ya concluido un proyecto de ley, que el Sr. Secretario de lo Interior presentaría muy en breve al Estamento. (*Pr.*, p. 501)

(After the conclusion of the reading, the Secretary of State explained that the Government, far from being opposed to the petition, had on its part worked a long time on this interesting and complicated matter, and that as a result of its efforts it had finished drafting a projected law, which the Secretary of the Interior would shortly present to the Chamber.)

As a result, the signers agreed to table, but not withdraw, the petition. Two months later, on December 13, when the government still had not presented a projected law, the signers requested that the petition be discussed, and the chairman ordered it to be printed (*Pr.*, pp. 885–886). On December 26 (in between the debates on the state and war budgets) the matter came up again. Martínez de la Rosa rose to say that

> al paso que es laudable esa impaciencia que muestran los Sres. Procuradores, y que el Gobierno considera muy justa, debe decir que éste tiene ya preparado el proyecto . . .
>   . . . habiendo tocado el Gobierno con nuevas dificultades, que ha tenido que vencer, no ha podido presentarse a la deliberación de las Cortes como hubiera deseado: nadie tiene más empeño en ello que el Gobierno mismo; y por lo tanto espera, en vista de las razones manifestadas, que se suspenda la discusión de esta petición, puesto que nada se adelantaría con ella, o bien que no se le dé curso . . . (*Pr.*, pp. 1013–1014)

> (while on the one hand the impatience shown by the Honorable Procuradores is laudable, and considered quite just by the Government, it must be pointed out that the latter has already prepared the project . . .
>   . . . the Government, having come upon new difficulties which it had to overcome, has not been able to present it to the Cortes for deliberation, as it had wished to. No one is more determined in this matter than the Government itself. Therefore it hopes, in view of the reasons exposed, that discussion of this petition will be suspended, since it would bring no progress, or rather, that it not be opened . . .)

Lasanta said that he was not convinced by the minister, and the petition was voted. On Sunday, January 4, possibly the date of writing of "Adelante," the prime minister sent to the Cortes the queen's resolution concerning this petition: "Mandaré examinarla, y determinaré lo conveniente"[11] ("I shall have it examined and shall determine what is convenient"). We should pause here to consider the fundamental importance of such a law. Any regulations concerning the election of *procuradores* depended on the organization of municipal governments, so that implementation of the representative principle in Spain rested solely on this project. As matters stood then, the government had enough power over the *ayuntamientos* to change them if they went athwart its wishes. Consequently, the *ayuntamientos* were in the habit of sending ministerialist representatives to Cortes in order to ingratiate themselves with the cabinet.[12] This is why Mártinez was in no hurry to put them on a more democratic foundation. Larra's sentence, "Todavía no ha salido la ley de ayuntamientos; pero como los que hay son a pedir de boca, *¡adelante!*" (4: 327—"the electoral district law hasn't been issued yet; but since the existing districts are there just for the asking, *let's go on!*"), provides an accusatory explanation for the delay.

Figaro also deals with the judicial system, a subject that came up in Procuradores on January 2 soon after the Gracia y Justicia budget went to the floor. The committee had followed the ministry's recommendations, with an apology to the chamber for the insignificance of the savings it had suggested in the expensive governmental proposal (*Pr.*, p. 1882); it felt, however, that any additional retrenchment would be hazardous. But if this committee thought it could avert Progressive ire by begging the chamber's forgiveness for its minute economies, it must have been sorely mistaken, because the left attacked as boldly as ever. As soon as his turn came, the Conde de las Navas let forth a brash onslaught which set the tone for Progressive argumentation during the whole debate. Starting with the premise that impunity and arbitrariness are two of the most destructive forces in society, he began to inveigh against corrupt legal practices in existence throughout the land: hasty termination of some cases and unwarranted delay in others, unjust or at least ill-founded judgments, recourse to antiquated laws in order to avoid responsible decisions, and, worst of all, inaction on the ministry's part to halt such practices. Then the count became so bold as to broach the subject of the Isabelinos accused of conspiracy:

cuando se ve a los jueces . . . valerse de fórmulas que están en leyes desusadas acaso para eludir lo que piden los fiscales y demás, y el Ministerio encargado del ramo no toma las medidas necesarias para evitar estos vicios, y poner la sociedad a cubierto de la arbitrariedad de los jueces, ¿qué se podrá decir? Cuando se ven reos o supuestos reos, cuyas causas políticas están sin ventilarse al cabo de cinco o seis meses que tienen de fecha, y a quienes una mano injusta, armada de la arbitrariedad y del despotismo, arrancó de la sociedad, ¿qué se dirá? El Estamento conocerá ya que hago alusión a la causa del 24 de Julio, acerca de la cual se me tiró, hace mucho tiempo, un guante que recogí y ahora saco a la palestra. Cinco meses hace que hablé aquí de esa causa ruidosa, y se me dijo que pronto se examinaría; pero aún no se ha hecho, y los presuntos reos siguen o presos o arrestados. En tanto tiempo ¿no se han encontrado medios de terminar dicha causa? ¿Es éste un buen sistema de administración judicial? ¿Es para esto para lo que vamos a disponer con mano franca del dinero de nuestros comitentes? ¿Podrán, al ver esto, dar con gusto subsidios los gobernados a los gobernantes? Me parece que la respuesta es muy sencilla. Si yo doy diez para que se me conserven veinte, y además de exigírseme los diez se me quitan los veinte, ¿no estaré quejoso? Pero esto es natural, es la ilación de las cosas mismas: si no hay vencedores ni vencidos, como se nos dice siempre; si no se quiere suavizar ciertas cargas por no ofender a varios individuos; si se mantienen en sus puestos muchos que no debían estar en ellos, es natural suceda así. Esto nace, como ya he dicho otra vez, del error en que se ha caído de que unas ruedas carcomidas que han servido al carro de la opresión y tiranía, se pueden adaptar para que sirvan a la brillante carroza de Isabel II, símbolo de la libertad y ventura de la nación española. ¿Qué resultado pues se puede esperar? ¿Cómo se han de corregir los abusos de los que no conociendo su dignidad ni la grandeza del papel que representan en la sociedad, abusan de su poder o por maldad o por debilidad? Y sobre este punto, débiles en asuntos políticos es tanto como decir criminales, en mi concepto, y tal vez en el de muchos de los Sres. Procuradores que me escuchan. Es preciso desconfiar de esos hombres que desprecian el principio, sin el cual no hay sociedad ni puede marchar el Gobierno representativo. Necesito, señores, serenarme mucho, pues me altero demasiado, para poderme explicar en un punto tan grave, tan vital, con toda franqueza.

El Estatuto Real, formado y concedido a la nación por una mano augusta y benéfica, concede la inviolabilidad por las opiniones emitidas en este recinto por los Procuradores. Lo mismo sucedía en la Constitución de año de 1812; y no hay la menor duda en que es sumamente necesaria esa garantía para la existencia de la libertad y del Gobierno representativo. Pero ¿podremos estar seguros de esa garantía al ver todavía en sus destinos a hombres que con mano parricida firmaron la sentencia de muerte contra los Diputados de 1822 por sus opiniones? ¿Podremos tener confianza en este particular? ¿Dónde está, si no hay confianza, ese principio inconcuso sin el cual no existe la libertad en las naciones? Y sin esa garantía ¿cómo podremos emitir nuestras opiniones para el mejor sostén del Trono de nuestra augusta Reina?

Niégueseme que de los individuos que firmaron esa sentencia ominosa, que cubrió de luto y amargura a la nación y de escándalo a toda Europa, algunos no ocupan altos puestos en la judicatura. Veamos más: ¿qué se ha hecho para limpiar y quitar ese borrón infame, ese monumento que sólo puede destruirse con otro monumento; esa sentencia de horca por la que pereció Riego, cuyo nombre aún no se atreven a tomar en boca muchos, y otros temen pronunciarle?

¿Qué se ha hecho para esto? ¿Qué se ha hecho para restaurar el honor, ya que no puede ser la vida, de tantos otros patriotas sacrificados? Nada absolutamente. ¿No están aún en su puesto muchos de esos jueces? Yo no quiero excitar pasiones, ni promover recuerdos de odio y de venganza. No; sólo indico estas cosas para que el Gobierno las tome en cuenta; para que se repare en lo posible dicha falta; para que no sea ilusoria la expresada garantía, y pueda emitirse por todos la opinión libremente, como exigen el mismo Estatuto Real y el bien del país. (*Pr.*, pp. 1088–1089)

(when judges are seen . . . making use of formulas from archaic laws, perhaps in order to elude what prosecutors and others are asking, and the Ministry in charge of this branch does not take the measures necessary to avoid these wrongs and to protect society from the arbitrariness of judges, what can one say? When there are culprits or accused persons whose political cases have still not come to trial after five or six months, and whom an unjust hand, armed with arbitrariness and despotism, has torn away from society, what can one say? The Chamber probably realizes that I am alluding to the case relative to the 24th of July, concerning which a gauntlet was thrown down to me some time ago. I took it up and now bring it to the arena. Five months ago I spoke here of this resounding case and was told it would soon be examined. But this has not been done yet and the accused are still either in jail or under arrest. After so much time has elapsed, have no means been found for putting an end to the case? Is this a good judicial administrative system? Is it for this that we are going to dispose of our constituents' money by the handful? Will the governed, on seeing this, be able to give subsidies with good grace to their rulers? It seems to me the answer is quite simple. If I give ten so that twenty can be preserved for me, and then, besides having the ten exacted, the twenty are taken away, shall I not have a grievance? But this is natural; it follows from the nature of things. If there are no vanquishers and vanquished, as we are told repeatedly; if, in order not to offend a few persons, certain tributes cannot be mitigated; if many persons who should not occupy their posts are kept in them, it is natural that this should happen. This is due, as I said before, to the erroneous notion that the wormeaten wheels used on the chariot of oppression and tyranny can be adapted to serve on the resplendent carriage of Isabel II, symbol of the freedom and good fortune of the Spanish nation. What results can then be expected? How will the abuses of those who, not recognizing their own dignity or the great role they play in society, overstep the bounds of their power either through wickedness or weakness? On this point, let me add that to be weak in political matters is like being criminal, in my view and possibly in that of many Procuradores who hear me. Men who scorn principle, without which society cannot exist and representative government cannot function, must be mistrusted. Gentlemen, since I have become so agitated, I need to calm down now, in order to explain such an important, such a vital point with frankness.

The Estatuto Real, formed and conceded to the nation by an august and beneficent hand, concedes inviolability for the opinions emitted in this hall by the Procuradores. This was also the case in the Constitution of the year 1812; and there is not the slightest doubt that this guarantee is wholly necessary for the existence of liberty and representative government. But can we be certain of this guarantee when we still see at their posts men who with a patricidal hand signed the death sentence against the deputies of 1822 for their opinions? Can we have any confidence in this respect? If there is no confidence, where then is that indisputable principle without which freedom cannot exist in a nation? And without this guarantee, how shall we be able to utter our opinions the better to uphold the Throne of our august Queen?

Let anyone deny that some of the individuals who signed the ominous sentence, which spread mourning and bitterness over the nation and scandal over all Europe, are not occupying high positions in the judiciary. Furthermore, what has been done to clean up and remove that infamous taint, that monument which can only be destroyed through another monument, the sentence to the gallows in which died Riego, whose name many still dare not speak, and others fear to pronounce?

What has been done about this? What was done to restore the honor, since it cannot be the lives, of so many other patriots who were sacrificed? Absolutely nothing. Are not many of those judges still in their posts? It is not my desire to incite passions or foment memories of hate and vengeance. No. I only indicate these matters so the Government will take them up, so that this flaw will be repaired as far as possible, so that the stated guarantee will not be illusory, and that all can express their opinion freely, as demanded by the Estatuto Real itself and the good of the nation.)

Later, directing his attack at the minister himself, the count made clear

el objeto que me proponía; y era este que por no haber remediado las arbitrariedades de los individuos que han traspasado los límites de sus facultades, no era [Garelly] muy acreedor a que se votase el presupuesto. . . . puede que S.S. ignore que algunos de los que firmaron esas sentencias ["de los años 24 y sucesivos" against liberals] están ocupando puestos elevados en la magistratura.

(the point I was aiming at; and it was that the minister of justice was not quite deserving of having his budget voted, since he had not remedied the arbitrary acts of the individuals who transgressed the limits of their faculties. . . . Perhaps His Lordship is unaware that some of those who signed those sentences [from 1824 on against liberals] still occupy high places in the judiciary.)

Garelly replied ably and discreetly to these thrusts (p. 1091), with Martínez de la Rosa and Saturnino Calderón Collantes coming to his aid. But the Progressives, Argüelles and Alcalá Galiano in particular, kept up the attacks. Argüelles, being an experienced orator, chose the more abstract method, debating with Garelly on the relation of the two principles of permanence in office and responsibility, while Galiano, following the lead of the Conde de las Navas, went so far as to bring up, without mentioning their names, the imprisoned Isabelinos, and to remind his audience of the fate of Riego, whose condemners still held their positions.

These Progressive arguments provided a roughhewn model for Figaro's meiotic remarks:

> Ahora andan en dudas en el Estamento sobre si son buenos los jueces o no. Es el caso que, según dicen, los hay todavía de los que sentenciaron en los pasados *diez años,* que siguen sentenciando. *¡Adelante!*
> En los periódicos verás un comunicado de uno de mis amigos. La cosa no es importante: parece que tenía un asuntillo pendiente, en el cual debía llevar razón, según lo mal que le ha salido; fue a verse con uno de los primeros empleados del ramo, y le contestó que no había más que un ligero inconveniente, a saber, que no estaba *purificado.* Este fue el día 3 de este enero de este 1835. A propósito de fechas, la Amnistía se publicó en 15 de octubre de 1833; luego ha habido también un decreto de 31 de diciembre de 1834 sobre rehabilitación de empleados. *¡Adelante!* (4: 327)

> (Now they're having their doubts in the Chamber on whether judges are good or not. The case is, so they say, that some of those who passed sentence during the *ten years* are still sentencing. So, *let's go on!*
> In the newspapers you'll find a letter from one of my friends. It's not an important matter. It seems he had a little business pending, in which he must have been in the right, because he came out so badly. He went to see one of the top administrators in this branch, who answered him that there was just a slight inconvenience; to wit, he wasn't *purified.* This happened on the third day of this January of this year 1835. Speaking of dates, the Amnesty was published on October 15, 1833. Then there was also a decree of December 31, 1834, concerning the rehabilitation of employees. So, *let's go on!*)

The two paragraphs just quoted evince the delicacy of Larra's pseudoepistolary style. They are apparently unrelated, yet linked by the obvious thought that those who issued unjust verdicts are still around to impede their rescission.

From an ideological viewpoint, Larra's essay is a paragon of moderation compared to his chief's oratory, if indeed Alcalá Galiano was still his editor-in-chief at the time.[13] Galiano, among other things, said that the debate had gotten off its track because "ha sucedido lo que debía ocurrir en toda Cámara que no tiene la iniciativa directa, y donde un Representante del pueblo está privado del derecho de petición" (*Pr.*, p. 1099—"what happened was bound to happen in any Chamber which has no direct initiative, and where a Representative of the people is deprived of the right of petition"). He ended his speech by further undermining the Estatuto Real:

> En las naciones que tienen Gobierno representativo, en que la ley coarta el derecho de petición como en la nuestra, y donde se ponen a la opinión pública diques que cuanto mayor es su número más se aumenta la fuerza que los destruye, hay que apelar a un remedio desesperado; pero en otras naciones no sucede lo mismo, pues hay mil modos de manifestar la desconfianza que merece el Ministerio, y de hacer que su poder se desplome sin necesidad de que se trastorne el Estado. Yo no creo que nosotros debamos echar mano de este remedio tan desesperado; pero sí que tenemos derecho de manifestar nuestra opinión, y que elevada ésta al Trono no dejará de hacer su efecto. (*Pr.*, p. 1101)

> (In nations which possess representative government, where the law restrains the right of petition as in ours, and where public opinion is so dammed up that the more this is done, the greater is the force that will burst through, then one must appeal to desperate remedies. But in other nations this does not occur, because there are a thousand ways to express the mistrust deserved by the Ministry, and to bring about its downfall without any need for an upheaval of the State. I do not believe that we must resort to so desperate a remedy; but I do believe we have a right to express our opinion, and that, once it has been taken up to the Throne, it will not fail to have its effect.)

This was unmistakably a hint that the Progressives were making a last attempt to obtain reforms legally, and that their failure would bring on a revolt—which, in fact, came on January 17.

Stylistically, "Adelante" exemplifies Tarr's observation that "the core of [Larra's] articles is often a single happy word or phrase, frequently a title ingeniously elaborated."[14] Though less concise than "Atrás," its relative extensiveness is compensated by full utilization of word plays. These word plays depend on three acceptations of *adelante*: political or social progress, which is the figurative meaning; an exclamation expressing the journalist's intention to persevere in spite of a stroke of bad luck; and the desire of Silva's correspondent to go on to another topic in the letter itself, being the most obvious and informal sense of the word. The occurrence of "adelante" at the end of each paragraph is accordingly an epistrophe of extraordinary ironic complexity. The first paragraph, for example, smacks of Voltairian wit: "Así es que me doy a todos los carlistas: tal es el humor que tengo. Pero... *adelante*" (4: 326—"So I'm possessed by all the Carlists; that's the kind of humor I'm in. But... *let's go on!*"). The word "adelante," in the sense of progress, frames the whole essay in irony while acquiring a distinct and significant shade of meaning in each paragraph. As we have noted, this essay is less compact than "Atrás." Nevertheless, there are subtle threads uniting its paragraphs and giving it continuity. A pregnant vehicle in the first, "parece mi existencia un Gobierno naciente," precedes mention in the second of Llauder's machinations to overhaul the cabinet. The troubles encountered in writing "Atrás," which form another topic of the second paragraph, seem to introduce the theme of the third, a different set of troubles, due this time to the publication of "Bailes de máscaras." The second and third paragraphs are also joined by the concept of suppression, since the third begins, "Luego le he tomado un miedo, no precisamente a escribir artículos, sino a que los lean mis amigos, un miedo tal, que no fuera fácil explicártelo, ni hay motivo para otra cosa" (4: 326 —"Then I was overcome with such fear, not exactly of writing articles, but of having my friends read them, such a fright that it wouldn't be easy to explain it to you, and there's no reason for anything else"). We cannot know, unfortunately, whether this suppression was effected by governmental censorship or editorial self-policing. "Amigo" could refer to the censor or, if it is taken literally, to Larra's editor. Perhaps Figaro sought a double irony; the uninformed reader would assume that "amigo" is an ironic term for the censor, but those in the know might realize that it was meant literally. We are faced with the same problem in "Un periódico nuevo" (January 26, 1835), taken up in the next chapter.

The fifth paragraph of "Adelante," dealing with the national budget, is cunningly placed after the one on financing masked balls. The eighth, criticizing the incredible anachronism of bureaucratic concern with "purification"—in the year 1835!—aptly follows one regarding the judges who are "holdovers" from the reactionary régime.

Structure is the last thing we would look for in a newspaper columnist's production, and perhaps for this reason we may not be conscious of structural unity in some of Larra's articles; but it is there nevertheless, not accidentally, but by the will and genius of the writer.

12

THE POST-OFFICE MUTINY

The first of Figaro's articles actually printed in the year 1835 was "La sociedad," which came out on January 16, just one month after "Bailes de máscaras" (December 17, 1834), his previous publication. "Bailes" is his last essay in *El Observador*, while "La sociedad" marks Larra's return to *La Revista Española*. Since we know almost nothing about the circumstances that prompted his changing papers, we can only conjecture on the relation between Larra and the editors and its effect on his writings. There are a few dubious clues. Both "La sociedad" and the next piece, "Un periódico nuevo" (January 26), were preceded in their newspaper column by the heading "Costumbres." Must we deduce from this that the author was welcomed back to *La Revista* on the condition that he submit only *artículos de costumbres?* He may have acceded to such a demand through financial desperation, not due merely to the halt in revenue from his journalistic production, but also to the pitifully inadequate remuneration for translating two Scribe comedies, *Las desdichas de un amante dichoso*, performed at the Príncipe on January 6, and *El arte de conspirar*, at the Cruz on January 17.[1] Such speculation can be considered seriously because it is possible that rejection of the three articles studied in chapter 11 was due to self-policing by the newspapers rather than to governmental censorship. If such is the case, we have a plausible explanation for Figaro's attempt to start a paper of his own, where he would have to cope with the censor only, and not, in addition, with a policy that imposed temporary editorial moderation to compensate for the editor's (that is, Galiano's) parliamentary boldness.[2]

Although "La sociedad" and "Un periódico nuevo" are labeled "Costumbres," this heading is deceptive. Despite appearances, both have political significance. In the first place, whatever is *costumbrista* about "La sociedad" concerns, not regional types or quaint customs, but fashionable society. Unlike the ordinary *costumbrista* Larra does not provide us here with much prosopography, but rather with a bleak ethopoesis communicated by a disillusioned young "nephew": "¡en la sociedad siempre triunfa la hipocresía!" (1: 444—"in society hypocrisy always triumphs!"); "Esa es la sociedad, una reunión de víctimas y de verdugos" (1: 445—"This is society, a reunion of victims and executioners!"). Over a third of the article consists in a sort of philosophical exordium, where "sociedad" is understood in an abstract sense, which leads the reader to believe that the article will advocate some positive social philosophy. The reader soon realizes, however, that any abstract solution leads to cynicism:

> La sociedad es, pues, un cambio mutuo de perjuicios recíprocos. Y el gran lazo que la sostiene es, por una incomprensible contradicción, aquello mismo que parecería destinado a disolverla; es decir, el egoísmo. (1: 442)

> (Society is thus an interchange of reciprocal offenses. And the great bond which upholds it is, by an incomprehensible contradiction, the very thing that would seem destined to dissolve it: selfishness.)

As often happens with Larra, the philosophical language of his prolegomenon merely provides a medium for satire. Here the immediate object of his satire is the thing known as "society" by antonomasia, the social life of the leisure class, here specifically that of Madrid. The philosophical prolegomenon, however, leads us to expect a discussion based on the general, not the specific acceptation of the term. Yet, after the exordium, Larra writes as though he were free to assume that in his essay the word "society" is still applicable to a particular entity designated by that name in common usage, that is, "high society." This ambiguity allows him to focus his argument on specific grounds, then to deduce generalizations without any preoccupation for possible semantic distinctions revolving on *sociedad*. Even in high society backwardness is evident, and he will expose it to demonstrate that crassness and ignorance produce malice and selfishness:

> ¿Hablar a las mujeres en Madrid? Como en general no se sabe hablar de nada, sino de intrigas amorosas, como no se habla de artes, de ciencias, de cosas útiles, como ni de política se entiende, no se puede uno ni dirigir ni sonreír tres veces a una mujer . . . En una palabra, en esta sociedad de ociosos y habladores nunca se concibe la idea de que puedas hacer nada inocente, ni con buen fin, ni sin fin. (1: 445)

> (Speak to women in Madrid? Since generally no one knows how to talk about anything except love affairs, since no one speaks of arts, sciences, useful things, since no one even understands anything about politics, you can't address or smile three times at a woman . . . In a word, in this society of loafers and gossipers the idea could never enter anyone's mind that you could be doing something innocent, either with honorable motives or without motives.)

"La sociedad" is thus another one of those *artículos de costumbres* to end all *artículos de costumbres;* it almost implies that the genre is not worth writing and is cultivated only because what really should be written cannot or may not. "La sociedad" is the *artículo de costumbres* which grudgingly admits its impotence; which, after attempting to become a political essay, expresses the futility of rebelling against its own nature:

> Ahora bien: convencidos de que todo lo malo es natural y verdad, no nos costará gran trabajo probar que la sociedad es natural, y que el hombre nació por consiguiente social; no pudiendo im-

pugnar la sociedad, no nos queda otro recurso que pintarla.
(1: 442)

(Now then, being convinced that everything bad is natural and
true, it will not be hard to prove that society is natural and that
consequently man was born a social being. As we cannot impugn
society, our only recourse is to paint it.)

And so with the author himself. Not having had a single article
published in one month, Figaro records his defeat. Yet the very
ability to record this defeat is a triumph, for it constitutes another
fling at his principal adversary, the censor, and another opportunity to advocate, by insinuation, freedom of expression, which, in
Larra's view, is the greatest national desideratum.

During the reign of Ferdinand, Larra had given his public two
so-called *artículos de costumbres* portraying the difficulty of innovation in Spain: "La fonda nueva" (August 23, 1833) and
"Las casas nuevas" (September 13, 1833). On January 26, 1835, he
produced "Un periódico nuevo," which explains the troubles he
faced in attempting to start his own paper. Again, the adversity
encountered trying to innovate is seen as a manifestation of a national affliction. Lack of press freedom is cautiously touched on,
as well as the unavoidably limited contents of censored newspapers. With such topics Larra finds an excuse to satirize some of
the oratory heard in Cortes on the day after the Post-Office
Mutiny.

Before we examine these echoes of politics in "Un periódico
nuevo," let us scan the historical events preceding its publication.
In the beginning of January Cortes passed on the justice department budget, then attended to a projected law to overhaul the
monetary system (*arreglo de la moneda*). Even on this matter the
lines were drawn between Moderates and Progressives, the former
wanting no more than an ad hoc remedy for each one of the
monetary system's more obvious defects, while the Progressives
insisted on a decisive change to the decimal system. Three days
(January 5, 7, 8) were taken up with the discussion. The Progressives, incidentally, showed more concern than the Moderates
about the financial plight of the common people, who, since they
were wont to hoard gold, would suffer the greatest losses as a re-

sult of alterations in the fineness of coins. The government, perceiving an impending defeat of its bill, decided to withdraw it, which gave rise to a polemic on the legality of such a move, since it had no precedent. This polemic, of course, afforded the Progressives an opportunity to attack the parliamentary system established under the Estatuto. They laid bare the defects of Martínez's charter, whose suitability for the nation was placed in doubt, first through the insinuations of Galiano, Argüelles, and Istúriz, and finally by the blunt statement of the Conde de las Navas that "el sistema constitucional que nos rige, dándole la versión que por el acto presente le ha dado el Sr. Secretario del Despacho, era nulo" (*Pr.*, p. 1165—"the constitutional system now ruling us was null, if the interpretation that the prime minister has applied to it by this act were attached to it").

On January 9, after discussing a minor petition concerning navigation of the Duero River, Procuradores turned to a much more important matter, the petition for judicial reforms. This debate continued on the 11th and 12th, being interrupted on the 10th for a discussion of emergency additions to the existing military budget. After the sessions on judicial reform, which consisted almost entirely in perorations against the judicial system, the judges, and the *Novísima recopilación*, the chamber took up a petition to abolish the Santa Hermandad.

The lower house's next topic found echoes in Larra's essay. It was the government's projected law concerning entailed property (*bienes vinculados*), which would have returned to their buyers lands sold to them during the Triennium and then confiscated during the Ominous Decade. The Liberal régime of 1820–1823 had allowed real property from *mayorazgos* to be sold, but the reaction which followed it, deeming them inalienable, restored the estates to their original owners without reimbursing the buyers.[3] Although debate did not begin until February 18, the committee had read its report on January 16 and the projected law was already a topic of conversation. Larra, commenting on the subject in "Un periódico nuevo," adroitly combines two unrelated topics, the *mayorazgos* and the official government paper, *La Gaceta*. A precedent for berating the latter had in fact been set by Fermín Caballero, on January 20, while impugning the ministry's arbitrariness:

Se ve la misma arbitrariedad en prescindir de ciertas fórmulas, de ciertas formalidades que en todo gobierno representativo están admitidos. ¿No hemos visto que ha sido preciso reclamar que no se publiquen en la *Gaceta* las leyes antes de promulgarse en las Cortes? (*Pr.,* p. 1272)

(The same arbitrariness is present in dispensing with certain formulas, certain formalities accepted in all representative governments. Was it not necessary to complain about laws being published in the *Gaceta* before they were promulgated in Cortes?)

The practice he denounced could indeed have brought on great confusion if people got the false impression that such projected laws were in force. Larra remarks:

Sólo diremos que los primeros periódicos fueron *gacetas;* no nos admiremos, pues, si fieles a su origen, si reconociendo su principio, los periódicos han conservado la afición a mentir, que los distingue de las demás publicaciones desde los tiempos más remotos; en lo cual no han hecho nunca más que administrar una herencia. Es su mayorazgo; respetamos éste como los demás, pues que estamos a esta altura todavía. (1: 447)

(We shall merely say that the first newspapers were *gazettes.* We should not be astonished then if, fatihful to their origins, recognizing their beginnings, newspapers have preserved their fondness for lying, which has distinguished them from other publications since the remotest times, having, in such wise, never done more than administer an inheritance. This is their heritage. Let us respect this entailed estate like the others, since we are still at that stage.)

For the purpose of irony Figaro exaggerates the government's conservatism; Martínez, to be sure, did not defend the inalienability of *mayorazgos*. Nevertheless, we should keep in mind that the status quo was still in effect one year after his coming to power. From a stylistic point of view, the above passage is enhanced by the antonomastic play on "gaceta," and by parody of Martínez's language, especially recognizable in the phrases, "fieles a su origen . . . reconociendo su principio," occasionally uttered by him to remind his audience that his régime's origin, far from being revolutionary, possessed the legality of royally sanctioned authority.

The last debate in Procuradores preceding the famous Post-Office Mutiny bore upon the navy budget. It took place January

15, 16, and 17, and resumed on the 23rd, after the three days it took Procuradores to ventilate its apprehension over the frustrated coup. The committee's recommendation had contained a preamble consisting mostly of a recital of ills afflicting the ruined Spanish fleet and the expression of hope that it might be restored, if not to its former grandeur, at least to a strength consistent with the needs of a colonial power having to defend its trade and its coasts. The principal savings proposed were on the monarch's two pleasure yachts, whose inclusion in the navy budget was deemed unjustifiable. The committee left intact the appropriations for repair of old ships and construction under way, but reduced by half the funds allotted to new construction. Larra jocularly records his impression of these sessions: *"De Marina.* Esto es más delicado. ¿Ha de ser *Fígaro* el único que hable de eso? No me gusta ahogarme en poca agua" (1: 448—"*Navy.* This is more delicate. Must Fígaro be the only one to mention this? I wouldn't want to sink in a teacup"). This passage provides evidence for dating the essay. It must have been written on the morning of January 22,[4] by which time the Procuradores had tabled the navy budget in order to take up the Post-Office Mutiny; and so Figaro would have been alone in talking about "Marina."[5] The humor of the sentence about Spain's depleted fleet stems from the familiar metaphor, "ahogarse en poca agua," which here incidentally acquires an ironic connotation. In this particular context, the metaphor happens to be antithetical to the literal meaning, because most of the navy had sunk in much water thirty years previously.

One extremely important aspect of the naval appropriations debate was the excuse it gave the Progressives to harass the ministers. The latter were impugned with unfounded accusations, which they refuted honorably, during a digression on the causes of the Spanish navy's decline. In fact, in one of his speeches Martínez de la Rosa ventilated the obvious truth that budgetary deliberations are frequently pretexts for such inculpations in any parliament (*Pr.*, p. 1224). In the present case, the Progressive accusations took on the appearance of threats, like those of the Conde de las Navas, who went so far as to hint at a forthcoming coup:

entraré en aquella protesta que sabe el Estamento tengo dicho que haré siempre que se trate de presupuestos. Por este año al menos,

hasta que la marcha de las cosas y la esperanza con que yo me lisonjeo de que los Sres. Secretarios del Despacho, sean los actuales
o los que fueren, nos llevarán por el camino de la felicidad pública:
hasta que la marcha que observe en las cosas, repito, no me haga
variar de sistema (y no se espanten S. SS. al oír sistema: sistema
es uno y otro, bueno o malo), consecuente a mis principios, yo
quisiera, y suplicaría al Estamento que no se pasase a los Sres.
Secretarios del Despacho más sueldo que el de 60.000 rs. . . . ya
se aproxima el día en que me pueda explicar más latamente . . .
(*Pr.*, p. 1223)

(I shall begin the protesting which the Chamber knows I do every
time budgets are dealt with. For this year at least, until the course
of affairs and the hope with which I look forward to the Secretaries of the Cabinet—the present ones or whoever they might
be—taking us along the path of public felicity; as long as the course
observed in national affairs, I repeat, does not make me change
systems [do not be shocked, Your Lordships, at hearing the
word system; system is one thing and another, good or bad],
consistent in my principles, I wish and beg the Chamber not to
vote the Secretaries of the Cabinet more than 60,000 reales
in salary. . . . the day is approaching when I can make myself
understood more fully . . .)

The above certainly corroborates an assertion of some historians
that many *procuradores* not only knew about but were involved
in the attempted Isabelina coup of January 17. And, for that matter, the government was likewise aware of it. It is even possible
that Martínez de la Rosa hoped to use its consequences in order to
rid himself of Llauder.

The revolt was prompted by the Progressives' increasing im-
patience with the government's slow pace in effecting reforms,
its arbitrary manner of proclaiming martial law in rebellious provinces without consulting Cortes, and especially its evident inability to cope with the threat of a rightist coup. To facilitate their
action, the Isabelinos probably entered into a pact with rightist
elements supporting a coup in favor of Llauder. The immediate
goal was to unseat the government; then each side hoped to gain
control by betraying the other. Results, however, fell far short of
expectations. The forewarned cabinet had taken precautionary
measures, one of which was to name the reactionary José Can-

terac captain general of Madrid. When it came to a showdown, the only conspiratory leader to carry out his part of the plot was a lieutenant of the seventh Aragonese regiment, Cayetano Cardero. Ironically enough, this was the regiment chosen by Canterac to keep order in the city on the night of the 17th. The 17th was also Cardero's turn of night duty. Instead of obeying instructions, he surreptitiously led, with the sergeants' help, over seven hundred men of the regiment to the main post office, where he proclaimed an insurrection.[6] Troops loyal to the government were rushed to the site, but it was soon recognized that only heavy cannon would dislodge the insurgents. Canterac feared that by the time artillery could be brought, the loyal troops would have gone over to Cardero's side. Consequently, the captain general decided to mark time by walking over unguarded to the Casa de Correos to harangue the rebels. He was so vehement, however, that some exasperated soldiers shot him in cold blood. When Llauder, the war minister, who had been sleeping soundly during most of the disturbance, finally arrived on the scene, all he could do was negotiate with the insurgents on terms humiliating to the government. Cardero's men were allowed to leave the post office with shouldered rifles, fixed bayonets, colors flying, and drums beating. They paraded through Madrid in this manner and started north to join their comrades fighting the Carlists.

It was about this incident that Larra included his famous laconic comment in "Día de difuntos de 1836. 'Fígaro' en el cementerio" (November 2, 1836). The author, looking upon the post office as if it were a tomb bearing symbols of conspiracy and mutiny, exclaims:

> Correos ¡Aquí yace la subordinación militar! Una figura de yeso, sobre el vasto sepulcro, ponía el dedo en la boca; en la otra mano, una especie de jeroglífico hablaba por ella: una disciplina rota. (2: 281)

> (Post Office. Here lies military subordination! A plaster figure standing on the vast sepulcher held a finger to its mouth. In its other hand a kind of hieroglyph, a shattered swagger-cane, spoke for it.)

But this was written more than twenty-nine months after the event. Figaro's views at the time of the insurrection may have been quite different.[7] We shall never know precisely how he felt in January 1835. Nevertheless, in "Un periódico nuevo" he appears to throw the blame on the government only. We also get this impression two weeks later, in "Por ahora":

> Palabras [hay] que valen más que un discurso, y que dan que discurrir; cuando uno oye, por ejemplo, la palabra *conspiración*, cree estar viendo un drama entero, y aunque no sea nada en realidad. (1: 454)

> (Some words are worth more than a speech and give you something to think about. For example, when you hear the word *conspiracy*, you think you're looking at an entire drama, even though in reality it's nothing.)

It is likely that Figaro shared the real opinions of his friends in parliament, which diverged considerably from the feigned shock they expressed in Cortes in order to protect themselves and condemn the cabinet.

As soon as the next meeting of Procuradores opened, on January 19, García Carrasco proposed that they convene into permanent session and request the war minister's presence to answer questions about the previous day's incidents (*Pr.*, p. 1241). The pretext for such a step was a proposal to draft a message to the queen. His suggestion overwhelmingly approved, García Carrasco delivered a speech recapitulating the preceding month's events and intimating Llauder's political maneuvers:

> Se ha dicho que un individuo del Gobierno trataba de presentar nuevos candidatos que reemplazasen a sus compañeros; y causa horror el decir los sujetos que designaba la opinión pública como tales.[8] (*Pr.*, p. 1243)

> (It was said that a member of the Government was trying to present new candidates to replace his colleagues; and mere mention of the individuals indicated as such by public opinion causes horror.)

The speaker accused Llauder, moreover, of undermining Mina by giving direct orders to his subordinates (an incrimination repeated by the Conde de las Navas [*Pr.*, p. 1253]). Broadening his rebuke, he went into the matter of French intervention, the Camarilla, foreign designs on Spain, and rumors of an agreement to marry Isabel to Carlos's son. Then he requested a change in the governmental system, consisting in a law to make the ministers responsible to Cortes, and even asked for a new cabinet holding views compatible with the representatives'. García Carrasco thus set the tone for the ensuing four days of debate, during which his demands and inculpations were reiterated.

Llauder defended himself the best he could by refuting the charges against him, but only Martínez's and Toreno's oratory could cope with the charges against the government. Yet even they found parliamentary thrusts hard to parry. Trueba, Caballero, Calderón Collantes, and Antonio González all expressed concern over the declaration of martial law in the rebellious provinces without prior consultation of Cortes (*Pr.*, pp. 1247, 1272, 1278, 1286). López criticized the police for failing to learn of Cardero's plans, and later Caballero and Argüelles asked rhetorically why the nation allotted to it eight and a half million reales a year (*Pr.*, pp. 1249, 1273, 1293). Mention of the police led to the topic of continued persecution of liberals, some of whom, according to Antonio González and Abargues, were still in jail and others abroad unamnestied (*Pr.*, pp. 1284–1286, 1298). On the subject of foreign intervention, López asserted that any government which so much as hinted its need of it was thereby exposing its own weaknesses (a remark specifically aimed at Llauder, reputed to be an interventionist). This topic was later dealt with at great length by Argüelles. How did it happen, asked "el divino orador," that each time news of a military defeat reached Madrid it was accompanied by rumors of a forthcoming intervention? (*Pr.*, p. 1294.) The cabinet was also reproved, this time by the Conde de las Navas, for delaying its enactment of the Milicia Urbana law, on which the queen's signature was still pending (*Pr.*, p. 1253). It is significant that the proposed law provided for civilian control of the militia, which had been temporarily placed under military authority; this step, according to Caballero and Calderón Collantes, was an affront to Cortes (*Pr.*, pp. 1272, 1278). The judicial system was once more given its share of blame, and the growth of the Carlist rebellion imputed to the deposed Zarco del Valle. Palarea, who brought up these particulars, likewise expressed his fears for the loss Spanish credit would suffer abroad (*Pr.*, pp.

1259–1261). In addition he asserted that division in the cabinet was the immediate cause of the revolt (*Pr.*, p. 1260), in which opinion he was anticipated by Arango (p. 1252). And, like the Conde de las Navas (*Pr.*, p. 1253), he attributed the abortive coup to restrictions on the press.

Two orators ventured to attack Martínez de la Rosa directly. Galiano said that "por segunda vez que estando S.S. a la cabeza de los negocios, han sido regadas con sangre las calles de Madrid, aunque por distinta causa" (*Pr.*, p. 1263—"for the second time during Your Lordship's direction of public affairs, the streets of Madrid have been bathed in blood, though for a different reason"). He also asked why a Frenchman had been made captain general at the very time when a petition was pending concerning employment of foreigners in government service. Calling Canterac a foreigner, however, showed bad faith on Galiano's part. As Llauder pointed out in reply (*Pr.*, p. 1271), Canterac had lived in Spain from a very tender age and served the nation all his life. Furthermore, he was married to a Spaniard and had Spanish children. Despite this defense of the dead general, Antonio González later rose to deplore the choice of Canterac (*Pr.*, p. 1284). The other *procurador* who directly criticized Martínez was Fermín Caballero. He accused the ministry of being as arbitrary as Calomarde. As illustrations for this reproach, Caballero cited the decrees on salt taxes and on subsidy of commerce issued by the treasury without the prior approval of Cortes (*Pr.*, p. 1272). He then reproved the government for being unable to obtain the Holy See's recognition of Isabel. Finally, Caballero uttered a saucy remark about Martínez's conviction that a "término medio" was necessary to conciliate the disparate segments of national opinion; he said: "Permítame S.S. que le diga que en este caso ha confundido a la nación con su pensamiento" (*Pr.*, p. 1274—"May Your Lordship allow me to say that in this case you have confused the nation with your ideas").

On its last day,[9] January 22, the debate turned into retrospective argumentation, which allowed orators to hint at analogies between régimes. For example, Abargues said that, had Zea been deposed upon Ferdinand's death, Spain's problems would be at an end. Behind this asseveration lies an idea which the audience had to discover for itself. By making such a statement, Abargues indicated his accord with Aviraneta, the Isabelina leader, who had advocated a plot against Zea.[10] Furthermore, Abargues remarked that Martínez de la Rosa "ha heredado las desconfianzas de Zea Bermúdez" (*Pr.*, p. 1298—"has inherited the mistrust that Zea Bermúdez inspired"). Now it is most likely that Aviraneta was behind the present abortive coup also. Hence, the implication of this speech is obvious: the speaker hints at his support of Cardero. And, in case there were any doubt about where he stood, Abargues further displayed his radicalism by suggesting the confiscation of Jesuit properties. The session ended with a speech by the Marqués de Montevirgen, the most daring of the Progressives, hinting that Llauder was involved in the plot (*Pr.*, p. 1315).

The predicament of the cabinet under this barrage of incriminations is cleverly used by Figaro as a comparison to illustrate the adversities confronting the journalist:

> ¿Por qué no pone usted un periódico suyo? ¿Cuándo sale Fígaro? ¡Es idea peregrina! Ya he visto en los demás periódicos la publicación del permiso para el periódico nuevo. ¿Saldrá por fin en febrero, en marzo? ¿Cuándo? ¿Nos hará usted reír, por supuesto?
>
> He aquí las preguntas que por todas partes se me dirigen, que me cercan, me estrechan, me comprometen, y a las cuales me veo más apurado para responder, que se ven hace tres días... Iba a hacer una mala comparación; y si me la había de suprimir algún amigo de estos que miran de continuo por mi tranquilidad, suprímomela yo. (1: 446)

> (Why don't you start your own paper? When will *Fígaro* come out? It's a great idea! I see other papers have already published the permit for the new paper. Will it finally come out in February, in March? When? You'll make us laugh, of course, won't you?
>
> These are the questions thrown at me from all sides, which besiege me, press me, bind me, and put me in even more of a dither to answer them than, for the past three days, have been... I was going to make a bad comparison; and in case one of those friends of mine who are constantly looking after my peace and quiet was going to suppress it, I'll do it myself.)

We may observe here that Larra begins his essay in such a way as to establish a sympathetic comparison between the ministers and

himself. Why did the government fail to take action in the face of revolt? Likewise, when is Figaro going to act on the project to start a paper of his own? The journalist and the ministers are both beset by questions and at a loss for satisfactory answers. But Larra makes sure that the comparison—along with the sympathy some of his readers might feel for the ministry—comes to an abrupt end: "Iba a hacer una mala comparación." A clever twist is apparent; the journalist's hardships are in fact caused by the ministers, so that the momentary temptation to regard them as fellow victims is soon overcome by the remembrance that they are his persecutors. "Y si me la había de suprimir algún amigo de estos que miran de continuo por mi tranquilidad, suprímomela yo"; the sufferer's self-restraint merely avoids repression by opponents who, for one moment perhaps, may be mistaken for fellow sufferers and friends in adversity.

It is, to be sure, the restrictions on freedom of the press that cause Larra's failure to start his own publication, and he goes into this at length in "Un periódico nuevo." But that is not all. In the eyes of the Progressives, the ultimate reason for the difficulties now facing the government were curbs on the press. During the debate about these difficulties, the ministers and their opposition weighed the advantages and disadvantages of press freedom, though, unlike Larra, on a political level only. The Conde de las Navas, who insisted the government had lost much "fuerza moral" because it did not place itself "francamente . . . en brazos de sus amigos" ("frankly . . . in the arms of its friends"), was the first to analyze the problem in this wise:

> ¿Cómo se ha conservado la fuerza moral, sin la cual no puede gobernar nadie, y mucho menos en un país donde se establece un sistema constitucional, donde hay una tribuna pública y periódicos, aunque con una libertad de imprenta bien coartada? (*Pr.*, p. 1254)

> (How has moral force been preserved, without which no one can govern, and much less so in a country where a constitutional system is established, where there is a public platform and newspapers, though with considerably restrained press freedom?)

Palarea, in turn, blamed the revolt on the distrust instilled into the people

hasta por los mismos periódicos; ¿y qué periódicos? Es menester decirlo: los mismos llamados ministeriales,[11] constituidos bajo la censura, han dicho que se trataba de un cambio de Ministros . . .

. . . Hemos reclamado, señores, desde el principio de esta legislatura que fuesen sancionados, como consecuencia del Estatuto Real, los derechos de los españoles: hemos reclamado la libertad de imprenta; ¿se nos ha concedido? No. ¿Es necesaria? Sí; precisamente los hechos de ayer son una confirmación de esta verdad. En el año de 1808 la opinión extraviada por manejos ocultos dio margen a iguales sucesos que el de antes de ayer. . . . Estas calumnias [against Generals San Juan and Blake, heroes of the Napoleonic war] se esparcían, y la opinión se extraviaba. ¿Y cómo se corrigieron tales abusos? ¿Y cómo se restableció la disciplina en los ejércitos? La libertad de imprenta que se sancionó en 1810 fue un poderoso correctivo que ilustró la opinión, rectificó muchos errores, y contribuyó a restablecer la disciplina, demostrando su necesidad y su importancia . . . ella es el correctivo de todos los males de un Gobierno constitucional . . . Si nosotros tuviéramos la libertad de imprenta, verdadera, sin previa censura, las calumnias que se han propagado estos días no hubieran producido el funesto efecto de haber sido asesinado el Capitán general de esta provincia por tropas que estaban a sus órdenes, o enemigos ocultos que han ocasionado esta insubordinación y este crimen. (*Pr.*, pp. 1260–1261)

(even through the newspapers themselves. And which newspapers? We'll have to say it: the so-called ministerialist papers themselves, created under censorship, said it was a matter of a change of ministers . . .

. . . We have insisted, gentlemen, since the beginning of this legislature, that the rights of Spaniards be sanctioned as a consequence of the Estatuto Real. We asked for freedom of the press. Was it granted? No. Is it necessary? Yes. Yesterday's events are indeed a confirmation of this truth. In the year 1808, public opinion, led astray by concealed maneuvers, provided the opportunity for events like those of the day before yesterday. . . . These slanders [against good generals] spread and public opinion was led astray. And how were such abuses remedied? How was discipline restored in the army? Freedom of the press, sanctioned in 1810, became a potent antidote which enlightened public opinion, rectified many errors, and contributed in restoring discipline, demonstrating its necessity and importance . . . This freedom is the corrective for all the ills of a constitutional government . . .

If we had real freedom of the press, without prior censorship, the calumnies propagated during the past few days would not have resulted in the dismal murder of the captain general of this province by troops under his command, or by hidden foes who brought about this insubordination and this crime.)

As we can see, Progressive orators insisted on a connection between mutiny and censorship. Larra has likewise linked the two topics in "Un periódico nuevo," as I shall point out later.

In the meantime, it will be profitable to examine the polemic on the validity of this connection. Alcalá Galiano, in his long discourse of January 20, charged that rumors started by the newspapers about a possible cabinet change had alarmed the populace. Owing to the limitations on the press, he added, it must be assumed that such alarm was far more intense than would be normally warranted by rumor. Instead of being accepted as gossip, the news was taken as fact, because "en los países donde existe la previa censura los periódicos llevan hasta cierto punto el sello de la aprobación gubernativa" (*Pr.*, p. 1264—"in countries where prior censorship exists, newspapers bear to a certain extent the government's seal of approval"). Martínez de la Rosa replied by affirming that the government was responsible only for ministerial newspapers, of which there was only one, *La Gaceta*, and added:

Ha añadido S.S. que con la censura basta para el objeto de oprimir la voz y el pensamiento de los periodistas. Si la censura fuese muy rigurosa, sería cierto; pero la experiencia le prueba a S.S. que no es tan severa que sólo pase lo que favorece o gusta a los Ministros, pues tolera lo que les es desfavorable, y ellos no dicen nada en favor de los principios, por amor a la libertad: aunque muchas veces es tal la amargura de los artículos, que los mismos periodistas no la sufrieran, si he de juzgar por la intolerancia que manifiestan en otros puntos. (*Pr.*, p. 1269)

(Your Lordship added that censorship suffices for the purpose of oppressing the voice and thought of journalists. If censorship were very rigorous, this would be true. But experience has shown Your Lordship that it is not so severe as to only allow passage of what favors or pleases the Ministers; indeed, it tolerates what is unfavorable to them, and they, owing to their love of freedom, say nothing in favor of the principles [of censorship?], though the articles' bitterness is often so great that the journalists themselves would not brook it, to judge by the intolerance they display on other issues.)

Martínez's remarks, as we can see, are really defensive and apologetic; Fermín Caballero adroitly rebutted him (*Pr.*, p. 1274). Mention was made of complaints from foreign governments against Spain's censored newspapers. On the last day of debate, Argüelles warmly defended freedom of the press (*Pr.*, p. 1292), after which Martínez sought to demonstrate that it could not endure without a jury system (p. 1304). Istúriz replied thereupon that this was clear proof of the immediate desirability of both (*Pr.*, p. 1311). The great dilemma faced by liberals but not mentioned specifically—because it constituted their "can of worms" —was that the jury system had failed miserably during the Triennium in all cases with political implications, especially those concerning journalistic libel. National inadaptability to the precept of impartiality, as well as tenacious habits of favoritism, made a sham of the jury system, the Achilles' heel of all Spanish political theories.[12]

In contrast to this skirting of a paradoxical issue, the Conde de Toreno attempted a firm justification of censorship. His statement of January 21 provides an example of the kind of thinking that Larra assiduously contravenes:

la libertad de imprenta . . . ha dicho el Gobierno que en principios estaba siempre dispuesto a sostenerla; pero en la aplicación era preciso atender a las circunstancias. El Gobierno hubiera podido usar de esa misma libertad en beneficio suyo, adoptando ciertas medidas de Francia o Inglaterra, pues en tal caso las circunstancias que se exigirían para poder publicar periódicos dejarían reducido casi a la nada el número de los que pudieran publicarlos, y sólo serían sus amigos, y es seguro que si se quitase la censura no habría un solo Procurador que no quisiera que se diesen prendas para que los periódicos no fuesen un germen de disensiones. (*Pr.*, p. 1280)

(the Government has said that in principle it is always disposed to uphold freedom of the press; but that in practice it was necessary to heed the circumstances. The Government could have used this very freedom to its own benefit by adopting certain measures from France and England, since in such cases the conditions required for permission to publish newspapers would reduce to almost nothing the number of persons allowed to do so, and they would only be its friends. One can be sure that if censorship were removed, every Procurador would without exception favor requiring security deposits in order to insure that the press not become a source of dissensions.)

Notwithstanding the vicissitudes of political alignments throughout his career, the one principle to which Larra showed absolute constancy was freedom of the press. Because he knew at first hand the hardships of Spanish journalists, Figaro must have been particularly provoked by this aspect of the debate and especially infuriated by any intimation that freedom of the press could aggravate national problems. This topic affected him personally and he must have been quite chagrined at seeing Toreno's contention go unanswered; for although the Conde de las Navas, Joaquín María López, Caballero, and Antonio González all spoke on that day after the secretary of the treasury, none bothered to refute him. The rebuttal would have been easy, however, since the number of persons enabled to publish newspapers in Spain was quite limited, as in England and France, owing to impediments devised by the government. Hence, removal of prior censorship while maintaining existing newspaper regulations would not make publishing easier than in those two nations. Probably moved by such considerations, Larra took it upon himself, the very next day, to point out in his essay the difficulties faced by anyone wanting to bring out even the most trifling periodical.

The first difficulty he will encounter, writes Figaro, is that there is almost nothing to say. Spain is not moving forward one whit, and the war in Navarre is at a standstill (1: 447); as for the treasury, it can only be used as a laughingstock, and the technicalities of the war department's functioning are a bore. With regard to the Interior, there is nothing to speak of save what has not been accomplished; as for the navy, there is not enough of it to bother about. And what is the use of writing on literature when no good books are published? The same goes for Spanish drama: "no diremos nada mientras no haya nada que decir" (1: 448—"we shall say nothing while there is nothing to say").

In any case there is a ray of hope: no one will object to the name of Larra's paper, because it does not imply such stated purposes as are found in the titles of other periodicals. Alluding to *El Observador*, *La Revista Española*, *El Eco del Comercio*, *La Abeja*, and *El Compilador*, the writer says:

> El periódico se titulará *Fígaro*, un nombre propio; esto no significa nada y a nada compromete, ni a *observar*, ni a *revistar*, ni a ser *eco de nadie*, ni a *chupar flores*, ni a *compilar*, ni a maldita de Dios la cosa.[13] (1: 448)

> (The paper will be entitled *Fígaro*, a proper name; it signifies nothing and does not impose any obligation, such as to *observe*, or *review*, or be anyone's *echo*, or *suck up flowery nectar*, or *compile*, or God only knows what.)

The next problem is obtaining a permit, for which financial surety must be given; since the author is poor, he has to seek a backer, who furthermore must be assured of a profit. Then a printer must be found. Some do not have the right type, others the right press. Some do not want their presses to run at night. The typesetters are almost illiterate and make innumerable mistakes. It is impossible to come across the right kind of paper, and if one orders it made, it will not dry on time in case of rain.

If starting a newspaper is almost unfeasible, avoiding delays is well nigh unthinkable. The blame for this falls, of course, on prior censorship, which the author artfully exposes at the end of his essay:

> —¿Qué hace usted?—le digo a mi escribiente, de mal humor.
> —Señor—me responde—, estoy traduciendo, como me ha mandado usted, este monólogo de su tocayo de usted, en el *Mariage de Figaro* de Beaumarchais, para que sirva de epígrafe a la colección de sus artículos que va usted a publicar.
> —¿A ver cómo dice?
> —"Se ha establecido en Madrid un sistema de libertad que se extiende hasta a la imprenta; y con tal que no hable en mis escritos, ni de la autoridad, ni del culto, ni de la política, ni de la moral, ni de los empleados, ni de las corporaciones, ni de los cómicos, ni de nadie que pertenezca a algo, puedo imprimirlo todo libremente, previa la inspección y revisión de dos o tres censores. Para aprovecharme de esta hermosa libertad anuncio un periódico..."

—Basta—exclamo al llegar aquí mi escribiente—, basta; eso se
ha escrito para mí; cópielo usted aquí al pie de este artículo; ponga
usted la fecha en que eso se escribió.
    —1784.
—Bien. Ahora la fecha de hoy.
—22 de enero de 1835.
—Y debajo: *Fígaro*. (1: 449–450)

(—What are you doing?—I ill-humoredly ask my secretary.
    —Sir—he answers—, I'm translating, as you told me to, this
monologue of your namesake's from Beaumarchais's *Marriage of
Figaro*, to be used as an epigraph for the collection of articles you
are publishing.
    —Let's see how it comes out.
    —"A system of liberty has been established in Madrid which
goes even as far as the press. So, provided I write nothing about
authority, religion, politics, morality, employees, religious orders,
actors, or anyone who belongs to anything, I can print it all freely,
as long as it is inspected and revised by two or three censors. In
order to take full advantage of this lovely freedom I am announcing a new paper..."
    —Fine; that's enough—I exclaim at this point—; this was writ-
ten just for me. Copy it here at the end of this article. Put down
the date when this was written.
    —1784.
—Good. Now today's date.
—January 22, 1835.
—And underneath: Figaro.)

To prove its backwardness, Larra casts into his country's present
a past bygone fifty years. But this is not all; he also casts the reader's world into the essay itself. The reader sees that the date on
his copy of *La Revista* is January 26; consequently there has been
a four-day delay, and the fate of the article becomes a proof of its
own argument. Could this literary device be inspired by Cervantes's manner of bringing the 1605 *Quijote* into the 1615 *Quijote?*
    Now that we have seen how the author went about controvert-
ing Toreno, let us examine other parliamentary reminiscences
found in the essay. During their four-day attack on the cabinet,
the Progressives elaborated, as they had already done in September and October, on the implications of the Crown speech that

opened the Cortes in August.[14] One of the oft-repeated terms they dwelt upon was "cimiento." It was revived by Rivas in Próceres on January 19:

Y si el ministerio no completa la regeneración de nuestra patria, no levanta el edificio de que es cimiento el Estatuto Real, por no aumentar el encono de los carlistas, de los partidarios del despotismo, se engaña . . ." (*Ilus.*, p. 191)

(And if the ministry does not complete the regeneration of our country, if it fails to raise the edifice whose foundation is the Estatuto Real, just to avoid increasing the rancor of the Carlists, of the partisans of despotism, then it is deceiving itself . . .)

The next day Fermín Caballero reintroduced the term in Procuradores:

Me ha decidido también a hacer esta oposición el ver que el cimiento que se nos ha dado y hemos recibido como tal, se halla en el mismo estado que hace un año, sin que se haya adelantado una línea en la obra, dejándonos expuestos a que este mismo cimiento se descarne y se pierda con la injuria del tiempo . . .

. . . He dicho también que no habíamos adelantado una línea en el cimiento que se había echado para nuestra regeneración política, y no es menos patente la verdad de esta proposición. Yo creo que los Sres. Secretarios del Despacho, es decir, aquellos que estaban en el Ministerio cuando aconsejaron a S.M. que se diese el Estatuto Real, estarán bien convencidos de que, como dice su mismo título, no es otra cosa que una ley orgánica para la convocación de las Cortes generales del reino; pero que de ninguna manera puede por sí solo, y sin acabarse de completar el cimiento, ser ley constitutiva de la nación. . . .

. . . aquí que estamos en los cimientos después de un año de trabajos, ¿no hay razón para que se quiera completar la obra? ¿No ha de haber personas que quieran ir más allá, puesto que la Reina nos dijo al abrir este santuario: "está echado el cimiento, acabad vosotros la obra"? (*Pr.*, pp. 1272–1273, 1274)

(I also decided to express opposing views when I saw that the foundation given us and received by us as such is still in the same state as a year ago, without having made any headway, of even a single row, in the work, making us run the risk of having the foundation itself chipped away and buried by the ravages of time . . .

. . . I also said that we had not progressed one inch above the foundation laid for our political regeneration, and the truth of this proposition is not less obvious. I believe that the Secretaries of the Cabinet, that is, those who were in the Ministry when they advised Her Majesty to have the Estatuto Real granted, are probably quite convinced that, as its very title says, it is no more than an organic law for the convocation of the general Cortes of the realm. But in no wise can it be of itself, and without the completion of the foundation, the constitutive law of the nation. . . .

. . . Since we are still at the foundations after a year of travails, is there no reason for wishing to complete the edifice? Will there be no one who wants to go on, since the Queen told us, when she opened this sanctuary, "the foundation is laid; finish the edifice"?)

Toreno replied to Caballero,[15] and Argüelles also broached this topic on the last day of debate. It finds an echo in "Un periódico nuevo": "Por un periódico sabe usted que hay Cortes reunidas para elevar sobre el *cimiento* el edificio de nuestra libertad" (1: 447; italics are Larra's—"By way of a newspaper you learn that there are Cortes summoned in order to raise above the *foundation* the edifice of our liberty"). Consequently, this remark does not constitute a criticism of the *procuradores*, as casual readers have been wont to believe, but of the cabinet, which denies the representatives power to carry out their role, while priding itself on reestablishing representative government. The sentence in "Un periódico nuevo" following the one quoted above refers to the upper house. Some *próceres*, like the cabinet, seem to have found undue satisfaction in their own function. Antonio Cano Manuel, for example, had stated his accord with the government while eulogizing the upper house:

S.M. ha apelado a la nación conociendo que Rey y pueblo es una misma cosa, que sus intereses son idénticos, unos sus derechos, unas sus obligaciones: ha restablecido nuestras leyes fundamentales, y ha cerrado por último aquella honda sima del despotismo. Además de estos pasos ha restablecido dos cuerpos; uno que puede ser llamado templador, y es el Estamento de Sres. Procuradores, para que el pueblo no haga por sí lo que le expone a pasar la raya o quedarse atrás; y además; otro **Cuerpo esencialmente conservador,**

cual es este ilustre Estamento, que pudiera servir para poner en armonía la máquina política. (*Ilus.*, p. 184)

(Her Majesty appealed to the nation in the knowledge that Monarch and people are the same thing, that their interests are identical, their rights and responsibilities one and the same. She has reestablished our fundamental laws and closed up once and for all the deep gulf of despotism. Besides these steps she has restored two bodies, one of which may be called tempering, the Estamento of Procuradores, so that the people will not do for itself what puts it in danger of going beyond limits or of remaining behind; and also another Body, essentially conservative, this illustrious Chamber, which could well serve to put in harmony the political machinery.)

When we review the Próceres' record, the pretentiousness of this statement is revealed immediately; they had, to all intents, met only once that year.[16] Larra comments: "Por ellos [the newspapers] se sabe que hay dos Estamentos, es decir, además del de Procuradores, otro de Próceres" (1: 447—"Through them you'll find out there are two chambers, that is, besides that of Procuradores, another one, of Próceres").

There is likewise a reminiscence of the debates in Larra's sentence following the one just quoted. It reflects a polemic on the nature of the debates themselves and the definition of the words "conversation" and "discussion" as applied to parliamentary procedure. The need to differentiate these two terms was prompted by Martínez de la Rosa's objections to the proceedings of January 19:

a pesar de las graves ocupaciones que nos impone aquel [destino], hemos estado contestando todos los días a cuantas preguntas se nos han hecho, improvisando las respuestas: cosa que no se verifica en otro país, en que no se halla establecido el régimen representativo. En la misma Inglaterra se dan plazos para estas contestaciones, y hasta se señala el asunto especial sobre que han de recaer; pero no se exigen explicaciones sobre todas las cuestiones, todos los días y a todas horas, ni sobre detalles que fatigan la memoria, y que versan sobre los puntos más minuciosos de la administración. Sólo aquí, por la lealtad y celo (cuidado, señores, que no hablo del acierto) de los Ministros, sólo esa lealtad y celo hace que se ocupen

de todos esos detalles, y puedan contestar de repente a cuantas preguntas y contestaciones se les dirigen. (*Pr.*, p. 1250)

(in spite of the serious duties imposed on us by our position, we have been answering every day all the questions put to us, improvising the replies. This does not happen in any country where a representative régime has been established. Even in England, time is accorded for the preparation of these replies, and the special subject to be dealt with is even indicated; but explanations for all questions, every day and at all hours, on details that tire the memory, concerning the most minute points of the administration, are not required. Only here, owing to the loyalty and zeal—notice, gentlemen, that I do not say good judgment—of the Ministers; only owing to this loyalty and zeal do they busy themselves with all those details and are able to reply quickly to all the questions and contradictions aimed at them.)

At this point the Progressives saw an opportunity to confound the prime minister. Assuming that Martínez sought to avoid answering questions by excusing himself with lack of preparation, Galiano suggested the next day that the proceedings be given another name:

Han sido tantos los puntos tocados en esta, que no llamaré discusión, pues creo que le cuadra mejor el nombre de conversación, que por tanto le daré; han sido, digo, tan diversas y tan importantes las especies suscitadas en esta conversación vaga, pero no inútil, que será muy difícil acordarse de todas ellas, coordinarlas y formar un cuerpo para sacar de las mismas una consecuencia formal. He dicho que esta discusión es una conversación; y para probarlo apelo sólo a una cosa. Ayer nos reunimos y en aquel momento, sin que el Ministerio nos hubiese hablado nada, no sólo por nosotros, sino por el público que asistía a las tribunas, se creyó que el Estamento debía tomar en consideración la situación actual. ¿Y por qué? Claro está; porque el resultado de esta discusión, y por eso he dicho que aunque conversación no es inútil, no puede ser otro que dar desahogo a ciertas doctrinas, y prestar en suma aquella influencia moral, que es la fuerza de este Estamento como de todos los cuerpos de la misma clase. He aquí la utilidad de esta discusión o conversación. (*Pr.*, p. 1262)

(So many points have been taken up in this—I shall not call it discussion, because I feel the name of conversation suits it better—

this conversation, then, which is the name I shall give it; so diverse and important have been the affairs brought up in this vague but not useless conversation, that it is probably quite difficult to remember them all, coordinate and form a corpus with them in order to come to a formal conclusion. I said that this discussion is a conversation, and to prove it I appeal only to one thing. We met yesterday and at that moment, without the Ministry's having said a word, it was felt, not only by us but by the public looking on, that the Chamber should take into consideration the present situation. Why? Clearly enough, because such a discussion—and for this reason I said that though it is a conversation it is not useless—can result in nothing less than giving vent to certain doctrines, and in the last analysis provide the kind of moral influence which constitutes the power of this Chamber, as it does of all similar bodies. Such, then, is the usefulness of this discussion or conversation.)

Only a parliament with power to initiate legislation can properly be said to hold conversations, since these conversations provide ideas for first drafts of proposed laws. Martínez was sufficiently informed to understand his opponent's implications, and he replied adroitly:

Largo tiempo ha tardado el Sr. Procurador que acaba de hablar en definir el debate que nos ocupa, apelando por último a un idioma extranjero para hacerlo, y llamándole conversación, según el uso parlamentario inglés. (*Pr.*, p. 1266)

(The Procurador who has just spoken took a long time to define the debate which now occupies us; he finally called upon a foreign language to do so, naming it a conversation, according to English parliamentary usage.)

He then tried to turn Alcalá Galiano's initiative to his own advantage, by saying that Galiano had to resort to the term in question because the Progressives' accusations were vague and founded on rumors, suspicions, exaggerations, malice, and ignorance. "¿Y qué prueba esto? Que no ha podido hacerse un cargo formal" (*Pr.*, p. 1267—"And what does this prove? That no formal charges could be made"). On the last day of the debate, however, a Progressive, Istúriz, desirous that these sessions should have some positive result, reversed Alcalá Galiano's argument and expressed

hope that the debate would be in the end more than a mere "conversation." Istúriz proposed that

> El Estamento de Procuradores del reino, si es que esta discusión no ha de ser una mera conversación, como ha dicho el Sr. Galiano; si ha de tener un objeto, un fin; el Estamento, repito, creo yo que está en el caso de elevar a los pies del Trono un respetuoso mensaje,

> (If this discussion is to be more than a mere conversation, as Mr. Galiano said; if it is to have a purpose, a goal, then I believe the chamber ought to elevate to the feet of the Throne a respectful message),

requesting the queen to make certain that the amnesty accorded to the insurgents not be violated,[17] and to point out to the cabinet the need for a system capable of bringing reforms to the country (*Pr.*, p. 1311). Progressive tactics were obviously very cunning. Forcing Martínez to defend the term "discussion," they took him at his word and insisted that something concrete be debated. Accordingly, Istúriz proposed something which, as we have observed, the prime minister had had his fill of, namely, another petition. The Marqués de Someruelos, a ministerialist, sensing the danger, immediately rose to accede to the term "conversation":

> Había pensado renunciar la palabra apenas oí el elocuente y razonado discurso del Sr. Presidente del Consejo de Ministros, respondiendo completa y satisfactoriamente a los cargos repetidamente hechos al Ministerio, y repetidamente contestados, que se han producido en los cuatro días que llevamos de discusión, o mejor dicho, de conversación, como acertadamente la llamó el Sr. Alcalá Galiano. (*Pr.*, p. 1312)

> (I had thought of relinquishing the floor as soon as I heard the eloquent and reasoned discourse of the President of the Cabinet, who answered completely and satisfactorily all the charges repeatedly leveled at the Ministry, and repeatedly answered, during the four days we have been carrying on the discussion, or rather conversation, as Mr. Alcalá Galiano so aptly called it.)

This polemic, incidentally, indicates that Galiano and Istúriz were working together closely and might already have formed a sort of caucus with which Larra may have been connected.[18] It

also helps to understand the journalist's intent when he writes in "Un periódico nuevo":

> Por los periódicos sabe usted, *mutatis mutandis*, es decir, quitando unas cosas y poniendo otras, lo que hablan los oradores, y sabe usted, como por ejemplo ahora, cuándo una discusión es tal discusión, y cuándo es meramente *conversación*, para repetir la frase feliz de un orador. (1: 447)

> (Through the newspapers you learn, *mutatis mutandis*, that is, taking out some things and putting in others, what the orators are saying, and you learn, as we can do now for example, when a discussion is indeed a discussion and when it is merely a *conversation*, to repeat the felicitous phrase of an orator.)

A superficial interpretation of this essay might tend to justify those critics who have painted a nonpartisan Larra satirizing members of parliament as a group, as well as the ministers. Nothing could be farther from the truth. Figaro deplores the Cortes' impotence with regard to initiating legislation, so that much of what should be discussion is in fact merely conversation. Alcalá Galiano's locution was indeed felicitous, whether or not it had anything to do with English parliamentary usage. Furthermore, Figaro seeks through his essay to point out the shallow content of a censored press. Instead of frankly informing the people about issues, newspapers can only repeat the oblique expressions and sophistries of circumspect oratorial skirmish. Only "quitando unas cosas y poniendo otras," says Larra, can the public comprehend the real issues, since interpretive journalism is impossible. The papers are forced to dwell on mere technicalities, like "conversation," which would be disregarded if the press were free to tackle real issues.

The conclusion that Larra attacks only the cabinet and its allies is unavoidable when we examine in the next paragraph the locutions "ministro responsable," "ley fundamental," "representación nacional," and "fantasma." Let us start with the first one. A great deal was said in Cortes on the responsibility of ministers, but the concept was never defined. Actually—but of course this was never frankly broached—the true nature of the problem was the inadequacy of the Estatuto Real. "Ministro responsable" in the 1812 constitution, for example, means that the minister is accountable to the parliament. In the present session, however, "responsabilidad" seems to mean responsibility for the Correos incident.

It was the Duque de Gor, in Próceres, who first used the word on January 19:

> El horror que le inspiran los acontecimientos del día de ayer, los deseos de aclarar la conducta del Gobierno para ejercer sobre ella una imparcial censura, ésta puede verificarse, o bien en una discusión como la presente o bien aplazando al Ministerio para otro día por la ausencia del Sr. Ministro de la Guerra [who was in the lower house at the time], para si hubiese caso de exigir la responsabilidad, para lo que aún no tenemos la ley necesaria. (*Ilus.*, p. 188)

> (The horror that the events of the day before yesterday inspired, the wish to clarify the Government's conduct in order to exercise impartial judgment over this conduct. Such an investigation can be realized either in a discussion like the present one or by summoning the Ministry for another day, because of the absence of the Secretary of War, in case responsibility were demanded, for which we still do not have the necessary law.)

Then the Duque de Rivas, speaking as if the Estatuto were a constitution rather than a *charte octroyée*, used the terms "responsable" and "responsabilidad" to hint at the discord in the cabinet and the guilt of Llauder (or Martínez):

> yo no reconozco en un Ministerio constitucional Ministros aislados, sino un cuerpo sólidamente responsable. Resulta pues de todo que la conspiración se supo, y no se atajó; resulta que habiendo fuerzas para atajarla, no se echó mano de ellas; resulta pues un misterio cubierto con un velo fatídico que nos deja en sombras. Dedúcese pues que hay sobre quien recaiga la responsabilidad; y si es que ésta puede recaer sólo sobre un individuo, y apelo a la opinión pública y a la de todos los que me escuchan, que metida la mano en su pecho, conocerán quién debe ser este responsable, aunque no pronuncien su nombre . . . (*Ilus.*, p. 191)

> (in a constitutional ministry I do not recognize isolated ministers, but a solidly responsible body. From all this, it turns out that the conspiracy was known about, and not curbed; that there were forces to check it, and they were not used; a mystery covered with a presaging veil leaving us in the shadows. Let it be deduced

that there is someone on whom responsibility falls; and if it can fall on one individual only—and I appeal to public opinion and that of all those who hear me, if they take their hand to their breast—, they will know who this responsible person must be, though they pronounce not his name . . .)

Shortly thereafter García Carrasco called for a law making the ministers responsible to Cortes (*Pr.*, p. 1243). The next day in Procuradores Martínez defended the ministry on this point:

Si estas discusiones han sido tan vagas, si no se ha fijado un cargo especial, es una prueba a favor del Ministerio que en vez de presentarse un hecho fijo con derivación de la ley, un delito, cuando más se ha presentado, y no una vez sola, un campo sin límites, en el que se ha recorrido siempre, no sólo lo pasado, sino lo presente y hasta lo futuro. Es claro que esto ha sido por no encontrarse un hecho determinado, positivo, para exigir la responsabilidad. . . .
. . . El Ministerio no es un instrumento cuyas cuerdas estén templadas al unísono; esto no cabe en lo humano. Pero después de examinar bien los asuntos, cuando se fija una decisión con la cual debe sostenerse el principio sobre que pesa la responsabilidad, todos están conformes; y el que no lo estuviese, por su mismo pundonor se retiraría. (*Pr.*, pp. 1267, 1269)

(If these discussions have been so vague, if no special charges have been made, it is a proof in the Ministry's favor. Instead of a specific instance of deviation from the law, an offense, what has been presented at most, and not just once, is a boundless field in which not only the past is gone over, but also the present and even the future. Clearly, the reason for this is that no determined, positive fact was found for demanding responsibility. . . .
. . . The Ministry is not an instrument whose strings are all tuned to one note; this would not be humanly possible. But after matters have been thoroughly examined, when a decision has been made to uphold the principle on which responsibility depends, all are in agreement; and if by any chance one of them were not, he would resign as a matter of honor.)

After the prime minister it was the turn of Caballero, who lost no opportunity to hint at the constitutional meaning of responsibility:

He dicho que existe la misma arbitrariedad en los mandatarios del poder que bajo la administración de Calomarde, y de hecho es así. No hay más ventaja que el de existir una tribuna donde se pueden denunciar al público los abusos, pero que no se pueden corregir sino con el efecto moral: ley no hay que los corrija. En el mes de Junio de 1834 se dieron los Reglamentos para las Cortes. En el artículo 139 del nuestro se dice que el Estamento podrá ejercer funciones judiciales para exigir la responsabilidad del Ministerio. Ésta es la hora en que no hay tal ley, a pesar de que allí se cita: de suerte que si en el día por los sucesos de antes de ayer se creyera el Estamento en la necesidad de exigir la responsabilidad al Ministerio, no tendríamos ley ni regla ni pauta por donde gobernarnos. . . .

. . . Si hubiera una ley de responsabilidad, si estuvieran marcados los derechos que tenemos los españoles, entonces sería fácil citar en qué se faltaba . . . (*Pr.*, pp. 1272, 1273–1274)

(I said that the same arbitrariness as in the Calomarde era prevails among those invested with power, and this is a fact. The only advantage now is that a platform exists where abuses can be denounced to the public, but they cannot be corrected save through their moral effect; there is no law to right them. In the month of June 1834 Regulations were issued for Cortes. Article 139 of ours states that the Chamber may exercise judicial functions to demand the responsibility of the Ministry. At this hour there is no such law, in spite of its mention there, so that if the Chamber now felt itself in the need to demand responsibility from the Ministry, owing to the events of the day before yesterday, we should have no law, regulation, or guideline to rule ourselves. . . .

. . . If there were a law of responsibility, if the rights of Spaniards were marked down, then it would be easy to show where the failure lay . . .)

After Martínez replied on January 22 that even France did not have such a law, and that England had not had one until Fox's time (*Pr.*, p. 1303), the Marqués de Montevirgen made a bold proposal, in the last speech of the debate:

Esta discusión debe terminarse por el solo hecho de no haber una ley de responsabilidad. Si la hubiese, pediría la de los dos Sres. Ministros de Guerra y de lo Interior, como responsables de la tranquilidad, porque habiéndolo podido impedir con tiempo, consintieron en que la insurrección estallase, y se turbase aquélla. Sin embargo, creo que el Estamento debe pedir que se juzgue de la conducta de dichos Sres. Ministros para ver si han correspondido a la confianza que S.M. la Reina Gobernadora ha depositado en ellos. (*Pr.*, p. 1325)

(This discussion must end for the mere fact that there is no law of responsibility. If there were, I would demand that of the Ministers of War and of the Interior, as responsible for public order, because they allowed it to be disturbed by consenting to the outburst of the insurrection, though they could have prevented it in time. Nevertheless, I believe the Chamber must request that the conduct of these Ministers be judged in order to see whether they responded to the confidence that Her Majesty the Queen Regent has placed in them.)

These remarks were not without repercussions. On January 24 the resignation of Llauder was announced (*Pr.*, p. 1325). A month later Moscoso and Garelly left the cabinet.

Another expression listed by Figaro is "ley fundamental." Here again there was diversity of interpretation. Whereas Progressives took this phrase to mean the sort of law they had demanded in the bill of rights petition, the ministers used it to denote the Estatuto Real itself. Martínez spoke of "el régimen representativo, fijado por el Estatuto Real, en que S.M. ha restablecido las antiguas leyes fundamentales" (*Pr.*, p. 1250—"the representative régime, made fast by the Estatuto Real, in which Her Majesty restored the ancient fundamental laws"); or again: "Plantear reformas políticas, fijar las bases de nuestras leyes fundamentales, y dar latitud a la libertad, sofocando la rebelión; ésta es la misión del Gobierno" (p. 1252—"To bring about political reforms, establish the bases of our fundamental laws, and give freedom room to expand while smothering rebellion, this is the mission of the Government"). The prime minister maintained this stance throughout the debate and, on its last day, to avert any confusion arising from discrepant definitions, he asseverated that by "leyes fundamentales" he meant only those sanctioned by the Throne. Referring to responsibility of ministers as conceived during the Triennium, Martínez asked:

¿qué sucedió cuando estuvieron consignados esos principios en la Ley fundamental? Sucedieron dos cosas: Primera, que por llevar a tan sumo grado esa libertad individual, tuvieron impunidad los conspiradores todos contra el sistema constitucional, prevaliéndose de esas mismas leyes que les servían de parapeto para minarle . . .[19] (*Pr.*, p. 1303)

(what occurred when those principles were stated in the fundamental law? Two things happened: First, because individual freedom was elevated to such an extreme degree, all the conspirators against the constitutional system were accorded impunity, availing themselves, to undermine it, of those same laws which they used as a parapet . . .)

"Representación nacional," the next term on Figaro's list, was uttered only once during the debate, in a speech by Calderón Collantes.[20] Here it is used as a synonym for Cortes:

Después de un sacudimiento tan terrible que ha comprometido evidentemente la suerte del Trono y de la libertad, los Secretarios actuales del Despacho no pueden continuar con las riendas del Gobierno, sin que la Representación nacional pronuncie la aprobación de su conducta y su decisión de continuarles el apoyo que hasta ahora han encontrado en ella. (*Pr.*, p. 1278)

(After a jolt so terrible that it evidently jeopardized the fate of the Throne and of freedom, the present Secretaries of the Cabinet cannot continue holding the reins of Government if National Representation is powerless to make pronouncements on its approval of their conduct and its decision to maintain the support they have found in it up to now.)

We must realize that a vote of confidence for the cabinet would have set a parliamentary precedent detrimental to the conservative principles of the Estatuto. On the other hand, such a vote would have been overwhelmingly in favor of the ministers. Hence, the introduction of the issue would have hurt both parties. It is understandable, therefore, that Calderón Collantes's suggestion was ignored. But would the Progressives have lost on such a motion if there had been a truly representative congress? If we remember how much they insisted on a *ley de ayuntamientos* to obtain fair representation, then we can surmise that Larra must have looked askance at using the term "representación nacional" to designate Cortes.

The word "fantasma" is comically placed at the end of Figaro's list. Let us trace the function of this noun in the debate. When on January 19 Llauder had to defend before Cortes his actions of the 17th, the Progressives' interpellations provoked him into uttering the preposterous canard that Canterac was killed by Carlists (*Pr.*, p. 1248). As could be expected, the next speaker, Joaquín María López, seized the opportunity to take advantage of the blunder:

> Nos ha dicho [Llauder] en seguida que los extremos contrarios nos baten por derecha e izquierda. Pero ¿cuáles son esos extremos opuestos? Fantasmas abortados por la ardiente imaginación de algunos visionarios, y que encontrando cabida en la de los Ministros, les hacen retroceder y estremecerse a la vista de estos soñados planes y peligros, dando a su marcha administrativa un carácter vacilante e incierto que de ningún modo se concilia con el paso seguro y firme de un Gobierno franco y pronunciado. (*Pr.*, p. 1249)

> (He told us just now that contrary extremes are beating us on the right and the left. But what are those opposite extremes? Phantoms aborted by some visionaries' ardent imaginations, which penetrated into that of the Ministers, make them recede and shake at the sight of these spectral plans and perils, giving the course of their administration a vacillating and uncertain character which can in no manner be reconciled to the sure and firm step of a frank and resolute Government.)

Martínez de la Rosa, probably feeling a need to save the day, attempted to confound López's figure of speech with a piece of solemn irony:

> Todavía está caliente la sangre derramada no muy lejos del Estamento; y cuando se ven tropas sublevadas que al grito de libertad privan de la vida al primer general de la provincia, se dice que son fantasmas; pues si lo son, son fantasmas que asesinan. (*Pr.*, p. 1251)

> (The blood spilled not far from the Chamber is still warm; and when rebellious troops, at the cry of freedom, take the life of the first general in the province, they are said to be phantoms. If so, they are phantoms who murder.)

The prime minister must have felt quite pleased at his newly-found oxymoron, for he soon repeated it:

Se insubordinan tropas; rehusan obedecer a sus jefes y se lanzan
a sorprender un puesto, donde entre la confusión y el orden se
comete el atentado más horrendo.... ¡y aun se dice que son
fantasmas! Si lo son (vuelvo a decirlo) son fantasmas que derra-
man sangre. (*Pr.*, p. 125)

(Troops become insubordinate. They refuse to obey their com-
manders and launch forth to surprise a post, where among confusion and order the most heinous crime is committed.... and
yet they are said to be phantoms! If so, I repeat, they are phantoms who spill blood.)

After this speech, López rose to say:

El Sr. Presidente del Consejo de Ministros me permitirá deshaga
varias equivocaciones e inexactitudes que ha cometido en su discurso. La primera es sobre fantasmas políticas; yo he dicho que
no existen los que se figura el Ministerio. El Sr. Presidente del
Consejo de Ministros dice que sí, y que son fantasmas que asesinan; pero añade que son los exaltados. El Ministro de la Guerra
ha dicho un momento antes que son los carlistas; yo dejo a cargo
de ambos señores el arreglar entre sí esta diferencia y esta contradicción. (*Pr.*, p. 1252)

(The President of the Cabinet will allow me to set aright a few
errors and imprecisions committed by him in his speech. The first
is about political phantoms; I said that those the Ministry imagines
do not exist. The President of the Cabinet says they do, and that
they are phantoms who murder, but he adds that they are the
exaltados. The Minister of War said a moment ago they were the
Carlists. I leave it up to these two gentlemen to decide between
themselves this difference and contradiction.)

And the next day Palarea prosaically analyzed Martínez's metaphor:

El Sr. Presidente del Consejo de Ministros ha manifestado que
hay un partido que se ocupa en promover la anarquía, y ha añadido que éstas no son fantasmas como las llamó mi digno compañero y paisano el Sr. López, y que si lo son, son fantasmas
que asesinan. Pero en mi concepto siempre son fantasmas; y yo
quisiera, y aun me atrevería a pedir que se averigüe del modo más
enérgico, y por todos los medios que el Gobierno tiene en su mano,

qué es lo que hay de realidad y de positivo. Así yo suplicaría al Gobierno que trate de examinar cuál ha sido la mano oculta que promovió el suceso de antes de ayer, cuál fue la que hizo más que los infelices ilusos de Correos. (*Pr.*, p. 1261)

(The President of the Cabinet declared that there is a party occupied in fomenting anarchy, and added that these are not phantoms, as my meritorious companion and neighbor Mr. López called them, and that if they are, then they are phantoms who murder. But in my opinion they are still phantoms, and I would like, and even be bold to request that whatever is real and concrete in the matter be investigated in the most forceful manner, and with all the means the Government has at its disposal. Therefore I beg the Government to try to examine what was the hidden hand that fomented the events of the day before yesterday, doing more than those deluded wretches in the Post-Office.)

Alcalá Galiano also took a turn at wiping up the floor with the prime minister's wit. If the government could only carry out the Progressives' ideas, he said, "no daría lugar a recriminaciones amargas ni a sucesos lamentables; no vendría a decirnos: ¿no habláis de que son fantasmas la anarquía? pues hay fantasmas que matan" (*Pr.*, p. 1265—"it would not give occasion for bitter recriminations or lamentable events. It would not come to tell us: Did you not say that anarchy is phantoms? Well, they are phantoms who kill"). And, putting forth the opinion that the Milicia Urbana should guard Madrid and the army be sent north, he concluded: "esos fantasmas que matan, no hubieran matado a Canterac si hubieran estado matando carlistas en Navarra" (*Pr.*, p. 1266—"those phantoms who kill would not have killed Canterac if they had been killing Carlists in Navarre").

Even Argüelles got into the act. Urging greater freedom of the press, he declaimed:

Por sostener estas doctrinas no creo que haya riesgo ninguno de incurrir en la nota de revolución, ni que esto contribuya directa ni indirectamente a fomentar los fantasmas de que se hizo ayer uso como figuras retóricas. No me arredrarán a mí esas recriminaciones, que son las verdaderas fantasmas con que se asusta siempre en tiempos como éste; y menos deben todavía asustar a hombres de Estado, que tienen tantos medios para desvanecerlas, sin comprometer la fuerza ni el rigor del Gobierno. (*Pr.*, p. 1292)

(In upholding these doctrines I do not feel there is any risk of slipping into a tone of revolution, or that this contributes directly or indirectly to the encouragement of the phantoms resorted to yesterday as rhetorical figures. Those recriminations, which are the real phantoms used to scare people in times like these, will not frighten me. And statesmen, who have so many means to make them vanish without jeopardizing the strength or rigor of the Government, have even less reason to fear them.)

But the prime minister could not let the crux of his argument be weakened in this manner. He decided on a forceful oration, announced that he would speak of the Isabelina, and started to hint at its complicity in the slaughter of the monks. Then he associated that calamitous event with the abortive coup which had occurred on the eve of the opening of Cortes. He read the titles of two subversive pamphlets, one penned by Aviraneta. There was a writer, he added, who had published in a newspaper the Isabelina's secret statutes; this man was later sent a murder threat on stationery bearing the society's seal. "¡Amenazar de muerte a un escritor los mismos que dicen que se reúnen en defensa de la libertad! ¡Y luego se dirá que éstos son fantasmas que no existen sino en la mente del Ministerio!" (*Pr.*, p. 1306—"A murder threat to a writer from the very same persons who say they gather in defense of liberty! And then it is said that these are phantoms who exist only in the Ministry's mind!"). After this broadside, the Progressive orators avoided any mention of phantoms, limiting their speeches to veiled demands for political reform and for the removal of Llauder.

Figaro, unlike his friends in parliament, did not let the matter drop. He ridiculed Martínez's phrase by inserting it into a mock praise of newspapers:

¿En qué libro encontraría lo que quiere decir un *ministro responsable*, y una *ley fundamental*, y una *representación nacional*, y una *fantasma*? ¿En qué universidad podría aprender la sutil distinción entre *las fantasmas que matan* y *las que no matan*? Distinción por cierto sumamente importante para nosotros, pobres mortales, que somos los que hemos de morir. (1: 447)

(In what book would he find the meaning of *responsible minister, fundamental law, national representation,* and *phantom?* At what university would he learn the subtle distinction between *phantoms who kill* and *those who don't?* Certainly a highly important distinction for us poor mortals, who are the ones that have to die.)

There is cunning banter in this passage. The writer, as we see, links the word "universidad" with talk of subtle distinctions supposedly of great importance to all mortals. This smacks of a Voltairian type of burlesque against scholasticism (the foundation of learning at the hopelessly backward Spanish universities). If so, then Larra means to insinuate the image of the prime minister into the shadow of obscurantism.

Another reference to parliamentary oratory is found in Figaro's repetition of the word "licencia." Here the author got his idea from a speech by Martínez de la Rosa, exalting the *juste milieu:*

> sin temor de ser desmentido, ni pretensión de pasar por profeta, añadiré que cualquier variación [of ministers] que se haga, se vendrá a parar, sobre poco o menos, en el sistema actual. De lo contrario, o se dará en el escollo de la licencia y anarquía, o se perderá la libertad. . . .
>
> . . . Todo esto ha convencido a la nación de que necesita huir de todos los extremos, pues el poder absoluto y la licencia o libertad desenfrenada, que conduce a la anarquía, son los dos extremos que se tocan. . . .
>
> . . . Creyó [the ministry] . . . que dando este régimen a la nación, se quitará el temor y recelo de caer en el extremo del absolutismo, o en el opuesto de la licencia. . . .
>
> . . . De la lucha encarnizada de los partidos nace la anarquía, el exceso de la licencia, y sólo ésta tiene el privilegio de llamar inmediatamente al despotismo. (*Pr.*, pp. 1267, 1268, 1269)

(without fear of being disproven, without pretense of passing for a prophet, I shall add that any variation of ministers that could be made would again result in the present system, more or less. Otherwise, either it will land on the reefs of license and anarchy, or freedom will be lost. . . .

. . . All this has convinced the nation that it must shun all extremes, since absolute power and unbridled freedom, which leads to anarchy, are the two extremes that touch one another. . . .

. . . The ministry has believed that by giving this régime to the nation it will remove the fear and suspicion of falling into the absolutist extreme, or its opposite, license. . . .

... Anarchy is born of cruel party strife. It is an excess of license and it alone bears the privilege of immediately calling upon despotism.)

Figaro's parody is especially ingenious. He weaves three themes into a pun: the "fantasma" topic; Martínez's insistence on the threat of political license; and the difficulty of obtaining a newspaper license, for which purpose he quotes the regulation.[21] The double meaning of "license," of course, links the oratorical theme even more closely, linguistically speaking, with the essay's main topic of the journalist's vicissitudes. We may also notice that the above-mentioned "university" theme finds an echo in the use of "catedrático":

> *o tener empleo con sueldo... . . . o ser catedrático...* pero so fuera catedrático sabría algo, y entonces no servía para periodista...
> Está decidido que no sirvo para pedir licencia. Otro al canto: un testaferro; un sueldo al testaferro; seguridades contra seguridades, fianza, depósito, licencia, en fin. He aquí ya a *Fígaro* con licencia; no esa licencia tan temida, esa licencia fantasma, esa licencia que nos ha de volver al despotismo, esa licencia que está detrás de todo, acechando siempre el instante, y el ministro, y el... No, sino licencia de imprimirse a sí mismo. (1: 449)

> (*either have a job with salary... . . . or be a university professor...* but if I were a professor I would know something, and thus I should be worthless as a journalist...
> Decidedly, I won't do for the purpose of requesting a license. Let's try someone else: a straw man; a salary for the straw man; surety bonds against surety bonds, guarantee, deposit, license. Now we have *Fígaro* with a license; not the bloodcurdling kind, the phantom license, the license that will take us back to despotism, the license that's behind everything, always lying in ambush for the right moment, the minister, the... No; the kind of license you need to put yourself in print.)

The pun on "licencia" is by no means a "bad" pun. It has ideological depth; the fantasy or ghostly fear of political license is precisely why the government issues newspaper licenses so grudgingly! Larra has found by means of this pun an opportunity to depict Martínez's concern as maniacal fear: he has used this opportunity quite successfully, composing an anaphorical crescendo ("esa licencia" and "y el"), interrupting the climax by aposiopesis ("y el..."), and falling off into something which appears, through his linguistic dexterity, to be an insignificant intimate activity, like begging someone's leave to scratch oneself. The contrast elaborated by the author on the two types of license prepares us for the final device, which is the contrast the reader himself must perceive between the dates of writing and printing (see above).

Let us not forget that "Un periódico nuevo" reflects Larra's own professional difficulties on a particular occasion. Perhaps he complained bitterly to his editor about the rejection of some articles ("Atrás," "Adelante," "Revista del año 1834"?), and was curtly told, "¿Por qué no pone usted un periódico suyo?" We know that he did try. If there had indeed been harsh words between him and his former editor, then his failure was not only frustrating but chastening. But the double blow to his pride is resolved through the composition of a witty, well-devised essay. While baring some of his adversities and veiling others, Figaro also touches upon his country's troubles, thus imbodying his homeland's suffering in his own.

13

FUNDS FOR THE
SECRET POLICE

O N February 7, 1835, there appeared in the *Revista Española* an essay by Larra entitled "La policía," the significance of which can be understood if we go back to the
parliamentary session of January 28. On that day the Comisión
de lo Interior of the Estamento de Procuradores presented to the
chamber a revised version of the government's budget for the interior, amounting to about 123 million reales. Next came the prescribed debate on the totality of the interior department's budget,
which had to precede discussion on its individual articles. Although this budget contained forty-eight items, debate soon began to revolve on two of them only, item number 6, "Policía,"
and item number 28, "Inspección general de Imprentas," that is,
censorship. Tempers rose quickly and the meeting was soon adjourned.[1]

During the subsequent period, in which the budget was taken
up item by item, the first five articles were approved in a day and
a half, whereas articles 6 and 28 each required two days of debate,

February 2 and 3 and February 9 and 10. Article 6, the most controversial, is an uncommonly ambivalent document; it is indeed astounding to see a request for money put in such a manner:

Artículo 6—Policía

Si la comisión por su objeto no estuviese estrictamente circunscrita al presupuesto y sus economías, con el mayor placer y la más sincera efusión de su corazón se extendería sobre los perjuicios morales, políticos y aun económicos que causa la policía, según la vulgar aceptación que se la da, y el modo que en el día se ejerce, que da motivo a tantas vejaciones, continuo objeto de quejas y reclamaciones, sin producir ninguno de los resultados que sirven de pretexto, y que pudiera producir si estuviese fundada en justicia y equidad. Esperando que el Estamento tendrá la bondad de disculpar esta digresión, contrayéndose al presupuesto, opina que debe rebajarse de la superintendencia general la cantidad de 191,055 rs., dejando, como en los demás artículos, a disposición del Gobierno el número de empleados, sus sueldos y la suma que destine para gastos, etc.... (*Pr.*, p. 1364)

(Article 6—Police

If the committee, owing to its purpose, did not have to limit itself strictly to the budget and its economies, it would, with the greatest pleasure and most sincere and heartfelt effusiveness, go at length into the moral, political, and even economic harm caused by the police, as it is commonly called, and the manner in which it operates nowadays, giving occasion to so many vexations, and being the continuous object of complaints and claims, without producing any of the results that serve as a pretext for its existence, which it could produce were it founded on justice and equity. Hoping that the Chamber will be kind enough to excuse this digression, the committee, circumscribing itself to the budget, is of the opinion that the amount of 191,055 reales must be cut from the general superintendency, leaving, as in the other articles, at the disposition of the Government the number of employees, their salaries, and the sum allotted for expenses and so forth...)

There are two tragic incongruities in this article. As we can see, though it had reduced the police budget merely from 8,422,172 reales to 7,928,288, the committee was in fact requesting funds for an institution which it declared, in the same sentence, to be harmful to the country. The second incongruity is a rational one, used to justify the first, and is inherent in the wording of article 6. It deems the police to be beneficial *in principle* though harmful *in fact*. Hence, a complete incongruence between fact and theory has been brought to the fore: funds, which are a concrete reality, are to be applied to something that is good only in the abstract. And yet, considering the state of the country at the time, a police force "fundada en justicia y equidad" is well-nigh impossible.

It is significant that not one *procurador* contested the committee's unfavorable portrayal of this institution. Even the most conservative, it appears, were agreed about the faults of the police as expressed in article 6. Consequently, despite its intensity, the debate concerned only the course of action that these faults might require.

Dissenting from the committee's recommendations, a core of Progressives were convinced that the secret police should be abolished. It ought to be pointed out that this opinion had already been voiced before the debate. This was on January 21, 1835, when Argüelles spoke of the government's inability to nip the post-office plot in the bud:

> ¿Y para qué es la policía? ¿Por qué figuran entre las partidas del presupuesto de lo Interior millones para este objeto? La policía ¿a qué se dirige? ¿Y por qué no vigila y cumple con su deber? ¿No es bastante esa terrible arma? Pues entonces deduciría yo que la policía es inútil.
>
> Al tratarse de este ramo en el presupuesto respectivo votaré condicionalmente. Si acompaña o se ofrece una ley para la seguridad individual, lo aprobaré; pero si no, desde ahora anticipo mi voto, no le daré para sostener un establecimiento inútil para el bien, y que es capaz de acabar con la libertad y con otra cosa que es peor, con la moralidad pública, porque yo no concibo que la sociedad pueda ser moral mientras abrigue en su seno el espionaje vil: ésta es mi opinión. (*Pr.*, p. 1293)

(And what is the police for? Why do millions for this purpose appear among the items of the Interior budget? What is the police used for? And why is it not watchful? Why does it not fulfill its duty? Is this terrible arm not enough? I can only deduce that the police is useless.

When this branch is dealt with in its respective budget, I shall vote conditionally. If a law guaranteeing individual security accompanies it or is offered, I shall approve it. If not, then from this moment I declare what my vote is. I shall not cast it in order to uphold an institution useless to the common good and capable of bringing liberty, and, what is worse, even public morality to an end, because I cannot conceive how society can be moral while it shelters in its bosom the vile practice of spying. This is my opinion.)

"El divino orador" also traced the history of the police in Spain, pointing out that several monarchs attempted unsuccessfully to set up such a force:

Esta policía, contraria a nuestras costumbres, a nuestros hábitos y a nuestro carácter, y sobre todo, porque hay en ella un no sé qué de olor a Inquisición, no puede ser nunca nacional. Pero si todavía se nos presentase como indispensable en el día, es menester, señor, una retribución; que a un voto vaya unido el otro. Yo creo deber exigir que se una el voto de la existencia de aquélla con el de la seguridad personal. En esto no pido para mi persona sola; lo pido también para los Sres. Secretarios del Despacho, que pueden estar seguros que tal vez no la necesitaran menos que yo. (*Pr.*, p. 1294)

(This police, contrary to our customs, our habits, our character, and especially because it has about it a certain odor of the Inquisition, can never be national. But if it is still presented to us as indispensable nowadays, a compensation is needed, sir. One vote must be tied to the other. I believe we must demand that the vote on its existence be joined to that on personal security. In doing this I ask it not for myself alone; I ask it for the Secretaries of the Cabinet, who can be certain that they may perhaps not need it any less than I.)

During the budget debate, other orators would reiterate Argüelles's comparison of the police with the Inquisition, as we shall see. It was a commonplace among Progressives and it finds an echo in Figaro's essay: "La Inquisición no era tampoco otra cosa que una policía religiosa" (1: 452). We should note Larra's reversal of tenor and vehicle, which gives the concept a satirical flavor not found with the orators. Larra, who sought a break with the past, is reluctant to argue from history, because, after all, historical argumentation is just what serves the purpose of Medieval

Revivalism in the manner of Martínez de la Rosa. Whereas Argüelles, an optimistic Doceañista, asserts that the existence of the police is contrary to national tradition, the journalist skeptically points to the continuous presence of such an institution in Spain. Unlike Argüelles's speech, moreover, Larra's essay was written after the Progressive defeat; therefore, their attitudes must differ. That of Larra is rather one of Romantic despair toward an evil which he begins to see, perhaps, as an ineluctable heritage.

Though the Progressives realized that the budget would be passed, they hoped to obtain a few nonmonetary concessions. Some, Argüelles among them, sought constitutional guarantees against police excesses, but their proposals were in vain. Others argued that funds should be withheld until the government reformed the police; they were told that a reform program could not be undertaken without such funds.[2] Toward the end of the debate, on February 3, it was pointed out by the secretary of the interior that if the government were not voted the money, it would be obtained by subtracting some here and there from other parts of the budget (*Pr.*, p. 1428). Many delegates must have decided at this point that it was a question of saving appearances and, realizing how powerless they really were, brought the debate to an end. Up to this moment some Moderates had favored money first and reforms later, but the predominant opinion on the right represented the police as a necessary evil. On February 3, four days before Larra's article appeared, the police budget as proposed by the committee was approved by 62 against 50 votes, with 10 abstentions.

Figaro plainly shows in his article that he opposed the existence of this institution and its corresponding appropriation. His stand, identical to that of the Progressives, is clear and simple, perhaps oversimple, compared to the ambivalent attitude of the Moderates, who would vote funds to something they considered good only in principle. Their position is satirically epitomized by Figaro in the expression "cosa buena," which he repeats over and over again in order to dissect it with consummate skill. Larra shows himself here to be an unrelenting wrecker of the amphibology with which he toys linguistically. In his essay we find the locutions "algo bueno," "algo ni bueno ni malo," "cosa buena y rebuena," "cosa buena es, y muy buena," and "cosa excelente," each used once. "Cosas buenas" appears four times, while the plain singular, "cosa buena," as much as eleven. Moreover, the adjective "bueno" or its feminine is used, in all but two instances, as an indirect qualifier, so to speak; that is, instead of serving as a predicate adjective, it modifies a vacuous predicate noun or pronoun. Rather than say "La policía es buena," Figaro writes humorously, "La policía es cosa buena." "Cosa buena" is thus an institution whose supporters dare not defend it by affirming that it is "buena," but who justify it only on principle, in the abstract, because its supposed goodness or integrity is belied by actual performance.

It is evident that we are faced here with a phenomenon consisting in rationalization and generalization, and whose verbal equivalent can best be given in the form of a hackneyed expression. Now the process of linguistic synthesis which culminates in such expressions is ridiculed by Larra in the essay immediately following "La policía." Entitled "Por ahora," it also examines oratorical bombast, but in a different manner:

> Ahora bien, cuando dos de estas palabras insignificantes y maleables se llegan a encontrar en el mismo camino una de otra, únense al momento y se combinan por una rara afinidad filológica; y entonces no toman por eso mayor sentido; todo lo contrario, juntas suelen querer decir menos todavía que separadas: entonces estas palabras buenas suelen convertirse en lo que vulgarmente llamamos *buenas palabras*. (1: 454)

> (Now, when two of these insignificant and malleable words happen to find themselves on the same course, they merge immediately and combine with each other through a rare philological affinity. And then they do not acquire greater meaning thereby; on the contrary, together they are wont to have even less meaning than when separate. These good words then turn into what we commonly call good *mots*.)

All of "Por ahora" is a burlesque of trite words and their combinations. In "La policía," on the other hand, Figaro concentrates on semantic analysis rather than synthesis, as we shall see on further examination of "cosa buena."

When we say about something that it is a "good thing," we usually mean that it is desirable, that its existence is welcome. Yet this is not equivalent to stating that it is "good." If we feel that an institution is good, we have to take for granted first of all that it is desirable; in addition, we must mean either that the institution is performing its task well or that its members are good men in a moral sense. Now, though not one of the *procuradores* would have dared aver that the Spanish secret police was "good," some did argue that it was a necessary evil. At this point we might expect their opponents to censure such an attitude. Indeed, we find Argüelles reviling the type of rationalization used by the ministers and their adherents to justify the secret police:

> Es hija de una especie de ateísmo político, de la inmoralidad que domina a la Europa desde el congreso de Viena, de unos principios que excluyen fría y cruelmente la moralidad de las acciones, en fin, de la doctrina jesuítica de que "con tal que el fin corresponda a la intención, poco importan los medios." (*Pr.*, p. 1408)

> (It is the offspring of a sort of political atheism, of the immorality that dominates Europe since the Congress of Vienna, of principles which coldly and cruelly exclude morality from actions; in sum, of the Jesuitic doctrine that "provided the ends correspond to the intent, the means matter little.")

In "La policía," where Moderate views are restated ironically, the rationalized justification is mocked by attributing to the phrase "good thing" the implied meaning of "necessary evil." From here on Larra can base his satire on the extraction from the phrase "cosa buena" of the adjective "buena," as I shall show. Finally, in the last paragraph of his article the journalist achieves maximum effect by the substantivization "bondad," which he has kept in store for the end.

As the essay unfolds, the reader may become aware of two waxing themes, induced by the text but in themselves extratextual. Inasmuch as several passages in "La policía" parody specific speeches, the reiteration of "cosa buena" in these paragraphs can be considered a satire of the impression of triteness imparted by the oratory. First of all, the ironic refutation of "cosa buena" gives rise in the reader's mind to its converse, "cosa mala." Simultaneously, when "good thing" has been reduced by iteration to a hackneyed locution, it can dichotomize into the original primary concepts *cosa* and *buena*. Now, because the dominant ironic tone of the essay induces the reader to dwell on concepts opposite in meaning to the locutions he reads, he will thereby perceive by analogy the concept of *mala*, as opposed to *buena*. He consequently discerns a range of five conceptual categories: *cosa mala*, *mala*, *cosa*, *cosa buena*, and *buena*. This revelation may come to the reader consciously or subconsciously during the course of his reading. In any case, in the first of the two instances in which "buena" appears alone as a predicate adjective, the "buena" concept is overtly used to cast an air of confusion on the "cosa buena" concept. About an imagined moot on censorship, Larra writes:

> Cosa buena es, y muy buena. Replicárannos los que viven de disputar que la tal previa censura no es igualmente buena para el que escribió el artículo que no puede correr, ni para el país que de él pudiera sacar provecho; pero en primer lugar, que al sentar nosotros la proposición de que hay cosas buenas, no hemos dicho para quién, y en segundo añadiremos que ése es el destino de las cosas de este mundo, en las cuales no hay una sola buena para todos. (1: 451)

> (A good thing it is, and very good indeed. Those who live by debating will probably reply that this prior censorship is not equally good for the writer of the unprintable article, or for the country that might benefit from it. But, in the first place, when we stated the proposition that good things exist, we did not say for whom; and in the second place, we shall add that this is the destiny of the things of this world, where not a single one of them is good for everyone.)

The author appears here to destroy the concept of "cosa buena" by the denial of its general applicability (as he explains further on, censorship is of unequal goodness for the writer and for the censor). In another instance, the two words "cosa" and "buena" have been separated, the noun being detached from the adjective and serving only an auxiliary grammatical function: "La Inquisición no era tampoco otra cosa que una policía religiosa; y si era buena la Inquisición, no hay para qué disputarlo" (1: 452—"Likewise, the Inquisition was nothing more than a religious police; and if the Inquisition was a good thing, there is no reason to dispute this"). Because "cosa" appears in the first half of the sentence, stylistic elegance, we might say, dictates its avoidance in the second. Yet this avoidance is effective in another respect; though the reader is already on guard for the weaker term "cosa buena," it is somewhat shocking to find the Inquisition called "good," even in protasis. Another stylistic device that bears mentioning in this respect is to leave the word order of "cosa buena" intact in the comparative: "La otra policía es urbana. Ésta es todavía más cosa buena que la otra" (1: 453—"The other police is urban. It is even more of a good thing than the other one").

From the very first, Larra's article reflects ideas expressed by Alcalá Galiano about the need to differentiate between men and institutions, which, as we shall see, can be designated respectively as "cosas buenas" and "hombres buenos." Galiano had said:

> no nos basta . . . saber que los actuales individuos del Gobierno son hombres de probidad y de ilustración, no; mañana pueden ser sustituidos por otros que no tengan, no digo sus ideas, sino su temperamento, su carácter dulce; y al contrario le tengan severo, inflexible, duro; de lo que podría citar ejemplos; pero no lo hago por ser siempre cosa odiosa las comparaciones.[3] (Pr., p. 1407)

> (it is not enough for us to know that the present members of the Government are upright and enlightened men. No. Tomorrow they can be replaced by others who do not possess, I shan't say their ideas, but their temperament, their mild character; who, on the contrary, are severe, inflexible, hard. I could give examples, but I shall not do it, for comparisons are always detestable.)

The first sentence of "La policía" makes use of Alcalá's differentiation between institutions and men:

> Así como hay en el mundo hombres buenos, también hay cosas buenas: no citaremos nombres propios en la primera clase por no ofender a la mayoría; pero en la segunda preciso será citar si queremos que nos crean. (1: 451)

> (Just as there are in this world good men, there are also good ideas. We shall not quote proper names for the first category in order not to offend the majority; but for the second, it will be necessary to quote if we want people to believe us.)

Here the author plays on the word "mayoría," which may refer to men in general ("en el mundo"), or to the parliamentary majority that voted for the police budget. The first interpretation indicates a skeptical attitude on Larra's part toward the nature of man; he probably affects it here for his immediate purpose. The second connotation implies caution with respect to the more powerful political faction. But this second meaning is ironic, because, as with all good puns, the two acceptations impinge on one another. Figaro is really directing a veiled slur against those voting Moderate; they are definitely not good men. In this manner, moreover, the essayist hints at his goals immediately. The antithesis of "hombres buenos" and "cosas buenas" intimates that they are conceptual opposites, not necessarily in a general way, as some cynical philosophers would have it, but specifically. First of all, it must be deduced that the "hombres buenos" are the parliamentary minority who opposed a "cosa buena," the police. Furthermore, in contrast with the unreasonable concept of an institution deemed good only in the abstract, Larra suggests that an institution can be good only if the men who comprise it are good. Institutions are molds and, in the long run, no better than their members, or, as Galiano indicates, than the rulers who use them. But Larra carries the matter further than his friend. Whereas the orator compares men to men, the journalist opposes men to institutions (that is, those deemed to be necessary evils). Etiquette prevents Galiano from citing examples, though it is probable that he had Llauder in mind. Figaro would find it even more difficult to give examples of people, for, as he says, "no somos desgraciadamente ni procuradores ni inviolables" (1: 453—"unfortunately we are neither a *procurador* nor inviolable"). Thanks to his satirical procedure, however, he can give examples of "cosas buenas" and, in fact, "preciso será citar si queremos que nos crean." Also, he has one advantage, stylistically speaking, over the *procurador*, namely, hindsight, for at the time of writing, the election results are known and he can play on the word "mayoría."

The redundancies found in the remainder of the first paragraph of "La policía" help to form in the reader's mind the aforementioned conceptual categories. First comes, "Cosa buena, por ejemplo, es la previa censura, y para algunos no sólo buena, sino excelente"[4] (1: 451—"Prior censorship, for example, is a good thing, and for some not only good but excellent"). We may note here that the words, "no sólo buena, sino" constitute a humorous redundance whose mock affectation the reader will recollect whenever he comes across the expression "cosa buena" in the essay.

At this point we find in the first paragraph the intercalation of another theme, that of command:

> Que manda usted y que manda usted mal, dos cosas que pueden ir juntas. ¿Pues no es cosa buena y rebuena que nadie pueda decirle a usted una palabra? Que manda usted y que no manda usted mal, pero que es usted hombre de calma; y como había usted de mandar algo bueno, no manda usted nada, ni bueno ni malo. ¿Pues no es un placer verdaderamente que si hay algún escritorzuelo atrevido que sale a decir: "Esto no marcha," salga por otra parte el censor que usted le pone, y le escriba en letra gorda y desigual al pie del folleto: *Esto no puede correr?* Vaya si es cosa buena. (1: 451)

> (That you're in charge and do badly, two things that can go together. Now, isn't it a good and extra good thing that no one can say a word to you? That you're in charge and don't do badly, but that you're a man with poise; and since you have to command something good, you command nothing, neither good nor bad. Now is it truly not a pleasure, when there's a petty writer who dares to come forth and say, "This isn't working," that some censor you assign to him should come forth and write with a clumsy and uneven hand at the bottom of the pamphlet, *This can't pass?* You bet it's a good thing.)

Who is meant by "usted" is not altogether clear. It could be the government, or Martínez de la Rosa himself, or, for that matter, Moscoso de Altamira, who, as secretary of the interior, was in charge of censorship. Such equivocalness indicates the need for a careful examination of the passage, because the stylistic ambiguity may be meant as a political clue. Let us imagine that the above excerpt were monothematic, that is, that the topic of command had not been interpolated in the "cosa buena" theme. In such a case the passage would still be dealing with censorship only, and its first sentence would be, "¿Pues no es cosa buena y rebuena que nadie pueda decirle a usted una palabra?"; likewise, the next sentence would be the other interrogation beginning, "¿Pues no es un placer . . . ?" But, to be sure, such is not the case. What then does the thematic intertwining accomplish? Mainly, I would say, it keeps the reader on the alert for more ideological interpolations, which, however, may not be so obvious stylistically. Furthermore, it hints strongly at the relation between censorship (or secret police methods) and bad government. The device is rather original; it allows the author to dispense with an immediate explication, although his meaning is clarified in the second paragraph by the words, "La policía se debe al miedo" (see below).

Let us now turn to the command theme in this passage. Its initial manifestation is expressed by what may seem at first to be a redundance: "Que manda usted y que manda usted mal . . ." Yet we have just observed a meaningful example of this device ("no sólo buena, sino excelente"). It may prove fruitful, therefore, to ponder the present redundance. The adverb "mal," grammatically speaking, is merely a modifier for "manda"; thus the simple statement, "that you command" and its modification, "that you command badly," are separable but not mutually exclusive concepts, "dos cosas que pueden ir juntas." In fact, the first subsumes the second. Now when we pass to the next interpolated sentence, "Que manda usted y que no manda usted mal . . . ," whose second member is the negative of that of the previous sentence just examined, the inconsistency and incongruity puzzles us until we perceive the puns on "manda" and "mal." The verb can be transitive or intransitive, while the adverb is also a noun. I shall attempt to clarify this by means of a translation designed to express the most significant interpretation of the passage: "That you are in command, and that you command badly—two things which are not incompatible. That you are in command and that you do not command evil to be done, but that you are a man of inaction; and as you should command something good to be done, you command nothing, neither good nor bad." This passage, moreover, reflects stylistically the vacillation and indecision for which Martínez was reputed. But the punning does not end here. "Esto no puede correr" is not only the censor's judgment that an article may not be printed, but also an amplification of the "escritorzuelo's" criticism of government policy, "Esto no marcha." Furthermore, this "escritorzuelo atrevido" is pitched against an ignorant and plebeian censor who writes "en letra gorda y desigual." In the next sentence, "Vaya si es cosa buena," Figaro begins to develop a conceptual play on the oft-repeated locution.

Between the censorship, the government's policy, the pleasure of observing the censor's blunders, need we decide which of them is the "cosa buena"?

The first paragraph of "La policía" also contains a remark about censors' salaries. It should be pointed out that this topic had been broached in Cortes by Istúriz during his peroration of January 28, one of whose targets was article 28 (censorship). This mercurial orator had said:

> No daremos un cuarto ni aconsejaremos al Estamento vote un maravedí hasta que desaparezca ese borrón de nuestro sistema representativo, que es el mayor que puede echarse en cualquiera. La comisión no ha debido pasar por sostener con los subsidios que propone el precio de la corrupción: cualesquiera que sean las calidades de los censores, nada más es el sueldo que se les señala que el precio con que se compra su adhesión a las ideas del Gobierno. (*Pr.*, p. 1376)

> (We'll not give a dime and we'll advise the Chamber not to vote a cent until this blot disappears from our representative system, for it is the biggest that can be made on any. The committee should not have allowed itself to uphold the subsidies proposed for the price of corruption. Whatever the censors' qualities may be, the salary assigned to them is nothing more than the price at which their adherence to the Government's ideas is bought.)

In the following passage, which reflects the words of Istúriz and López, Fígaro turns to another person whom he calls "usted":

> Que es usted un sujeto de luces por otra parte, amigo del Gobierno, y que tiene usted poco sueldo, o no tiene usted ninguno, como suele suceder; vaya si es cosa buena que le den a usted 20.000 reales de sueldo u opción a los primeros que vaquen, sólo por poner: *Esto no puede correr*, que al cabo es decir una verdad como un templo... Cosa buena es y muy buena. (1: 451)

> (That you are, on the other hand, a man of learning, a friend of the Government, and that you get little salary, or none, as is wont to happen; then you can bet it's a good thing if they give you a 20,000 reales salary or a right to the first vacant job, just for putting down *This can't pass*, which, after all, is to utter a truth as big as a shrine... A good thing it is and very good indeed.)

This passage follows immediately the last one quoted from Larra, with its "command" theme. The change in the person addressed is the first of three apostrophic mutations in the paragraph, and is indicated by the words, "por otra parte." The third apostrophe will be to an informer, the fourth to a traveller. The present one is, of course, the censor. What sort of a person is he? It is hinted to us (or, rather, to him) that he got the job through influence and servility, that his personal motives are solely mercenary, and that he is not really qualified for the position. This information enables Larra to repeat the pun, "esto no puede correr," while adding to it a third meaning. The literal acceptation is that "this article may not be printed"; besides that, it is an amplification of the remark, "esto no marcha" made about the government; it is also an added criticism that giving a fellow like "you" a censor's job is outrageous. The point is driven across by the affirmation "que al cabo es decir una verdad como un templo." The repetition of the pun is therefore an ideologically relevant tautology, analogous to other such devices in the paragraph. Finally, it must be noted that the words "Cosa buena es, y muy buena" are cleverly ambiguous. Do they ironically refer to the existence of censorship, or even more ironically to the fact that Figaro himself has been able to speak "una verdad como un templo"?

The reason for intercalating sentences about governmental authority within a passage on censorship now becomes clearer. First of all, this process indicates unequivocally that the words "esto no marcha" apply to the government. Secondly, it helps ventilate an opinion about the kind of people working for Martínez. And, incidentally, if the ministry uses men of this type as censors, those working for the secret police will not be much better. This demonstrated feasibility of applying the same criticism to any aspect of the Martínez government leads to an eventual elimination of categories in dealing with the political scene, and thereby of the "good thing" concept.

By the end of the first paragraph, Larra has effectively demolished this idea of "cosa buena." He is thus ready to begin the second paragraph with an ironic discussion of the secret police as, of course, a "good thing": "convengamos únicamente en que hay cosas buenas. Sabido esto, pocas hay que se puedan comparar con la policía" (1: 451—"Let's just agree on the fact that good things

do exist. Once this is known, few can be compared with the police"). Any such assertions must naturally be corroborated by
historical precedent. In his review of *La conjuración de Venecia*
(April 25, 1834), Larra had referred to the Republic of Venice
as "el imperio del terrorismo, por tantos años triunfante contra
todas las leyes de la naturaleza" (1: 384—"an empire of terrorism,
triumphant for so many years over all the laws of nature"). We
might keep in mind this echo of Rousseau as we observe the
journalist writing about the police what seems at first to be a totally contrary opinion:

> Su origen está en la naturaleza; la policía se debe al miedo, y miedo
> es cosa tan natural, que poco o mucho no hay quien no tenga al-
> guno; y esto sin contar con los que tienen demasiado, que son los
> más. (1: 451)

> (Its origin can be found in nature itself; the police is due to fear,
> and fear is such a natural thing that there is no one who does not
> have it to a greater or lesser degree; without even counting those
> having too much, who are in the majority.)

But, in the first place, Larra is not a philosopher; moreover, in
"La policía" he is not speaking of the fearfulness of the governed
but of the rulers.[5] We might note here also that "los más" may
be an allusion to the majority who voted for the police appropriation.

Larra continues to discuss the topic of fear and concludes his
paragraph with two verses from *La Araucana*. But why does he
go to such lengths as to include a quotation from Ercilla to accuse
the ministry of cowardice? The answer to this is found only by
going through the *Diario de las sesiones*. What Larra has done is
to avail himself of oratorical reminiscences. The citation happens
to be a parody of remarks made two weeks previously by Toreno,
which Larra's contemporary readers would have been likely to
recall. Here is what happened. During the debate following the
Correos incidents, Alcalá Galiano had stated that the ministry's
policy towards the militia was based on fear. It was Toreno who
answered him with the words:

> Me parece que dijo el señor Galiano que nosotros tenemos miedo
> de los enemigos de la libertad y recelos de la Milicia urbana. El

Gobierno no tiene miedo de los amigos de la libertad, ni de los amigos del desorden, no; lo que hace es estar prevenido para que no puedan destruir esa misma libertad. (*Pr.*, p. 1280)

(It seems to me that Mr. Galiano said we were afraid of the enemies of freedom and suspicious of the Urban Militia. The Government fears neither the friends of liberty nor the friends of disorder, no. What it does do is to be prepared so that they cannot prevent the destruction of this very liberty.)

Then, after amplifying his ideas, the secretary of the treasury attempted to counter some arguments of Caballero. Caballero had alleged about the Estatuto Real, as pointed out in the previous chapter, that

el cimiento que se nos ha dado y hemos recibido como tal, se halla en el mismo estado que hace un año, sin que se haya adelantado una línea en la obra, dejándonos expuestos a que este mismo cimiento se descarne y se pierda con la injuria del tiempo. (*Pr.*, p. 1272)

(the foundation given to us and received by us as such is still in the same state as a year ago, without having made a headway of even one row in the work, thus making us run the risk of having the foundation itself chipped away and buried through the ravages of time.)

Toreno replied thus:

Dice el Sr. Caballero que el Estatuto Real es un cimiento; pero que ahí se está el cimiento. Afortunadamente ahí se está; el gran mal sería que no estuviese, y se hace todo lo posible para que esté; y no se verifique un verso de Ercilla en la Araucana, que dice, si mal no me acuerdo:
    "Danos licencia, rompe el Estatuto
    Con tu poder sin límite absoluto."
    Pero lo primero para levantar ese edificio y que no sea de naipes, es que el cimiento se siente bien, y es imposible que un edificio cuyos cimientos se han echado hace siete meses se haya coronado ya y recibido todos sus adornos hasta el entablamento. (*Pr.*, p. 1281)

(Mr. Caballero says that the Estatuto Real is a foundation, but that the foundation is still there as such. Fortunately, I say, it is still there, and everything possible is done so that it may still be there, and that a verse of Ercilla's in *La Araucana* may not be fulfilled, which says, if I recall correctly: "Give us permission, break the Statute / by thy limitless power absolute."

But the first thing needed to raise this edifice so that it will not be a house of cards, is for the foundation to sit well, and it is impossible for an edifice whose foundations were laid seven months ago to have been topped off by now, with all its ornaments, including the entablature.)

The verses quoted by the secretary of the treasury are from Canto XX, st. 53, and are spoken at the jousts by Crepino, the unknown foreign knight, to Tegualda, daughter of the chieftain Brancol. Crepino asks her to override the decision of the judges, based on the statutes of the game, forbidding him to wrestle a second time with the champion Mareguano, whom he has defeated but who likewise wants to fight again. Though Toreno's citation may seem out of context, and used merely because it contains the word "Estatuto," it insinuates nevertheless that whenever strife occurs, a faction can attempt to persuade a ruler to exercise absolute power, overrule decisions and suspend privileges. The quotation from Ercilla therefore serves to warn subtly about the possible abolishment of the Estatuto Real, which, after all, is only a *charte octroyée* and hence theoretically subject to revocation by the Throne. Accordingly, the fact that Larra in turn quotes two verses from *La Araucana* shows that he is parodying Toreno, even though they are not the same verses:

> Todos tenemos miedo; los cobardes a todo; los valientes a parecer cobardes; en una palabra, el que más hace es el que más lo disimula, y esto no lo digo yo precisamente; antes que yo lo ha dicho Ercilla, en dos versos, por más señas, que si bien pudieran ser mejores, difícilmente podrían ser más ciertos.
>
> > El miedo es natural en el prudente,
> > Y el saberlo vencer es ser valiente. (1: 451)

(We are all afraid; the cowards, of everything; the brave of appearing cowardly. In a word, he who does most hides it most. I'm not really the one who says this. Ercilla said it before me, in two verses to be exact, which, though they might be better, could hardly be truer: "Fear is natural in a wise man; / valor is knowing how to overcome it.")

The verses quoted by Figaro serve sarcastic, not minatory ends, as with Toreno.[6]

Larra's parodying of the secretary of the treasury, moreover, goes beyond the quotation from Ercilla; indeed, the quoting of Ercilla fits another purpose, that of paragraph transition, because the next paragraph, as I shall demonstrate, is in itself a parody of a speech by Toreno on the police budget. This is his famous discourse of February 3 in favor of the dreaded institution, sententious and overloaded with polysyndeton. On the two pages of the *Diario* where it is reproduced, the conjunction "y" appears seventy-nine times, often after a semicolon. The following passage, which Larra parodied, is from this oration:

> Si se censurase que el Gobierno procura averiguar lo que se trama contra él, diríamos al señor preopinante que no ha habido gobierno que no se vea forzado a hacer otro tanto, sin exceptuar los más libres de la antigüedad, y no nos faltarán textos en nuestro apoyo. En la conspiración tan conocida y traqueada de Catilina, Cicerón ¿no tenía sus Curios y sus Fulvias? ¿No daba instrucciones a sus agentes, en que se les decía observasen a los sospechosos, *adeant, bene polliceantur, dentque operam ut eos quam maxime manifestos habeant*, según dice Salustio? ¡Y esto en Roma, y bajo un consulado como el de Cicerón! (*Pr.*, p. 1424)

> (If the Government were to be censured for attempting to inquire into plots against it, we would reply to the previous speaker that there has never been a government which did not find itself obliged to do this, including the freest ones of antiquity; and there is no dearth of texts to support our statement. In the well-known and oft-mentioned Catiline conspiracy, did Cicero not have his Curiuses and his Fulvias? Did he not give instructions to his agents, in which they were told to observe suspicious persons, *to approach people, to promise well, and do their best to have them convicted as much as possible,* according to Sallust? And this, in Rome! And under a consulship like Cicero's!)

By "Curios" and "Fulvias" Toreno refers to a loose talker among the conspirators named Curius, who was betrayed by a girl named Fulvia with whom he cohabited in *stuprum*.[7] As for the minister's Latin quotation, it must be shown in context to bring out Sallust's original meaning: "Cicero per Sangam consilio cognito legatis praecipit, ut studium coniurationis vehementer simulent, ceteros adeant, bene polliceantur, dentque operam uti eos quam maxume manifestos habeant"[8] ("Cicero, having learned of the stratagem through Sanga, orders his lieutenants to strongly simulate enthusiasm for a conspiracy . . ."). There is a considerable difference between Cicero's spies ad hoc and a powerful, organized, unchecked, and permanent political police. The comparison of the Spanish situation with the Catiline conspiracy can be made to appear far-fetched, unless the public becomes convinced of the government's contention that it is in constant danger of being overthrown.[9]

The secretary of the treasury also sought precedents in Portugal:

> Lo mismo sucede en Portugal, donde también son más latos los principios de libertad que concede su Carta; y a pesar de haberse hecho infinitas proposiciones por los Sres. Diputados sobre puntos diversos, y todas en el sentido de mayores ensanches, no pienso se haya hecho ninguna importante hasta ahora para destruir la policía, bastante rigorosa en aquel país, y notable en Lisboa mismo el cuerpo, perteneciente, si no mal me engaño, a este establecimiento, y al que dan el nombre de *os morcegos*. (*Pr.*, p. 1425)

> (The same thing occurs in Portugal, where the principles of liberty conceded by its Charter are likewise more ample. And despite the endless proposals made by the Deputies on several subjects, and all in the direction of greater latitude, I believe that no important one so far has been made to destroy the police, which is quite rigorous in that country. If I recall correctly, the Lisbon brigade of this establishment is considered noteworthy, having been nicknamed *the bats*.)

The word *morcegos* was obviously not the official name for the Lisbon secret police, but their nickname; and Larra, in his lampoon of Toreno's bombast, wittily clarifies this point:

> Preclaro es, pues, el origen de la policía. No nos remontaremos a las edades remotas para encontrar apoyos en favor de la policía. Trabajo inútil fuera, pues ya nos lo han hecho; un orador ha dicho que en todos los países la ha habido con *este o aquel nombre* [doubtlessly referring to "Curios" and "Fulvias"], y es punto sa-

bido y muy sabido que la había en Roma y en el consulado de Cicerón: no se sabe si con este o con aquel nombre, no precisamente con su subdelegado al frente y sus celadores al pie; pero ello es que la había, y si la había en Roma, es cosa buena; si a esto se añade que la hay en Portugal, y que el pueblo da a sus individuos el nombre de *morcegos*, ya no hay más que saber. (1: 451–452)

(Illustrious therefore is the origin of the police. We need not go back to remote ages for documentary evidence favoring the police. A useless task it would be indeed, since this has already been done for us. An orator said that it has existed in all nations *under one name or another*, and it is known, quite well known, that it existed in Rome, and during the consulship of Cicero. We know not whether with this name or that, nor exactly whether with its subdelegate at the top and its watchdogs at the bottom; but the fact is that it existed. And if it existed in Rome, it's a good thing. If to this is added the fact that it exists in Portugal, and that the populace gives its members the name of *bats*, what more need one know?)

In this parody we should also observe the repetition of "y,"[10] and the word "apoyo" (cf. Toreno's "no nos faltarán textos en nuestro apoyo"). The last remark, "no hay más que saber," alluding perhaps to the minister's discernment, is ironically belied by the statement of further examples in the next paragraph.

For these further examples Larra uses three sources. First comes *La conjuración de Venecia*, by Martínez de la Rosa, thus throwing back at the prime minister his own play; secondly, James Fenimore Cooper's *Bravo*, of which a Spanish translation had appeared the previous year;[11] thirdly, a comparison of the police to the Inquisition. The precedent for the latter, we might add, was set by Argüelles, Antonio González, and Istúriz in speeches made only four days previously.[12] Figaro writes:

Venecia ha sido el Estado que ha llevado a más alto grado de esplendor la policía; pues ¿qué otra cosa era el famoso tribunal pesquisidor de aquella República? A ella se debía la hermosa libertad que se gozaba en la reina del Adriático, y que con colores tan halagüeños nos ha presentado un literato moderno en la escena, y un célebre novelista en su *Bravo*. La Inquisición no era tampoco otra cosa que una policía religiosa; y si era buena la Inquisicion, no hay para qué disputarlo. Aquí se prueba lo que ha dicho el orador ci-

tado, de que siempre ha existido en todos los países *con este o aquel nombre.* (1: 452)

(Venice is the State that brought the police to its highest level of splendor. After all, what else was that Republic's famous investigatory tribunal? To it was due the lovely freedom enjoyed inside the Queen of the Adriatic, which a modern writer has presented to us on the stage in such flattering colors, and a famous novelist in his *Bravo.* Likewise, the Inquisition was nothing other than a religious police; and, if the Inquisition was good, there is no reason to dispute this. So this proves what the abovementioned orator said, that it has always existed in all nations *under one name or another.*)

By ending this passage with the same italicized phrase introduced in the previous paragraph, Figaro hints that Toreno has set a precedent in finding instances of secret police organizations; hence we need not limit ourselves to his examples and are justified in referring to the police as "Inquisición" or "Tribunal de los Diez," a comparison really more valid than "Curios" and "Fulvias."[13] Through repetition, the phrase *"con este o aquel nombre"* helps to connect the two paragraphs, or, better yet, to create a relation of parallelism between them, because one parodies Moderate arguments while the other ironically exaggerates them. This process is similar to the intertwining of the "que manda usted" sentences at the beginning of the essay.

To begin the next paragraph, Larra refers back to Toreno's example, and then goes on to bring up more unfavorable analogies: "Otra prueba de que es cosa buena la policía es su existencia, no sólo en Roma y en Portugal, sino también en Austria . . ." (1: 452—"Another proof that the police is a good thing is its existence, not only in Rome and Portugal, but also in Austria . . ."). Yet, to understand its full significance, we must keep in mind González's speech of February 2:

La policía se ha establecido en España para sustituir a la Inquisición; y como se estableció por un ejército enemigo que vino a destruir las libertades patrias y los derechos que nos consignaba el Código de aquella época, éste es otro motivo más para que la odiemos. (*Pr.,* p. 1404)

(The police was created in Spain to replace the Inquisition; and as it was established by an enemy army which had come to destroy our national freedoms and the rights written down in the Code of that period, this is one more reason for us to detest it.)

Another pertinent discourse is Alcalá Galiano's of February 3:

La policía no puede jamás ser favorable a un sistema de instituciones liberales; y yo me atrevo a emitir una opinión que está confirmada por la práctica; dondequiera que hay policía bajo instituciones más o menos libres, siempre propende a favorecer un tanto a los que se inclinan al Gobierno absoluto con preferencia a los que quieren un sistema liberal, porque tiene una simpatía invencible por el absolutismo: en fin, la policía siempre propende, cuando ve dos clases de enemigos, a batir a los que se empeñan en apoyar un sistema extremadamente liberal, porque con su establecimiento deja de existir la policía: esto sucede en Francia, sucederá en España y en todas partes. (*Pr.*, p. 1421)

(The police can never be favorable to a system of liberal institutions; and I shall be bold to offer an opinion confirmed by practice: wherever there is a police under more or less free institutions, it always tends to favor somewhat those who lean toward an absolute government, in preference to those who want a liberal system, because it has an unflagging sympathy for absolutism. In sum, the police always tends, when it sees two kinds of enemies, to strike against those who persist in backing a thoroughly liberal system, because when it becomes established the secret police ceases to exist. This is happening in France; it will happen in Spain and everywhere else.)

Now Larra has assumed ironically the opposite point of view. After mentioning the Austrian police in northern Italy, he writes:

Óigase otro ejemplo. Ahí está la Polonia, que debe su actual felicidad—¡vaya si es feliz!—a la policía rusa. Que la policía es, pues, una institución liberal se deduce claramente de su existencia en Polonia y Austria.[14] (1: 452)

(Let's look at another example. Here is Poland, which owes its present felicity—and my, is she happy!—to the Russian police.

That the police is a liberal institution is clearly deducible from its
existence in Poland and Austria.)

To be sure, the Holy Alliance, headed by Austria and Russia, had
for years been the Spanish liberals' worst foreign enemy.

Napoleon was mentioned several times during the debate, so
that Larra could not fail to include his name in "La policía." In
this connection it will be profitable to quote a lengthy passage
from the speech of Moscoso de Altamira, who praised Spain's
most famous oppressor:

> Desde la revolución francesa la sociedad conmovida en sus cimien-
> tos vino a ser víctima sucesivamente de las opiniones particulares
> llevadas en los primeros momentos al mayor extravío. Épocas hubo
> en que se dudaba si era mejor menester pertenecer a la sociedad
> humana que retirarse a vivir entre los irracionales habitadores de
> los bosques. En tal conflicto se presentó en la escena uno de aque-
> llos genios que de tarde en tarde aparecen en medio de las socie-
> dades con bastante superioridad para dar la ley a los demás hom-
> bres. Napoleón, conociendo el caos en que se precipitaba el Estado,
> concibió la idea de retirarlo del borde del abismo y pensó en or-
> ganizarlo de nuevo. Bien penetrado de que el trastorno de la Fran-
> cia había nacido de la diversidad de pasiones puestas en violenta
> lucha, formó particular empeño en conocer las opiniones de los
> diferentes partidos, sus intrigas secretas y todo cuanto conceptuaba
> conveniente para consolidar el orden público que se proponía res-
> tablecer. A este fin organizó la policía de tal modo que jamás se
> había conocido en ningún país de Europa. Es verdad que tuvo la
> fortuna o habilidad de encontrar genios capaces de llevar a cabo
> semejante organización; genios que conocían el corazón humano,
> y hombres de un temple cual requerían las circunstancias y deseaba
> el mismo Napoleón. Los motivos para el establecimiento de la poli-
> cía existen y existirán mientras los hombres, para hacer triunfar
> las opiniones del partido político a que pertenecen, busquen como
> auxiliares a otros, que cubriéndose con la capa de las mismas opi-
> niones, no son más que viles intrigantes a quienes es necesario per-
> seguir por el bien de la sociedad que aspiran a trastornar. (*Pr.*, p.
> 1414)

(Ever since the French revolution, society, shaken to its foundations, became successively victim to particular opinions carried to
the wildest extremes. There were periods when some wondered

whether it was really better to belong to human society than to go live among the irrational inhabitants of the forest. During this conflict there came on the world scene one of those geniuses who occasionally appear in the midst of societies with sufficient superiority to lay down the law for their fellow men. Napoleon, sensing the chaos the State was plunging into, gave thought to pulling it back from the edge of the precipice and organizing it anew. Keenly aware that France's upheaval had sprung from a diversity of passions put into violent play, he zealously took it upon himself to learn the opinions of the several parties, their secret intrigues, and everything he deemed convenient for the consolidation of the common good he proposed to restore. To this end he organized the police in a manner such as had never been known in any European country. It is true that he had the good fortune or ability to find geniuses capable of carrying out an organization of this kind; geniuses who understood the human heart, men cut out for what the circumstances required and what Napoleon himself wanted. Reasons for the establishment of the police do exist, and always shall when men, in order to bring about the victory of the political party they belong to, seek the help of others who, hiding under the mantle of the same opinions, are nothing more than vile intriguers whom it becomes necessary to persecute for the good of the society they attempt to put into disarray.)

The next day Alcalá Galiano retorted in the following manner:

Yo me lisonjeo . . . de que la doctrina del Sr. Secretario del Despacho de lo Interior, cuya persona no trato de ofender, pues no tengo enemistad con S.S., será mirada por los demás señores Secretarios del Despacho, aunque no lo digan, como altamente anticonstitucional, y me lisonjeo de que aunque esta reprobación, por razones que yo venero y estimo como justas, no se manifieste con palabras, se manifestará con el silencio.

El Sr. Secretario del Despacho de lo Interior, abogando por la policía, fue a buscar su origen, y dijo haber sido creada o formada por Napoleón Bonaparte. Ninguno más que yo conoce el extraordinario talento de aquel hombre insigne, y ninguno detesta más su carácter: el mayor enemigo que ha tenido la libertad ha sido Napoleón Bonaparte. (Pr., p. 1420)

(I believe I can expect to my satisfaction . . . that the doctrine of the Secretary of the Interior, whose person I wish in no way to

offend, since I have nothing against him, will be looked upon by
the other members of the Cabinet, though they might not say so,
as highly unconstitutional; and I expect that although this repre-
hension, for reasons I venerate and deem just, will not be expressed with words, it shall be expressed by silence.

The Secretary of the Interior, in advocating the police, sought
its origin, and said it had been created or formed by Napoleon
Bonaparte. No one knows better than I do the extraordinary
talent of this famous man, and no one detests more his character:
the worst enemy freedom ever had was Napoleon Bonaparte.)

Four days later Larra wrote:

y si nos venimos más acá, veremos que en Francia la instaló Bonaparte, uno de los amigos más acérrimos de la libertad, y tanto, que
él tomó para sí toda la que pudo coger a los pueblos que sujetó; y
a España por fin, la trajo el célebre conquistador del Trocadero el
año 23, y fue lo que nos dio en cambio y permuta de la Constitución que se llevó; prueba de que él creía que valía tanto por lo
menos la policía como la Constitución.[15] (1: 452)

(and as we come closer, we see that in France it was installed by
Napoleon Bonaparte, one of liberty's fiercest friends, and so much
so, that he grabbed for himself every bit he could take from the
peoples he subjected. And it was given to Spain at last in the year
1823 by the famous conqueror of the Trocadero, trucking it for
the constitution he took away; ample proof that he felt the police
was worth at least as much as the Constitution.)

We should note the pun on "amigo" (that is, *aficionado*), and
likewise the one on "Trocadero" and "en cambio y permuta" in
the next line, assuming a *figura etymologica* with *trocar* in ellipsis.
Angoulême's "transaction" thus echoes, both stylistically and historically, Napoleon's "thievery."

The journalist now proceeds to bring his discussion of the secret police down to the more human level of individual cases. He
mentions the tragic cases of Miyar, the bookdealer who was betrayed and executed during the Omnimous Decade, and of Torrijos, who, after landing a small band in Andalusia, was summarily shot with his followers. Again, the precedent for bringing
up these cases was an oration of Alcalá Galiano's:

Había un digno oficial, un militar benemérito que derramó su sangre en la guerra de la Independencia, el cual creyó, como otros muchos (no se escandalice nadie de oírlo), que bajo un gobierno absoluto o de fuerza, sentado en la nación por mano extranjera, todo acto dirigido a derribarle era digno de alabanza; tenía esta doctrina; otros la teníamos también; disimúlese pues que yo la abone. Él, en consecuencia, formaba proyectos para dar la libertad a su patria, hallándose en la plaza de Gibraltar: ¿y qué hizo la policía? ¿Le cortó el paso por la mar para que no viniera a producir el derramamiento de sangre? No tuvo este sentimiento generoso: lo que hizo fue traerle al matadero, y querer echar sobre él un borrón, que es de gloria, y arrancar el alma a aquel hombre grande. (*Pr.*, 1421)

(There was a meritorious officer, a worthy soldier who shed his blood in the War of Independence. He believed, as many others did—and no one should be scandalized at this—that under an absolute government, or one forced on the people, established in the land by foreign arms, every act aimed at overthrowing it was praiseworthy. He held this doctrine; others among us held it too. So let us not go into the possibility that I might also subscribe to it. He, consequently, made plans to give his country freedom while he was in Gibraltar. And what did the police do? Did it cut off his access by sea in order to prevent bloodshed? No, this generous feeling did not occur to it. It led him to the slaughter, hoping to heap shame upon this great man, and snatched away his life; but it was glory that was heaped upon him.)

Larra does not fail to follow Galiano's lead:

A la policía debió el desgraciado Miyar su triste fin; y como ha dicho muy bien otro orador, a la policía se debió sin duda alguna aquella inocente treta por la cual se sonsacó de Gibraltar a un célebre patriota para acabarlo en territorio español con toda nobleza y valentía. (1: 452)

(The unfortunate Miyar owed his sad end to the police; and, as another orator said quite aptly, to the police was undoubtedly due the innocent trick by which a famous patriot was lured from Gibraltar to finish him off on Spanish soil with complete loyalty and frankness.)

It is also possible that Figaro's remark about Miyar was prompted by a speech of the Marqués de Montevirgen. On February 2 this *procurador,* without mentioning names, had exposed police methods: a secret agent posing as a conspirator would induce a number of people to join him in a plot. Once they agreed, he would denounce them to the authorities and collect the reward money (*Pr.,* p. 1413). This is supposedly how Miyar was misled.

Larra now brings up topics which lead up to the old "vencedores y vencidos" theme that he eventually takes up in the next paragraph. He seems at first to find his inspiration in an oration given by Argüelles, who had said:

> La mayor parte de los empleados en ese ramo son los que estaban desde la reacción de 1823, lo cual se verifica en él como en otros, sin poderse evitar, pues soy el primero en reconocerlo en razón de que no habiendo una causa probada, no conviene nunca ocasionar una desgracia.
>
> Dichos individuos han de tener sus relaciones por parentesco, amistad, beneficio o simpatía, y más bien simpatías, puesto que parece más grato el plural. (*Pr.,* pp. 1407–1408)

> (Most of the employees of this department are the very same ones who have been there since the reaction of 1823. This deduction is unavoidable, and I am the first to be willing to recognize it, because when something has not been proven in court, it is never suitable to bring about a misfortune.
>
> These individuals must have connections through kinship, friendship, favor, or sympathy, or rather sympathies, because the plural seems more fitting.)

Argüelles's incriminations, however, obliged Moscoso de Altamira to defend those who worked under him:

> Podrá tal vez haber algunos que hayan sido en la época pasada empleados en la policía y que lo sean ahora; pero si estos individuos han cumplido en aquella época con su deber, sin excederse de sus facultades, y cumplen en el día de la misma manera, no encuentro una razón para que se les prive de continuar en este servicio; el buen empleado es aquel que sirve a su patria sin traspasar los límites de la ley que la rige; y con tal que lo haga fielmente y con integridad, no alcanzo la razón por que haya de prescribírsele. (*Pr.,* p. 1416)

(There may be some perhaps who were employed by the police in past epochs and still are. But if these individuals did their duty then, without exceeding their authority, and are doing their duty likewise nowadays, I can find not one reason for preventing them from staying in this service. A good employee is one who serves his country without going beyond the limits of the laws that govern it; and if he does it faithfully and with integrity, I see no reason why it should now be forbidden to him.)

At this point the clerk inserted in parentheses: "(Murmullo)."

All this is reflected in Larra's essay immediately after the reminiscence of Torrijos:

De cuantos liberales han muerto judicialmente asesinados en los diez años, acaso no habrá habido uno que no haya tenido algo que agradecer a esa brillante institución. Ahora bien: continuador el año 35 y heredero universal, como se ha pretendido, de los diez años, mal pudiera rehusar herencia tan legítima; así hemos visto a nuestra policía recientemente hacer prodigios en punto a conspiraciones. (1: 452)

(Among all the liberals who were judicially murdered during the ten years, there is probably not a single one who could not have thanked that brilliant institution for its part. Consequently, since the year 1835 is supposedly the continuator and residuary legatee of the ten years, it could hardly refuse such a legitimate heritage. And so we saw our police recently perform prodigies with respect to conspiracies.)

The latter remark refers to the Correos events, of course, and the writer must have found a precedent for it in Francisco Antonio Mantilla's speech of February 2:

Dice S.S. que la policía ha traído una porción de beneficios; y yo preguntaría: si estos beneficios son tan grandes y tan públicos, ¿por qué no nos evitó la policía las desgraciadas ocurrencias del día 18 de enero? (Pr., p. 1411)

(His Lordship says that the police has brought us a number of benefits. I should like to ask: If these benefits are so great and so public, why didn't the police prevent the unfortunate incidents of January 18th?)

Turning now from inspiration back to parody, we find ample material in the oratory of February 3, when Toreno, in defense of the police, started his argument with an irrelevant semantic analysis:

> Hay varios géneros de policía; la hay urbana, la hay judicial, la hay política; las dos primeras, la urbana y la judicial, han merecido la aprobación de todos los señores que me han precedido en la palabra. (*Pr.*, p. 1422)

> (There are several types of police, the urban, the judiciary, and the political. The first two, the urban and judiciary, have deserved the approval of all the previous speakers.)

Figaro parodies the secretary of the treasury thus: "La policía se divide en política y urbana. Y es cosa tan buena una como otra" (1: 452—"The police is divided into political and urban. And one is just as much of a good thing as the other"). And further down he writes: "La otra policía es urbana. Ésta es todavía más cosa buena que la otra"[16] (1: 453—"The other police is urban. This one is even more of a good thing than the other"). Then, after pointing out that false denunciations to the police are used in private vendettas, the journalist puts forth a burlesque recital of qualifications necessary to exercise various professions (doctor, lawyer, soldier), remindful of Quevedo or Molière. At the end he writes:

> pero para ser de policía, basta con no ser sordo. ¡Y es tan fácil no ser sordo! Ahora, si fuera preciso hacerse el sordo, ya era otra cosa: era preciso saber entonces casi tanto como para ser ministro. (1: 452)

> (but to belong to the police, the only requirement is not to be deaf. And it's so easy not to be deaf! Now, if it were necessary to play deaf, that's another matter: one would then have to know almost as much as is required to be a minister.)

We may notice here that Larra takes the opportunity of a pun to banter the cabinet, which is heedless of the nationwide clamor for reform.[17] The burlesque in this case depends on a pregnant vehicle and on the word "casi," which Figaro always uses deftly.

Through his sentence calling the year 1835 the heir of the

Ominous Decade, Figaro leads up to a variation on the "vencedores y vencidos" catch phrase in his next paragraph:

> Por otra parte, decía un ilustre amigo nuestro que la España se había dividido siempre en dos clases; gentes que prenden y gentes que son prendidas: admitida esta distinción, no se necesita preguntar si es cosa buena la policía. (1: 452)

> (On the other hand, an illustrious friend of ours said that Spain had always been divided into two classes: those who catch and those who are caught. Once this distinction is granted, it's needless to ask whether the police is a good thing.)

The "ilustre amigo" is, of course, Martínez de la Rosa, whose caution is converted by Larra into pessimistic resignation: since the country will always remain divided, it would be disastrous to disrupt a long tradition.

In continuing with the topic of apprehension, Larra makes use of an address of February 2 by the Marqués de Montevirgen, who spoke of the role of the police in the conspiracies of July 24, 1834, and January 18, 1835, with which he hinted that he sympathized. Montevirgen mentioned two cases where a member of the police had received a reward for informing:

> Sea cual fuere el premio que merezca este infame delator, désele enhorabuena; pero no un destino público, como se ha dado; pues éstos sólo deben encomendarse a un hombre de probidad y que inspire la confianza que el Gobierno no puede tener en semejante monstruo. Ni cito el destino, ni cito el nombre, porque son bien conocidos.

> En el otro caso en que se supone haber prevenido el Gobierno por una delación de la policía una conspiración que tendía a conducirnos a un mayor grado de libertad, el delator de esta conspiración que se supone, y que no quiero decir que sea cierta, ha sido también premiado con un buen destino, los cuales, repito y repetiré mil veces, no deben darse sino a los hombres de conciencia y pundonor, y nunca jamás por servicios que provengan de la policía. (Pr., p. 1413)

> (Whatever be the reward coming to that infamous informer, let him have it! Fine. But not public office, which is what was awarded, because this type of position must only be entrusted to

a man of integrity who inspires the kind of confidence that the Government cannot possibly place in such a monster. I shall name neither the job nor the man, for they are well known.

In the other case in which the Government supposedly forestalled, by means of police information, a conspiracy that tended to lead us to a greater degree of freedom, the informer on this supposed conspiracy—for I don't mean to say it is certain—was also rewarded with a good job. These, I repeat and shall keep on repeating a thousand times, must be given only to men of conscience and honor, and never for services originating from police work.)

Recasting the above opinion in an ironic mold, Larra makes use of "refranes" in a manner similar to Quevedo:

Acerca de los premios destinados a la delación, y para cuyos gastos será sin duda gran parte de los millones del presupuesto, esto es indispensable: primero, porque uno no ha de delatar de balde, y segundo, porque *no se cogen truchas*, etcétera, refrán que pudiéramos convertir en *no se cogen anarquistas*, etc. En una palabra, o se ha de prender, o no se ha de prender: si se ha de prender, es preciso que haya quien delate; y si ha de haber delatores, éstos han de comer, porque tripas llevan pies. Por consiguiente, no sólo es cosa buena la policía, sino también los ocho millones. (1: 452–453)

(Concerning the reward money earmarked for informing, whose expenses doubtlessly make up a large part of the millions in the budget, it's indispensable; because, in the first place no one is going to inform for nothing, and secondly, *trout aren't caught*, etc. [in dry breeches], a proverb we could change into *anarchists aren't caught*, etc. In a word, you're either going to catch or you're not going to catch; if you're going to catch, it's necessary to have someone for informing; and if there are going to be informers, they have to eat, because they can't creep around on an empty stomach. Ergo, not only is the police a good thing, but also the eight million.)

The theme of Figaro's next passage, which begins, "En los Estados Unidos y en Inglaterra no hay esta policía política; pero sabido es en primer lugar el desorden de ideas que reina en aquellos países" (1: 453—"In the United States and England, this police does not exist; but, in the first place, it's well known that in those countries there's a reign of chaos as far as ideas go"), definitely mirrors in an ironic way Galiano's words: "Pero ¿es posible que podamos subsistir sin policía? Sí; hay muchas naciones sin ella. ¿Y cuáles son estas naciones? Los Estados Unidos y la Inglaterra" (Pr., p. 1421—"But, is it possible we could subsist without police? Yes; there are many nations without it. And which are they? The United States and England"). After the sentence based on Galiano's oration comes the next to last paragraph of Figaro's article, which deals with passports and *cartas de seguridad*. Both Argüelles and Mantilla had inveighed against them, the former saying:

En otras épocas en que no ha existido tal policía, había facultades para viajar sin impedimento ni traba de ninguna clase, y no por eso se alteraba la tranquilidad, ni el Gobierno dejaba de vigilar sobre los puntos que eran de su inspección. Después se ha visto que los más solícitos en cumplir hasta las más minuciosas formas de los reglamentos de policía eran los malévolos; casi todos los que han sufrido sentencias y ejecuciones por justicia tienen sus documentos corrientes, como cartas de seguridad, partes y demás, al paso que el hombre de bien, que descansa en el testimonio de su conciencia, descuida tal vez esas impertinencias, exponiéndose a reconvenciones no merecidas. (Pr., p. 1418)

(In former times, when this police did not exist, there were travel privileges without impediments or obstacles of any sort. Despite this, peace in the land was not disturbed, and the Government did not cease to watch over its inspection points. Later it was realized that those who were most diligent in fulfilling police regulations down to the most minute details were malefactors. All those who have served sentences or been issued major fines have their documents in order, such as safe-conducts, despatch papers, and so forth; while honest men, who rest on the testimony of their consciences, perhaps overlook some of this nonsense at times, laying themselves bare to undeserved accusations.)

Mantilla had said:

¿A qué viene esta carta, señores? Yo entiendo que no sirve más que para sacarle a cada individuo 2 rs. de contribución: éste es un censo que gravita sobre nuestros intereses y al cual hay que agregar el coste de los pasaportes y las multas; no sirviendo todos estos sacrificios que hacen los ciudadanos honrados más que para ponerles trabas para que no puedan viajar libremente de un punto a otro, y por último para pagar una multitud de agentes . . .[18]

(What is this safe-conduct, gentlemen? It seems to me that it serves no other purpose than to levy 2 reales on every individual. This tribute is a burden on our welfare; and so is the cost of passports and fines. All these sacrifices made by honorable citizens only have the function of impeding them from travelling freely from one point to another, and ultimately to pay for a multitude of agents . . .)

Figaro's humor, in this case, produces a more caustic effect than anything pronounced in Cortes. After setting down an antithetical incongruity, he compares the lack of facilities to the abundance of formalities:

los pasaportes, con los cuales va usted adonde quiere y adonde le dejan. Paga usted su peseta y ya sabe usted que tiene pasaporte. Suponga usted que, a imitación de Inglaterra, no hubiera pasaportes. En verdad que no se concibe cómo se puede ir de una parte a otra sin pasaporte: si fuera sin caminos, sin canales, sin carruajes, sin posadas, ¡vaya! ¡pero sin pasaportes! Por el mismo consiguiente saca usted su carta de seguridad, y ya está usted seguro de haber gastado dos reales; pero en cambio hay otro que desde que usted los tiene de menos los tiene de más. (1: 453)

(passports, with which you go where you want and wherever they let you. You pay your peseta; now you know you have a passport. Imagine that, as in England, there were no passports. In truth it's inconceivable that anyone can go from one place to another without a passport. If it were without roads, without canals, without carriages, without inns, all right, granted. But without passports! By the same token, you get yourself a safe-conduct and you know that two reales have been safely conducted out of your pocket. But, on the other hand, there's another fellow, for whom it's a surplus from the very moment it's your deficit.)

We should note, among other things, that the ironic incongruity of the first sentence of the above passage anticipates stylistically the illogic of the first sentence of the last paragraph: "Probada, pues, hasta la evidencia la bondad de la policía, ¿cómo pudiéramos no agregarnos al voto de los cincuenta procuradores que han perdido la última votación?" (1: 453—"Now that the goodness of the police has been proven to the point of self-evidence, how could we fail to side with the vote of the fifty *procuradores* who lost in the last balloting?"). Here the author has not only dropped "cosa" from the mot "cosa buena," which would indicate that he were proceeding from the "cosa buena" category to the next higher one in the aforementioned scale of values; he has substantivized the adjective by using the word "bondad," thus totally abstracting the concept—the acme of dehumanization. Furthermore, it is obvious that he has proven nothing, since the evidence he adduces is ironically counterproductive. In the middle of the sentence, however, Larra puts an end to his humor by ranking himself frankly with the fifty representatives who voted against the police budget. If he had wanted to maintain the ironic tone of the initial absolute clause, he could have left his main clause affirmative, omitting the "no." But the writer knows at this point that he must cease to jest, and his usual literary irony must not be allowed to veil the underlying tragic and real irony of aligning himself with the losers. This is the last paragraph, the partisans of progress have been defeated, and flippancy would be inconsistent with his disappointment and honest revulsion. The break in mood therefore occurs not only in the last part of the article, but, even more significantly, in the last part of a sentence, thus duplicating the means of effecting the contrast. In addition, the irony of the absolute clause is a bridge between the last paragraph and the humorous ones which precede it. The impact of the last few lines of the essay is quite forceful. The journalist not only condemns the resolution in angry words, but definitely sides with the "hombres buenos" of his first sentence, the fifty "procuradores que han perdido la última votación."

14

CLIMAX BEFORE
DEPARTURE

Between the appearance of "La policía" and his departure
from Madrid on or about April 5, 1835, seven articles of
Larra's were published by *La Revista Española* and *La Revista–Mensajero*, the name it acquired after a merger: "Por ahora"
(February 10), "Poesías de Juan Bautista Alonso" (February 19),
"Carta de Fígaro a su antiguo corresponsal" (March 2), "El
hombre globo" (March 9), "La alabanza, o que me prohíban
éste" (March 16), "Un reo de muerte" (March 30), and "Una
primera representación" (April 3). In March Larra also composed a burlesque synopsis of a bad French play by Ernest Legouvé entitled in Spanish *La muerte de Abel*, which could be
seen on the Madrid stage at the time, but this hilarious piece of
theatrical criticism remained unpublished until 1851.[1]

The first article we must consider here is, therefore, "Por
ahora." It was printed in *La Revista* ten days after "La policía,"
to which Larra significantly refers in the first sentence: "En
nuestro último artículo, en que defendíamos la policía, dejamos

ligeramente apuntado que hay *cosas buenas* en el mundo . . ."
(1: 454—"In our last article, in defense of the police, we pointed
out offhandedly that there are *good things* in this world . . .").
In spite of this initial reference, it would be misleading to conclude that "Por ahora" is no more than a mere sequel.[2] Far from
this, the essay seems to summarize parodically all the Moderate
oratory uttered in these Cortes. And even from a chronological
point of view only, we could consider "Por ahora" as the climax
of this phase in Larra's career, because none of the other essays
mentioned above contains any satire of parliamentary speeches,
and parliamentary satire is, after all, the hallmark of this period
of his production. But it is also a climax qualitatively. First of all,
the title is in itself a satirical summary because it embodies the
spirit of the *juste milieu*, especially since the phrase can be found
among Moderate speeches. Those quoted in this study provide
a few examples of the locution. Another instance should be mentioned; the ministerialist Medrano, speaking about the jury system, said on August 3, 1834, that "en España, según mi opinión,
no puede establecerse por ahora" (*Pr.*, p. 22—"in my opinion, it
cannot be established in Spain for the time being"). This attitude,
as we saw, was ridiculed in "El ministerial," who, according to
Figaro, "anda a paso de reforma; es decir, que más parece que se
columpia, sin moverse de un sitio, que no que anda" (1: 439—
"The ministerialist walks at reform's pace; that is to say, he seems
to swing and sway, without moving from any one place, rather
than walk"). Yet, journalistic attacks never deterred Martínez de
la Rosa from making such statements as: "en materia de reformas
. . . es menester buscar el tiempo, la oportunidad, la sazón de
hacerlas; y si no se compromete, se aventura su éxito" (*Pr.*, p. 546
—"In the matter of reforms . . . it is necessary to seek the moment, the opportunity, the time to make them; and, if their success is not endangered, at least it is risked"); or "No se debe dar a
una nación instituciones que no esté preparada a recibir, adelan-
tándose imprudentemente a la acción del tiempo . . ." (ibid.—
"Institutions that a nation is not prepared to receive should not
be given to it, imprudently preempting the action of time"); or

En abstracto estoy de acuerdo con esta libertad, y más digo: sería
menester ser muy enemigo de los hombres y de las luces el que

quisiese grillos para las personas y trabas para la imprenta. Pero la cuestión actual no es en abstracto . . . (p. 1302; January 22, 1835)

(In the abstract I agree with this freedom; moreover, I say one would have to be quite an enemy of mankind and enlightenment to wish fetters on persons and shackles on the press. But the present question is not in the abstract . . .)

The views exemplified by these statements of the prime minister are certainly epitomized in Figaro's phrase, "por ahora." Around this locution the author develops his satire of the verbal palliatives uttered to justify ministerial inaction. He proceeds to dissect the term relentlessly, then focuses on it from several angles and against a changing background. In this background figures "La policía," of which "Por ahora" is in some measure a sequel, adopting its style and technique. Whereas "La policía" centered on "cosas buenas," the present essay revolves around "palabras buenas," "palabras que parecen cosas." And just as there could exist a "cosa buena" that was "más cosa buena" than another, so can certain "palabras buenas" stand above their fellows because they are, in addition, "buenas palabras." Moreover, the exordia of these two essays are about equal in length and serve the same formal purpose. Both articles introduce the main theme, the police in one, procrastination in the other, after lengthy verbal play on the comprehensive but vacuous concepts of "cosas buenas" and "palabras buenas."

The relation of "cosas buenas" to the police provides a pattern for establishing the relation of "palabras buenas" to the term "por ahora," symbol of procrastination. Delay of political reform is, of course, the crux of Moderate policy. Hence, almost all the important parliamentary discussions of the period are brought in to illustrate this theme: the debates on the Correos events, freedom of the press, the bill of rights, the judicial system, and, indeed, on all the petitions in general, since most of them had not been acted upon by the Crown.

"Por ahora," as I pointed out above, culminates the journalist's "oratorical" satire during the Martínez ministry. Because of its general nature it is perhaps his most appealing political article written in this period. Its retrospective character allows for both comprehensiveness and profundity, so that it approximates the true essay more than any other article dealt with here.

The political events witnessed by Larra between the publication of "Por ahora" and the "Carta de Fígaro a su antiguo corresponsal" (March 2), though important, were not of the kind to invite satire.[3] Garelly and Moscoso announced their resignations on February 21, the date of their replacement by Juan de la Dehesa and Diego Medrano. On the same day a Progressively inclined general, Jerónimo Valdés, was appointed war minister. This was a concession to the left, of course, but it fell short of heralding the start of bipartisan government. If there was talk of bipartisanship or fusion, as it was called, few believed that it would genuinely occur with Martínez in power even though he had been the first to use the term. According to Luis Sánchez Agesta, the prime minister had said that with his system he wanted to unite all Spaniards and merge all opinions into one ("unir a todos los españoles y fundir todas las opiniones en una").[4] The word came up again much later in a speech by Antonio González on civil servants: "nosotros debemos ser los primeros en hacer una franca fusión de principios, para que no haya desunión entre los españoles" (*Pr.*, p. 540—"we must be the first to bring about a frank fusion of principles in order to prevent disunity among Spaniards"). Larra's first mention of the topic is contained in the "Segunda y última carta de Fígaro al bachiller" (August 13, 1834): "entonces malicia encontrarían hasta en una fusión cordial del Estamento y del Ministerio" (1: 428—"then they'd even find malice in a cordial fusion of the Chamber and the Ministry"). In the present "Carta," although there was little political activity to discuss, Figaro did see an opportunity for some word play on "fusión": "La fusión sigue en boga por todas partes; dentro de poco conseguirán que se junten el agua y el aceite. Pero ¡qué químicos! Así nos refundiéramos como nos fundimos" (2: 54—"Fusion is still in vogue everywhere. It won't be long before they can get oil and water to mix. But, oh what chemists! If we could only be recast as nicely as we're being cast down!"). This paronomasia is also skillfully used to introduce a disquisition on the merger of *El Mensajero* and *La Revista*. It should be noted that *El Mensajero* had been constant in its Progressive policy, while *La Revista* had vacillated with respect to conservatism. Larra writes:

A propósito, también se me olvidaba la gran novedad, la verdadera novedad del día. *La Revista* y *El Mensajero* se han fundido, es decir, se han casado. Si ha sido casamiento por amor o por interés no te lo diré; pero yo creo que se querían; ya sabes que hace tiempo que se conocían; dónde se han visto, y dónde se han tratado, nadie lo sabe, porque al fin los padres siempre han andado por distinto lado, pero los chicos son el diablo; ello es que de la noche a la mañana nos hemos encontrado hecha la boda. (2: 54)

(By the way, I almost forgot about the great news, the true novelty of our day. *La Revista* and *El Mensajero* have merged; in other words, they've gotten married. Whether it was for love or interest I shan't tell you, but I think they loved each other. They've known one another for a long time, as you're aware. Where they met and got acquainted no one knows, because, after all, the parents were always on different sides. But aren't children the very devil? The fact is that overnight we found out the wedding had taken place.)

The humorous allegory continues for a few more paragraphs, until Figaro ends his letter by stating that nothing is happening, neither in Navarre nor in Cortes: "se acabará probablemente la sesión sin presentarse la ley de ayuntamientos, y sin lograr una buena ley de imprenta, ya me parece que te digo bastante" (2: 55 —"the session will probably come to a close before the electoral district law gets presented, and before a good press law is obtained. I think I've said enough"). This last paragraph, as we can see, deals with a topic of personal relevance to Larra. Freedom of the press had been broached during the debate on article 28 of the interior budget, which took place on February 10 and 11. The proceedings made it quite obvious that a new *ley de imprentas* would not be forthcoming.

In this "Carta" Figaro also utters a few words about cabinet changes. What he says on the topic is rather obvious, but his remarks on individual branches of the government need explanation. On February 28 a proposed petition was presented to put the absurdly low naval officers' salaries on a par with those of their army counterparts. Its defeat in Procuradores may have prompted Larra's comment: "La Marina, sin novedad, que por cierto, es lástima" (2: 54—"As for the Navy, nothing new; it's a pity indeed"). Likewise, the discussion of the treasury budget on February 14 and 16 revealed more than ever the nation's continuing state of near-bankruptcy, which explains Figaro's sentence, "Lo que es la Hacienda sigue lo mismo, y el Estado *in statu quo*" (2: 54—"What there is of the Treasury goes on as usual; and in State, *the status quo*").

A whole paragraph of the essay is devoted to the music conservatory, for which an allocation of 673,000 reales had been specified by the government in article 39 of the interior budget. The committee in turn had proposed a reduced amount of 400,000 (*Pr.*, p. 1393). Then, on February 13 Procuradores voted to postpone discussion on all parts of the budget dealing with public instruction (*Pr.*, p. 1540). When at last the time came for debate on the conservatory, Progressive leaders came out against government support. Galiano felt that it was a luxury and hence an inordinate burden on the taxpayers (*Pr.*, p. 1675). Trueba said that the conservatory was badly run, and that the students were pressed to show immediate results rather than encouraged to study patiently before attempting public performances. It would have been more sensible, the speaker went on, to assign funds to a naval academy (*Pr.*, p. 1678). González, García Carrasco, and Istúriz also opposed the allocation. Then Martínez (*Pr.*, p. 1677) and Toreno (pp. 1678–1679) came to the defense of the conservatory, pointing out that it trained actors as well as singers. In spite of their efforts, on February 25 this article of the budget was defeated 52 to 42 (*Pr.*, p. 1680). Trueba had suggested, however, that he would not object to an "Escuela Normal de Música," and to this end he proposed on February 26 that his colleagues apportion 80,000 reales for such a school. This measure floundered likewise. Larra's comment is clever and ironic:

> El Conservatorio de Música no ha podido sacar un maravedí a la nación. Primero se contentó con 600,000 reales, luego ya pidió 400,000, después subió hasta 80,000. Pero nada. Sin embargo, a él se le dan dos cominos de todo eso. Anoche se cantó allí la *Norma*, y se asegura que siguen cantando. Siempre se ha dicho que *el español cuando canta, o rabia o no tiene blanca*. Mira tú lo que es: yo era de opinión que le hubieran votado alguna friolera. (2: 54)

> (The Music Conservatory hasn't been able to get a cent out of the nation. At first it was satisfied with 600,000 reales, then it asked

for 400,000; later it went up to 80,000. Still, nothing. But it doesn't
care a fiddle about all this. Last night *Norma* was sung there, and
it appears they're still singing. It's always been said that *Spaniards,
when they sing, / are either raging or haven't a farthing.* You figure out which it is. I felt they could have voted it a trifle.)

An "Escuela Normal de Música" would really have amounted to
the same thing as a conservatory, and Larra recognizes this by
mentioning the 80,000 reales as if they were destined for the conservatory. Consequently, the first sentence in his next paragraph
could allude in part to this situation: "Ya vamos mudando los
nombres a las cosas" (2:54—"Now we're changing the names of
things"). Although he seems to treat the whole subject very
lightly, the defender of culture and artistic betterment may very
well have been in disagreement with the Progressive *procuradores*
—perhaps for the first time. Figaro did want to have his say on
the matter, but the apparent indifference sensed in his tone at this
point might have been meant to mitigate such a disagreement, and
to minimize the satirical bent which he probably felt was put to
better use against the Moderates. After all, some Progressive politicians may have been secretly in favor of the conservatory, though
none could have gone against the wishes of his taxpaying constituents.

A week after this "Carta de Figaro a su antiguo corresponsal,"
the writer produced "El hombre globo," one of his most famous
political articles which, as E. Herman Hespelt pointed out, is in
part an allegorical satire of Martínez de la Rosa.[5] It belongs to the
same pseudonaturalist type as "La planta nueva;" and it derives its
topicality from a current interest in balloons, which Larra had
recorded in three pieces entitled "Ascensión aerostática" (April
30 and July 16, 1833, in *La Revista Española*, and July 17, 1833,
in *El Correo de las Damas*). The first of these articles is serious,
giving a historical summary of experimentation with balloons and
explaining the possible causes in the failure of Rozo's attempt to
rise. But the journalist is not so charitable the second time, as can be
seen from the ironic nature of his main paragraph:

Es circunstancia precisa en toda ascensión que el globo no ha de
subir. En un punto dado pónese un globo bien subjeto, no sea que

se escape antes de tiempo el que nunca se ha de escapar, que es como si pusiesen grillos a un ojo. A cosa de las cuatro hace que se hincha; pero esto es una mera formalidad. A las cinco vienen los espectadores, que, como dice Víctor Hugo, constituyen en las más de las funciones el espectáculo. A las seis se impacienta el pueblo; a las seis y cuarto suben varios batidores a anunciar sin duda a los cielos que se aparten, que va el aeronauta. A las siete se lanza el atrevido mortal en la frágil barquilla; el globo, entonces, padece un rapto, una feliz inspiración, y por medio de un proceder horizontal hace un pinito o dos; y como una persona obesa que ha subido el primer tramo de una escalera, se vuelve fatigado a su posición, donde le atan de nuevo por atrevido. (2: 9–10)

(It is a necessary condition of every ascent that the balloon has to rise. At a given point a balloon is put in place, well-fastened, lest what is never going to escape should escape ahead of time, which is as if an eye were put in irons. Around four o'clock, it makes believe it's swelling, but this is a mere formality. At five, the spectators arrive. As Victor Hugo says, they constitute the spectacle itself at most functions. At six, people become impatient. At six-fifteen several scouts climb in, undoubtedly to tell the heavens to get out of the way because the aeronaut is leaving. At seven the daring mortal jumps into the fragile bark. Then the balloon goes into an ecstasy, a joyful inspiration, and by means of a horizontal procedure takes its first couple of steps; and, like an obese individual who has just gone up one flight of stairs, it returns exhausted to its original position, where it is again tied down for having been so bold.)

The same light tone informs the satire of "El hombre-globo":

He aquí, sin embargo, a nuestros *hombres-globos* probando de nuevo otra ascensión; pero escarmentados ya nuestros antiguos y derretidos Ícaros, tienen miedo hasta al gas que los ha de levantar; y en una palabra, nosotros no vemos que suban más alto que subió Rozo. Para nosotros todos son Rozos.

Vean ustedes, sin embargo, al *hombre-globo* con todos sus caracteres. ¡Qué ruido antes! "¡La ascensión! Va a subir. ¡Ahora, ahora sí va a subir!" Gran fama, gran prestigio. Se les arma el globo; se les confía; ved cómo se hinchen. ¿Quién dudará de su suficiencia? Pero como casi todos nuestros globos, mientras están abajo entre nosotros asombra su grandeza, y su aparato y su fama;

pero conforme se van elevando, se les va viendo más pequeños; a la altura apenas de Palacio, que no es grande altura, y el *hombre-globo* no es nada; un poco de humo, una gran tela, pero vacía, y por supuesto, en llegando arriba, no hay dirección. ¿Es posible que nadie descubra el modo de dar dirección a este globo?

Entretanto el *hombre-globo* hace unos cuantos esfuerzos en el aire, un viento le lleva aquí, otro allá, descarga lastre... ¡inútiles afanes! Al fin viene al suelo: sólo observo que están ya más duchos en el uso del paracaídas; todos caen blandamente, y no lejos; los que más se apartan van a caer en el Buen Retiro. (2: 59)

(Nevertheless, our *balloon-men* are again attempting another ascent. But our ancient and molten Icaruses, having profited from a good lesson, are afraid even of the gas which is to lift them; and, in a word, we don't see them rising any higher than Rozo. As far as we're concerned, they're all Rozos.

Despite all this, look at the *balloon-man* with all his characteristics. What noise beforehand! "The ascent! He's going to get in! Now he's just about to climb in!" Great fame, great prestige. Their balloon is readied for them; they're entrusted with it; look how they swell up! Who can doubt their ability? But like almost all our balloons, while they're down among us their greatness, preparation, and fame causes wonderment; but as they climb they begin to look smaller. When he's as high as the Palace, which in truth is not very high, the *balloon-man* is nothing by now: a bit of smoky air; a large sheet, empty and blank. And of course, once up, there's no direction. Is it possible that no one can find a way to direct and steer this balloon?

The *balloon-man* meanwhile makes a few tries in the air; one wind takes him hither, another thither; he drops some ballast... It's useless! At last he comes down to earth. I can observe at least that they're more expert now at using the parachute. They all fall softly, and not too far. Those who go farthest land in the *Retiro* [park where the Estamento de Próceres is located].)

All this may remind us of a remark of Voltaire's which may have inspired Larra: "l'amour propre est un ballon gonflé de vent, dont il sort des tempêtes quand on lui a fait une piqûre" (*Zadig*, chapter 1—"self-esteem is a wind-filled balloon, from which tempests emerge when it is pricked").

Another week went by, and *La Revista-Mensajero* published "La alabanza o que me prohíban éste" (March 16), an article criticizing censorship. It begins with an ironically cynical exordium in which the author "proves" that only in nations where there is no freedom of the press can one write for others, because in all other instances people write for themselves. His first paragraph is a tour-de-force, demonstrating that those who keep diaries do it neither for themselves nor for anyone else, though they may appear to do it for themselves, in which case they are not very smart ("No diré precisamente que sea necio el decirse las cosas a sí mismo" [1: 60—"I shan't say precisely that it is stupid to say things to oneself"]). As for Figaro, having a good memory, he does not forget what is worth remembering; and the rest is not worth the trouble of recording. Therefore he has never written either for himself or for anyone else—at least this is what the paragraph insinuates—since he never gets a chance to write what is deemed better forgotten ("cosas que debo olvidar").

The next paragraph deals with those who make out petitions for employment. They likewise do it only for themselves, because decisions for filling positions are based on personal considerations. Those who issue reports also do it for themselves, since the recipients have already made up their minds. And he who sends letters to his beloved is really writing only for himself, because if the two break up, he stops writing her. As for authors who say in their prologues that they write for the public, they deceive themselves, because "los no leídos y silbados escriben evidentemente para sí; los aplaudidos y celebrados escriben por su interés, alguna vez por su gloria" (2: 61—"the unread and hissed evidently write for themselves; the applauded and respected ones write for their own interest, sometimes for their glory"). In a nation like Spain, on the other hand, at least you can write for the censor. But this is really not enough, and, as Julio Nombela y Campos so succinctly summarized the problem,

> Era triste cosa que así como muchos escriben para una sola persona, para sí mismos, el periodista tuviera que escribir también muchas veces para ser leído por un solo sujeto, el censor. *Fígaro*, decidido a no verse en este trance, apelaba al arbitrio de alabarlo todo.[6]

(Sadly enough, while many write for only one person, themselves, the journalist often had to write in order to be read by one individual, the censor. Figaro, determined not to find himself in this predicament, looked to the expedient of praising everything.)

Consequently, the author goes through several topics, uttering mock praise for government action or inaction in each instance. The first anniversary of the Estatuto Real is approaching (it was proclaimed on April 10, 1834; "La alabanza" was published on March 16, 1835). Hence, a recapitulation of accomplishments is in order. We should note that this had already been done by Larra in "Adelante" and "Revista del año 1834," which were censored; it thus appears that he awaited this anniversary as an opportunity to attempt once more the publication of such a recapitulation, which he had not succeeded in doing three months previously. For example, Figaro states in "La alabanza" that "En menos de un año se ha abolido el voto de Santiago" (2: 62—"In less than a year the Oath of Saint James was abolished"), and that

> soy poco amigo de los cumplimientos. Los de los censores me hacen el mismo efecto que le hacían al portugués los del casteçao. El cuento es harto sabido para repetirlo. Esto sería no escribir para nadie. (2: 61)

> (I'm not in the least fond of compliments. The censors' have the same effect on me as the Castilian's on the Portuguese. The tale is too well known to be repeated. It would be like writing for no one.)

These passages reiterate some ideas from "Adelante": "hemos echado abajo el voto de Santiago, y no es poco hacer en un año" ("we have cast down the Oath of St. James, and that isn't little work for one year"); and "ya sabes que estos *complimentos dos casteçaos me reventan*" (4: 26—"you know that these *formalities from Castilians make me sick*"). There are several other examples of such restatement.

"La alabanza" seems to be the last political article Larra wrote before leaving Madrid, thus bringing to a close the phase which had begun on January 15, 1834, with the appointment of Martínez de la Rosa as prime minister. Of the two essays labeled "Costumbres" which may have been published before his departure, only "Un reo de muerte" can be considered political; yet it shows general social concern rather than a specific political attitude. This is the stage of Figaro's career where he found himself further to the left than at any other time. Beforehand, he had been a liberal waiting in the wings for the downfall of Zea while issuing anti-Carlist articles. Afterwards, upon his return from France at the end of 1835, he maintained his loyalty to the Istúriz clique by criticizing Mendizábal. During the period we have studied, however, Figaro's essays reflect the attitude and policies of the leftist liberals designated as Progresistas, opposed to the Moderate ministerialists who upheld Martínez's efforts to delay reforms, maintain a *juste milieu*, and retard social changes.

REFERENCE
MATTER

NOTES

CHAPTER I: LIFE AND TIMES OF LARRA

1. H. Butler Clarke, *Modern Spain 1815–1898* (Cambridge: Cambridge University Press, 1906), p. 26.
2. Francisco Pi y Margall and Francisco Pi y Arsuaga, *Las grandes conmociones políticas del siglo XIX en España*, 2 vols. (Barcelona: Seguí, n.d.), 1: 169.
3. Quoted by Ramón de Mesonero Romanos, *Obras*, vol. 7 (Madrid: Renacimiento, 1926), p. 48; and by Francisco Pi y Margall, *Historia de España en el siglo XIX*, 7 vols. (Barcelona: Serguí, 1902), 2: 396.
4. Quoted by Federico Suárez, *La crisis política del antiguo régimen en España (1800–1840)* (Madrid: RIALP, 1950), p. 85.
5. Larra's articles are usually referred to here as essays. This usage should not be interpreted as implying disagreement with critics who, in distinguishing between the two terms, claim, strictly speaking, that Larra did not write essays. The word is used here mostly for variety's sake, and in some instances specifically to avoid confusion with articles of legislative documents. An example of the latter case is "Lo que no se puede decir no se debe decir" (October 1834), where Figaro quotes article 12 of the censorship regulation bearing on newspaper articles. If Larra's piece were to be designated as an article in our analysis, the word would have to be used in three acceptations: Larra's, article 12, and articles in general as regulated by article 12.
6. Frederick Courtney Tarr, "Larra's *Duende satírico del día*," *Modern Philology* 26 (1928): 33.

7. See Domingo Delmonte, "Centón epistolario de Domingo del Monte," *Anales de la Academia de la Historia* (Cuba), 2 (1920): 124; and Wenceslao Ramírez de Villa-Urrutia, *La reina gobernadora, Doña María Cristina de Borbón* (Madrid: Beltrán, 1925), p. 76.

8. Some historians give the date of his death as September 30.

9. Edgar Quinet, *Mes Vacances en Espagne*, in *Oeuvres complètes*, vol. 9 (Paris: Pagnerre, 1857), pp. 71–72.

10. Sir Herbert Maxwell, *The Life and Letters of George William Frederick, Fourth Earl of Clarendon*, 2 vols. (London: Edward Arnold, 1913), 1: 173–174.

11. Augusto Conte, *Recuerdos de un diplomático*, 3 vols. (Madrid: Imprenta de J. Góngora y Álvarez, 1901–1903), 1: 365.

12. Vicente Lloréns, "Jovellanos y Blanco. En torno al *Semanario Patriótico* de 1809," *Nueva Revista de Filología Hispánica* 15 (1961): 262–278. Joseph Blanco White (1775–1841), known in Spain as José María Blanco y Crespo, was a Liberal priest who initiated freedom of the press in his country during the early years of the Peninsular War by publishing the *Semanario Patriótico*, the first Spanish paper which dared to criticize the authorities. When the French invaded Seville he fled to England, where he became an Anglican and later Unitarian. Blanco White, whose paternal grandfather had immigrated to Spain from Ireland, soon acquired an excellent command of English, just as he had of Latin, Greek, French, and German; his prose works, *Letters from Spain* and *Letters from England* earned him high praise at the time. One of his poems, "Night and Death," was deemed by Coleridge the best sonnet in the English language. Blanco White expressed himself in his various Protestant, Unitarian, abolitionist, and anticolonialist treatises with as much enthusiasm and elegance as he formerly had in his brilliant Spanish sermons, thus acquiring an international host of enemies and disciples. The Spanish-language paper which he published in England, *El Español*, enjoyed great influence. Its main purpose was to encourage friendship and understanding between the two nations.

13. Antonio Alcalá Galiano, *Historia de España* . . . , 7 vols. (Madrid: Sociedad Líteraria y Tipográfica, 1844–1846), 7: 343, 356: "disponer mal los ánimos . . . en un tono de hueca solemnidad."

14. Quinet, *Mes Vacances en Espagne*, 9: 77.

15. Ibid., p. 81.

16. "El Día de difuntos de 1836" (November 2, 1836), "La Noche-

buena de 1836" (December 26, 1836), "Horas de invierno" (December 25, 1836), and "Exequias del Conde de Campo-Alange" (January 16, 1837).

17. Quinet, *Mes Vacances en Espagne*, 9: 43-44.
18. Ibid., pp. 77-78.
19. We should note that the author makes no mention of his first period, that of *El Duende*, which was likewise published during the Calomarde ministry. Moreover, only three issues of *El Pobrecito Hablador* were printed under Calomarde, and almost half of Larra's production in *La Revista Española* came out during the Martínez ministry.
20. Those who attempt despite such evidence to dissect Larra's work by genre are grasping at a concept suggested by the title of the first edition of his collected essays: *Fígaro, Colección de artículos dramáticos, literarios, políticos y de costumbres* . . . (Madrid: Repullés, 1835-1837). Yet the five volumes of this edition are not divided according to genre. It was only later publishers who decided to bring about the separation. Some persons then began to classify the writer in that manner. Perhaps they were impressed by the adjectives in the title of the first edition, even though its grammatical structure does not rule out the possibility that every article might possess more than one of the four qualities indicated. Of course, these later publishers and their editors found a few stumbling blocks. In one instance, an editor solved the problem in a peculiar fashion. He classified Larra's review of Bellini's opera *I Capuletti ed i Montechi* as theatrical (we can be thankful he did not set up an operatic subgroup). Now, the first four paragraphs of the review consist in a satire of the contemporary political situation by means of musical metaphors. And so, what better solution to the editor's categorizing dilemma than to exscind these initial paragraphs! The book in question is Larra, *Artículos completos*, ed. Melchor de Almagro San Martín (Madrid: Aguilar, 1951), p. 1211. Other defects in this edition of incomplete articles have been pointed out by Aristide Rumeau in his review of it in *Bulletin Hispanique* 49 (1947): 106-109.
21. Emilio Pastor Mateos, "Larra y Madrid," *Revista de la Biblioteca, Archivo y Museo* (Ayuntamiento de Madrid), 18 (1949): 327.
22. Frederick Courtney Tarr, "Mariano José de Larra (1809-1837)," *Modern Language Journal* 22 (1937): 47.
23. [Louis-] Charles de Mazade [-Percin], *L'Espagne Moderne* (Paris: Michel Lévy, 1855), p. 342.

24. This passage is from Larra's review (June 20, 1836) of the first two volumes of Ramón de Mesonero Romanos's *Panorama matritense*, 3 vols. (Madrid: Repullés, 1835–1838).

25. Tarr, "Mariano José de Larra," p. 48.

26. José R. Lomba y Pedraja, *Mariano José de Larra (Fígaro). Cuatro estudios que le abordan o le bordean* (Madrid: Tipografía de Archivos, 1936), pp. 184, 186. Lomba's historical bias, originating from overreliance on [Francisco] Javier de Burgos's notoriously one-sided *Anales del reinado de Doña Isabel II*, 6 vols. (Madrid: Mellado, 1850–1851), can best be understood by reading a keen appraisal of the latter work in Luis Sánchez Agesta, *Historia del constitucionalismo español* (Madrid: Instituto de Estudios Políticos, 1955), pp. 218–219.

27. Ismael Sánchez Estevan, *Mariano José de Larra . . .* (Madrid: Hernando, 1934), p. 128.

28. Frederick Courtney Tarr, "More Light on Larra," *Hispanic Review* 4 (1936): 109.

29. The pertinent certificate is found in Manuel Chaves, *Don Mariano José de Larra . . .* (Seville: Imprenta de la Andalucía, 1898), p. 13: "Certificamos los abajo firmados, que el caballero don Mariano de Larra y Sánchez de Castro, hijo de don Mariano de Larra y doña María de los Dolores Sánchez de Castro, seminarista que ha sido de este Real Colegio de Escuelas Pías de San Antonio Abad, ha estudiado en él las facultades de **gramática castellana y latina, retórica, principios de poesía latina y castellana, ritos romanos, mitología, aritmética, álgebra y geometría,** con aplicación y aprovechamiento, en cuyo tiempo ha sostenido los exámenes acostumbrados para pasar de una clase a otra, etc.; igualmente por lo que toca a su conducta ha sido constantemente buena durante su residencia en dicho Seminario.—Y para que así conste, etc.—Colegio de Escuelas Pías de San Antonio Abad de Madrid, a 3 de Agosto de 1822.—Ambrosio Romero de San Francisco, Vice-Rector.—Isidro Peña de la Concepción, **Director y maestro de latinidad.**—Eustaquio Tonico de Jesús María, **Vice-Secretario.**"

30. Tarr, "Mariano José de Larra," p. 48.

31. The copy in my possession is: "ELEMENTOS | DE RETÓRICA | CON EXEMPLOS LATINOS | DE CICERON, | Y CASTELLANOS | DE FR. LUIS DE GRANADA, | PARA USO | DE LAS ESCUELAS PÍAS, | *POR EL P. CALIXTO HORNERO* | *de la Resurección del Señor,* *de las Escuelas* | *Pías de Madrid.* | SEPTIMA IMPRESION. | *MADRID* | POR IBARRA, IMPRESOR DE CAMARA DE S.M. | *1828.*" Antonio Palau y

Dulcet, *Manual del librero hispano-americano*, 18 vols. to date (Barcelona: Palau, 1948—), 6: 648, lists the following editions: Valencia, 1777; Madrid, 1791, 1801, 1815, 1828, 1833. If the 1828 edition is the seventh, it is most likely that the sixth edition was printed somewhat before young Mariano entered the course.

32. The progymnasmata are translation, variation, narration, ethology, rendering of verse into prose, fable, chria, and amplification. The latter, considered most important, is divided into two broad categories. Amplification of words is attained through epithets, verbs, repetition, synonyms, metaphors, periphrasis, and lofty words; amplification of objects, through multiple definitions, explanation of circumstances, enumeration of parts, consequences, antithesis, similes, and examples, causes and effects, negation of other causes, and climax. The chria, a series of exercises devised by Aphthonius of Antioch, consists of eight parts: praise, paraphrase, cause, contradiction, similarity, example, testimony from the ancients, and epilogue.

The rhetoric proper begins with an introductory section advising the orator to dissimulate his knowledge of rhetoric so as not to give away ostentatiously the artifice contained in his speeches. It also tells him about the three types of oratory, demonstrative, deliberative, and judicial, and about the nature of imitation (in the best sense of the word). Later, he learns that the four parts of rhetoric are elocution, invention, disposition, and pronunciation. Now the student is told that "the ornament of speechmaking consists in the ordered and prudent use of tropes, figures, sentences, and adages" ("el ornato de la Oración consiste en el uso arreglado y prudente de los tropos, y figuras, sentencias y adagios") (*Elementos de retórica*, p. 111). The following tropes are presented: metaphor, allegory, metonymy, synecdoche, irony, antonomasia, periphrasis, enigma, hyperbaton (alteration of the normal order of words in a sentence), hyperbole, catachresis (an indispensable metaphor). The author recognizes two kinds of figures, one of words, the other of concepts. The word figures are anaphora; epistrophe (the opposite of anaphora, that is, the repetition of a word at the end of adjoining clauses); symploce (combination of anaphora and epistrophe); epanalepsis (a cross between anaphora and epistrophe, that is, a sentence begins and ends with the same word); polyptoton (repetition of a verb in different tenses, or of a noun in different cases); paronomasia (almost a pun but not quite, because it uses similar words, not the same one); polysyndeton; asyndeton; antimetabole (or *retruécano*, in which the second phrase reverses the order of terms in the first, such as: ask not what your country can do for you but what you can do for your country); zeugma; homoeoteleuton (*cadencia igual*); isocolon (a series of antithetical clauses of similar construction); synonymy; antanaclasis (repetition of a word, but with a different meaning); and pun (*equívoco*). Hornero then lists ten more figures without defining them. It should be pointed out that the English word *epanalepsis* is in Spanish *epanadiplosis* and vice versa.

The figures of concept listed by Hornero are exclamation; interrogation; rhetorical question (*sujeción*); communication (whereby the speaker assumes the hearer as a partner in his sentiments); gradation (in Spanish, *climax*, which is the original meaning of this word in English also; for climax in its modern English acceptation, the Spanish use *catastasis* or *punto culminante*); litotes; apostrophe; epanorthosis (where a word is recalled to substitute a more accurate term); preterition or apophasis; antithesis; epitrope (*concesión*, where an opponent is ironically given permission to carry out what he proposes); prosopopoeia (a sort of personification); epiphonema (a concluding exclamation); prolepsis (where an opponent's objections are anticipated); dubitation (where the orator presents himself as perplexed before beginning; an excellent example is Larra's famous "Día de difuntos"); adynaton or impossible (for example, the Tiber shall flow backwards before I cease to love thee); dissimilarity; hypotyposis (vivid description); metabole and exergasia (*frecuentación* and *expolición*, accumulation of similar ideas); simile; distribution (the orderly enumeration of propositions relating to the same topic); and suspense. The manual then goes into transitions, theatrical figures, pneuma, types of style (simple, medium, sublime), invention, oratorical syllogisms, enthymemes, memory, and pronunciation.

This description of Fr. Hornero's textbook is by no means intended as an exhaustive list that will enable us to analyze Larra's style. For this purpose, the scholar is advised to consult José Coll y Vehí, *Compendio de retórica y poética* (Barcelona: Imprenta Barcelonesa, 1892), and many other editions of this work; James De Mille, *The Elements of Rhetoric* (New York: Harper, 1882); the *Shorter Oxford Dictionary;* Julio Casares, *Diccionario ideológico de la lengua española*, 2d ed. (Barcelona: Gustavo Gili, 1963), s.v. *literatura;* and H. W. Fowler, *A Dictionary of Modern English Usage*, 2d ed. (New York: Oxford University Press, 1965).

33. I. A. Richards, *The Philosophy of Rhetoric* (New York: Oxford University Press, 1936), pp. 96–97, passim.
34. Tarr, "Mariano José de Larra," p. 48.

CHAPTER 2: THE POLITICAL SCENE

1. "que nunca había sido más cercana la posibilidad de recobrar nuestras antiguas posesiones" (Wenceslao Ramírez de Villa-Urrutia, *La reina gobernadora, Doña María Cristina de Borbón* [Madrid: Beltrán, 1925], p. 73, note 1).
2. Ibid., p. 66.
3. See A. Cánovas del Castillo, *"El Solitario" y su tiempo*, 2 vols. (Madrid: Pérez Durrull, 1883), 1: 90.
4. Teniente General Fernando Fernández de Córdova, *Mis memorias íntimas*, 3 vols. (Madrid: "Sucesores de Rivadeneyra," 1886–1889), 1: 129.
5. See José Eugenio Eguizábal, *Apuntes para una historia de la legislación española sobre imprenta desde el año de 1480 al presente* (Madrid: Imprenta de la Revista de Legislación, 1879), pp. 243–255.
6. That is, a kind of scholasticism that goes far beyond the theological domain (as we would regard it nowadays) and infringes on everything else. See the anonymous history *Panorama español*, 4 vols. (Madrid: Imp. de El Panorama Español, 1842–1845), 1: 163.
7. Villa-Urrutia, *La reina gobernadora*, pp. 64–65.
8. See Vicente Lloréns, "Jovellanos y Blanco. En torno al *Semanario Patriótico* de 1809," *Nueva Revista de Filología Hispánica* 15 (1961): 262–278.
9. See Antonio Pirala y Criado, *Historia de la guerra civil y de los partidos liberal y carlista*, 5 vols. (Madrid: Mellado, 1853–1856), 1: 132; Juan Rico y Amat, *Historia política y parlamentaria de España* . . . , 3 vols. (Madrid: Impr. Escuelas Pías, 1860–1861), 2: 332–335; Juan Donoso Cortés, *Historia de la regencia de María Cristina*, in *Obras completas*, vol. 1 (Madrid: Editorial Católica, 1946), p. 902; *Panorama español*, 1: 33, 35, 90, 93, 97, 143; [Francisco] Javier de Burgos, *Anales del reinado de Doña Isabel II*, 6 vols. (Madrid: Mellado, 1850–1851), 1: 193.
10. See Rico y Amat, *Historia de España*, 2: 346; Villa-Urrutia, *La reina gobernadora*, p. 79; Anonymous, *Historia contemporánea de la revolución de España* . . . , 5 vols. (Madrid, 1843), 4: 30 ff.;

Manuel Pando Fernández de Pinedo, Marqués de Miraflores, *Reseña histórico-crítica de la participación de los partidos en los sucesos políticos de España en el siglo XIX* (Madrid: Espinosa, 1863), pp. 98, 114; and Burgos, *Anales*, 1: 200.

11. For the difficulties faced by Burgos in effecting reforms, see Pirala, *Historia de la guerra civil*, 1: 156.

12. See the anonymous *Historia contemporánea de la revolución de España*, 4: 60.

13. In "Segunda carta de un liberal de acá" (2: 17); "Primera contestación" (2: 20); and "Atrás" (4: 325). See chapter 11.

14. Villa-Urrutia, *La reina gobernadora*, pp. 89–91. Larra also uses this topic for humorous purposes in "Tanto vales cuanto tienes" (1: 416).

15. For the decree, see J. Castillo y Ayensa, *Historia crítica de las negociaciones con Roma desde la muerte del Rey Fernando VII*, 2 vols. (Madrid: Tejado, 1859), 1: 165, quoted in Henry Charles Lea, *A History of the Inquisition in Spain*, 4 vols. (New York: Macmillan, 1906–1907), 4: 545.

16. See the comments on "Lo que no se puede decir no se debe decir" in chapter 10.

17. Tomás Quintero in a letter to Domingo Delmonte, in "Centón epistolario de Domingo Delmonte," *Anales de la Academia de la Historia* (Cuba), 2: 292.

18. Pirala, *Historia de la guerra civil*, 1: 271.

19. See the comments about his review of *Numancia* (1: 409) in chapter 3.

20. [Fermín Caballero], *El gobierno y las Cortes del Estatuto* (Madrid: Yenes, 1837), pp. xx–xxi.

21. See chapter 9.

22. It is reproduced in Burgos, *Anales*, 1: 358–373; Francisco Pi y Margall and Francisco Pi y Arsuaga, *Las grandes conmociones políticas del siglo XIX en España*, 2 vols. (Barcelona: Seguí, n.d.) 2: 347–353; Juan Valera y Alcalá Galiano, *Historia general de España . . . por Don Modesto Lafuente . . .*, 25 vols. (Barcelona: Montaner y Simón, 1887–1890); and in many other histories.

23. See Luis Sánchez Agesta, *Historia del constitucionalismo español* (Madrid: Instituto de Estudios Políticos, 1955), p. 223. See also Luis Díez del Corral, *El liberalismo doctrinario*, 2d ed. (Madrid: Instituto de Estudios Políticos, 1956), pp. 449–450.

24. See Antonio Alcalá Galiano, *Historia de España . . .*, 7 vols. (Madrid: Sociedad Literaria y Tipográfica, 1844–1846), 7: 326.

25. See Vicente Lloréns, *Liberales y románticos* (Mexico City: Co-

legio de México, 1954), pp. 246–248, 260–261; and ibid., 2d ed. (Madrid: Castalia, 1968), pp. 292–294, 308–309. See also Sánchez Agesta, *Historia del constitucionalismo*, pp. 220, 223–224; and Jean Sarrailh, *Un Homme d'Etat espagnol: Martínez de la Rosa (1787–1862)* (Bordeaux: Feret, 1930), pp. 19, note 4, 95, 152–153, 253. Martínez had tried before to establish a second chamber. This was in 1822 when he attempted to put a brake on Exaltado legislation; but when he spoke of it to Ferdinand, the king replied: "No puedo gobernar con una y quieres que haya dos" (Villa-Urrutia, *La reina gobernadora*, p. 95). For the influence of Bentham, see Lloréns, *Liberales y románticos*, passim.

26. [Caballero], *El gobierno*, pp. xiii, xxiv.
27. Burgos, *Anales*, 1: 365.
28. Ibid.
29. See the comments on this question in chapter 4.
30. Sarrailh, *Un Homme d'Etat espagnol*, p. 197.
31. Ibid., pp. 200–204.
32. Villa-Urrutia, *La reina gobernadora*, p. 103.
33. Baron de Barante, *Souvenirs*, 8 vols. (Paris: Calmann-Lévy, 1890–1901), 5: 138.
34. Ibid., pp. 154–155. See also a conversation of Louis-Philippe with Esterhazy, in Metternich, *Mémoires du prince de Metternich*, vol. 5 (Paris: H. Javal, 1959), p. 606, quoted by Sarrailh, *Un Homme d'Etat espagnol*, p. 203, note 5.
35. Villa-Urrutia, *La reina gobernadora*, pp. 107–108.
36. See the comments on Larra's disillusionment with this aspect of foreign policy in chapter 4.
37. See Pierre Henry de La Blanchetai [pseud. Pierre de Luz], *Isabelle II, reine d'Espagne* (Paris: Plon, 1934), p. 12.
38. Ibid., p. 44.
39. Ibid.
40. Augusto Conte, *Recuerdos de un diplomático*, 3 vols. (Madrid: Imprenta de J. Góngora y Álvarez, 1901–1903), 1: 365.
41. For various views on the "matanza de los frailes," see: Valera, *Historia general de Espana*, 20: 70; Burgos, *Anales*, 1: 272–278; Rico y Amat, *Historia de España*, 2: 378–379; Pío Baroja y Nessi, *Aviraneta; o, la vida de un conspirador*, 2d ed. (Madrid: Espasa-Calpe, 1931), pp. 183–186; Sarrailh, *Un Homme d'Etat espagnol*, p. 207; [Caballero], *El gobierno*, p. li; Vicente de la Fuente, *Historia de las sociedades secretas antiguas y modernas en España y especialmente de la francmasonería*, 3 vols., new ed. (Barcelona: Prensa Católica, 1933), 2: 270; *Panorama español*, 2: 273.

42. Valera, *Historia general de España*, 20: 86. Baroja, *Aviraneta*, pp. 174–182, gives some additional information on the organization of the Sociedad Isabelina.
43. Pirala, *Historia de la guerra civil*, 1: 287.
44. Sarrailh, *Un Homme d'Etat espagnol*, pp. 189–192.
45. H. Butler Clarke, *Modern Spain 1815–1898* (Cambridge: Cambridge University Press, 1906), p. 6.
46. Cánovas, *"El Solitario,"* 1: 244.
47. Ibid., pp. 295–296.
48. Barante, *Souvenirs*, 5: 106.

CHAPTER 3: LARRA'S PREPARLIAMENTARY ARTICLES

1. Julio Nombela y Campos, *Larra (Fígaro)* (Madrid: Imprenta Particular de "La Ultima Moda," 1906–1908), pp. 266–267.
2. Ibid., pp. 267–268.
3. Jerónimo Merino (1769–1844), Spanish priest, and guerrilla leader during the War of Independence. He became general and military governor of the province of Burgos until 1833, when he formed a Carlist band.
4. Gabriel Boussagol, *Ángel de Saavedra, duc de Rivas* (Toulouse: Privat, 1926), p. 30.
5. Ramón de Mesonero Romanos, *Obras*, vol. 2 (Madrid: Renacimiento, 1886), pp. 100–101.
6. This becomes a *topos* in "El hombre menguado" (October 27, 1833) (1: 301) and "La planta nueva" (November 10, 1833) (1: 304).
7. Cf. "Antony" (June 25, 1836) (2: 251). For further evidence of Larra's democratic attitudes, see a letter to the editor of *El Castellano*, quoted by Carmen de Burgos Seguí, *"Fígaro"* (Madrid: Imprenta de "Alrededor del mundo," 1919), p. 34. Also, 1: 14–15, 411–412, 2: 41.
8. Nombela, *Larra*, p. 266.
9. See ibid., pp. 266–276. Lomba concurs in this judgment and adds that it was Martínez's biography of Hernán Pérez del Pulgar which gave the journalist the idea to clothe its author thus. See José R. Lomba y Pedraja, *Mariano José de Larra (Fígaro)* (Madrid: Tipografía de Archivos, 1936), pp. 98–99.
10. [Fermín Caballero], *El gobierno y las Cortes del Estatuto* (Madrid: Yenes, 1837), p. lxxi. See Antonio Alcalá Galiano, *Historia*

de España . . . , 7 vols. (Madrid: Sociedad Literaria y Tipográfica, 1844–1846), 7: 332–333, on the political position of these newspapers. In addition, Larra writes in *"El Siglo* en blanco" (March 9, 1834): "si hay quien culpe todavía de poco carácter a la *Revista*, desafiamos por esta vez al *Siglo* a que tenga más que nosotros" (1: 353).

11. For a brief account of the incident, see E. Rodríguez Solís, *Espronceda; su tiempo, su vida y sus obras* (Madrid: Imp. de Fernando Cao y Domingo de Val, 1883), pp. 119–130. The most informative analysis to date, which includes a partial elucidation of Larra's reaction, is Robert Marrast, "Fígaro y *El Siglo*," *Insula* 17, nos. 188–189 (July–August, 1962): 6.

12. José Eugenio de Eguizábal, *Apuntes para una historia de la legislación española sobre imprenta desde el año de 1480 al presente* (Madrid: Imprenta de la Revista de Legislación, 1879), p. 258.

13. Ibid., p. 244.

14. Rodríguez Solís, *Espronceda*, p. 127.

15. Frederick Courtney Tarr, "More Light on Larra," *Hispanic Review* 4 (1936): 98. As for the problem of chronology, I was unable to locate the *Diario de Avisos* for this period. Segovia's article on *Hernán Pérez del Pulgar* came out in March 1834 (Antonio María Segovia, *Colección de composiciones serias y festivas en prosa y en verso, escogidas entre las publicadas e inéditas del escritor conocido por "El Estudiante*," vol. 1 [Madrid: I. Sancha, 1839], p. 48). As the article was available to me only in this collection, where solely the month of appearance is listed, I could not learn its exact date. Larra's article appeared on March 30 (see Ismael Sánchez Estevan, *Mariano José de Larra* . . . [Madrid: Hernando, 1934], p. 235); consequently there are twenty-nine out of thirty chances that it was written after Segovia's. Moreover, if it is true, as Lomba states (*M. J. de Larra*, p. 300), that *Hernán Pérez del Pulgar* inspired Larra's satirical description of Martínez's clothes in "Los tres no son más que dos" (February 18, 1834), then the book had been out for quite some time before the reviews were written (unless Larra had seen the manuscript of Martínez's work before he wrote "Los tres no son más que dos").

16. Segovia, *Colección de composiciones*, pp. 50–51.

17. Ibid., p. 49.

18. Found on p. 36 of original edition. Changed to "de ella" in *BAE*, 150: 285.

19. Found on p. 26 of original edition. Also *BAE*, 150: 281.

20. Segovia, *Colección de composiciones*, p. 50.

21. Ibid., p. 51.
22. I have found no evidence to confirm this, however.
23. Francisco Martínez de la Rosa, *Hernán Pérez del Pulgar* (Madrid: Jordán, 1834), pp. 7, 38, 82. The other page references are to this, the original edition, unless *BAE* is specified.
24. Augusto Conte, *Recuerdos de un diplomático*, 3 vols. (Madrid: Imprenta de S. Góngora y Álvarez, 1901–1903), 1: 43. Note that Figaro had used this figure of speech before Conte: "En disenciones civiles, el que no es *montesco* o *capuleto* merece la execración de Verona . . ." (1: 389).
25. *BAE*, 19: 368.
26. "Centón epistolario de Domingo del Monte," *Anales de la Academia de la Historia* (Cuba), 2 (1921): 362.
27. Ibid., p 361.
28. Sánchez Estevan, *M. J. de Larra*, pp. 92–94.
29. "Los tres no son más que dos, y el que no es nada vale por tres. Mascarada política" (February 18, 1834); "*El Siglo* en blanco" (March 9); "Ventaja de las cosas a medio hacer" (March 16); "*Hernán Pérez del Pulgar*" (March 30); and "El hombre propone y Dios dispone o lo que ha de ser el periodista" (April 4).
30. "*I Capuletti ed i Montechi*" (May 3, 1834), and "Las palabras" (May 8). See Nombela, *Larra*, pp. 278–280, for an analysis of the latter with reference to the prime minister.
31. Sánchez Estevan does not seem to sense this; he writes: "No cabe elogio mayor en aquellos días" (*M. J. de Larra*, p. 93).
32. Tarr, "More Light on Larra," p. 98, note 34.
33. Anonymous, *Historia contemporánea de la revolución de España* . . . , 5 vols. (Madrid: [Of. del Establecimiento Central], 1843), 4: 48.
34. [Caballero], *El gobierno*, p. lxxi.
35. Wenceslao Ramírez de Villa-Urrutia, *La reina gobernadora, Doña María Cristina de Borbón* (Madrid: Beltrán, 1925), p. 96. For further evidence, see the ambiguous statement apparently concerning *La conjuración*, in Larra's review of Martínez's *Aben Humeya* (June 12, 1836) (2: 225).
36. Though Larra spelled her name *Grissi*, it actually has only one *s*. In the Aguilar edition the first three paragraphs have been omitted.
37. Two months later Larra said frankly that there was room for improvement (1: 414–415, 426).
38. *El Eco* probably stood to the left of *La Revista*. Fermín Caballero writes that "el decidido Boletín, que tan ardientemente y sin cesar

había combatido el despotismo ilustrado, cayó el 30 de marzo de 1834, cuando su popularidad le había granjeado el mayor número de suscritores que tuvo periódico español. Volvió a aparecer con el nombre de *Eco* luego que el Sr. Burgos dejó el Fomento; pero a poco más de un año recibió otro golpe de poder el 17 de agosto de 1835, siguiendo las mismas alternativas que la marcha de la libertad" ([Caballero], *El gobierno*, pp. lxxi–lxxii).

39. [Javier de Burgos], *Historia pintoresca del reinado de Da. Isabel II y de la guerra civil*, 4 vols. (Madrid: Castello, 1846–1847), vol. 2, bk. 5, pp. 281–284. During the debate of August 2 in Próceres about the reply to the address of the Crown, the Duke of Rivas proposed that "se debería insinuar la necesidad de fijar por medio de una decisión solemne el modo de destruir real y positivamente la división de partidos." These so-called parties centered on secret societies (Masons, Isabelinos, etc.). The duke himself, though, was implicated in the Palafox conspiracy (cf. Jean Sarrailh, *Un Homme d'Etat espagnol: Martínez de la Rosa (1787–1862)* (Bordeaux: Feret, 1930), p. 210, note 6; and Juan Valera y Alcalá Galiano, *Historia general de España . . . por Don Modesto Lafuente . . .* , 25 vols. (Barcelona: Montaner y Simón, 1887–1890), 20: 86.

CHAPTER 4: THE QUEEN OPENS THE CORTES

1. See Luis Sánchez Agesta, *Historia del constitucionalismo español* (Madrid: Instituto de Estudios Políticos, 1955), p. 127.
2. His contract with *El Mundo* and *El Redactor General* specified that free tickets should be given him (Carmen de Burgos Seguí, "*Fígaro*" [Madrid: Imprenta de "Alrededor del mundo," 1919], p. 112).
3. See Antonio Alcalá Galiano, *Historia de España . . .* , 7 vols. (Madrid: Sociedad Literaria y Tipográfica, 1844–1846), 7: 332.
4. Wenceslao Ramírez de Villa-Urrutia, *La reina gobernadora, Doña María Cristina de Borbón* (Madrid: Beltrán, 1925), pp. 10–11; and "Centón epistolario de Domingo Delmonte," *Anales de la Academia de la Historia* (Cuba), 2: 325–326.
5. Jean Sarrailh, *Un Homme d'Etat espagnol: Martínez de la Rosa (1787–1862)* (Bordeaux: Feret, 1930), p. 210.
6. Francisco Pi y Margall and Francisco Pi y Arsuaga, *Las grandes conmociones políticas del siglo XIX en España*, 2 vols. (Barcelona:

Seguí, n.d.), 1: 213, states that "en el discurso de la corona no se hizo otra cosa que recomendar paciencia." This is a misleading exaggeration. The anonymous *Historia contemporánea de la revolución de España . . .* , 5 vols. (Madrid: [Of. del Establecimiento Central], 1843), 4: 63, remarks that in the address of the Crown "ni la más ligera mención se hizo de la milicia urbana, lo cual produjo algún disgusto en los ánimos de los progresistas."

7. This type of simile might be dubbed "depersonification." For the influence of Quevedo on Larra, see Emilio Pastor Mateos, "Larra y Madrid," *Revista de la Biblioteca, Archivo y Museo* (Ayuntamiento de Madrid), 18 (1949): 315; Edgar Quinet, *Mes Vacances en Espagne*, in *Oeuvres complètes*, vol. 9 (Paris: Pagnerre, 1857), p. 108; R. Benítez Claros, "Influencia de Quevedo en Larra," *Cuadernos de Literatura* (Madrid), 1 (1947): 117–123; Mariano Baquero Goyanes, "Barroco y romanticismo," *Anales de la Universidad de Murcia*, curso 1949–50, pp. 733–738; and Ismael Sánchez Estevan, "Quevedo y Fígaro," *Diario Universal*, February 26, 1914.

8. Quoted by Villa-Urrutia, *La reina gobernadora*, p. 96, note 1.

9. Alcalá Galiano, *Historia de España*, 7: 338.

10. George Villiers, *A Vanished Victorian, Being the Life of George Villiers, Fourth Earl of Clarendon, 1800–1870, by his grandson* . . . (London: Eyre and Spottiswoode, 1938), p. 94.

CHAPTER 5: A REPLY TO THE CROWN

1. Paul-Louis Courier de Méré, *Oeuvres complètes*, ed. Maurice Allem (Paris: Gallimard, 1951), p. 61.

2. This locution from *Don Quixote* is also adapted in "Ascensión aerostática" (July 16, 1833) (1: 255).

3. Rivas's proposal to find means of putting an end to political cliques is quoted in chapter 3, note 39.

4. Tomás Navarro Tomás, *Manual de pronunciación española*, 4th ed. (Madrid: Consejo Superior de Investigaciones Científicas, 1932), par. 35.

5. "Siguiendo esta misma idea, se ha hablado de no ser oportuno el jurado en España, porque salió mal el ensayo anterior. La comisión ya ha dicho que no fija tiempo; pero además debo añadir que los abusos de las instituciones no son efecto de ellas mismas: una mala práctica no prueba que la teoría de que es parte esté mal ordenada.

La utilidad del jurado es innegable; y no porque a su sombra, como a la de todas las cosas, se hayan cometido defectos e injusticias, debe deducirse que no es ventajoso" (*Pr.*, p. 35). This may have given Larra the idea of writing in his paragraph, "y si es en vano, peor que peor."

6. The Jesuit Fr. Jerónimo Martínez de Ripalda (1586–1618), whose *Catecismo y exposición breve de la Doctrina cristiana* (1618) has undergone hundreds of editions and is still used in elementary schools. The *third* commandment, "Non assumes nomen Domini Dei tui in vanum," is given as the *second* commandment, so that "Non facies tibi sculptile, neque omnem similitudinem . . . non adorabis ea . . ." may be left out. Ripalda's second commandment is given as: "No jurarás en el nombre de Dios en vano." See Juan M. Sánchez, *"Doctrina cristiana" del P. Jerónimo de Ripalda e intento bibliográfico de la misma. Años 1591–1900* (Madrid: Imprenta Alemana, 1909), p. 16 verso.

7. In Larra's period, the subject of religious education could only be hinted at. A hundred years passed before another famous author wrote: "De la enseñanza religiosa decía mi maestro: 'La verdad es que no la veo por ninguna parte.' Y ya hay quien habla de sustituirla por otra. ¡Es lo que me quedaba por oír!" (Antonio Machado, *Juan de Mairena* [Madrid: Espasa-Calpe, 1936], chap. 47, p. 326).

8. See *Enciclopedia Universal europeo-americana*, 70 vols. (Barcelona: Espasa-Calpe, 1907?–1930), s.v. *Recopilación.*

9. The only historian to mention this specifically is [Francisco] Javier de Burgos, *Anales del reinado de Doña Isabel II*, 6 vols. (Madrid: Mellado, 1850–1851), 1: 328–329: "Al presidente de éstos [Procuradores] oficiaban desde Martorell algunos de los nombrados por las provincias catalanas que, en camino para Madrid, habían tenido que suspender su viaje por haber recibido (con notable atraso, por cierto) la noticia de los estragos que en la capital estaba haciendo el cólera." On September 11, a resolution was read concerning the absent *próceres*. It brought about a short but controversial debate (*Pr.*, pp. 234, 237).

10. Another pun by Larra on *representación* appears in 2: 10.

11. "Centón epistolario de Domingo Delmonte," *Anales de la Academia de la Historia* (Cuba), 3: 315. Quintero, however, later obtained employment with the official *Gaceta* (ibid., p. 325).

12. Antonio Alcalá Galiano, *Historia de España . . .* , 7 vols. (Madrid: Sociedad Literaria y Tipográfica, 1844–1846), 7: 334.

CHAPTER 6: ABSENTEEISM AND INACTION

1. [Fermín Caballero], *El gobierno y las Cortes del Estatuto* (Madrid: Yenes, 1837), p. 24.
2. The verb "oficiar" is used with the acceptation, "comunicar una cosa oficialmente y por escrito." The substantive "oficio" in the essay's third paragraph has an equivalent definition.
3. 1: 448. The pertinent definition of *flor* is found only in Real Academia Española, *Dicc. de Autoridades*, 6 vols. (Madrid, 1726–1739): "el dicho agudo y elegante con que se adorna algún escrito u oración. Úsase regularmente en plural." Cf. Pierre L. Ullman, "The Baroque Poems which Frame the *Quijote*," *Anales Cervantinos* 9: 216.
4. "Bad" because it is merely linguistic, and not conceptual. Cf. James Brown, "Eight Types of Puns," *PMLA* 71 (1956): 16, note 4.

CHAPTER 7: A BILL OF RIGHTS

1. The latter part of the session was secret. It dealt with the Marqués de Villahermosa's excuse for his absence (*Ilus.*, pp. 52–53).
2. *Pr.*, pp. 84–85 and appendix to no. 22.
3. Juan Valera y Alcalá Galiano, *Historia general de España . . . por Don Modesto Lafuente . . .*, 25 vols. (Barcelona: Montaner y Simón, 1887–1890), 16: 139. The tax was based on the legend that when Ramiro, king of Asturias, fought the Moslems at Clavijo in 845, Saint James the Less came to his aid in white garments. The victorious Ramiro accordingly pledged eternal tribute. There is, however, sufficient evidence to show that the battle of Clavijo never took place.
4. The Marqués de Falces was *corregidor* of Madrid at the time of the slaughter of the monks (see [Fermín Caballero], *El gobierno y las Cortes del Estatuto* [Madrid: Yenes, 1837], p. xxii).
5. "Mais quoi! je vous le dis, ce sont les gens de cour dont l'imaginative enfante chaque jour ces merveilleux conseils; ils ont plus tôt inventé cela que le semoir de Fehlenberg, ou bien le bateau à vapeur. On a eu l'idée, dit le ministre, de faire acheter Chambord par les communes de France, pour le duc de Bordeaux. On a eu cette pensée! qui donc? Est-ce le ministre? il ne s'en cacherait pas, ne se contenterait pas de l'honneur d'approuver en pareille occasion. Le prince? à Dieu ne plaise que sa première idée ait été celle-là, que

cette envie lui soit venue avant celle des bonbons et des petits moulins! Les communes donc apparemment? non pas les nôtres, que je sache, de ce coté-ci de la Loire, mais celles-là peut-être qui ont logé deux fois les Cosaques du Don. Ici nous nous sentons assez des bienfaits de la Sainte-Alliance: mais c'est tout autre chose là où on a joui de sa présence, possédé Sacken et Platow; là naturellement on s'avise d'acheter des châteaux par les princes, et puis on songe à refaire son toit et ses foyers" (Paul-Louis Courier de Méré, *Oeuvres complètes*, ed. Maurice Allem [Paris: Gallimard, 1951], pp. 73–74).

6. José Eugenio de Eguizábal, *Apuntes para una historia de la legislación española sobre imprenta desde el año, de 1480 al presente* (Madrid: Imprenta de la Revista de Legislación, 1879), p. 75.

7. Lobster, reptile, reed, camel, mine, water, thorn, and sunflower were used as similes in "El hombre pone y Dios dispone" (1: 364–365).

8. He quotes the Latin apophthegm again for a similar purpose in an article of February 8, 1836 (2: 153). For the several interpretations of this apophthegm, see José Ferrater Mora, *Diccionario de filosofía*, 5th ed., vol. 2 (Buenos Aires: Sudamericana, 1966), pp. 288–289.

9. See the quotation above from *Pr.*, p. 137.

10. Cf., however, note 7 above, where we can see that the sunflower analogy was used in a much earlier article.

11. In his speech (*Pr.*, pp. 178–180), López actually never said what Toreno imputes to him. In fact, after Toreno's speech, the following entry is found in the *Diario:* "El Sr. López deshizo algunas equivocaciones que dijo haber padecido el Conde de Toreno" (*Pr.*, p. 182).

12. See L. Rodríguez Aranda, "La recepción y el influjo de la filosofía de Locke en España," *Revista de Filosofía* 14, nos. 53–54, (1955); and Vicente Lloréns, *Liberales y románticos* (Mexico City: Colegio de Mexico, 1954), p. 275.

13. Larra had already used the same source of banter in his "Segunda carta" (1: 429), as noted in chapter 5.

CHAPTER 8: THE GUEBHARD LOAN

1. See Frederick Courtney Tarr, "More Light on Larra," *Hispanic Review* 4 (1936): 104–105; Ismael Sánchez Estevan, *Mariano José de Larra . . .* (Madrid: Hernando, 1934), pp. 125–128.

2. See Sánchez Estevan, *M. J. de Larra*, p. 127; or Carmen de Burgos Seguí, *"Fígaro"* (Madrid: Imprenta de "Alrededor del mundo," 1919), pp. 188–190.

3. Sánchez Estevan, *M. J. de Larra*, p. 128, note 1.

4. Ramón de Mesonero Romanos, *Memorias de un setentón natural y vecino de Madrid*, 2 vols. (Madrid: Oficinas de la Ilustración Español y Americana, 1881), 2: 176, and Antonio Asenjo, *La prensa madrileña a través de los siglos* (Madrid: Artes Gráficas Municipales, 1933), p. 45.

5. The ministerialists had an answer for this; the Marqués de Falces expressed it: "Ha dicho el Sr. Torremejía que fue tal el vejamen con que fue contraído el empréstito, que está doblemente pagado el capital, y aun siguen cobrándose los réditos. No dificulto que así sea; pero esto de reembolsar el capital y seguir pagando los réditos, es común a todas las negociaciones de esta clase" (*Pr.*, p. 364).

6. Even in 1835 and 1836, only 157,000 of the 475,000 *guardias nacionales* were armed. See [Fermín Caballero], *El gobierno y las Cortes del Estatuto* (Madrid: Yenes, 1837), p. lvii.

7. García Carrasco replied the next day to this line of argument: "se sancionará la obligación de reconocer más tarde los empréstitos contraídos por Don Carlos y Don Miguel . . . Los que han de prestar auxilios a Don Carlos ya lo hacen. Por el contrario, sería una nueva esperanza para Don Carlos el reconocimiento de estos empréstitos, pues en su virtud encontraría dinero a un precio más ventajoso" (*Pr.*, p. 268).

8. The "de" after víctimas seems to be interposal and does not express the agent. See M. Ramsey and Robert K. Spaulding, *A Textbook of Modern Spanish* (New York: Holt, 1956), par. 2.26.

9. Caballero insisted that the "Memoria sobre los presupuestos" be presented to the Cortes before any decision on the debt was made. The "Memoria," however, was not issued until October 11 (see *Pr.*, Apéndice al núm. 60).

10. The figure of speech persisted even while the "Segunda carta" was going to press. On October 6 Trueba waxed metaphorical as he described his own position: "La luz derramada sobre la materia la coloca en un terreno ventajoso para mí; y removidos los obstáculos, la maleza, que pudiera entorpecer mi marcha, camino por una senda llana y recta, en que fuera difícil tropezar, imposible el caer. Entraré pues con menos desconfianza en la cuestión . . ." (*Pr.*, p. 466)

11. Espoz y Mina's previous record as a famous liberal guerrilla leader

was mentioned in chapter 1. In chapter 11 we shall see what occurred once he was appointed to the cabinet.

12. Cf. "Carta de Fígaro a un bachiller su corresponsal" (July 31, 1834) (1: 424): "Quedo, pues, rogando, señor Bachiller, que los facciosos de las gavillas que hace un año se están destruyendo todos los días completamente no intercepten por esas *veredas* esta carta . . ." The italics are Larra's.

13. The paragraph is quoted here exactly as given in Larra's *Fígaro; Colección de artículos dramáticos, literarios, políticos y de costumbres . . .*, 5 vols. (Madrid: Repullés, 1835–1837), 3: 121. Seco Serrano's rearrangement in *BAE* (2: 18) does not seem justified.

14. This is a moot point, of course. In any case, the important thing here is to understand clearly Larra's views. Cf. Antonio Alcalá Galiano, *Historia de España . . .*, 7 vols. (Madrid: Sociedad Literaria y Tipográfica, 1844–1846), 7: 339: "Fuese como fuese, su presencia en España causó grande efecto. Saludáronla sus parciales de dentro y fuera de la monarquía como una victoria, o como pronóstico infalible de futuro triunfo, y los liberales descontentos desahogaron su furia en imprecaciones contra el gobierno, como si éste tuviese culpa en un acaecimiento que le era tan adverso, y que no había sido en su mano impedir de modo alguno. Queriendo el ministro Martínez de la Rosa disminuir el mal efecto producido por la entrada del pretendiente, e infundir confianza con aparentarla grande, dijo 'que D. Carlos en España era sólo un faccioso más,' expresión no desnuda de mérito aunque repetición o copia de otras que siempre han pasado por ingeniosas y a veces por sublimes; pero que en esta ocasión no tuvo la dicha de agradar, equivocándose con un necio descuido del peligro, y llevándose la injusticia al extremo de tacharla como un dicho vituperable."

15. Augusto Conte, *Recuerdos de un diplomático*, 3 vols. (Madrid: Imprenta de J. Góngora y Álvarez, 1901–1903), 1: 36.

16. There is also another possibility. On August 9 in the Chambre des Paires the French foreign minister, Count de Rigny, had preceded Martínez with some remarks in the same vein: "Ce n'est pas lui [Don Carlos] . . . qui a soulevé les provinces basques; elles s'étaient soulevées sans lui, avant lui, et pour une cause qui n'était pas d'abord la sienne.

Ce qu'il a fait depuis, vous le savez; je ne vous rappellerai pas les chants de victoire, les fanfaronnades de parti. Il semblait que son drapeau marchait de clocher en clocher, et arriverait jusqu'à Madrid sans obstacle; que ce serait une marche triomphale. Je ne vous dirai pas où il est maintenant, mais je vous dirai qu'il est beaucoup plus près de notre frontière que de la capitale de l'Espagne . . . On nous a demandé si nous interviendrons . . . Les circonstances . . . ne se sont pas présentées, . . . et nous avons bien lieu d'espérer qu'elles ne se présenteront pas" (*Archives Parlementaires de 1787 a 1860*, vol. 91 [August 7, 1834–January 17, 1835] [Paris: Dupont, 1895], p. 34).

CHAPTER 9: CIVIL SERVANTS

1. The "Tercera carta" is in *Fígaro; Colección de artículos dramáticos, literarios, políticos y de costumbres . . .* , 5 vols. (Madrid: Repullés, 1835–1837), 2: 170–174, where it was first published. It bears the signature "El liberal de acá." Ismael Sánchez Estevan, *Mariano José de Larra . . .* (Madrid: Hernando, 1934), p. 239, thus commits an obvious error by giving "Fígaro" as the signature. On the other hand, the *Colección* commits an anachronism by entitling the article, "Inédito.—Setiembre.—1834," and Sánchez Estevan seems to be on the right track when he indicates that it was written in October. Yet the *Colección*'s chronological error may have swayed him to list the "Tercera carta" before "La cuestión transparente." Internal evidence indicates that "La cuestión transparente" is the earlier essay.

2. Argüelles had finally taken his seat in Procuradores on October 15, and was sworn in the next day (*Pr.*, pp. 530, 537). According to a strict interpretation of the law, he should not have been admitted, because of his poverty, but the Procuradores made an exception in his case owing, as Manuel María Acevedo said, to "el escándalo que causaría a España y a toda Europa el oír que don Agustín Argüelles, tan conocido desde las columnas de Hércules hasta el Vístula, fue rechazado del Congreso de su nación, en donde hizo un papel tan sobresaliente en todos los que han existido desde el año 1810, porque no se observaron todos los ápices que la comisión se persuade prescribe una ley reglamentaria con carácter de interina" (*Pr.*, p. 526). Argüelles's certificates of ownership depended on what amounted to fictitious gifts from his constituents.

3. For information on the staff of the *Eco,* see Ramón de Mesonero Romanos, *Memorias de un setentón natural y vecino de Madrid,* 2 vols. (Madrid: Oficinas de la Ilustración Española y Americana, 1881), 2: 176; Eugenio Hartzenbusch e Hiriart, *Apuntes para un catálogo de periódicos madrileños . . .* (Madrid: "Sucesores de Rivadeneyra," 1894), pp. 44, 46; Antonio Asenjo, *La prensa madri-*

leña a través de los siglos (Madrid: Artes Gráficas Municipales, 1933), p. 45.

4. Perhaps there was nothing else for him to do but compose the "Memoria." The following table indicates the number of pages in the report of each minister. The appendices of the *Diario de las sesiones* are individually paginated, even though, in most copies, they are inserted among the regular pages of the volume:

Ministry	Date	Page reference	No. of pages	Name of minister
Hacienda				
State of treasury	Aug. 7	Ap. 2 to No. 12	8	Toreno and Martínez
Budget	Oct. 10	Ap. to No. 60	11	Toreno
Estado	Aug. 9	Ap. to No. 13	10	Martínez
Marina	Aug. 11	Ap. to No. 14	21	Vázquez
Interior	Aug. 14	Ap. to No. 17	9	Moscoso
Guerra	Aug. 16	Ap. to No. 18	16	Zarco
Gracia y Justicia	Aug. 18	Ap. to No. 19	18	Garelly

5. The Moderates had already been satirized for expressing this idea. In "El ministerial" one of the parrot's favorite phrases is "No es oportuno" (1: 438).

6. The Progressives' victory was mostly oratorical, with meager legislative results. According to one source, two royal decrees favoring the Triennium employees were issued, on December 30, 1834, and January 8, 1835 (see *Historia contemporánea de la revolución de España* . . . , 5 vols. [Madrid, 1843], 4: 76), but their consequence is a moot point. One author claims, however, that "el gobierno no la llevó [la petición] a efecto porque según su presidente la época constitucional no debía enlazarse con la del Estatuto" ([Fermín Caballero], *El gobierno y las Cortes del Estatuto* [Madrid: Yenes, 1837], p. 30).

CHAPTER 10: THE EXPULSION OF BURGOS

1. Larra, *Fígaro; Colección de artículos dramáticos, literarios, políticos y de costumbres* . . . , 5 vols. (Madrid: Repullés, 1835–1837), 2: 163, dates it August 1834, an obvious error.

2. This will have to remain a mere hypothesis until the letter is found in the newspapers of the period.

3. Javier de Burgos, *Observaciones sobre el empréstito de Guebhard*

(Madrid: Imprenta de D. Miguel de Burgos, 1834), p. 2 (in the "Advertencia"). Considering their true opinion of Burgos, the Progressives were, in fact, comparatively reserved in their attack. Cf. Antonio Alcalá Galiano, "Literature of the Nineteenth Century—Spain," *Athenaeum* (London), no. 344 (May 31, 1834), p. 413: "he has also written one or two comedies. Of these, *Calzones en Alcolea,* of a political character, enjoyed some celebrity; it was written with the intention of throwing ridicule upon those renowned guerrilla chiefs, who proved so harassing to the French during the Peninsular War, and, with them, upon the popular cause. Burgos was a *sous-préfet* under Joseph Bonaparte; he wrote to please his master; and received the applause of an audience, consisting of men attached to his interests. In proportion, as he was popular with them, he became odious to the bulk of the population, devoted to the men and the principles he reviled. However, in the midst of all the persecutions of which Spain has been the theatre, the fortunes of the poet have never suffered—far otherwise: he affords an example (particularly rare in Spain), of the paths of literature leading to opulence. By flattering Ferdinand from the year 1814 to 1820, he managed to evade the law which condemned him to exile, and was permitted to remain a resident in Madrid: by writing, as a zealous constitutionalist in the year 1820, he obtained a transient success for a periodical which he was then editing: by lending his pen to a third or *juste milieu* party against the violent patriots of 1822, he became a favourite with the King: by a succession of fierce attacks on the fallen liberals, in the year 1823, he made himself yet dearer to the ruling powers at home and abroad. His reward for these manifold services has been a substantial one. In common with the others, who joined the party of the usurper of Ferdinand's throne, he was allowed a share in those Spanish loans, which, on the Paris exchange, proved the source of enormous wealth to the favoured few. The poet, metamorphosed into a Croesus, has sunk into idleness, his voice, formerly so loud, is no more lifted in praise or in censure, for the happy, or for the unfortunate . . ." Professor Vicente Lloréns has pointed out to me a base diatribe against patriots, which appeared in no. 36 of the *Gazeta Oficial del Gobierno de Vizcaya,* reproduced in Manuel Gómez Imaz, *Los periódicos durante la Guerra de la Independencia* (Madrid: Tipografía de la Revista de Archivos, 1910), p. 187, and bearing the signature "F.X.B." The initials indicate that its author was in all likelihood Francisco Xavier de Burgos.

4. See the preceding note. The document was later reproduced by

Javier de Burgos in *Anales del reinado de Doña Isabel II*, 6 vols. (Madrid: Mellado, 1850–1851), 1: 111–125.

5. Advertised in the *Diario de Avisos de Madrid*, October 18, 1834, under "Publicaciones periódicas." This is *El Observador*'s October 15 issue, containing likewise Larra's "Primera contestación de un liberal de allá."

6. Juan Rico y Amat, *Historia política y parlamentaria de España . . .*, 3 vols. (Madrid: Impr. Escuelas Pías, 1860–1861), 2: 417, says that the expulsion was due to "intrigas de las sociedades secretas, cuya amistad y apoyo había despreciado Burgos cuando ocupaba el poder." Cf. [Javier de Burgos], *Historia pintoresca del reinado de Da. Isabel II . . .*, 4 vols. (Madrid: Castello, 1846–1847), vol. 1, bk. 2, pp. 383–385. We do know, in any case, that a royal commission had been appointed to examine all transactions connected with the Guebhard loan, but Burgos was expelled before it could finish its investigation.

7. See Burgos, *Anales*, 1: 28–34, 2: 28.

8. [Fermín Caballero], *El gobierno y las Cortes del Estatuto* (Madrid: Yenes, 1837), pp. lxxi–lxxii, 175. See also José Eugenio Eguizábal, *Apuntes para una historia de la legislación española sobre imprenta desde el año de 1480 al presente* (Madrid: Imprenta de la Revista de Legislación, 1879), pp. 175–178, 245–246.

9. The regulation is quoted in Eguizábal, *Apuntes*, pp. 255–260.

10. Larra, *Colección*, 2: 175.

11. Excellently annotated by Herman Hespelt, ed. *Artículos de costumbres y de crítica de Mariano José de Larra* (New York: S. F. Crofts, 1941). Hespelt points out Larra's Encyclopedic bent in the reference to God as "el Ser supremo" (p. 118).

12. See Frederick Courtney Tarr, "More Light on Larra," *Hispanic Review* 4 (1936): 105–106; and Ismael Sánchez Estevan, *Mariano José de Larra . . .* (Madrid: Hernando, 1934), pp. 139–146.

CHAPTER 11: MACHINATIONS IN THE CABINET

1. Their first printing was in *Semanario Pintoresco Español*, 16 (1851): 2–3, 28–29.

2. Ismael Sánchez Estevan's appendix (*Mariano José de Larra . . .* [Madrid: Hernando, 1934], p. 239) places "Atrás" in January 1835. Nevertheless, I feel there is sufficient indication that it was written in December. In the first place we know that Larra wrote "Atrás" before "Adelante," because "Adelante" contains the fol-

lowing observation: "escribí un artículo titulado *Atrás*, el cual no se llegó nunca a imprimir, por cuatro etiquetas que ocurrieron entre la persona del censor y la mía" (4: 326). But we can bring the putative date of composition even further back by examining the ironic passage: "un ministerio que sea el justo medio entre Cea y el justo medio; que se coloque entre setiembre del año pasado y setiembre de éste . . ." (4: 325). It is obvious that "setiembre del año pasado" is equivalent to "Cea." Now, Zea Bermúdez was prime minister from December 1832 to January 1834; hence "el año pasado" is 1833, whose September is the only one during which he was in power. Likewise, "setiembre de éste" is obviously equivalent to "el justo medio," the political philosophy attributed to Martínez de la Rosa, who came to power in January 1834; hence *éste* is 1834 (it would have to be in any case, since the choice we must make is between December 1834 and January 1835). As for "Revista del año 1834," the author speaks, in his first sentence, of "el 31 de este diciembre que expira," and, at the end of the essay, of "el próximo y naciente 1835." Figaro may be overstepping the bounds of reality for the purpose of literary effect, but in any case he writes as if it were December 31, composing a piece that should be printed as soon as possible in order to be topical. "Adelante" could not have been finished before January 3 because it mentions an incident occurring on that date: "Esto fue el día 3 de este enero" (4: 327). Larra also refers to the debate on judges: "Ahora andan en dudas en el Estamento sobre si son buenos los jueces o no" (4: 327). The most heated of these debates took place on January 2; others, more staid, on January 9 and 12. This is additional corroboration that the essay could not have been written before January 3. As for the terminal date, "Adelante" could not have been penned after January 17, because this is the day of the Post-Office Mutiny, which altered the political situation so thoroughly that its occurrence would necessarily have affected any article written after it; there is no evidence of this whatsoever in "Adelante."

3. For references to Larra's illness, see chapter 10, note 12.

4. Wenceslao Ramírez de Villa-Urrutia, *La reina gobernadora, Doña María Cristina de Borbón* (Madrid: Beltrán, 1925), p. 92.

5. See Juan Valera y Alcalá Galiano, *Historia general de España . . . por Don Modesto Lafuente . . .*, 25 vols. (Barcelona: Montaner y Simón, 1887–1890), 20: 121; and Antonio Pirala y Criado, *Historia de la guerra civil y de los partidos liberal y carlista*, 5 vols. (Madrid: Mellado, 1853–1856), 2: 116.

6. From a letter of Andrés de Arango, in "Centón epistolario de Domingo del Monte," *Anales de la Academia de la Historia* (Cuba), 3: 170.

7. Of course, since "Adelante" remained unpublished, the validity of the statement, "ni me lo dejaran decir tampoco" is unverifiable, as is the possibility that the newspaper, and not the censor, was responsible for the suppression of "Atrás."

8. Alcalá Galiano did not attend this session owing to illness. He returned to the chamber on December 26.

9. "Dice que el más débil e inferior es al que van a parar siempre las desdichas." *Refranero español,* ed. José Bergua, 4th ed. (Madrid: Ediciones Ibéricas, n.d.), s.v. *último.*

10. The Conde de las Navas was especially virulent during the state department debate, which he used as a pretext to impugn the government for the escape of Carlos ("cuando se introdujo en España un faccioso más, ¿pudo evitar que saliera . . . ?" [*Pr.,* p. 961]) and asked if the cabinet was really deserving of confidence. Argüelles had to rise to the defense of the ambassador to London, his friend Miraflores (*Pr.,* p. 964).

11. It was not until April 23, 1835, that the government presented its projected law, and even this law was to have only a provisional nature. The Comisión de lo Interior announced its readiness on April 28. The debate on this temporary law lasted from May 8 to 11.

12. Jean Sarrailh, *Un Homme d'Etat espagnol: Martínez de la Rosa (1787–1862)* (Bordeaux: Feret, 1930), p. 197: "le Ministère voulait qu'on lui préparât une majorité. On sait avec quelle fidélité cette méthode a été suivie en Espagne jusqu'à nos jours."

13. We cannot be sure of it, since Larra's next article, "La sociedad," appeared in *La Revista Española* on January 16, 1835. Is it possible, then, that the government did not censor these articles, but rather that *El Observador* refused to print them? There are indications that Larra originally went over to *El Observador* because *La Revista* would not print a hypothetical "Primera carta de un liberal de acá"; a similar explanation could possibly be given for Figaro's return to *La Revista.* It is not beyond reason to suppose that at that time some Progressives decided to leave their newspapers unimpeachable in order to speak with impunity in the congress. The government would thus find no excuse to retaliate by shutting down the newspapers. The more ardent Progressives, on the other hand, seem to have chosen the opposite course; neither

the fiery López nor Fermín Caballero, editor-in-chief of *El Eco del Comercio*, said a word during the debate on Gracia y Justicia appropriations.

14. Frederick Courtney Tarr, "More Light on Larra," *Hispanic Review* 4 (1936): 109.

CHAPTER 12: THE POST-OFFICE MUTINY

1. Ismael Sánchez Estevan notes (*Mariano José de Larra* . . . [Madrid: Hernando, 1934], p. 137): "Dio la singular coincidencia de que su estreno sirvió de prólogo a una sublevación militar . . ." There are no available data, however, which allow us to see this as anything more than coincidence, so that the idea of its being a signal for revolt, with Larra's possible implication, is mere speculation. *El arte de conspirar* was the most played and apparently the best of Larra's translations from Scribe (see Frederick Courtney Tarr, "More Light on Larra," *Hispanic Review* 4 [1936]: 105, note 68). Figaro had to make some changes in order to avoid comparisons of the royal couple in the drama with recent Spanish Bourbons (see E. H. Hespelt, "The Translated Dramas of Mariano José de Larra and their French Originals," *Hispania* [Stanford], 15 [1932]: 128).

2. A permit was granted to Larra, who only carried the matter to the point of writing a prospectus for this publication, which never came to fruition. The prospectus begins: "Dos años hace que 'Fígaro' comenzó su carrera periodística, modestamente escondido entre las dilatadas columnas de la *Revista Española*. Apartándose de las altas cuestiones políticas, caminó los primeros meses de su existencia a paso de reformar, es decir, lentamente de bastidor en bastidor y de teatro en teatro" (quoted by Carmen de Burgos Seguí [pseud. Colombine], *"Fígaro"* [Madrid: Imprenta de "Alrededor del mundo," 1919], p. 106). "Colombine" does not date the prospectus, but Larra's reference to a two-year period is sufficient internal evidence for us to do so. Larra is not concerned here with his first piece in the *Revista Española*, "Teatros" (1: 363–364), unsigned and merely attributed to him (see Sánchez Estevan, *M. J. de Larra*, p. 228); nor with three other such unsigned articles, dated December 19 and 31, 1832, and January 4, 1833; nor with one signed "M. J. de Larra" of December 26, 1832. Larra refers specifically to a piece in which he makes use of his *persona*,

"Fígaro," and which he signs accordingly, entitled, "Variedades teatrales. Mi nombre y mis propósitos" (1: 173–176). It appeared on January 15, 1833. This is approximately two years before "Un periódico nuevo." As further evidence, "Un periódico nuevo" states that "El periódico se titulará *Fígaro*" (1: 448), the very title given it in the projected prospectus.

3. On the significance of entailed estates in the history of economic theory, cf. John K. Galbraith, *The New Industrial State* (Boston: Houghton Mifflin, 1967), p. 56.

4. This can be surmised from the article's last three lines, which read, "la fecha de hoy,—22 de enero de 1835" (1: 450), and also from the phrase "hace tres días" of its second paragraph. The fourth day of debate on the post-office insurgency began at 12:30 P.M., Thursday, January 22.

5. The budget debate resumed, however, on January 23, the day after Larra wrote "Un periódico nuevo"; but because the article did not appear in print until January 26, the sense of his remark was obsolete long before the public got to read it.

6. It has not been determined whether Cardero possessed more temerity or less information than his fellow conspirators. Were the plans unbeknownst to him? The "Esposición de los individuos del regimiento de Aragón al presidente del estamento de procuradores," reproduced in [Fermín Caballero], *El gobierno y las Cortes del Estatuto* (Madrid: Yenes, 1837), pp. 101–103, asserts that "Llenos de estos nobles sentimientos los que suscriben tomaron el partido que han tomado y que desgraciadamente otros que debían seguirlo han faltado a sus palabras y juramentos" (p. 102).

7. In *El gobierno*, which Caballero wrote at about the same time that Larra published "El día de difuntos," we can also find a disapproving attitude toward the rebellion. Caballero, as has been pointed out, apparently belonged to a more progressive clique than Larra and, unlike him, felt no qualm about insinuating that an unsuccessful plot is more harmful than either a successful one or no plot at all: "Herido de muerte quedó el prestigio del gabinete con esta humillación; mas no es menos seguro que habría acabado más presto su administración a no suceder el hecho de Correos, el del 11 de mayo siguiente y otros que sostenían la creencia de que se le atacaba por medios ilegales y pecaminosos, cuando los parlamentarios bastaban para combatirle" (p. 100).

8. For historical information on Llauder's maneuvers, see chapter 11.

9. January 22 was the last day of discussion of these events in Procu-

radores. In Próceres, however, the debate took place on Monday, January 19, and Monday, January 26.

10. Wenceslao Ramírez de Villa-Urrutia, *La reina gobernadora, Doña María Cristina de Borbón* (Madrid: Beltrán, 1925), pp. 64–65.

11. Manuel Llauder, *Memorias documentadas del Teniente general* . . . (Madrid: Ignacio Boix, 1844), appendix, pp. 50–52, reproduces the pertinent articles from *La Abeja* of January 8, 12, and 18, 1835.

12. For information on the failure of the jury system during the Triennium to deal properly with such abuses as journalistic libel, see José Eugenio Eguizábal, *Apuntes para una historia de la legislación española sobre imprenta desde el año de 1480 al presente* (Madrid: Imprenta de la Revista de Legislación, 1879), pp. 74–77, 184.

13. The Aguilar edition erroneously reads "chapar flores." Cf. a similar pun on "flores" in "Modas" (1: 432), discussed in chapter 6, especially note 3.

14. See, above, pp. 91 and 117.

15. *Pr.*, p. 1281. Part of this speech is quoted in chapter 13.

16. The first session, January 3, was a mere formality devoid of discussion. The next meeting, in which the post-office insurgency was broached, took place on the 19th. But the chamber did not bother to reconvene until January 26, when, rather belatedly, discussion of this all-important matter was resumed.

17. The rebels had sent a plea to Procuradores, which was tabled by the vice-president of the chamber. It reads in part: "Los que suscriben en la crítica situación en que se hallan se dirigen al estamento por conducto de V.E. para implorar que con su poderoso influjo obtengan de S.M. el indulto de todos los individuos que se hallan en esta real casa de Correos . . ." (quoted by [Caballero], *El gobierno*, pp. 101–103).

18. Cf. Tarr, "More Light on Larra," pp. 97–98: "Not even his purely literary friendships . . . are so important, for the detailed history of his life and works, as are the vicissitudes of his personal and professional relations to . . . the editors of *El Observador*, to Andrés Borrego (editor and publisher of *El Español*), Alcalá Galiano, the Duque de Rivas, and the other members of the Istúriz clique."

19. Cf. Antonio Cano Manuel's speech quoted above from *Ilus.*, p. 184, where the locution "leyes fundamentales" is used with the same acceptation (*Ilus.*, p. 184). (This ministerialist *prócer* should not be confused with Vicente Cano Manuel, *procurador* for Álava, and Vicente Cano Manuel y Chacón, *procurador* for Cuenca).

20. [Caballero], *El gobierno*, p. 8, lists Saturnino Calderón Collantes in Roman type, thus indicating that he was a ministerialist.

21. The regulation can be found in Eguizábal, *Apuntes*, pp. 255–260.

CHAPTER 13: FUNDS FOR THE SECRET POLICE

1. The discussion on this first day became vehement. Istúriz expressed such ire against the police that a motion was made to close debate on article 6 temporarily. It was passed unanimously but for one vote, Istúriz's. Augusto Conte writes of him that "tenía mal genio y se enfadaba con facilidad" (*Recuerdos de un diplomático*, 3 vols. [Madrid: Imprenta de J. Góngora y Álvarez, 1901–1903], 1: 53). When Larra was elected to the Cortes in 1836, this politician had become prime minister.

2. The police was created by Calomarde on February 8, 1824, with the name of Vigilancia Pública (Antonio Ballesteros y Beretta, *Historia de España y su influencia en la historia universal*, 2nd ed., 10 vols. [Barcelona: Salvat, 1943–1956], 10: 224). The reforms proposed here would have been the second ones during the regency of María Cristina, because the police laws had already been revised during the Zea ministry (*Historia contemporánea de la revolución de España* . . . , 5 vols. [Madrid, 1843], 4: 9). During both the Calomarde and Zea ministries the superintendent of police was José Zorrilla's father.

3. This Progressive argument was used in other instances, such as the one discussed in chapter 7.

4. It should be pointed out that this criticism of censorship anticipates the February 9 discussion of article 28 in the Estamento de Procuradores.

5. This is evidenced by Larra's previous writing, where the matter is stated quite bluntly. In "Representación de *La mojigata* de Moratín" (February 2, 1834), he asserts: "La mayor parte de las obras de nuestros autores que han corrido y corren en manos de todos constantemente, no hubieran visto jamás la luz pública si hubieran debido sujetarse por primera vez a la censura parcial y opresora con que un partido caviloso y débil ha tenido en nuestros tiempos cerradas las puertas del saber. Y decimos débil, porque sabido es que tanto más tiránico es un partido cuanto menos fuerza moral, cuanto menos recursos físicos tiene de que disponer. Desprovisto de fuerzas propias, va a buscarlas en ajenas conciencias, y teme la palabra. Sólo un Gobierno fuerte y apoyado en la pública opinión

puede arrostrar la verdad, y aun buscarla: inseparable compañero de ella, no teme la expresión de las ideas, porque indaga las mejores y las más sanas para cimentar sobre ellas su poder indestructible" (1: 341). In a more ironic vein, he satirizes the government's fear in his review of *Norma* (July 2, 1834): "En el día no se puede vivir sin tener miedo: o a los revolucionarios que nadie ha visto y que nos llevan sin embargo a la anarquía, no se sabe por dónde, según ciertas gentes, o a las sociedades secretas, que van a hacer un daño tremendo a la sordina, según la *Revista* y el *Eco*" (1: 415). Likewise, in his "Segunda carta" (October 9, 1834) the "liberal de acá" writes that "por acá los liberales son tremendos; así es que les tenemos, no diré un miedo cerval, pero sí un miedo ministerial" (2: 19). Six days later, on October 15, the "liberal de allá" replied: "Háceme reír por último en tu carta lo que del miedo que a los liberales se tiene por ahí, me dices. En cuanto a eso, y en cuanto a los muchos que han andado de cárcel en cárcel y de destierro en destierro por conspiradores, así como a los que andan sin colocación todavía, por anarquistas . . ." (2: 20).

6. We should note that it was not Larra who thought up the theme of cowardice in a political context. The subject was broached by the Duque de Rivas and Joaquín María López. The first brought it up with regard to freedom of the press: "Pasaré a desvanecer ciertos temores que la idea sola de esta institución saludable ha hecho nacer en algunas personas" (*Ilus.*, p. 156). The second orator introduced the topic on October 16, 1834, while describing the distress of the Triennium employees and the undeserved good fortune of Calomarde's former henchmen: "Entre tanto muchos empleos parece que se han acumulado o como circunscrito a manos sospechosas o ineptas; no parece sino que al emplear esos individuos se ha consultado sólo a la templanza; digo mal, parece que el cálculo de la cobardía sea el solo título necesario para obtener ciertos empleos" (*Pr.*, p. 549).

7. Gaius Sallustius Crispus, *Catilina Iugurtha*, § 23.

8. Ibid., § 42.

9. Fermín Caballero makes light of the government's fears of such a conspiracy: "El decir que no teníamos seguridades, el procurar que se afianzasen los derechos políticos por medio de un pacto, y el sostener que debía partirse de la Constitución que la nación se dio en 1812, por ser el único acto legítimo de su soberanía, se miraba por el ministerio como sedición y anarquía. Dábase importancia a sociedades secretas, o fraguadas por la policía, o ideadas por cuatro jóvenes sin séquito: se suponían maquinaciones horri-

bles, planes demagógicos . . . Porque algunos genios fogosos idearon una sociedad, de que todo el mundo se reía, y cuyos secretos se imprimieron con el título de *Estatutos de la confederación de guardadores de la inocencia o isabelinos,* hubo motivo para la circular del ministerio de estado, previniendo que se velase contra los enemigos del trono y del reposo público que maquinaban en los oscuros clubs; y todo Madrid conocía a la media docena de jóvenes que jugaban a lo conspirador sin séquito ni transcendencia alguna" ([Fermín Caballero], *El gobierno y las Cortes del Estatuto* [Madrid: Yenes, 1837], pp. lxxvi–lxxvii).

10. This does not mean that Larra was averse to using polysyndeton for primary stylistic effect, independent of parody. Cf.: "con sus señoras, y sus niños, y sus capas, y sus paraguas, y sus chanclos, y sus perritos" ("El castellano viejo" [December 11, 1832] [1: 116]). Here polysyndeton helps to create a humorous impression of accumulation.

11. See J. F. Montesinos, *Introducción a una historia de la novela en España en el siglo XIX* (Valencia: Castalia, 1955), p. 215.

12. When Larra writes, "Venecia ha sido el Estado que ha llevado a más alto grado de esplendor la policía," he is merely using the picture of splendor that Venice conveys. The expression "más alto grado de esplendor," though seemingly hackneyed, could not have been considered ridiculous of itself, since the author uses it in all seriousness in his novel, for example: "En tiempos de paz, y cuando posteriormente hubo llegado esta famosa institución a su más alto grado de esplendor y a su verdadero apogeo, se solía aprovechar, para conferirla a los escuderos que se habían hecho de ella merecedores, alguna solemnidad" (3: 124).

13. The Marquis de Custine, who witnessed Miyar's execution, remarks: "En regardant du côté d'où s'approchait la procession, je vis paraître d'abord des hommes a cheval, habillés a peu près comme des prêtres; que font là ces cavaliers ecclésiastiques? dis-je à mon voisin. —Ce ne sont pas des prêtres, ce sont des alguazils. Je demande alors pourquoi ces sbires portent un costume religieux. On ne peut me répondre. C'est par ses accointances de tout genre avec la police que la religion catholique sera discréditée en Espagne" (*L'Espagne sous Ferdinand VII,* 4 vols. [Brussels: Sociéte Typographique Belge Ad. Wahlen et Cie., 1838], 1: 184).

14. Cf. in "Exequias del Conde de Campo-Alange" the word "mediodía" used to signify the constitutional half of Europe menaced by the North, which connoted absolutism (2: 293).

15. The phrase "amigos más acérrimos" (corrected to "amigos acérri-

mos" in the *Colección*) was not invented by Larra. There is an example of this locution in a speech of Galiano's on December 13, 1834, during the royal household budget debate. He was replying to Toreno, who had attempted to explain away the smallness of Louis-Philippe's allowance in comparison to María Cristina's as a necessary compensation for the illegitimacy of his claim to the French throne. Alcalá Galiano said: "Debo decir que a mi parecer no pudiera haber elegido S.S. argumento más fatal y opuesto a su idea, pues los más acérrimos amigos de revoluciones no hubiesen empleado otro para hacer ver las ventajas de ellas. Pues que, si fuera necesario para que los pueblos disfrutasen de los beneficios de la economía hacer revoluciones, ¿habría argumento mejor para probar la utilidad de éstas?" (*Pr.*, p. 893).

16. In an essay composed during Ferdinand's reign (April 30, 1833), Figaro uses the term "policía" with this meaning. "—¡Qué basura! En este país no hay policía," says Don Periquito, an ignoramus who criticizes everything about his own country (Larra intends an effect of ironic perspectivism, of course). See "En este país" (1: 218).

17. Cf. in "El ministerial": "Pues bien, hombres conozco yo en Madrid de cierta edad, y no uno ni dos, sino lo menos cinco, que así ven y oyen claro como yo vuelo" (1: 437).

18. For more information on the nuisance of *cartas de seguridad*, see the *Real decreto para el establecimiento de subdelegaciones de Fomento en las provincias*, capítulo VI, artículo 32. Reproduced in [Francisco] Javier de Burgos, *Anales del reinado de Doña Isabel II*, 6 vols. (Madrid: Mellado, 1850–1851), 1: 92.

CHAPTER 14: CLIMAX BEFORE DEPARTURE

1. Larra's son allowed it to appear in the *Semanario pintoresco español* 16 (1851): 2–3. It is also in *BAE*, 4: 316–317. A contemporaneous unsigned version has also been attributed to Larra. See Ismael Sánchez Estevan, *Mariano José de Larra* . . . (Madrid: Hernando, 1934), p. 240, note 1. Larra's approbation of the new government policy allowing theaters to remain open during Lent, and his puzzlement over the continuing prohibition of folk dancing, are the only aspects of the review that could possibly be deemed political.

2. The editor of the Aguilar edition unfortunately took the liberty of giving "Por ahora" the subtitle, "Continuación del anterior."

3. Between the two appeared "Poesías de Juan Bautista Alonso" (February 19), thoroughly analyzed by Narciso Alonso Cortés, *Sumandos biográficos* (Valladolid: Santarén, 1939), pp. 119-137. Some uncertainties in Alonso Cortés's investigation are resolved by Carlos Montilla, "Tres cartas inéditas de 1837," *Insula* 12, no. 123 (1957): 3.

4. Quoted by Luis Sánchez Agesta, *Historia del constitucionalismo español* (Madrid: Instituto de Estudios Políticos, 1955), p. 222.

5. M. J. de Larra, *Artículos de costumbres y de crítica de Mariano José de Larra*, ed. E. Herman Hespelt (New York: F. S. Crofts, 1941).

6. Julio Nombela y Campos, *Larra (Fígaro)* (Madrid: Imprenta Particular de "La Última Moda," 1906-1908), p. 285.

A SELECTED
BIBLIOGRAPHY

EDITIONS USEFUL FOR SCHOLARLY PURPOSES

García Calderón, Ventura. "Larra, écrivain français," *Revue Hispanique* 72 (1928): 592–604.

———. "Pages inédites de Larra," *Hispania* (Paris), 5 (1922): 289–291.

Larra, Mariano José de. *Artículos de costumbres y de crítica de Mariano José de Larra.* Edited by E. Herman Hespelt. New York: F. S. Crofts, 1941.

———. "La empresa nueva," *Semanario Pintoresco Español* 19 (1854): 11–12.

———. *Fígaro; Colección de artículos dramáticos, literarios, políticos y de costumbres . . . .* 5 vols. Madrid: Repullés, 1835–1837.

———. *Obras de D. Mariano José de Larra (Fígaro),* edited by Carlos Seco Serrano. In *Biblioteca de Autores Españoles.* Vols. 127–130. Madrid: Atlas, 1960.

Rumeau, A. "Larra, poète—fragments inédits. Esquisse d'un répertoire chronologique," *Bulletin Hispanique* 50 (1948): 3–4, 510–529, 53 (1951): 115–130.

Taylor, Baron Isidore-Justin-Séverin. *Voyage pittoresque en Espagne, en Portugal et sur la côte d'Afrique, de Tanger à Tétouan.* Paris: A. F. Lemaître, 1827–1866.

SIGNIFICANT STUDIES PERTAINING TO LARRA

Adams, Nicholson B. "A Note on Larra's *El doncel*," *Hispanic Review* 9 (1941): 218–221.

———. "A Note on Larra's *No más mostrador*." In *Romance Studies Presented to William Morton Dey*, edited by Urban Tigner Holmes, Alfred G. Engstrom, and Sturgis E. Leavitt, pp. 15–18. Chapel Hill, N.C.: University of North Carolina Press, 1950.

Alonso Cortés, Narciso. "Un dato para la biografía de Larra." In *Viejo y nuevo*, pp. 67–71. Valladolid: Viuda de Montero, 1915.

———. "El suicidio de Larra." In *Sumandos biográficos*, pp. 119–146. Valladolid: Santarén, 1939.

Banner, J. Worth. "Concerning a Charge of Plagiarism by Mariano José de Larra," *Studies in Philology* 48 (1951): 793–797.

Baquero Goyanes, Mariano. "Barroco y romanticismo," *Anales de la Universidad de Murcia*, curso 1949–1950 (cuarto trimestre), pp. 725–740.

———. *Perspectivismo y contraste*. Madrid: Gredos, 1963.

———. "Perspectivismo y crítica en Cadalso, Larra y Mesonero Romanos," *Clavileño* 5, no. 30 (1954): 1–12.

Barja, César. "Mariano José de Larra." In *Libros y autores modernos*, pp. 144–155. Rev. ed. Los Angeles, Calif.: Campbell, 1933.

Bellini, Giuseppe. *L'opera di Larra e la Spagna del primo ottocento*. Milan: Giolardica, 1962.

Benítez Claros, R. "Influencia de Quevedo en Larra," *Cuadernos de Literatura* (Madrid), 1 (1947): 117–123.

Buchanan, Milton A. "Mariano José de Larra." Address delivered at the Johns Hopkins University, February 12–14, 1913. Typewritten copy at the University of Toronto Library.

Burgos Seguí, Carmen de (pseud. Colombine). *"Fígaro" (Revelaciones, "ella" descubierta, epistolario inédito)*. Epílogo de Ramón Gómez de la Serna. Madrid: Imprenta de "Alrededor del mundo," 1919.

Casalduero, Joaquín. "La sensualidad en el romanticismo: sobre el *Macías*." In *Estudios sobre el teatro español*, pp. 219–231. 2d ed. Madrid: Gredos, 1967.

Centeno, Augusto. " 'La nochebuena de 1836' y su modelo horaciano," *Modern Language Notes* 50 (1935): 441–445.

Chaves y Rey, Manuel. *Don Mariano José de Larra (Fígaro). Su tiempo, su vida, sus obras*. Seville: Imprenta de la Andalucía, 1898.

Escobar, José. "Un soneto político de Larra," *Bulletin Hispanique* 71 (1969): 280–285.

Fox, Inman. "Historical and Literary Allusions in Larra's 'El hombre menguado,' " *Hispanic Review* 28 (1960): 341–349.

Hendrix, William S. "Notes on Jouy's Influence on Larra," *Romanic Review* 11 (1920): 37–45.

Hespelt, E. H. "Another Note on 'El Ladrón,' " *Modern Language Notes* 48 (1933): 325–327.

———. "The Translated Dramas of Mariano José de Larra and their French Originals," *Hispania* (Stanford), 15 (1932): 117–134.

Johnson, Robert. "Larra, Martínez de la Rosa, and the *Colección de artículos* of 1835–37," *Neophilologus* 50 (1966): 316–324.

Kercheville, F. M. "Larra and Liberal Thought in Spain," *Hispania* (Stanford), 14 (1931): 197–204.

Larra, Fernando José. *Mariano José de Larra (Fígaro)*. Barcelona: Amaltea, 1944.

Leslie, John Kenneth. " 'Fígaro en Lisboa,' an Unpublished Article by M. J. de Larra," *Modern Language Notes* 68 (1953): 96–100.

———. "Larra's 'Tirteida primera,' " *Hispanic Review* 21 (1953): 37–41.

———. "Larra's Unpublished Anacreontic," *Modern Language Notes* 61 (1946): 345–349.

Lomba y Pedraja, José R. *Mariano José de Larra (Fígaro). Cuatro estudios que le abordan o le bordean*. Madrid: Tipografía de Archivos, 1936.

———. "Notas breves, obtenidas de testimonios orales, con destino a una biografía de Mariano José de Larra (Fígaro)." In *Homenatge a Antoni Rubió i Lluch. Miscellània d'estudis literaris, històrics i lingüístics*, 1: 605–611. Barcelona: Impremta Elzeviriana, 1936.

Lorenzo-Rivero, Luis. *Larra y Sarmiento*. Madrid: Guadarrama, 1968.

Marrast, Robert. "Fígaro y El Siglo," *Insula* 17, nos. 188–189 (July–August 1962): 6.

Martínez Ruiz, José (Azorín). *Rivas y Larra*. Madrid: Renacimiento, 1916.

Matters, Virginia Corrie. "A Comparison of *El doncel* and of *Macías*." Master's thesis, Oberlin College, 1926.

Mazade [-Percin], [Louis-] Charles de. "Un Humoriste espagnol au XIXe siecle—Larra." In *L'Espagne moderne*, chap. 8. Paris: Michel Lévy, 1855.

McGuire, Elizabeth. *A Study of the Writings of D. Mariano José de Larra, 1809–1837*. University of California Publications in Modern Philology, 7: 87–130. Berkeley, Calif.: University of California Press, 1918.

Montilla, Carlos. "Tres cartas inéditas de 1837, a los 120 años de la muerte de Larra," *Insula* 12, no. 123 (1957): 3.

Nombela y Campos, Julio. *Autores célebres. Larra (Fígaro)*. Madrid: Imprenta Particular de "La Última Moda," 1906–1908.

Nunemaker, J. Horace. "Note on the 'Últimos amores de Larra,' " *Romanic Review* 23 (1932): 37–38.

Oliver, Miguel de los Santos. "Larra." In *Hojas del sábado*, 2: 29–85. Barcelona: Gustavo Gili, 1918.

Pastor Mateos, Emilio. "Larra y Madrid," *Revista de la Biblioteca, Archivo y Museo* (Ayuntamiento de Madrid), 18 (1949): 297–331.

Peral, Juan del. *El Laberinto* (Madrid), 1, no. 13 (1844).

Pons, J. S. "Larra et Lope de Vega," *Bulletin Hispanique* 42 (1940): 123–131.

Rumeau, Aristide. "Une Copie manuscrite d'oeuvres inédites de Larra: 1886," *Hispanic Review* 4 (1936): 111–123.

———. "Un Document pour la biographie de Larra. Le romance 'Al día primero de mayo,' " *Bulletin Hispanique* 37 (1935): 196–208.

———. "Larra et le Baron Taylor," *Revue de Littérature Comparée* 16 (1936): 477–493.

———. "Le Premier Séjour de Mariano José de Larra en France (1813–1818)." In *Mélanges offerts à Marcel Bataillon*, pp. 600–612. Bordeaux: Féret, 1962.

———. Review of Sánchez Estevan's Biography of Larra, *Bulletin Hispanique* 37 (1935): 519–521.

———. Review of the Aguilar Edition of Larra's Articles, *Bulletin Hispanique* 49 (1947): 106–109.

———. "Una travesura de Larra, o dos dramas y una comedia a un tiempo," *Insula* 17, nos. 188–189 (July–August 1962): 3.

Sánchez Estevan, Ismael. *Mariano José de Larra (Fígaro), ensayo biográfico redactado en presencia de numerosos antecedentes desconocidos y acompañado de un catálogo completo de sus obras*. Madrid: Hernando, 1934.

———. "Quevedo y Fígaro," *Diario Universal*, February 26, 1914.

Tarr, Frederick Courtney. "Larra. Nuevos datos críticos y literarios (1829–1833)," *Revue Hispanique* 77 (1929): 246–269.

———. "Larra's *Duende satírico del día*," *Modern Philology* 26 (1928): 31–46.

———. "Mariano José de Larra (1809–1837)," *Modern Language Journal* 22 (1937): 46–50.

———. "More Light on Larra," *Hispanic Review* 4 (1936): 89–110.

———. "*El Pobrecito Hablador*: estudio preliminar," *Revue Hispanique* 81, pt. 2 (1933): 419–439.

———. "Reconstruction of a Decisive Period in Larra's Life (May–November 1836)," *Hispanic Review* 5 (1937): 1–24.

Trueblood, Alan S. *"El castellano viejo* y la *Sátira III* de Boileau," *Nueva Revista de Filología Hispánica* 15 (1961): 529–538.

Ullman, Pierre L. Review of *Obras de Mariano José de Larra*, edited by Carlos Seco Serrano, *Revista Hispánica Moderna* 29 (1963): 298–299.

Vanderford, Kenneth H. "Macías in Legend and Literature," *Modern Philology* 31 (1933): 35–63.

———. "A Note on the Versification of Larra," *Philological Quarterly* 13 (1934): 306–309.

Zangano, Mario. La *"Nochebuena"* di M. J. de Larra (*riflessi oraziani e motivi personali*). Catania: Studio Editoriale Moderno, 1928.

COMMEMORATIVE ISSUES

Insula, 17, nos. 188–189 (July–August 1962). Articles by Ricardo Gullón, Guillermo de Torre, Federico Álvarez Arregui, Aristide Rumeau, Carlos Seco Serrano, Arturo del Hoyo, Robert Marrast, Ricardo Senabre Sempere, David Torres.

Revista de Occidente. Número extraordinario en homenaje a Larra, 2da. época, 5, no. 50 (May 1967).

GENERAL WORKS

Alcalá Galiano, Antonio. *Historia de España desde los tiempos primitivos hasta la mayoria de la reina doña Isabel II, redactada y anotada con arreglo a la que escribió en inglés el Dr. Dunham*. 7 vols. Madrid: Sociedad Literaria y Tipográfica, 1844–1846.

———. *Memorias . . . publicadas por su hijo.* 2 vols. Madrid: Imprenta de Enrique Rubiños, 1886.

Artola, Miguel. *Los orígenes de la España contemporánea.* 2 vols. Madrid: Instituto de Estudios Políticos, 1959.

Asenjo, Antonio. *La prensa madrileña a través de los siglos (apuntes para su historia desde el año 1661 al de 1925)*. Madrid: Artes Gráficas Municipales, 1933.

Ballesteros y Beretta, Antonio. *Historia de España y su influencia en la historia universal,* 2d ed. 10 vols. Barcelona: Salvat, 1943–1956.

Barante, Baron de. *Souvenirs.* 8 vols. Paris: Calmann-Lévy, 1890–1901.

Baroja y Nessi, Pío. *Aviraneta; o, la vida de un conspirador.* 2d ed. Madrid: Espasa-Calpe, 1931.

Bécker, Jerónimo. *Historia de las relaciones exteriores de España durante el siglo XIX.* 2 vols. Madrid: Estab. tip. de J. Ratés, 1924.

Blanco García, P. Francisco. *La literatura española en el siglo XIX.* 3d ed. 3 vols. Madrid: Sáenz de Jubera, 1909–1912.

Boileau-Despréaux, Nicolas. *Oeuvres complètes.* Edited by Charles-H. Boudhors. 7 vols. Paris: Société les Belles Lettres, 1939–1952.

Borrow, George. *The Bible in Spain.* Notes and glossary by Ulick Ralph Burke. New York: G. P. Putnam's Sons [1914].

Boussagol, Gabriel. *Angel de Saavedra, duc de Rivas; sa vie, son oeuvre poétique.* Toulouse: E. Privat, 1926.

Brown, James. "Eight Types of Pun," *PMLA* 71 (1956): 14–25.

Burgo, Jaime del. *Fuentes de la historia de España. Bibliografía de las guerras carlistas y de las luchas políticas del siglo XIX.* 3 vols. Pamplona: C.S.I.C., 1954–1955.

Burgos [Francisco], Javier de. *Anales del reinado de Doña Isabel II.* 6 vols. Madrid: Mellado, 1850–1851.

[————]. *Historia pintoresca del reinado de Da. Isabel II y de la guerra civil. Obra original.* 4 vols. Madrid: Castello, 1846–1847.

————. *Observaciones sobre el empréstito Guebhard.* Madrid: Imprenta de D. Miguel de Burgos, 1834.

[Caballero, Fermín]. *Fisonomía natural y política de los procuradores en las Cortes de 1834, 1835 y 1836, por un asistente diario a las tribunas.* Madrid: Boix, 1836.

[————]. *El gobierno y las Cortes del Estatuto. Materiales para su historia.* Madrid: Yenes, 1837.

Cánovas del Castillo, A. *"El Solitario" y su tiempo. Biografía de D. Serafín Estébanez Calderón y crítica de sus obras.* 2 vols. Madrid: Pérez Durrull, 1883.

Carné, L. de. "L'Espagne au XIXe siècle," *Revue des Deux-Mondes,* December 15, 1836.

Castillo y Ayensa, J. *Historia crítica de las negociaciones con Roma desde la muerte del Rey Fernando VII.* 2 vols. Madrid: Tejado, 1859.

Castro, Américo. *Les Grands Romantiques espagnols.* Paris: La Renaissance du Livre, 1923.

Cejador, Julio. "Azorín y Larra," *La Tribuna,* May 13, 1917.

Clarke, H. Butler. *Modern Spain 1815–1898.* Cambridge: Cambridge University Press, 1906.

Conte, Augusto. *Recuerdos de un diplomático.* 3 vols. Madrid: Imprenta de J. Góngora y Álvarez, 1901–1903.

Courier de Méré, Paul-Louis. *Oeuvres complètes.* Edited by Maurice Allem. Bibliothéque de la Pléiade, no. 59. Paris: Gallimard, 1951.

Custine, Marquis de. *L'Espagne sous Ferdinand VII*. 4 vols. Brussels: Sociéte Typographique Belge Ad. Wahlen et Cie., 1838.

Delmonte, Domingo. *Centón epistolario de Domingo del Monte*. Edited by Domingo Figarola Caneda. 7 vols. Havana: Academia de la Historia, 1923–1950. Also found in *Anales de la Academia de la Historia* (Cuba), 1 (1919): 92–159, 270–339, 2 (1920): 76–125, 286–361, 3 (1921): 117–181, 313–363, 4 (1922): 182–240.

De Mille, James. *The Elements of Rhetoric*. New York: Harper, 1882.

Diario de las sesiones de Cortes. Estamento de Ilustres Próceres. Legislatura de 1834 a 1835. Madrid: Imprenta Nacional, 1865.

Diario de las sesiones de Cortes. Estamento de Procuradores. Legislatura de 1834 a 1835. 3 vols. Madrid: Imprenta de J. A. García, 1867.

Díaz-Plaja, Fernando. *La vida española en el siglo XIX*. Madrid: Afrodisio Aguado, [1952].

Díaz-Plaja, Guillermo. *Introducción al estudio del romanticismo español*. Madrid: Espasa-Calpe, 1936.

Didier, Charles, "L'Espagne depuis 1830," *Revue des Deux-Mondes*, December 15, 1835, and February 1, 1836.

Donoso Cortés, Juan, Marqués de Valdegamas. *Historia de la regencia de María Cristina*. In *Obras completas*, 1: 807–908. Madrid: Editorial Católica, 1946.

Eggers, Eduardo R., and Colombí, E. Feunede. *Francisco de Zea Bermúdez y su época, 1799–1850*. Madrid: C.S.I.C., 1958.

Eguizábal, José Eugenio. *Apuntes para una historia de la legislación española sobre imprenta desde el año de 1480 al presente*. Madrid: Imprenta de la Revista de Legislación, 1879.

Enciclopedia universal ilustrada europeo-americana. 70 vols. Barcelona: Espasa-Calpe, 1907?–1930, s.v. "Recopilación."

Fernández de Córdova y Valcárcel, Teniente General Fernando. *Mis memorias íntimas*. 3 vols. Madrid: "Sucesores de Rivadeneyra," 1886–1889. Also found in *Biblioteca de Autores Españoles*. Vols. 192–193. Madrid: Atlas, 1966.

Ferrer del Río, Antonio. *Galería de la literatura española*. Madrid: Mellado, 1846.

Fowler, H. W. *A Dictionary of Modern English Usage*. Oxford: The Clarendon Press, 1937.

Fuente, Vicente de la. *Historia de las sociedades secretas antiguas y modernas en España y especialmente de la francmasonería*. 3 vols. New ed. Barcelona: Editorial Prensa Católica, 1933.

González Molleda, María Luisa. "Antonio María Segovia," *Revista de Literatura* 24 (1963): 101–124.

González Palencia, Angel. *Estudio histórico sobre la censura guberna-*

tiva en España, 1800–1833. 3 vols. Madrid: Tipografía de Archivos, 1934–1941.

Hartzenbusch e Hiriart, Eugenio. *Apuntes para un catálogo de periódicos madrileños desde el año 1661 al 1870.* Madrid: "Sucesores de Rivadeneyra," 1894.

Historia contemporánea de la revolución de España. Esta obra comprende la historia de la revolución de España hasta los últimos acontecimientos de Barcelona, para servir de continuación a la historia de Mariana, y a la del Levantamiento, guerra y revolución de España, debida a la pluma del celébre Conde de Toreno, publicada por una sociedad de literatos. (Anon.). 5 vols. Madrid: [Of. del Establecimiento Central], 1843.

Hornedo, Calixto. *Elementos de retórica.* 7th ed. Madrid: Ibarra, 1828.

Jouy, Etienne-Antoine. *La Chaussée d'Antin, esquisses contemporaines.* 2 vols. Paris: Lachapelle, 1838.

La Blanchetai, Pierre Henry de (pseud. Pierre de Luz). *Isabelle II, reine d'Espagne.* Paris: Plon, 1934. Also *Isabel II, reina de España.* Translated by Gabriel Conforto Thomas. Barcelona: Juventud, 1937.

Lea, Henry Charles. *A History of the Inquisition in Spain.* 4 vols. New York: Macmillan, 1906–1907.

Le Gentil, Georges. *Le Poète Manuel Bretón de los Herreros et la société espagnole de 1830 a 1860.* Paris: Hachette, 1909.

Llauder, Manuel. *Memorias documentadas del Teniente general . .* Madrid: Ignacio Boix, 1844.

Lloréns Castillo, Vicente. "De la elegía a la sátira patriótica." In *Studia philologica. Homenaje ofrecido a Dámaso Alonso.* 2: 413–422. Madrid: Gredos, 1961.

———. "Jovellanos y Blanco. En torno al *Semanario Patriótico* de 1809," *Nueva Revista de Filología Hispánica* 15 (1961): 262–278.

———. *Liberales y románticos. Una emigración española en Inglaterra (1823–1834).* Mexico City: Colegio de Mexico, 1954 [2d ed. Madrid: Castalia, 1968.]

———. "Sobre la aparición de liberal," *Nueva Revista de Filología Hispánica* 12 (1958): 53–58.

López, Joaquín María. *Colección de discursos parlamentarios, defensas forenses, y producciones literarias.* 7 vols. Madrid: Minuesa, 1856–1857.

M. M. "The Late King of Spain," *New Monthly Magazine and Literary Journal* (London), 39, pt. 3 (1833): 324–334.

M. N. O. "Reflections on the Politics of Spain," *New Monthly Magazine* 29, pt. 2 (1830): 484–495.

Martínez de la Rosa, Francisco. *Bosquejo histórico de la política de España, desde los tiempos de los Reyes Católicos hasta nuestros días.* 2 vols. Madrid: Rivadeneyra, 1857.

―――. *Hernán Pérez del Pulgar, el de las hazañas.* Madrid: Jordán, 1834. Also found in *Biblioteca de Autores Espanoles,* vol. 150. Madrid: Atlas, 1962.

Maxwell, Sir Herbert. *The Life and Letters of George William Frederick, Fourth Earl of Clarendon.* 2 vols. London: Edward Arnold, 1913.

Mesonero Romanos, Ramón de. *Memorias de un setentón natural y vecino de Madrid.* 2 vols. Madrid: Oficinas de la Ilustración Española y Americana, 1881. Also found in his *Obras.* Vol. 7. Madrid: Renacimiento, 1926.

[Miñano y Bedoya, Sebastián de]. *Lamentos de un pobrecito holgazán que estaba acostumbrado a vivir a costa agena.* Madrid: Roldán, 1820. Also Madrid: Ciencia Nueva, 1968.

Montesinos, J. F. *Introducción a una historia de la novela en España en el siglo XIX.* Valencia: Castalia, 1955.

Ochoa, Eugenio de. *Apuntes para una biblioteca de escritores españoles contemporáneos en prosa y verso.* 2 vols. Paris: Baudry, 1840.

―――. "La Littérature espagnole au XIXe siecle," *Revue de Paris* 20 (1840): 35–37.

Ossorio y Bernard, Manuel. *Ensayo de un catálogo de periodistas españoles del siglo XIX.* Madrid: Imp. J. Palacios, 1903.

Pando Fernández de Pinedo, Manuel, Marqués de Miraflores. *Memorias para escribir la historia contemporánea de los siete primeros años del reinado de Isabel II.* 2 vols. Madrid: Calera, 1843–1844.

―――. *Reseña histórico-crítica de la participación de los partidos en los sucesos políticos de España en el siglo XIX.* Madrid: Espinosa, 1863.

Panorama español. 4 vols. Madrid: Imp. de El Panorama Español, 1842–1845.

Peers, E. Allyson. *A History of the Romantic Movement in Spain.* 2 vols. Cambridge: The Cambridge University Press, 1940.

Pi y Margall, Francisco. *Historia de España en el siglo XIX.* 7 vols. Barcelona: Seguí, 1902.

―――, and Pi y Arsuaga, Francisco. *Las grandes conmociones políticas del siglo XIX en España.* 2 vols. Barcelona: Seguí, n.d.

Piñeyro, Enrique. *El romanticismo en España.* Paris: Garnier, [1904].

Pirala y Criado, Antonio. *Historia de la guerra civil y de los partidos liberal y carlista.* 5 vols. Madrid: Mellado, 1853–1856. The 3d ed. rev. (1893) was not available.

Quinet, Edgar. *Mes Vacances en Espagne.* In *Oeuvres complètes,* vol. 9. Paris: Pagnerre, 1857.

Répide, Pedro de. *Isabel II, reina de España.* Madrid: Espasa-Calpe, 1932.

Richards, I. A. *The Philosophy of Rhetoric.* New York: Oxford University Press, 1936.

Rico y Amat, Juan. *Historia política y parlamentaria de España (desde los tiempos más remotos hasta nuestros días)* . . . *dedicada a S.M. la Reina Doña Isabel II.* 3 vols. Madrid: Impr. Escuelas Pías, 1860–1861.

Rodríguez Solís, E. *Espronceda; su tiempo, su vida y sus obras.* Madrid: Imp. de Fernando Cao y Domingo de Val, 1883.

Romanones, Conde de. *Obras completas.* 3 vols. Madrid: Plus-Ultra, 1947.

Sánchez Agesta, Luis. *Historia del constitucionalismo español.* Madrid: Instituto de Estudios Políticos, 1955.

Sánchez Alonso, Benito. *Fuentes de la historia española e hispano americana.* 3d ed. Madrid: Consejo Superior de Investigaciones Científicas, 1952.

San José, Diego. *Vida y "milagros" de Fernando VII.* Madrid: Renacimiento, 1929.

Sarrailh, Jean. *Un Homme d'Etat espagnol: Martínez de la Rosa (1787–1862).* Bordeaux: Feret, 1930.

Segovia, Antonio María. *Colección de composiciones serias y festivas en prosa y en verso, escogidas entre las publicadas e inéditas del escritor conocido por "El Estudiante."* Vol. 1. Madrid: Sancha, 1839.

Soldevilla, Fernando. *Los hombres de la libertad.* Madrid: "Fernando Fe," 1927.

Suárez, Federico. *La crisis política del antiguo régimen en España (1800–1840).* Madrid: RIALP, 1950.

Tarr, Frederick Courtney. "Romanticism in Spain and Spanish Romanticism," *Bulletin of Spanish Studies* 16 (1937): 46–50.

Valera y Alcalá Galiano, Juan. *Historia general de España desde los tiempos primitivos hasta la muerte de Fernando VII, por Don Modesto Lafuente. Continuada desde dicha época hasta nuestros días por* . . . 25 vols. Barcelona: Montaner y Simón, 1887–1890.

Villarroya, Joaquín Tomás. *El sistema político del Estatuto Real (1834–1836).* Madrid: Instituto de Estudios Políticos, 1968.

Villa-Urrutia, Wenceslao Ramírez de, Marqués de Villa-Urrutia. *La reina gobernadora, Doña María Cristina de Borbón.* Madrid: Beltrán, 1925.

_____. *Fernando VII, rey absoluto. La ominosa década de 1823 a 1833.* Madrid: Beltrán, 1931.

Villiers, George. *A Vanished Victorian, Being the Life of George Villiers, Fourth Earl of Clarendon, 1800–1870, by his grandson* . . . . London: Eyre and Spottiswoode, 1938.

Zorrilla [y Moral], José. *Recuerdos del tiempo viejo.* 3 vols. Madrid and Barcelona, 1880–1882.

INDEX

Abarca, Joaquín, bishop of León, 22, 51
Abargues, Joaquín, 122, 291, 292–93
La Abeja, 77, 88, 135, 136, 183, 247, 299, 396
Aben Humeya, 380
Absolutists, 9, 13, 14, 20–23, 27, 47, 48, 63, 108, 186, 219, 220, 341. *See also* Conservatives; Enlightened despotism; Reactionaries; Serviles
Absurd legislation (administration), 126–34
A cada paso un acaso, 71
Acevedo, Manuel María, 388
Additional Articles, 57
"Adelante," 257, 263–80, 319, 364, 391–92, 393
Adynaton, 177, 374
Afrancesados, 7, 8, 9, 14, 17, 32, 60, 390
Agraviados, 15, 258
Aguado (banker), 17, 46, 99, 188, 245
"La alabanza, o que me prohíban éste," 354, 362–64
Alagón, Duke of, 9
Alava, Miguel Ricardo de, 247, 248
Alcalá Galiano, Antonio, 33, 35, 36, 107, 137, 184, 221, 222–23, 224, 229, 230, 232, 233–34, 238, 262, 266, 276, 277, 282, 285, 292, 296, 304, 305, 306, 307, 315, 328, 329, 334, 341, 343–44, 344–45, 351, 359, 376, 378, 381, 382, 383, 387, 389, 393, 396, 400
Alcudia, Conde de la, 246

Alfred the Great, 125
Alhambra, 24
Allegory, 239, 358, 373
Alliteration, 123
Almagro San Martín, Melchor de, 371, 400
Alonso, Juan Bautista, 354, 401
Alonso Cortés, Narciso, 401
Álvarez Guerra, Juan, 142
Amadeo I, king of Spain, 21
Amadís de Gaula, 78
Amalia of Saxony, queen of Spain, 18
Amarillas, Marquess de las, 118, 143
Ambiguity, 72, 94, 224, 283, 330, 333
American colonies, 9, 10, 16, 47, 118, 262
"Los amigos," 67
Los Amigos del Orden, 11
Amnesties, 16, 20, 47, 49, 52, 62, 162, 224, 277, 306
Amphibology, 324
"Ana Bolena," 43, 97
Analogy, 94
Anaphora, 319, 373
Angoulême, Duc d', 13, 19, 50, 169, 186, 198, 340, 344
Anticlericals, 48
Anticlimax, 80, 177
Antimetabole, 253, 374
Antithesis, 94, 115, 147, 176, 224, 287, 329, 352, 373, 374
Antonomasia, 286, 373
"Antony," 378

Aphthonius of Antioch, 373
Apophasis, 263, 374
Aposiopesis, 319
Apostolics, 13, 15, 20. *See also* Carlists; Inquisitorials; Reactionaries
Apostrophe, 333, 374
Aquinas, Thomas, 172
Aranalde, José, 50
Aranda del Duero, 14
Arango, Andrés de, 85, 86, 393
Arango, Manuel, 259, 292
Ardoin, 194, 208
Argüelles, Agustín, 36, 101, 217, 222, 261, 265, 267, 276, 285, 291, 297, 314, 322, 323, 324, 326, 339, 346, 351, 388, 393
Aristocracy, 4, 33, 54, 58, 63, 69, 70, 107, 108; of talent, 70; power of, 5, 46, 47
Aristotle, 172
Armijo de Cambronero, Dolores, 22, 28, 30, 31
Army of the Faith, 12
El arte de conspirar, 282, 394
Artículos de costumbres, 17, 37, 38, 66, 67, 255, 281–84, 364, 371
Artigas, 59
"Ascensión aerostática," 360, 382
Asenjo, Antonio, 386, 388
"Atrás," 257, 259, 264, 279, 319, 376, 391–92, 393
Austria, 11, 23, 47, 55, 340, 341, 342
Auto Acordado, 19
Ávila, 30
Aviraneta, Eugenio de, 48, 60, 61, 293, 316
Ayuntamientos, 95, 260, 261, 264, 270–72, 312, 358

Badajoz, 28
"Bailes de máscaras," 69
"Bailes de máscaras. Billetes por embargo," 255, 264, 279, 281
Bails, 160
Ballesteros, 246
Ballesteros y Beretta, Antonio, 397
Bandits, 6, 17
Barante, Baron Guillaume-Prosper de, 63, 377, 378
"Los barateros o el desafío," 70
Barcelona, 5

Bardají y Azara, Eusebio, 118
Baroja y Nessi, Pío, 377
Baquero Goyanes, Mariano, 382
Basque provinces, 17, 49
Bazán, 193
Beaumarchais, Pierre Auguste Caron de, 22, 96, 299
Belda, Francisco, 197
Belgium, 28
Bellini, Vincente. See "I Capuletti ed i Montechi"; Norma; "La Straniera"
Benítez Claros, R., 382
Bentham, Jeremy, 53, 151, 154, 171, 377
Berlin, 8
Bézout, Étienne, 160
Bienes mostrencos, 262
Bill of rights, 111, 116, 118, 151, 215, 242, 260, 295, 311, 356, 398
Blake, Joaquín, 295
Blancos, 213
Blanco y Crespo, José María, 32, 33, 370
Blood, cleanliness of, 5, 29
Boletín del Comercio, 52, 380
Bonaparte, Joseph, 6, 7, 266, 390
Bonaparte, Napoleon. *See* Napoleon I
Bordeaux, 8
Borrego, Andrés, 396
Bourbons, 4, 19
Bourgeoisie, 5, 29
Boussagol, Gabriel, 378
Brazil, 23
Bretón de los Herreros, Manuel, 15, 21, 102
Broglie, Duc de, 47
Brown, James, 384
Brutus, M. Junius, 136
Budgets, 262, 279, 389, 395; Interior, 320–24, 332, 358, 359; Justice, 272–77, 284, 394; Navy, 286; royal household, 264–70, 400; State, 268, 270, 271; Treasury, 358, 359; War, 268, 270, 271, 285
"Buenas noches," 50, 102
Buffon, Georges-Louis Leclerc, Comte de, 167, 176
Bullfighting, 16, 18, 19
Burgos, Carmen de, 378, 381, 386, 394
Burgos, Francisco Javier de, 17, 50, 60, 76, 98, 118, 188, 245–55, 372, 375, 376, 377, 381, 383, 389–90, 391, 400

Burgos, Ignacio Rives y Mayor, archbishop of, 141, 142

Burlesque, 163, 172, 176; low, 212

Butrón, Fernando, 51

Caballero, Fermín, 89, 122, 146, 151, 157, 158, 194–96, 203, 266, 267, 285, 291, 292, 297, 298, 301, 302, 309, 335, 376, 377, 378, 380–81, 384, 386, 389, 391, 394, 395, 396, 397, 398

Cabeza de partido, 53

Cabrera, University of, 14

Cadalso, José, 70

Cádiz, 8, 9, 10, 13, 18, 32; rise of middle class in, 5. *See also* Constitution of Cádiz

"El café," 17

"La calamidad europea," 244, 249–51, 254

Calatrava, José María, 11, 30, 150

Calderón Collantes, Saturnino, 276, 291, 293, 312, 397

Calomarde, Francisco Tadeo, 15, 16, 19, 20, 22, 37, 43, 49, 52, 93, 98, 108, 117, 194, 210, 213, 215, 219, 223, 225, 226, 239, 292, 310, 371, 397, 398

Camarasa, Marquess de, 141, 142

Camarilla, 290

Cambronero, Manuel María de, 22, 28

Camino, Antonio del, 150

"Camino(s)," 97, 207–9

Campo-Alange, José Negrete, Conde de, 28, 34, 371, 399

Candelaria, Marquess de la, 118

Candolle, Augustin de, 8, 167

Canning, Stratford, 23

Cano Manuel, Antonio, 55, 118, 142, 149, 302, 396

Cánovas del Castillo, Antonio, 62, 93, 375, 378

Canterac, José, 288, 289, 292, 313, 315

Capmany, Antonio de, 41

Capulets, 85, 88

"*I Capuletti ed i Montechi*," 93–95, 371, 380

Carbonari, 16

Cardero, 291, 395

Carlists, 15, 19, 20, 22, 23, 43, 47–49, 51, 52, 57–59, 62, 67, 68, 74, 86, 108, 148, 163, 164, 189, 191, 210, 212, 214, 220, 224, 226, 237, 258, 260, 279, 289, 291, 301, 313–15, 365

Carlist War, 15, 23, 28, 29, passim

Carlos, Infante Don, 9, 15, 16, 18–20, 22, 23, 48, 49, 51, 55, 57, 58, 86, 87, 97, 107–9, 140–42, 149, 150, 162, 187, 193, 211, 235, 237, 239, 242, 254, 265, 291, 386, 387. *See also* "Un faccioso más"

Carlota, Infanta, 18–20, 46, 267

Carondelet, Luis Ángel, 212

Carrères, 245

"Carta de Fígaro a su antiguo corresponsal," 354, 357–60

"Carta de Fígaro a un bachiller su corresponsal," 102–10, 214, 387

Carta otorgada, 52, 53, 113, 308, 336; promise of, in 1823, 12–14

Cartas de seguridad, 351, 352, 400

El casamiento por convicción, 111

Casares, Julio, 374

"El casarse pronto y mal," 21, 139

"Las casas nuevas," 284

"Casi," 83, 84, 348. *See also* "Cuasi"

Castaños, Francisco Javier, Duque de Bailén, 248

El Castellano, 378

"El castellano viejo," 399

Castillo y Ayensa, J., 376

Castroterreño, Duque de, 142

Catalonia, 16, 56

Catiline conspiracy, 337, 338

Cato, M. Porcius, 136

Cea. *See* Zea Bermúdez, Francisco

Censorship, 22, 27, 28, 30, 38, 39, 41, 48, 51, 52, 65, 68, 76, 86, 88, 89, 95, 97, 115–21, 123, 136, 145, 163, 164, 166, 168–70, 173, 177, 180, 182, 183, 224, 242, 251, 252, 254, 257, 260, 262, 263, 279, 282, 284, 292, 294–99, 307, 320, 321, 327, 329–33, 355, 356, 358, 363, 364, 369, 392, 393, 397, 398; and freedom of press, 115–19; Zea's decree concerning, 47–48. *See also* Press

Cervantes Saavedra, Miguel de, 97, 109, 117, 242, 300, 382

Charles III, king of Spain, 4, 7

Charles IV, king of Spain, 6, 7, 19, 32

Charte octroyée. See Carta otorgada

Chateaubriand, François-René de, 26

Chaves, Manuel, 372

Cholera epidemic, 59, 99, 103, 104, 108, 134, 140, 141, 150, 185, 212, 249, 383
Church. *See* Roman Catholic Church
Cicero, 42, 134, 337–39, 372
"Cimiento," 91, 92, 235, 238, 239, 301, 302, 335
"Las circunstancias," 68
Civil code, 47, 51
Civil servants, 52, 69, 98, 108, 148, 164, 165, 209, 210, 213, 255, 273, 277, 346, 357, 389, 398
Civil War, 15, 23, 28, 29, passim
Clarke, H. Butler, 62, 369, 378
Clericals, 23. *See also* Inquisitorials; Reactionaries
Climax, 81, 319, 373
Closed meetings. *See* Secret sessions
Colegio Imperial, 14, 15
Coleridge, Samuel Taylor, 370
Coll y Vehí, José, 374
Columbus, Christopher, 176
El Compilador, 299
Comuneros, 16, 17, 60
La conjuración de Venecia, 87–93, 334, 339, 380
Conservatives, 48, 52, 63. *See also* Absolutists; Enlightened despotism; Serviles
Conspiracies, 17, 19, 22, 31, 49, 58–60, 135, 141, 219, 224–26, 257, 272, 273, 290, 316, 346, 347, 349, 381, 398; feigned, 15; of Palafox, 60, 99, 103, 141, 349, 381; of the Triangle, 9. *See also* Fear, of plots; Post-Office Mutiny
Constant, Benjamin, 151
Constitution of Bayonne, 7, 36
Constitution of Cádiz, 8, 9, 12, 30, 32, 36, 48, 170, 273, 307, 344, 398
Constitution of 1837, 27
Consular employees' salaries, 261
Conte, Augusto, 25, 59, 85, 212, 370, 377, 380, 387, 397
Continuity, principle of, 229. *See also* Fusion
"Conversation" or "discussion," 303–7
Cooper, James Fenimore, 339
Copernicus, 161
Corellas, 12
El Correo de las Damas, 139, 360

El Correo Literario y Mercantil, 18, 20, 22, 175
Cortes, 8, 12, 19, 27, 40, 41, 49, 51–53, 60, 64, 65, passim; bylaws of, 255, 261; convocation of, 260; medieval, 128, 133; of Cádiz, 24, 150, 151; of 1843, 35; opening of, 91, 93, 95, 101–8, 301; power of, 157, 158, 307; regulations for, 310. *See also* Diario de las sesiones de Cortes; Próceres; Procuradores
Cortina, Manuel de la, 27
Costumbres, costumbrismo. See Artículos de costumbres
La Cotorrita, 12
Council of Regency, 8
Council of State, 46
Courier de Méré, Paul-Louis, 112, 162, 382, 385
Cousin, Victor, 53, 95
Cristina. *See* María Cristina of Bourbon
Cristinos, 20. *See also* Liberals
"Cuasi," 57, 83
Cuesta, Sebastián, 222
"La cuestión transparente," 214, 227–43, 388
Custine, Marquis de, 399
Cuvier, Georges, 167

Dante Alighieri, 39
Decazes, Elie, Duc, 57, 63
Dehesa, Juan de la, 50, 357
Deianira, 35
Delmonte, Domingo, 136, 370, 376, 380, 381, 383, 393
De Mille, James, 374
Depersonification, 382
Derechos fundamentales. *See* Bill of rights
Descarte, 184, 206, 207
Las desdichas de un amante dichoso, 281
Destutt de Tracy, Antoine, 175
"El día de difuntos de 1836. Fígaro en el cementerio," 44, 45, 289, 370, 374, 395
Diario de Avisos, 86, 90, 379, 391
Diario de las sesiones de Cortes, xi; proposed publication of, 255
Díez del Corral, Luis, 376

Díez González, Francisco, 206
El diplomático, 254
Disinterested observer. *See Artículos de costumbres*
Doceañistas, 30, 36, 95, 324
Domecq y Víctor, Francisco, 267
El Doncel de Don Enrique el Doliente, 77, 78, 83, 84
Donizetti, Gaetano, 43, 97, 149
Don Quixote. See Cervantes Saavedra, Miguel de
Donoso Cortés, Juan, 375
"Dos liberales o lo que es entenderse," 255
Double entendre, 118
Double irony, 279
Ducange, Victor, 18, 28, 96
El Duende Satírico del Día, 17, 18, 21, 42, 371
Duero River, 285
Dumas, Alexandre, 378

El Eco de la Opinión, 75, 89
El Eco del Comercio, 60, 61, 89, 98, 224, 299, 380, 388, 394, 398
"La educación de entonces," 69
Eguizábal, José Eugenio, 167, 375, 379, 385, 391, 396, 397
Election procedures. *See* Ayuntamientos; Procuradores, election of
Elizondo, 58
Empecinado, El. *See* Martí, Juan
Encyclopedism, 5, 391
Enero (banking house), 49
"En este país," 400
Enlightened despotism, 5, 22, 32, 46, 49
Entailed estates. *See Mayorazgos*
Epistolary style, 110, 112, 115, 135, 244, 277
Epistrophe, 279, 373
Ercilla y Zúñiga, Alonso de, 334–37
"Errar y enmendar," 184, 202–6
Escolapios. See Piarists
Espagne poétique, 87
El Español (London), 370
El Español (Madrid), 29, 30, 396
Espoz y Mina, Francisco Javier, 17, 208, 210, 214, 222, 258, 290, 386–87
Espronceda, José de, 17, 75, 76, 93
Estado. See State, Ministry of
Estatuto Real, 11, 27, 52, 54, 55, 60, 87–

91, 93–95, 113, 133, 152, 162, 235, 239, 253, 273, 274, 278, 285, 295, 301, 307, 308, 311, 312, 335, 336, 364. *See also Carta otorgada*
Estébanez Calderón, Serafín, 47
Esterhazy, 377
Ethopoesis, 282
Exaltados, 11–13, 32, 34, 314, 377
Exchequer. *See* Treasury
Exclamation, 278, 374
"Exequias del Conde de Campo-Alange," 371, 399
Exhibition, 15, 16
Exiles. *See* Liberals
Expatriation decrees, 52
Extremadura, 28

"Un faccioso más," 184, 210–12, 240, 387, 393
Falces, Pedro Manuel Velluti y Navarro, Marquess de, 116, 117, 154, 160, 161, 164, 172, 173, 178, 203, 220, 221, 228, 230, 384, 386
"Fantasma," 307, 312–16, 318
Fear, 263, 279, 318, 331, 334–36, 397, 398; of plots, 96, 98, 99
Federation of Pure Royalists, 15
Ferdinand VII, king of Spain, 6, 8–20, 22–24, 26, 27, 46–51, 58, 65, 70, 191, 192, 195, 199, 246, 258, 284, 292, 370, 377, 390
Fernández de Córdoba, Fernando, 375
Fernández de Córdoba, Luis, 47, 49
Ferrater Mora, José, 385
Fígaro (projected newspaper), 282, 284, 293, 299, 395
Figura etymologica, 344
Fina, 134
"El fin de la fiesta," 68
First Exhibition of Spanish Arts and Crafts, 15, 16
Fleix, Joaquín, 267
Flórez Calderón, 17
Fomento. *See* Interior, Ministry of the
"La fonda nueva," 284
Foreign debt and loans, 14, 17, 46, 51, 99, 184–213, 216, 219, 221, 229, 232, 245–51, 265, 386, 390, 391
Foreign relations, 108
Foreign trade, 261
Fowler, H. W., 42, 374

Fox, Charles James, 310
France, 9, 47–49, 53, 55, 56, 125, 151, 155, 192, 194, 245, 261, 266, 297, 298, 310, 341, 342, 344, 365, 387
Francisco de Paula, Infante Don, 10, 18, 20, 264, 265, 267
Freedom of the press. *See* Censorship; Press
Freemasons. *See* Masons
French revolution, 6, 7, 32; of 1830, 16
Freud, Sigmund, 39
Frías, Bernardino Fernández de Velasco, Duque de, 11, 21, 28, 48
Fuente, Vicente de la, 377
Fueros, of Navarre, 49, 58
Fusion, 116, 208, 229, 231, 232, 357, 358

La Gaceta, 256, 285, 286, 296
Galbraith, John Kenneth, 395
Galiano. *See* Alcalá Galiano, Antonio
Gall, Franz Josef, 167
Gallego, Juan Nicasio, 52
Gándara Real, Marqués de la, 179
García Carrasco, Rufino, 148, 191, 193, 194, 199, 200, 210, 245, 246, 263, 309, 359, 386
García Herreros, Manuel, 149
Garelly, Nicolás María, 50, 53, 276, 311, 357
Garotte, 45
Gassendi, Pierre, 161
Generation of '98, 3, 202
Género, 94, 97
Ghibellines, 85
Gibraltar, 345
Gil de la Cuadra, Ramón, 54, 118
Globe (of London), 47
Gloss, 242
Godoy, Manuel, 6, 7, 9, 10, 19, 32, 150
Gómez Imaz, Manuel, 390
González, Antonio, 158, 220, 229, 259, 291, 292, 298, 339, 340, 357, 359
Gor, Duque de, 308
Government employees. *See* Civil servants
Government officials, 47
Goya y Lucientes, Francisco, 6
Gracia y Justicia. *See* Justice, Ministry of
Granada, 24, 81
Granada, Duke of, 108

La Grande Aventure, 253
La Granja, 20, 30, 103, 162, 200, 266, 267
"La gran verdad descubierta," 149–64
Great Britain, 16, 23, 28, 29, 49, 55–58, 132, 266, 297, 298, 303, 305, 307, 310, 350–52
Gregory XVI, pope, 51
Grey, Lord Charles, 23
Grisi, Giudita, 88, 94, 97, 184, 350
Guebhard, 17, 182–213, 229, 245–51
Guelphs, 85
Guerra. *See* War, Ministry of
Guizot, François, 57

Hacienda. *See* Treasury
Hapsburgs, 4, 19, 128, 131
Hartzenbusch e Hiriart, Eugenio, 388
Helen of Troy, 250
Herculaneum, 176
Heresy, 5
Hernán Pérez del Pulgar, 77–83, 243, 380
Herschel, William, 175
Hespelt, E. Herman, 360
Highwaymen, 6, 17
Holbach, Paul-Henri Dietrich, Baron d', 168, 171
Holland, 8, 246
Holy Alliance, 186. *See also* Northern Powers
Holy Office. *See* Inquisition
Holy See. *See* Papacy
"El hombre globo," 354, 360–62
"El hombre menguado," 48, 67, 68, 378
"El hombre pone y Dios dispone," 68, 86, 167, 380, 385
Homoeoteleuton, 176, 374
"Horas de invierno," 371
Hornero, Calixto, 42, 372
Hugo, Victor, 361
Human rights. *See* Bill of rights
Humboldt, Karl Wilhelm, Baron von, 167
Hundred Thousand Sons of Saint Louis, 13
Hyperbole, 104, 373

Iliad, 10
"Inoportunidad," "inoportuno," 239, 240. *See also* "Por ahora"

Inquisition, 4, 5, 8, 13, 14, 16, 193, 323, 327, 328, 339, 340; abolished, 7, 51; restored, 58

Inquisitorials, 9, 14. *See also* Apostolics; Carlists; Reactionaries

Insurrection, 59, 62, 259, 278. *See also* Post-Office Mutiny

Intercalation, interpolation, 330, 331, 333

Interior, Ministry of the, 50, 245, 260, 298, 357. *See also* Budgets

Intervention, 56, 57, 290

Iriarte, Tomás de, 42

Isabella María, queen of Sicily, 9, 27

Isabel the Catholic, 47, 81

Isabel II, queen of Spain, 19, 23, 46–48, 50, 51, 64, 67, 68, 195, 200, 223, 264–66, 273, 291, 292, 372

Istúriz, Francisco Javier, 29, 30, 265, 267, 285, 297, 305, 306, 332, 339, 359, 365, 396, 397

Italy, 341

Jacobins, 48, 96, 168

Jado, Laureano de, 60

James, Jesse, 6

Jerez, 59

Jesuits, 59, 293, 326; expulsion of, 412; superior general of, 22. *See also* Colegio Imperial

Josefinos. *See* Afrancesados

Joseph I, king of Spain. *See* Bonaparte, Joseph

Jouy, Etienne-Antoine, 67, 179

Jovellanos, Gaspar Melchor de, 7, 32, 33, 53

Joyce, James, 39

Judiciary, reform of, 11, 51, 150, 264, 272–77, 285, 291, 356, 392

Julia, 70, 71

Junta Central, 32, 49

"La junta de Castel-o-Branco," 68

Juntas de fe, 14

Jury system, 12, 116, 123, 125, 126, 167, 297, 355, 382, 383, 396

Jussieu (family of botanists), 167

Justice, Ministry of, 50, 357. *See also* Budgets; Judiciary, reform of

"Justo medio," 74, 95, 97, 259, 317, 355, 365, 390, 392

La Blanchetai, Pierre Henry de, 377

Lacroix, Sylvestre François, 160

El Lairón, 12

Langelot, Eulalia Joaquina da Concepçaõ, 7

Larra, Antonio Crispín de, 7

Larra y Langelot, Eugenio de, 15, 21

Larra y Langelot, Mariano de, 7, 8, 10, 12, 14, 15, 28, 372

Larra y Sánchez de Castro, Mariano José de: adopts pen-name of Figaro, 22; allegiance to Progressives of, 324, 360; and Dolores Armijo de Cambronero, 21–22, 28, 30, 31, 34; and Istúriz clique, 29, 35, 36, 306, 396; and Mendizábal, 29; as novelist, 40; as playwright, 20, 40, 182; as poet, 15, 16, 18, 20, 40, 88; as translator, 21, 28, 255, 281, 394; attendance at parliamentary sessions of, 102; becomes associate editor of *La Revista Española*, 22; birth of, 8; candidacy for Cortes of, 30; children of, 15, 21, 31; commemoration of death of, 3; education of, 8, 10, 12, 14, 15, 372; election to Cortes of, 397; encyclopedism of, 391; first job of, 15; first love of, 14, 15; first publication of, 15; funeral of, 31; illnesses of, 29, 255, 258; in Corellas, 12; joins *La Revista*, 22, 394; leaves *La Revista* for *El Observador*, 182–84, 393; leaves Madrid, 28, 37; leaves Spain, 8; marriage of, 21; meets men of letters, 15; possibly deviates from Progressive line, 360; publishes *El Duende*, 17; publishes *El Pobrecito Hablador*, 21; return to *La Revista* of, 281; return to Madrid of, 14, 29; return to Spain of, 10; suicide of, 15, 31, 32, 34; writes for conservative papers, 31

Larra y Wetoret, Adela de, 21, 31

Larra y Wetoret, Baldomera de, 21

Larra y Wetoret, Luis Mariano de, 21

Lasanta, Damián de, 199

Latorre, Carlos, 17, 117

Laudatio ad absurdum, 94

Lea, Henry Charles, 376

La Legitimidad, 22

Legouvé, Ernest, 354

Leibnitz, Gottfried Wilhelm, 109, 201

Leipzig, 8
León, Joaquín Abarca, bishop of, 22, 51
León Bendicho, Francisco Javier de, 220
"Ley fundamental," 307, 311, 312, 316
Libel, 297; laws, 166
Liberals, 8, 14, 29, 31, 32, 43, 66, passim; "a la inglesa," 26; and tradition, 33, 34; as exiles, 19, 52, 62, 162, 222, 291; as repatriates, 219, 220, 221, 228, 277, 279, 389; attitude of, toward Zea, 47, 48; during Triennium, 11; fading hopes of, 57; of Portugal, 23; persecution of, 9, 13, 24, 62, 63, 224, 291, 398; plots and incursions by, 15, 17, 258; property restored to, 47; repression of, 15; reputation of politicians as, 62
Libertarians, 29
Liberty, 112, 114, 115, 120, 121, 127, 151, 154, 158, 159, 161, 166, 168, 172, 173, 180, 193, 195, 196, 225, 250, 273, 274, 284, 296, 299, 316, 317, 322, 334, 335, 338, 339, 343, 344
"Licencia," 317–19
Linnaeus, Karl, 161
Lisbon, 7, 23, 28, 338
Litotes, 104, 134, 161, 260, 374. See also Meiosis
Llano Chavarri, Ramón, 208
Llauder, Manuel, 49, 50, 222, 258, 263, 279, 288–93, 308, 310, 311, 313, 314, 316, 329, 395, 396
Lloréns Castillo, Vicente, 32, 370, 375, 376–77, 385, 390
Locke, John, 169–71, 174, 180, 385
Lomba y Pedraja, José R., 40, 372, 378
López, Joaquín María, 24, 121–25, 127, 128, 134, 151–53, 158, 173–75, 190, 191, 196, 198, 221–24, 265, 267, 291, 298, 313, 314, 332, 385, 394, 398
López de Ayala, Pero, 106
López del Baño, Agustín, 178
"Lo que no se puede decir no se debe decir," 254, 369, 376
Louis-Philippe, king of France, 17, 56, 57, 62, 377, 378, 400
Louis XVIII, king of France, 8, 13, 312
Loyalty oaths, 12

Luisa Carlota, Infanta, 18, 19, 20, 46, 267
Luis de Granada, 42, 372
Luther, Martin, 250

Machado, Antonio, 383
Macías, 78, 182
Madrid, 23, 45, passim; famine in, 8; middle class in, 5; uprising of May 2, 1808, 8
Madrid, Archdeacon of, 15, 18
"Mal aconsejado," 235, 240
Malvina, 111
Manifesto of October 14, 1833, 47
Manila, 28
Mantilla, Francisco Antonio, 347, 351
María Cristina of Bourbon, queen of Spain, 18, 20, 23, 27, 30, 46–48, 50–52, 57, 60, 64, 88, 93, 103, 107, 141, 142, 192, 198–200, 258, 261, 264–67, 301, 311, 400
Maria da Gloria, queen of Portugal, 23, 58
María Francisca of Braganza, 18, 19
Le Mariage de Figaro, 96
María Luisa of Parma, queen of Spain, 6, 9, 19, 27
Marina. See Navy, Ministry of the
Marliani, 56
Marrast, Robert, 397
Martí, Juan, "El Empecinado," 13
Martí, Pedro, 134
Martínez de la Rosa: passim; appointed prime minister, 24; as Moderado leader during Triennium, 11; character and life of, 24–28; epithet for, 166; general appraisal of ministry of, 59, 61–64; part in halting Berganzist plot of, 19; political credo of, 53; principal features of ministry of, 49–64; replacement by Toreno of, 28. See also Aben Humeya; "Cimiento"; La conjuración de Venecia; "Conversation"; Cuestión transparente"; Estatuto Real; "Un faccioso más"; "Fantasma"; Hernán Pérez del Pulgar; "El hombre globo"; "Inoportunidad"; "Justo medio"; "Ley fundamental"; Liberty; "Mal aconsejado"; Medieval Revivalism; "Ministro responsable"; Moderates; La

niña en casa; "Rama podrida"; "Regeneración"; "Representación nacional"; State, Ministry of; "Los tres no son más que dos"; "Vencedores y vencidos"
Martínez de Ripalda, Jerónimo, 125, 126, 177, 383
Martorell, 134, 383
Masons, 11, 16–18, 23, 26, 48, 49
Maury, Juan María, 87
Maximilian, emperor of Mexico, 6
Maxwell, Herbert, 370
Mayorazgos, 47, 261, 285, 286, 395
Mazade-Percin, Charles de, 39, 371
Medical metaphors, 85
Medieval Revivalism, 53, 78, 83, 106, 114, 197, 232, 234, 235, 266, 323
Medrano, Diego, 50, 124, 177, 217, 355, 357
Meiosis, 191, 261, 262, 277. *See also* Litotes
Melón, Juan Antonio, 150
Mendizábal, Juan Álvarez, 29, 30, 56, 62, 365
El Mensajero. See La Revista Española
Mérida, 28
Merino, Jerónimo, 68, 378
Mesonero Romanos, Ramón de, 22, 24, 369, 372, 378, 386, 388
Metaphor, 85, 287, 314, 373
Metternich, 377
Mexico, Pedro José Fonte, archbishop of, 118
Middle class, 5, 29
Miguel, Dom, 23, 58, 254, 386
Militia, 12, 52, 97, 109, 118, 166, 170, 189, 190, 191, 242, 256, 260, 291, 314, 334, 382, 386. *See also* Voluntarios Realistas
Milton, John, 168, 171
Mina. *See* Espoz y Mina, Francisco Javier
"El ministerial," 51, 68, 76, 95, 164–80, 182, 355, 389, 400
"Ministro responsable," 307, 312, 316
Miraflores, Manuel Pando Fernández de Pineda, Marquis of, 49, 56, 57, 376, 393
Miyar, 17, 193, 344–46, 399
"Modas," 139–49, 396
Moderates, 11, 15, 18, 24, 31–33, 35–37,

66; disillusionment latent in, 181; temporization of, 96, 111, 148, 177, 178, 216, 255
La mojigata, 72
Molière, Jean-Baptiste Polequin, 348
Monarchy: types of, 4
Monetary system: reform of, 284
Monks: hide weapons, 49; slaughter of, 59, 60, 103, 316
Montagues, 85, 88
Monterrón, Count de, 118
Montesinos, José F., 399
Montevirgen, José Vigil de Quiñones, Marqués de, 189, 190, 192, 198, 293, 310, 345, 349
Montilla, Carlos, 401
Moratín, Leandro Fernández de, 7, 32, 72, 397
Moreto, Agustín, 71, 72
Moscoso de Altamira, José María, 50, 143, 148, 254, 310, 311, 324, 330, 342, 343, 346, 357
La muerte de Abel, 354
El Mundo, 381
Muñoz, Fernando, 27, 103
Murillo, Bartolomé Esteban, 69
Music: and politics, 94, 95; conservatory, 9, 359, 360

El Nacional, 89
"Nadie pase sin hablar al portero," 67
Naples, 11, 47
Napoleon I, 6, 7, 32, 36, 169, 249, 342–44
Napoleon III, 6
National assembly, 60, 64
National Militia. *See* Militia
National representation. *See* "Representación nacional"
Navalcarnero, 28
Navarre, 12. *See also Fueros,* of Navarre
Navarro Tomás, Tomás, 382
Navas, Luis Pizarro, Conde de las, 151, 194, 199, 207, 208, 246, 247, 259, 261, 264, 266, 267, 272, 276, 285, 287, 290–92, 294, 298, 393
Navy, Ministry of the, 50, 227, 298, 358. *See also* Budgets
Negros, 213
Newton, Isaac, 160, 161

New World. *See* American colonies
Ni el tío ni el sobrino, 93
Los Niños de Écija, 6
Nobiliary system, 5, 46, 47
Nobility. *See* Aristocracy
"La nochebuena de 1836," 370–71
Nombela y Campos, Julio, 66, 73, 74, 363, 378, 380, 401
Norma, 97, 223, 359, 398
Northern Powers, 55, 56, 399
Novísima recopilación, 131, 133, 285
Nueva recopilación, 131
Numancia, 97
Núñez Arenas, Isaac, 75

Obscurantism, 317
El Observador, 37, 182–84, 247, 299, 393
Ocios de Españoles Emigrados, 53
Ocistas, 53
O'Donnell, José, 22
Olavarría, 60, 93
Olózaga, Salustiano, 49
Ominous Decade, 15, 77, 169, 191, 193, 194, 197, 212, 213, 216–33, 244, 263, 285, 344, 347, 349; press during, 18
One percent law, 52, 97
"Oportuna," 254. *See also* "Inoportunidad"; "Por ahora"
Oratory, 35–37, 40–42
Orfila, Mateo, 8
Orléans, Duc d', 57
Oxymoron, 99, 313

Pablo, Joaquín de, "Chapalangarra," 17
"Las palabras," 95, 167, 380
Palafox y Melzi, José de, Duke of Zaragoza, 60, 99, 103, 141, 381
Palarea, Juan, 220, 228, 235, 246, 251, 291, 294, 314
Palaudarias, Joaquín, 134
Palau y Dulcet, Antonio, 372
Palmerston, Henry John Temple, Third Viscount, 49
Papacy, 12, 51, 292
Paralipsis, 79
Parallelism, 177, 340
Paris, 28
Parisina, 149
Parison, 176
Partidas, 131, 132, 235
Passports, 351, 352

Pastor Mateos, Emilio, 38, 371, 382
La Pata de Cabra, 103
Pathos, 122, 126, 161, 163, 202, 242
Peninsular War. *See* War of Independence
"Un periódico nuevo," 146, 279, 281, 282, 284, 395
Peter of Braganza, 19, 23
Petitions, 116, 356; government response to, 261, 270, 271; right of, 278
Philippines, 225
Philip V, king of Spain, 19
Physiological analogies, 132
Piarists, 10, 12, 41, 42, 59, 372
Piedmont, 11
Pigault de l'Espinay, Guillaume (Pigault-Lebrun), 139
Pineda, Mariana, 17
Pirala y Criado, Antonio, 375, 376, 378, 392
Pi y Arsuaga, Francisco, 369, 376, 381
Pi y Margall, Francisco, 369, 376, 381
Plandolid, 134
"La planta nueva o el faccioso," 68, 159, 164, 167, 360, 378
Plots. *See* Conspiracies
Plutarch, 80
El Pobrecito Hablador, 21, 37, 42, 371
"Poesías de Juan Bautista Alonso," 354, 401
Poland, 341
Police. *See* Secret police
"La policía," 320–53, 354, 356
Polo, Miguel, 193
Polo y Monje, Ángel, 208
Polyptoton, 242, 337, 339, 373, 374, 399
Popes. *See* Papacy; Gregory XVI
"Por ahora," 37, 95, 290, 325, 354–57, 400
Portugal, 6, 22, 23, 29, 49, 55–58, 87, 97, 151, 204, 211, 338–41
Post-Office Mutiny, 227, 257, 263, 284, 286–96, 308, 311, 314, 322, 334, 347, 349, 356, 392, 394–96
Pragmática Sanción, 19, 20
Pregnant vehicle, 42–45, 70, 96, 97, 190, 227, 279, 323, 348
Press, 41, 60; during Ominous Decade, 13, 18; during Triennium, 12; Freedom of, 33, 37, 39, 40, 47–48, 115–19; persecution of journalists of, 30, 39;

suspension of publications of, 33. *See also* Censorship

Preterition. *See* Apophasis

"Primera contestación de un liberal de allá," 182, 191, 201, 202, 206, 207, 210–12, 223, 376, 391, 398

"Primera piedra," 90–93

"Una primera representación," 354

"Primera representación de la comedia refundida y puesta en cuatro actos titulada *Juez reo de su causa o Don Jaime el Justiciero*," 71

Próceres, xi, 91, 105, 117–19, 140–45, 149, 162, 184, 209, 210, 235, 239, 245–51, 301–3, 308, 362, 381, 396; appearance of, 102, 103, 105; inaction of, 104; qualifications for, 54, 107

Procuradores, xi, passim; appearance of, 103; election to, 53–55, 95; excuses of absent members of, 104; involvement in Palafox conspiracy of, 60; qualifications for, 54, 104

Progressives, 30, 32, 34, 93; attitude of, toward amnesties, 52; attitude of, toward Carlist War, 258; criticism of war policy by, 49; dissatisfaction of, with Martínez, 60, 97; displeasure of, with Crown address, 103; eventual disillusionment and recantation of, 33, 35, 36, 257; in Próceres, 54; in Procuradores, 55; Larra's allegiance to, 48, 66, 74, 88; parliamentary tactics of, 91–93, 111, 118, 148, 196, 200, 216, 217, 287

Prosopography, 282

Provence, 19

Pseudoautobiographical style, 255

Pseudonaturalist allegory and style, 159, 167, 173, 174, 176, 177, 179, 360

Pseudophilosophical prolegomenon and style, 76, 95, 167, 171, 282, 283

Pseudoscientific style, 68, 86

Pulgar, Hernando del. *See Hernán Pérez del Pulgar*

Puns, 104, 134, 139, 145–47, 177, 269, 270, 306, 318, 329, 331, 333, 344, 348, 373, 374, 383

Quadruple Alliance, 49, 55–57, 110, 162, 227, 254

"¿Qué hace en Portugal su Majestad?", 87

Quesada, Vicente Jenaro de, 49

Quevedo y Villegas, Francisco Gómez de, 105, 168, 348, 350, 382

Quinet, Edgar, 24, 33, 34, 36, 370, 371, 382

Quintana, Manuel José, 7, 32, 36, 85, 86, 118

Quintero, Tomás, 136, 376

Quixotism, 77, 81

Raisin tax, 261

"Rama podrida," 235, 237, 240

Ramsey, Marathon Montrose, 386

Reactionaries, 12, 29. *See also* Apostolics; Carlists; Inquisitorials

Reales Estudios de San Isidro, 15

Real Sociedad Económica de Amigos del País, 14

El Redactor General, 381

Redundance, 79, 329–31, 333

Refundiciones. *See* Rifacimenti

Regency of Urgel, 12, 186

"Regeneración," 112–14, 301

"Rehiletes," 149, 159

Reiteration, 326

Religious freedom, 125

Religious orders. *See* Jesuits; Piarists; Roman Catholic Church; Trappists

"Un reo de muerte," 354, 364

"Representación de *La mojigata*," 72, 397

"Representación de *La niña en casa y la madre en la máscara de Don Francisco Martínez de la Rosa*," 87

"Representación de *Norma*," 97, 223, 398

"Representación nacional," 53, 60, 64, 112, 120, 121, 307, 312, 316

Retruécano. See Antimetabole

"Revista del año 1834," 257, 262, 263, 319, 364, 392

La Revista Española, 22, 37, 44, 71, 75, 98, 99, 135, 247, 299, 354, 357, 358, 371, 379, 380, 398

Rhetoric, 10, 41, 42, 315, 372–75

Richards, I. A., 42, 43

Rico y Amat, Juan, 375, 391

Riego, Rafael de, 10, 274, 276

Rifacimenti, 71, 72

Rights of Man, 5. *See also* Bill of rights
Rigny, Henri Gauthier, Comte de, 57, 387
Ripalda. *See* Martínez de Ripalda, Jerónimo
Ripoll, 14
Rivas, Ángel Saavedra, Duque de, 54, 70, 99, 118, 149, 235–37, 301, 308, 376, 381, 382, 396, 398
Rodil, José Ramón, 58, 211
Rodríguez Aranda, Luis, 385
Rodríguez Solís, E., 379
Roman Catholic Church: abolition of religious orders of, 12, 27, 60; and Roman curia, 60; and social change, 34; as only acceptable faith, 8; confiscation of lands and monasteries of, 12, 27, 29, 31, 45, 265, 293; hierarchy of, in Próceres, 54; influence of clergy of, on Carlos, 58; power of, 4, 12, 31; reform of clergy of, 51. *See also* Inquisition; Jesuits; Monks; Papacy; Piarists, Religious freedom; Trappists
Romanticism, 4, 7, 24, 83, 84, 93, 324
Ros de Olano, Antonio, 75, 93
Rothschild, Baron James, 51, 99, 185, 189, 194, 202, 208, 216
Rousseau, Jean-Jacques, 113, 152, 334
Rozo, 360, 361
Rumeau, Aristide, 371
Russia, 9, 12, 23, 47, 55, 249, 341, 342

Saavedra. *See* Rivas, Ángel Saavedra, Duque de
Sáez, Víctor, 13
Saint-Hilaire, Comte de, 56
Saint-Sylvain, Auguet de, 58
Salic law, 19, 47, 57
Sallust, 337, 399
Salt taxes, 292
Samponts, Ignacio, 264, 266, 267
San Antonio Abad, 10, 372
San Ildefonso. *See* La Granja
San Juan, General, 295
Sánchez, Juan M., 383
Sánchez Agesta, Luis, 357, 372, 376, 377, 381, 401
Sánchez de Castro y Delgado, María de los Dolores, 7, 372
Sánchez Estevan, Ismael, 40, 87, 88, 183,

372, 379, 380, 382, 385, 386, 388, 391, 394, 400
Santafé, Pablo, 118, 121, 125, 130, 158, 178, 180, 181
Santa Hermandad, 285
Santiago. *See* Voto de Santiago
Sarrailh, Jean, 61, 377, 378, 381, 393
Saxony, Princess of, 264, 265, 268
Scholasticism, 48, 159, 160, 317
Scientific allusions, 152, 159–61, 163, 167, 168, 172, 173, 175
Scribe, Augustin, 20, 28, 70, 111, 253–55, 281
Sebastián, Infante Don, 264, 265, 267, 268
Seco Serrano, Carlos, xi, 58, 387
Secret police, 15, 22, 118, 291, 320–53, 397, 398
Secret sessions, 115–17, 146
Secret societies, 11, 22, 48, 98, 381, 391, 398
Secularization of Church property, 12, 27, 29, 31, 45, 265, 293
Segovia, Antonio María, 77, 79, 379
"Segunda carta de un liberal de acá a un liberal de allá," 182–85, 189–91, 202, 204–10, 376, 386, 398
"Segunda y última carta de Fígaro al bachiller, su corresponsal desconocido," 112, 357, 385
"Seguridad individual," 112
Semanario Patriótico, 33, 370
Semanario Pintoresco Español, 391, 400
Seo de Urgel, 12, 186
Serrano, Francisco, 219, 226, 245, 252, 253
Serviles, 8
Seville, 13, 20, 59
Sicilies, Kingdom of the Two. *See* Naples
Sierra Morena, special privileges of, 261
El Siglo, 75–77, 86
"*El Siglo* en blanco," 75–77, 379, 380
Simile, 43, 44, 45, 68, 79, 97, 105, 176, 177, 179, 382
Siscar, Ramón, 134
"La sociedad," 182, 281, 393
Sociedad Isabelina, 48, 60, 66, 93, 98, 103, 134, 135, 226, 272, 276, 288, 298, 316, 399
Society of Jesus. *See* Jesuits

Someruelos, Joaquín José de Muro, Marqués de, 265, 306
Soret, 245
State, Ministry of, 50, 209, 358. *See also* Budgets
"*La Straniera*," 182, 184
Strassburg, 8
Structural unity, of Larra's essays, 280
Suárez, Federico, 369
Subsidies, 292
Substantivization, 326, 353

Tabla de derechos. *See* Bill of rights
Tacitus, 80
Talleyrand-Périgord, Charles Maurice de, 56
"*Tanto vales cuanto tienes*," 99, 376
Tarr, Frederick Courtney, 18, 38, 40, 42, 43, 77, 369, 371, 372, 375, 379, 380, 385, 391, 394, 396
Tatitscheff, 9
Tautology. *See* Redundance
Taxes, 51, 292
"Tercera carta de un liberal de acá a un liberal de allá," 214–27, 388
La Tercerola, 12
Theater, 101; and politics, 43, 70, 71, 86, 88, 90, 92, 93, 97, 99, 134, 191, 226, 253, 254, 390, 400; state of the, 18, 22, 26, 43, 44, 88, 298. *See also* Rifacimenti
Thematic intertwining, 330, 331, 333, 340
Thiers, Adolphe, 57
El Tiempo, 75, 89
Tie vote: not foreseen in Procuradores regulations, 158, 162
Times (London), 47
Tirso de Molina, 72
Toreno, José María Queipo de Llano, Conde de, 11, 28, 29, 50, 53, 91, 120–23, 125–27, 134, 137, 149, 152–54, 157, 159, 162, 164, 174–76, 192, 194, 202, 203, 222, 265, 291, 297, 298, 300, 302, 334, 336–39, 385, 400
Torremejía, Alberto Felipe Valdrich, Marqués de, 189, 192, 198, 200, 386
Torrijos, José María, 17, 193, 344, 347
Toulouse, 49
Tournefort, Joseph Pitton de, 167

Traditionalism, 7. *See also* Apostolics; Carlists; Clericals; Inquisitorials
Trafalgar, 7
La Trágala, 12
Transitions, 110
Translations, 13
Trappists, 12
Treasury, 16, 29, 50, 51, 246
"Los tres no son más que dos y el que no es nada vale por tres—mascarada política," 70, 71, 73, 213, 379, 380
Triangle Conspiracy, 9
Triennium, 11, 13, 24, 32, 47, 52, 70, 169, 186, 191, 213, 215–41, 285, 297, 311, 377, 396; acts of, abrogated, 14; liberals during, 166; press during, 12, 166
Trocadero, 13, 344
Trueba y Cosío, Telesforo, 151, 154, 161, 184, 188, 204, 206, 217, 219, 228, 235, 245, 265, 291, 359, 386
Tu quoque, 68

"El último adiós," 97
Union. *See* Fusion
United States, 350, 351
El Universal, 75, 89, 136
Universities, 14, 16, 20, 47, 48, 159
Urbanos. *See* Militia

Valdés, Jerónimo, 50, 357
Valencia, University of, 15
Valera y Alcalá Galiano, Juan, 376, 377, 378, 384, 392
Valladolid, José Antonio Ribadeneira, archbishop of, 141
Vallejo, José Mariano, 160
Valmont de Bomare, 167, 176
El vampiro, 252, 253
"Variedades teatrales. Mi nombre y mis propósitos," 395
"Varios caracteres," 66
Vatican. *See* Papacy
Vázquez Figueroa, José, 50
Vega, Ventura de la, 15, 75, 253
Vega y Río, José Rosendo de la, 178
"Vencedores y vencidos," 184, 191–202, 210, 212, 218, 223, 273, 346, 349
Venice, 399. *See also La conjuración de Venecia*
"Ventajas de las cosas a medio hacer," 77, 380

Veragua, Duke of, 118
El verdugo de Amsterdam, 96
"Veredas," 208, 209, 387
Verona, Congress of, 12, 13
"La vida de Madrid," 255
Vienna: Dr. Larra in, 8; Congress of, 9, 326
Villahermosa, Marqués de, 384
Villa-Urrutia, Wenceslao Javier de, Marqués de, 26, 92, 370, 375, 376, 377, 380, 381, 382, 392, 396
Villiers, George, Fourth Earl of Clarendon, 25, 49, 56, 370, 382
Virgil, 250
Virgin Mary, 58
Vitoria, 57
Voltaire, François-Marie Arouet, 26, 109, 168, 171, 201, 212, 279, 317, 362
Voluntarios Realistas, 23, 52, 199
Voto de Santiago, 150, 151, 260, 262, 364, 384
"¡Vuelva usted mañana!", 21

War, Ministry of, 23, 49, 50, 59, 189, 258, 259, 298, 357. *See also* Budgets
War of Independence, 6, 8, 29, 32, 48, 258, 295, 345
Washington, George, 136
Watt, James, 175
Wellington, Duke of, 8
Wetoret y Martínez, Josefa Anacleta, 21
White, Joseph Blanco, 32, 33, 370

"Yo quiero ser cómico," 44

Zarco del Valle, Remón, 50, 59, 190, 291
Zea Bermúdez, Francisco, xi, 22–24, 37, 46–49, 52, 60, 67, 68, 76, 200, 258, 259, 292, 293, 365, 392, 397
Zorrilla, José, 31, 397
Zumalacárregui, Tomás de, 49, 58, 191, 227, 258
Zurita, Jerónimo de, 106
El Zurriago, 12, 166, 167, 179